Issues and Practices in Inquiry-Oriented Teacher Education

Dedication

To: Aaron, Jordan and Noah — KZ
To: Jeanne — BRT

Issues and Practices in Inquiry-Oriented Teacher Education

Edited by

B. Robert Tabachnick
and
Kenneth M. Zeichner

 The Falmer Press

(A member of the Taylor & Francis Group)
London • New York • Philadelphia

UK   The Falmer Press, 4 John Street, London WC1N 2ET
USA   The Falmer Press, Taylor & Francis Inc., 1900 Frost Road, Suite
            101, Bristol, PA 19007

© B. Robert Tabachnick and Kenneth M. Zeichner 1991

First published 1991

British Library Cataloguing in Publication Data
Issues and practices in inquiry-oriented teacher education.
1. Teachers. Professional education
I. Tabachnick, B. Robert   II. Zeichner, Kenneth M.
370.71

ISBN 1-85000-815-9
ISBN 1-85000-816-7 pbk

Library of Congress Cataloging-in-Publication Data
Issues and practices in inquiry-oriented teacher education /
    edited by B. Robert Tabachnick, Kenneth M. Zeichner.
        p.   cm.
    Includes bibliographical references and index.
    ISBN 1-85000-815-9:—ISBN 1-85000-816-7 (pbk.):
    1. Teachers—Training of—United States.   I. Tabachnick,
B. Robert.   II. Zeichner, Kenneth M.
LB1715.I87   1991
370'.71'0973—dc20   90-48612
                                                     CIP

Typeset by Graphicraft Typesetters Ltd, Hong Kong

Printed in Great Britain by Burgess Science Press, Basingstoke on paper which has a specified pH value on final paper manufacture of not less than 7.5 and is therefore 'acid free'.

Table of Contents

Table of Contents

Preface

Issues and Practices in Inquiry-Oriented Teacher Education is an excellent collection of essays written by practising teacher educators, who are dedicated to helping their colleagues better understand the work they do. The book is very timely, given the growing interest in reflective teaching and inquiry-oriented practices in teacher education and is an important addition to the Wisconsin Series on Teacher Education.

Editors Tabachnick and Zeichner and their distinguished group of essayists provide a rich description and discussion of inquiry-oriented practices that have been implemented in teacher education programs in the United States. Readers receive a first hand account of what happens when reflective teaching is introduced into a regular teacher education program. Chapter authors contribute to the understanding of inquiry-oriented practices, as they explain how they defined this concept and have applied it to teacher preparation. The chapter authors are very deliberate and forthright in sharing their experiences. They do not hesitate to describe the lessons they learned from their students and others. They discuss modifications they need to employ in their own practice. Methods course professors and other education professors will appreciate how several of the chapter authors define, describe and discuss how reflection and inquiry is put to the test in their courses. Other members of the teacher preparation team, for example, supervisors and cooperating teachers, will also benefit from reading the book, because it presents an analysis and discussion of how members of these role groups use reflection to nurture the development of critical inquiry in their student teachers. The writings are primary resources for teacher educators considering inquiry-oriented teaching.

Issues and Practices in Inquiry-Oriented Teacher Education is an important contribution to the Wisconsin Series on Teacher Education.

Carl A. Grant
University of Wisconsin-Madison

Introduction

In the last decade or so, there has been a growing acceptance within the US teacher education community of what has been referred to by many as inquiry-oriented teacher education.[1] This general approach to preparing teachers emphasizes the development of knowledge, skills and dispositions by prospective teachers and teachers that enable them to be reflective about their teaching *and* the social contexts in which their teaching takes place (e.g., the classroom, the school, the local community, the society).[2] Although there has been much discussion in recent years about various inquiry-oriented approaches and frequent use of such terms as 'reflection', 'action research' and 'teacher empowerment', there has also been: (1) a lack of clarity about the different intellectual traditions and political commitments underlying the use of this terminology in particular situations; and (2) very little specific information made available to the teacher education community about the pedagogy and practices in inquiry-oriented teacher education programs.

One purpose of this book is to describe a variety of inquiry-oriented practices that are currently being used within a small group of US teacher education programs. These practices are all situated at the preservice level and emphasize the development of dispositions and capabilities among prospective teachers and teacher educators to engage in particular forms of 'reflective teaching'. The recent efforts of teacher educators who have been developing inquiry-oriented teacher education strategies within their own preservice programs have largely been inaccessible to teacher educators outside of these institutions who are interested in incorporating inquiry-oriented strategies into their programs. Many of the recent descriptions of inquiry-oriented programs have (including some of our own descriptions of work at the University of Wisconsin-Madison) been written at a fairly general level which has not revealed the specific ways in which teacher educators work with their students. The practices that are presented in this volume are described in a way that is intended to give the reader very specific information about what these teacher educators do in their courses as well as making explicit the rationales for the practices that are described.

A second purpose of this book is to explore various meanings of the term 'reflective teaching' that are associated with inquiry-oriented practices. In addition to the first chapter which explores a variety of ways in which the slogan of reflective teaching can be interpreted, each author describes the commitments underlying their work and the particular traditions from which they draw. Tom (1985) distinguishes inquiry-oriented approaches to teacher education along three dimensions: the arena of the problematic (i.e., what in the teaching situation is considered problematic), the model of inquiry (i.e., the process through which the arena of the problematic is explored) and the view within an approach about the ontological status of educational phenomena. According to Tom's framework of inquiry-oriented approaches, the practices represented in this book all take a relatively broad view of the arena of the problematic (encouraging prospective teachers to consider alternatives with regard to more than just teaching strategies), employ models of inquiry that unite thought and action and view educational phenomena as social constructions rather than as natural and enduring events.

Although the teacher educators represented in this book draw upon a variety of intellectual traditions and traditions of practice, they are all committed to enabling prospective teachers to engage in reflection of a particular quality. The use of the term 'reflective teaching' in this text represents a focus on all three domains of reflection that have been discussed by Carr and Kemmis (1986) and by Van Manen (1977).[3] First, in the technical domain, the concern is with the efficiency and effectiveness of the means used to attain ends which themselves remain unexamined. Second, in the domain of the practical, the task is one of explicating and clarifying the assumptions and predispositions underlying the teaching activity and assessing the adequacy of the educational goals toward which actions are aimed. Here every action is seen as linked to particular value commitments and the actors consider the worth of different educational ends as well as how well the particular learning goals that they are working toward are achieved by students. Finally, the critical domain incorporates moral and ethical criteria into the discourse about practical action. Here the central questions are which educational goals, activities and experiences contribute toward forms of life that can be characterized by equity, justice and concrete fulfillment for all students. For example, the critical domain would extend a concern with the worth of educational goals and with how efficiently they are being accomplished, to a consideration of whose interests are represented in what it is that is being learned, and which groups of students are and are not accomplishing the goals. In this book, 'reflective teaching' involves reflection and action in all three of these domains. Although technical skill is an important element in our conception of reflective practice, this book does not include descriptions of teacher education practices in which teacher educators view reflection and inquiry as *merely* technical skills divorced from consideration of the broader purposes of schooling and issues of equity and social justice.

All of the authors in this book are practising teacher educators who are writing about their own work. A deliberate decision was made early in the conceptualization of the book to exclude accounts of inquiry-oriented teacher education practices by those who are not themselves engaged in an active way in a preservice teacher education program. Too little of the current research literature in teacher education, such as that which has been recently compiled in the *Handbook for Research on Teacher Education* (Houston, 1990), has been produced by practising teacher educators.[4] Just as the concerns, questions and voices of teachers have frequently been ignored in research on teaching, so too the perspectives of teacher educators have often been absent from research on teacher education. Much of the extant research in teacher education in the US is not at all sensitive to the institutional and political realities faced by teacher educators and is frequently rejected as superfluous by teacher educators. Furthermore, scholarship in teacher education is often cast in a language that is inaccessible to those who are outside of the particular 'club' from which the scholarship has emerged. There is a certain elitism and arrogance that is unavoidable here (even among those who espouse a rhetoric of democracy and liberation) as long as those who produce scholarship in teacher education remain personally detached from the consequences of their proposals and try to reform teacher education from the outside looking in.

Over the last decade there has been much effort to democratize the research process with regard to studies of teaching and teachers. We have seen a substantial increase in research projects that involve some form of collaboration between university-based researchers and classroom teachers and growing acceptance of the action research efforts of teachers as contributory to the 'knowledge base' for teaching.[5] Nell Noddings (1987) has described this shift as one from 'research *on* teaching' to 'research *for* teaching'. This same process of democratization also needs to occur with regard to research on teacher education. We need to see greater representation of the perspectives of teacher educators in teacher education scholarship, more genuinely collaborative research efforts involving external researchers and teacher educators, and greater support for and recognition of the action research efforts of teacher educators who engage in serious study of their own practices and programs.

All of the chapters in this book, with the exception of Chapter 1 (which attempts to set the context for what is to follow), represent examples of the action research efforts of US teacher educators. These accounts, while explicit about the specific practices that are used by teacher educators and about the contexts in which they are used, represent more than merely descriptive accounts or celebratory testimonials. All of the authors of Chapters 2–15 have sought to emulate in their work as teacher educators the reflectiveness that they seek to develop in their students. These accounts of practices in inquiry-oriented teacher education are often self-critical, and illuminate many tensions and contradictions that are experienced in implementing inquiry-oriented teacher education courses and programs. The authors give us realistic rather than romaticized accounts of how their inquiry strategies play out in the face of many factors which serve to undercut their aspirations. They refer repeatedly to the ways in which they can continue to improve upon their current practices in the future.

While many of the practices described in this book have benefited from the work of teacher educators outside of the US, the book is limited to a focus on US teacher education programs.[6] Also, the chapters in this book describe representative examples of current work in the US. There is clearly other similar work now underway in the US that has not been included in this volume.[7]

Although many of the authors are currently working or have worked at one time in their careers in the elementary teacher education program at the University of Wisconsin-Madison, the work that is described in this book represents teacher education practices from a variety of colleges and universities across the US in graduate and undergraduate programs that seek to prepare both elementary and secondary teachers. The examples of inquiry-oriented practices included in this volume represent work that is currently underway or that has recently taken place at the following institutions: Gustavus Adolphus College, Indiana University, Knox College, Mills College, Rockhurst College, the State University of New York at Binghamton, Syracuse University, the University of Maryland-Baltimore County, the University of Wisconsin-Madison, the University of Utah and Wheaton College.

After the opening chapter which discusses the concept of reflective teaching, the book covers a variety of efforts to develop inquiry-oriented teacher education practices. These efforts focus on entire teacher education programs such as at the University of Utah and Wheaton College or on particular program components such as methods courses, foundations courses and clinical experiences. They involve the introduction of various structural innovations such as student cohort groups, curricular reforms such as the introduction of case studies or imaginative literature, and instructional innovations such as collaborative learning, action research and autobiography. It is important to remember that all of these attempted innovations are linked to particular educational and social/political agendas. Because journals, case studies, action research, autobiography and the rest of these innovations can be used in many different ways within teacher education programs, they cannot be interpreted or assessed apart from the assumptions and commitments that underly their use (Zeichner, 1987).

In the first chaper 'Reflections on Reflective Teaching', we explore various ways in which the slogan of reflective teaching has been interpreted and used within the US teacher education community. In the first part of the chapter, we discuss the limits of several 'generic' models of reflective teaching and draw upon a recent analysis by Zeichner and Liston (1990) of traditions of practice in twentieth-century US teacher education to describe four different orientations to reflective teaching that are visible in the current teacher education reform movement in the United States. In the second part of the chapter, we explore the question of the different meanings that can be given to reflective teaching as we examine it being acted out in specific classroom situations. This question of the meaning of reflective teaching in concrete and specific instances of classroom teaching is explored through an examination of several examples of the teaching of social studies.

In Chapter 2, Frances Maher describes the various ways in which she has attempted to infuse feminist/gendered approaches to reflective inquiry into her teaching of three foundations and methods courses in the secondary teacher education program at Wheaton College. She also discusses the varied effects of different student teaching contexts on her feminist inspired goals for her students. Maher characterizes her approach in these three courses as student-centered, collaborative and autobiographical. As her students consider the history of American education, adolescent development or planning for their own teaching, Maher emphasizes approaches which can help them make personal, experiential connections to course themes. The themes in these courses emphasize issues of gender, race, social class and culture and reflect particular attention to the perspectives of marginalized groups. Specific examples of course assignments (e.g., the writing of personal and family autobiographies) and teaching strategies such as small group work are described, together with student reactions to these approaches. In the final section of the chapter, Maher reflects about the long-term impact of her program on her students and discusses several stories of Wheaton graduates who have moved on to various careers.

In Chapter 3, 'Educative Communities and the Development of the Reflective Practitioner', Robert Bullough and Andrew Gitlin describe the rationale underlying current teacher education programs at the University of Utah. These programs are built upon a commitment to both critical and interpretative orientations to reflective practice and emphasize the development of educative communities within each program that are characterized by a dual commitment to reasoned dialogue and caring. The authors present case studies from two of their programs that illustrate the various ways in which teacher educators at the University of Utah have been attempting to break from a 'training orientation' to teacher education. These cases describe the use of a variety of structural, instructional and curricular innovations which seek to promote their vision of educative communities. These innovations include the use of student cohort groups, the supervisory method of 'horizontal evaluation', the writing of personal and school histories, and the identification and continuing examination of personal teaching metaphors by students. In the final section of the chapter, the authors provide us with a critical account of their efforts to date and their reflections about the directions that they need to emphasize in the future.

In Chapter 4, 'Using a Methods Course to Promote Reflection and Inquiry Among Preservice Teachers', Jesse Goodman of Indiana University describes the ways in which he has attempted to promote critical inquiry and reflection among preservice teachers in an elementary social studies methods course. Following a discussion of reflection and its relation to teacher education which emphasizes the integration of rational and intuitive thought processes, Goodman discusses how he attempts to help his students integrate their reflections about substantive educational questions with their teaching practice through the course assignments. The central assignment of the course requires students to develop and implement (in their early field experiences) an original social studies unit that encourages inquiry and reflection by both teacher and pupils. This project is based on a model of curriculum development that is presented to the preservice students as an alternative to the pervasive 'objectives first' approach. This model of curriculum development asks the preservice teachers to consider the social and political dimensions of what they teach. Goodman describes this five-phase process of curriculum development and cites many examples of work that his students have produced. Goodman's students also write papers in which they discuss the general approach to the teaching of social studies that their unit represents together with their rationale for using such an approach. In the final part of the chapter, Goodman discusses the relationships between the methods course and the concurrent practicum and explores the impact of the methods course on his students' development as teachers.

In Chapter 5, 'Forming a Critical Pedagogy for the Social Studies Methods Class: The Use of Imaginative Literature', Susan Adler of the University of Missouri-Kansas City discusses how she used imaginative literature in her social studies methods class at Rockhurst College in Kansas City to stimulate reflection by her students about the nature of social studies, and their own personal knowledge and assumptions, within ethical, political and cultural frameworks. Adler discusses two of the works of literature that she used in her class: Arthur Miller's *The Crucible*, and Chinua Achebe's *Things Fall Apart*, and gives examples of how each work raises questions appropriate to social education and asks preservice students to consider enduring questions about what it means to live in the social world. In the second part of the chapter, Adler presents a case study describing the use of the Achebe novel with her students in three class sessions and explores the impact of her use of imaginative literature on her students' work during student teaching. She cites several examples of students who integrated literature and other art forms into their teaching of social studies during student teaching and argues that using literature in the social studies methods class helped to expand her students' conceptions of the sources of knowledge for social studies instruction beyond an exclusive reliance on textbooks.

In Chapter 6, 'Teaching a Language of Opportunity in a Language Arts Methods Class', Mary Gomez of the University of Wisconsin-Madison describes the ways in which she has attempted to help her elementary teacher education students develop dispositions and skills to teach diverse learners in ways that value and build upon the different cultures and traditions that their pupils bring to school. These goals are contrasted by Gomez with a 'cultural deprivation' view which recognizes the different values and experiences that pupils bring to school, but that tries to replace them with the school's values. Following a discussion of the changing demographics in US classrooms where she concludes that US teachers will increasingly be faced with the task of teaching pupils with backgrounds unlike their own, Gomez criticizes US teacher education programs for failing to attend in a central way to issues of race, class, gender and multiculturalism. Gomez then describes the way in which she uses specific readings and assignments in her own course to help her well-intentioned but often naive students develop capabilities to teach the language arts (with an emphasis on writing) to children with different cultural, language and economic backgrounds. The course encourages both a critique of the ways in which current schooling practices fail to educate many pupils of color and in poverty, and on the development of alternative practices that build important links between home and school. Gomez includes a discussion of the various ways in which her students have responded to particular readings and assignments, including two instances where students sought to change school practices that they concluded were harmful to students.

In Chapter 7, 'Teacher Education, Reflective Inquiry and Moral Action', Lanny Beyer describes the ways in which he has sought to facilitate critical reflection by his students in the Knox College course 'School and Society'. Following a discussion of the concept of reflection in which Beyer analyzes six different forms of reflection (escapist, therapeutic, commonsense, procedural/ technical, ameliorative and critical), the assumptions underlying the teacher education program at Knox College are presented. This teacher education program is based on the concepts of critical reflection and praxis. A central curricular theme in the program is concerned with the dynamics and consequences of social inequality. Beyer is concerned that his students learn how to engage in 'relational thinking' in which educational issues are seen as conjoined with economic, political and social issues, *and* that his students become committed to working to overcome the effects of social inequality. The second half of the chapter describes a central assignment in the School and Society course, a human service project. In this project, students complete a minimum of twenty-five hours of volunteer work with an individual or small group of people either in a social service agency or in a more informal setting. Beyer feels that this personal encounter with people who have experienced the effects of social inequality is a necessary supplement to academic study if a moral commitment to work to overcome social inequality is to be generated. Beyer then presents three examples at the end of the chapter, drawing from students' journals, that illustrate the powerful impact of this project on some students, at least in the short run.

In Chapter 8, 'Case Methods and Teacher Education: Using Cases to Teach Teacher Reflection', Anna Richert of Mills College discusses the use of case methods as one strategy for preparing reflective teachers. Following a general discussion of reflective teaching that considers why it is important for teachers to be reflective, what it is teachers need to know and how they might come to know it, the author discusses two specific characteristics of cases (their artifactual and social nature) and some of the benefits that she believes can and cannot be gained through the use of case methods in teacher education. She then describes a number of different ways in which she currently uses case methods in her teacher education classes at Mills College. This work involves students at various times in both writing cases (based on observations, interviews and various participatory experiences in schools) and in studying cases. In all of this work, Richert emphasizes that working with cases is a social process that helps student teachers develop dispositions to work collaboratively with their colleagues and to be actively involved in determining the substance and context of their work. In the final section of the chapter, she cautions us about some of the difficulties that are involved in using case methods, including its labor intensive nature.

In Chapter 9, 'But is it teaching? The Use of Collaborative Learning in Teacher Education', Michelle Comeaux of Gustavus Adolphus College in Minnesota describes the different ways in which she has incorporated collaborative learning experiences into her course 'Social Foundations of Education'. Following a general discussion of collaborative learning and its relationship to cooperative learning and reflective teaching, Comeaux draws on her experience with the approach and presents a series of guidelines for teacher educators interested in using collaborative learning that considers such issues as group composition, task definition and task monitoring. Comeaux also describes the four ways in which she uses collaborative learning with her teacher education students: as a structure for students to use when they respond to each other's writing; for discussion of material read; for peer teaching; and, for the creation of projects (e.g., multicultural lessons). Comeaux argues that if student teachers are to develop dispositions and skills to create more democratic classrooms that are based on a view of knowledge as a social construction, then they need personally to experience teacher education classrooms that reflect these same assumptions. Throughout the chapter, Comeaux incorporates comments indicating her students' reactions to collaborative learning activities.

In Chapter 10, 'Reading and Doing Ethnography: Teacher Education and Reflective Practice', Ken Teitelbaum and Deborah Britzman of the State University of New York at Binghamton discuss the ways in which they work with educational ethnography in their teacher education courses. Following a general discussion of ethnographic research and of the ways in which they feel educational ethnography can help establish teachers' ownership of and centrality in the research process, the authors describe two specific examples from their work that illustrate how they help their students engage in reflective practice using educational ethnography. In the first example, Ken Teitelbaum discusses his recent work at Syracuse University where his students employed ethnographic methods, read ethnographic accounts and wrote 'mini-ethnographies' focusing on various 'cultural problematics' of school life such as the hidden curriculum, gender equity and grouping practices. In the second example, Deborah Britzman describes a course (Introduction to Educational Anthropology) that she teaches in the graduate teacher education program at State University of New York (SUNY) Binghamton in which teachers and prospective teachers are introduced to educational ethnography and to the politics of reading ethnographic accounts. In the final section of the chapter, the authors assess the progress that they feel they have achieved with their students and discuss some of the tensions they have experienced in working to develop 'ethnographically-informed' teacher education programs.

In Chapter 11, 'Student Teachers Use Action Research', Susan Noffke and Marie Brennan provide an historical account of how they have used action research in their roles as supervisors in the elementary student teaching program at the University of Wisconsin-Madison to promote critical and reflective teaching by their student teachers. Noffke and Brennan view action research as a collaborative process that involves a focus on one's own practices *and* the wider situation in which that practice occurs. Following a discussion of their rationale for using action research with their students, the authors describe how they use the device of the 'cosmic egg' to help their students engage in relational thinking across different layers of social context and present an example of the action research project of one of their student teachers. The final section of the chapter discusses some of the continuing dilemmas that the authors have faced in using action research in a student teaching program. This chapter is part of the continuing 'researching action research' efforts that were initiated at the University of Wisconsin-Madison in 1986 by Susan Noffke.

In Chapter 12, 'The Cooperating Teacher's Role in Nurturing Reflective Teaching', Patricia Wood, a classroom teacher in the Madison Metropolitan School District and a cooperating teacher in the University of Wisconsin-Madison elementary teacher education program, shares her beliefs about the role of cooperating teachers in encouraging student teachers to become reflective teachers. Wood's view of reflective teaching emphasizes the learning from experience that student teachers can gain from focusing on individual children within the classroom as they interact with the curriculum. Wood describes a number of strategies that she has used with University of Wisconsin-Madison student teachers over the last fourteen years including the collaborative development of curriculum units, focused classroom observations by student teachers, the strategic questioning of student teachers by the cooperating teacher, the use of video technology in the supervision process and action research. In the final section of the chapter, Wood describes several of the tensions and obstacles that she has experienced as a cooperating teacher who has tried to encourage reflective teaching by her student teachers.

In Chapter 13, 'Writing and Reflection in Teacher Education', Jeffrey Maas, an elementary teacher in the Madison Metropolitan School District and formerly a university supervisor in the elementary student teaching program at the University of Wisconsin-Madison, describes the various ways in which he has utilized writing to promote collaborative learning among his student teachers. Maas's focus in this work has been on helping his students become more aware (and hence to gain more control over) the practical theories implicit in their teaching. Following a critical discussion of perspectives on writing as mainly a cognitive process, Maas provides us with his own view of the writing process which also addresses the emotional and social dimensions of writing. Throughout the chapter, he provides specific examples of how different kinds of writing (e.g., newsletters, teaching journals and two academic papers) are used along with small group work in the seminar to help create a more democratic learning community among his student teachers. Maas discusses how he had to work to help his students overcome the 'spectator' roles that they assumed in the writing process at the beginning of the semester and how he tried to establish connections among the student teachers' writing, the seminar and bi-weekly supervisory conferences.

In Chapter 14, 'War Stories: Invitations to Reflect on Practice', Jane White of the University of Maryland-Baltimore County explores the potential of teachers' narratives or 'war stories' for facilitating reflection about teaching and the social conditions of schooling. White argues that the 'war stories' of teachers provide a structure for the expression of the problematic nature of teaching. According to White, by using teachers' and student teachers' 'war stories' in field experience seminars, student teachers become more able to articulate principles on which their actions are based, examine premises and assumptions underlying their arguments and explore alternative perspectives. She believes that using 'war stories' as the basis for initiating discussion in the seminar causes both the story teller and others to reflect about their own practices. The chapter includes several examples of the ways in which 'war stories' told by a program graduate and by student teachers provoked discussion in the field experience seminar. White draws upon Bettelheim's work on the function of folk fairy tales to interpret the 'war stories' of her students.

In Chapter 15, 'Practicing What We Preach: Action Research and the Supervision of Student Teachers', Jennifer Gore, formerly a supervisor of elementary student teachers at the University of Wisconsin-Madison, describes an action research project that she conducted focusing on her own supervisory practice. Gore's research is concerned with power relations in the student teaching triad and explores how the rhetoric of the Wisconsin elementary student teaching program, as stated in program documents and implicit in program symbols (such as an equilateral triangle for the student teaching triad), were acted out in the context of several specific triad relationships. This research project was stimulated by Gore's desire to work toward the establishment of democratic relationships with her student teachers and their cooperating teachers. Throughout the chapter, she draws upon incidents that occurred in several specific triads to illustrate her claims about the actual functioning of student teaching triads. In the last section of the chapter, Gore uses the insights that she gained during her action research to formulate a view of the student teaching triad as potentially similar to collaboration in chamber music. She also discusses the value of collaborative action research as a vehicle for improving student teacher supervision.

The effect of these chapters is to explore meanings for reflective teaching and for inquiry-oriented teacher education. The authors identify theoretical positions and then challenge these through an interpretation of their experiences of inventing practical activities that put the theories to work. It is for readers to make the relevant connections to their own situations, to judge whether the issues selected for analysis are central to teacher education and the extent to which the analyses of the practices described contribute to resolving issues of preparing reflective teachers.

B. Robert Tabachnick
Kenneth M. Zeichner
Madison, Wisconsin
January, 1991

Notes

1 The term that is used in Australia and in the UK to describe 'inquiry-oriented' teacher education is 'research-based' teacher education. For example, see Ruddick (1985).

2 Zeichner (1983) distinguished this approach from behavioristic teacher education which emphasizes the development of specific and observable skills of teaching that are presumed (on the basis of research) to be related to pupil learning; from personalistic teacher education which seeks to promote the psychological maturity of prospective teachers; and from traditional-craft teacher education which seeks to transfer the wisdom of experienced practitioners to novices through an apprenticeship experience. Other typologies of conceptual alternatives in teacher education that address various aspects of 'inquiry-oriented' teacher education include those developed by Feiman-Nemser (1990), Hartnett and Naish (1980) and Kirk (1986).

3 Van Mannen (1977) presents these as 'levels' of reflection. The hierarchical notion of levels conveys the mistaken impression, however, of a developmental framework where technical and practical reflection are eventually transcended and critical reflection prevails. This devalues technical skill and the position of the teacher. The stance taken in this volume is that reflective teaching practice involves inquiry in all three domains of reflection. From this perspective, technical issues are not transcended, but become linked to deliberations about the nature of and justification for educational goals.

4 Heavy teaching loads and difficulty in gaining access to extramural funding for research on teacher education are two of the many factors that have helped create this situation (See Schneider, 1987).

5 See Elliott (1985), Kemmis (1988) and Noffke (1990) for discussion of the tremendous growth in many countries of the teacher-as-researcher movement.

6 For examples of similar practices in teacher education programs outside of the US see Ashcroft and Griffiths (1989), Lucas (1988) and Robottom (1988). An excellent source for descriptions of non-US examples of inquiry-oriented practices in teacher education is the volume edited by Nias and Groundwater-Smith (1988).

7 For example, see Armaline and Hoover (1989), Ayers (1989), Henderson (1989) and King and Ladson-Billings (in press).

References

ARMALINE, W. and HOOVER, R. (1989) 'Field experience as a vehicle for transformation: Ideology, education and reflective practice', *Journal of Teacher Education*, **40**, 2, pp. 42–8.

ASHCROFT, K. and GRIFFITHS, M. (1989) 'Reflective teachers and reflective tutors: School experience in an initial teacher education course', *Journal of Education for Teaching*, **15**, 1, pp. 35–52.

AYERS, W. (1989) 'Headaches: On teaching and teacher education', *Action in Teacher Education*, **11**, 2, pp. 1–7.

CARR, W. and KEMMIS, S. (1986) *Becoming critical: Education, Knowledge, and Action Research*, Basingstoke: Falmer Press.

ELLIOT, J. (1985) 'Education action research', in NISBET, J. and NISBET, S. (Eds) *Research, Policy and Practice: World Yearbook of Education* (pp. 231–50), London: Kogan Page.

FEIMAN-NEMSER, S. (1990) 'Teacher preparation: Structural and conceptual alternatives', in HOUSTON, W.R. (Ed.) *Handbook of Research on Teacher Education* (pp. 212–33), New York: Macmillan.

HARTNETT, A. and NAISH, M. (1980) 'Technicians or social bandits: Some moral and political issues in the education of teachers', in WOODS, P. (Ed.) *Teacher Strategies*, (pp. 254–74), London: Croom Helm.

HENDERSON, J. (1989) 'Positioned reflective practice: A curriculum decision', *Journal of Teacher Education*, **40**, 2, pp. 10–14.

HOUSTON, W.R. (Ed.) (1990) *Handbook of Research on Teacher Education*, New York: Macmillan.

KEMMIS, S. (1988) 'Action research in retrospect and prospect', *The Action Research Reader* (Third edn) (pp. 27–40), Geelong: Deakin University Press.

KING, J.E. and LADSON-BILLINGS, G. (forthcoming) 'The teacher education challenge in elite university settings: Developing critical perspectives for teaching in a democratic and multicultural society', *European Journal of Intercultural Studies*.

KIRK, D. (1986) 'Beyond the limits of theoretical discourse in teacher education: Towards a critical pedagogy', *Teaching and Teacher Education*, **2**, pp. 155–67.

LUCAS, P. (1988) 'An approach to research-based teacher education through collaborative inquiry', *Journal of Education for Teaching*, **14**, 1, pp. 55–73.

NIAS, J. and GROUNDWATER-SMITH, S. (1988) *The Enquiring Teacher: Supporting and Sustaining Teacher Research*, Basingstoke: Falmer Press.

NODDINGS, N. (1987) 'Fidelity in teaching, teacher education and research for teaching', *Harvard Educational Review*, **56**, 4, pp. 496–510.

NOFFKE, S. (1990) Action research: A multidimensional analysis. Unpublished doctoral dissertation, University of Wisconsin-Madison.

ROBOTTOM, I. (1988) 'A research-based course in science education', in NIAS, J. and GROUNDWATER-SMITH, S. (Eds) *The Enquiring Teacher: Supporting and Sustaining Teacher Research*, (pp. 106–20), Basingstoke: Falmer Press.

RUDDOCK, J. (1985) 'Teacher research and research-based teacher education', *Journal of Education for Teaching*, **11**, 3, pp. 281–9.

SCHNEIDER, B. (1987) 'Tracing the provenance of teacher education', in POPKEWITZ, T. (Ed.) *Critical Studies in Teacher Education*, Basingstoke: Falmer Press.

TOM, A. (1985) 'Inquiring into inquiry-oriented teacher education', *Journal of Teacher Education*, **35**, 5, pp. 35–44.

VAN MANEN, M. (1977) 'Linking ways of knowing with ways of being practical', *Curriculum Inquiry*, **6**, pp. 205–28.

ZEICHNER, K. (1983) 'Alternative paradigms of teacher education', *Journal of Teacher Education*, **34**, pp. 3–9.

ZEICHNER, K. (1987) 'Preparing reflective teachers', *International Journal of Educational Research*, **11**, 5, pp. 565–76.

ZEICHNER, K. and LISTON, D. (1990) 'Traditions of reform in US teacher education', *Journal of Teacher Education*, **41**, 2, pp. 3–20.

1 Reflections on Reflective Teaching

Kenneth M. Zeichner and B. Robert Tabachnick

In the last decade, concurrent with the growth of research on teacher thinking and with the increased respect for teachers' practical theories (Clark, 1988), the 'reflective practitioner' has emerged as the new zeitgeist in North American teacher education. One consequence of this phenomenon is that terms such as 'action research', 'reflective teaching', 'reflection-in-action', 'teacher as researcher' and 'research-based' or 'inquiry-oriented' teacher education have now become fashionable throughout all segments of the US and Canadian teacher education communities. Among the signs of this ascendancy are two recent national conferences in the US focused primarily on reflective inquiry in teacher education (e.g., Clift, Houston and Pugach, 1990), a special issue of the *Journal of Teacher Education* devoted to 'Critical Reflection in Teacher Education' (*JTE*, 1989) and the recent proliferation of books and monographs on reflective practice in teaching and teacher education (e.g., Grimmett and Erickson, 1988; Posner, 1989; Waxman, *et al.*, 1988).[1]

It's come to the point now that we don't know very much at all about a practice if it is merely described as something aimed at facilitating the development of reflective teachers. We agree with Calderhead's (1989) assessment that the full range of beliefs within the teacher education community about teaching, schooling, teacher education and the social order has now been incorporated into the discourse about reflective practice. There is not a single teacher educator who would say that he or she is not concerned about preparing teachers who are reflective. The criteria that have become attached to reflective practice are so diverse, however, that important differences between specific practices are masked by the use of the common rhetoric.

On the one hand, the recent work of teacher educators such as Cruickshank (1987), who has drawn upon Dewey (1933) for inspiration, gives us some guidance. The distinction that is often made between reflective and routine practice is not trivial and enables us to make some important qualitative distinctions among different teachers and teaching practices.[2] Similarly, the enormously popular work of Schon (1983, 1987, 1989) which has challenged the dominant technical rationality in professional education and argued for more attention to promoting artistry in teaching by encouraging 'reflection in action' and 'reflection on action' among teachers, also directs our attention to the preparation of particular kinds of teachers and not others. These generic approaches to reflective teaching lose their heuristic value, however, after a certain point and begin to hide more than they reveal.[3]

After we have agreed with Cruickshank and Schon, for example, that thoughtful teachers who reflect about their practice (on and in action) are more desirable than thoughtless teachers, who are ruled primarily by tradition, authority and circumstance, there are still many unanswered questions. Neither Cruickshank nor Schon have much to say, for example, about what it is that teachers ought to be reflecting about, the kinds of criteria that should come into play during the process of reflection (e.g., which help distinguish acceptable from unacceptable educational practice) or about the degree to which teachers' deliberations should incorporate a critique of the institutional contexts in which they work (Richardson, 1990). In some extreme cases, the impression is given that as long as teachers reflect about something, in some manner, whatever they decide to do is all right since they have reflected about it.

> *How* to get students to reflect can take on a life of its own, and can become *the* programmatic goal. *What* they reflect on can become immaterial. For example, racial tension as a school issue can become no more or less worthy of reflection than field trips or homework assignments. (Valli, 1990b, p. 9)

One of the reasons that these generic conceptions of reflection have become so popular is that they can (and have been) employed by teacher educators of every ideological persuasion.[4] Everyone can identify with them and they offend no one, except those who seek to tightly control teachers' actions through external prescription. Despite the important distinctions between reflective and routine practice on the one hand, and between technical rationality and an epistemology of practice on the other (Schon, 1983),[5] both of which affirm the value of teachers' practical knowledge, we do not think that it makes much sense to encourage or to assess reflective practice in general without establishing clear priorities for the reflections that emerge out of a reasoned educational and social philosophy. We do not accept the implication that exists throughout much of the literature, that teachers actions are necessarily better just because they are more deliberate or intentional.

This chapter will examine several aspects of reflective teaching practice in an attempt to push the discussion among teacher educators beyond an attempt to prepare reflective teachers in general. We hope that this analysis will encourage teacher educators to identify clearly the educational and political commitments that stand behind their own and others' proposals regarding reflective teaching so that we can move beyond the current situation where important differences in our motives and passions are hidden from view by the use of popular slogans. In the next section, various conceptions of reflective teaching practice will be described utilizing a framework that has emerged out of our analysis of four traditions of reform in twentieth-century US teacher education: an academic tradition, a social efficiency tradition, a developmentalist tradition and a social reconstructionist tradition. We will then explore the relationships between these different (but also overlapping) orientations to reflective teaching practice and the descriptions of inquiry-oriented teacher education practices that are presented in the remaining chapters of the book. Following this discussion, the question of the different meanings that reflective teaching practice can take on as it is acted out in classrooms will be examined through an analysis of specific examples of the teaching of social studies.

Conceptions of Reflective Teaching Practice

There are various ways in which we can distinguish particular proposals for reflective teaching from one another. One way in which we can think about differences among proposals for reflective teaching is in light of different traditions of practice in teacher education.[6] Zeichner and Liston (1990) have identified four varieties of reflective teaching practice based on their analysis of traditions of reform in twentieth-century US teacher education:

1   an academic version that stresses reflection upon subject matter and the representation and translation of subject matter knowledge to promote student understanding (Shulman, 1987);
2   a social efficiency version that emphasizes the thoughtful application of particular teaching strategies that have been suggested by research on teaching (Ross and Kyle, 1987);[7]
3   a developmentalist version that prioritizes teaching that is sensitive to students' interests, thinking and patterns of developmental growth (Duckworth, 1987), and;
4   a social reconstructionist version that stresses reflection about the social and political context of schooling and the assessment of classroom actions for their ability to contribute toward greater equity, social justice and humane conditions in schooling and society (Beyer, 1988; Maher and Rathbone, 1986).

In each of these views of reflective teaching practice, certain priorities are established about schooling and society that emerge out of particular historical traditions and educational and social philosophies.

None of these traditions is sufficient by itself for providing a moral basis for teaching and teacher education. Good teaching and teacher education need to attend to all of the elements that are brought into focus by the various traditions: the representation of subject matter, student thinking and understanding, teaching strategies suggested by research conducted by university academics and classroom teachers, and the social contexts of teaching. These elements do not take the same form, however, or receive the same emphasis within each tradition. For example, technical competence in teaching, when viewed as an end in itself apart from its ability to promote student understanding (a fairly common phenomenon in the US)[8] is not synonymous with technical competence that is sensitive to and builds upon student understandings (see MacKinnon and Erickson, 1988). Also, the employment of teaching practices that lead to student understanding does not necessarily mean that all students share the benefits of the exemplary teaching. In fact, much evidence suggests that the continued existence of a serious 'crisis of inequality' in US public schooling corresponds to a similar situation of inequality in the society as a whole (e.g., Kelly and Nihlen, 1982; Ornstein and Levine, 1989).

Despite the differences in the emphasis given to various factors within the different traditions of reflective teaching, these traditions are not mutually exclusive. In practice, the traditions overlap in many ways and each one attends in some manner to all of the issues that are raised by the traditions as a group. The differences among the traditions of reflection are defined in terms of the emphasis and priority that is given to particular factors within traditions. For example, although social reconstructionist teacher educators are frequently critical of those from other traditions for failing to emphasize a concern for reflection about the institutional, social and political contexts of schooling, it is not reasonable to conclude (without further analysis) that individuals who express allegiance to another version of reflective teaching are unconcerned with issues of social justice and equity.[9] Similarly, although there has been frequent criticism of social reconstructionist teacher educators for their strong emphasis on institutional and societal critique as a fundamental part of reflective teaching, it is not reasonable to conclude (again without further analysis) that they are unconcerned with teaching skills and techniques. Following is a brief discussion of each of these traditions of reflective teaching.

The Academic Tradition of Reflective Teaching

The academic tradition of reform within twentieth-century US teacher education has historically emphasized the role of the liberal arts and disciplinary knowledge in teacher preparation and belittled the contribution of schools, departments and colleges of education, with the exception of practice teaching and other clinical experiences (e.g., Flexner, 1930; Koerner, 1963; Damerell, 1985). This orientation to teacher education emphasizes the teacher's role as a scholar and subject matter specialist and has taken different forms throughout the twentieth-century. In recent years, Lee Shulman (1986, 1987), and Margaret Buchmann (1984) among others,[10] have advocated views of reflective teaching that emphasize the teacher's deliberations about subject matter and its transformation to pupils to promote understanding. Shulman and Buchmann, unlike many others within the academic tradition who advocate merely more exposure to subject matter content for teachers, recognize the contribution that pedagogical knowledge (and professional education course work) can make to a teacher's formal education. Their views represent a challenge to historically dominant notions of academically oriented reform in teacher education (see Zeichner and Liston, 1990).

For example, Shulman (1986a) has described subject matter knowledge as the 'missing paradigm' in research on teaching and teacher education. Reacting to a neglect of this issue by scholars in the field, Shulman (1987) and his colleagues in the 'Knowledge Growth in Teaching Project' (e.g., Wilson, Shulman and Richert 1987; Wilson and Wineburg, 1988; Grossman, Wilson and Shulman, 1989), have proposed a model of pedagogical reasoning and action and of the professional knowledge base for teaching that clearly places the emphasis on the intellectual basis for teaching and on the transformation of subject matter knowledge by teachers. Shulman and his colleagues have raised the important question of what kind of subject matter knowledge teachers need to teach in a way that leads to student understanding. Rather than assuming that more exposure to liberal arts courses, as they are currently conceived, is a solution to problems related to teachers' subject matter expertise,[11] they have proposed a model of the components of the professional knowledge base for teaching that includes three major categories of content knowledge: subject matter content knowledge, pedagogical content knowledge and curricular knowledge. A key component of the knowledge base for teaching that gives it its special identity according to Shulman and his colleagues is pedagogical content knowledge. According to Shulman (1986b), pedagogical content knowledge

> embodies the aspects of content most germane to its teachability. Within the category of pedagogical content knowledge I include, for the most regularly taught topics in one's subject area, the most useful forms of representation of those ideas, the most powerful analogies, illustrations, examples, explanations, and demonstrations — in a word, the ways of representing and formulating the subject that make it comprehensible to others ... [it] also includes an understanding of what makes the learning of specific topics easy or difficult: the conceptions and preconceptions that students of different ages and backgrounds bring with them to the learning. (p. 9)

This group has also proposed a model of pedagogical reasoning and action that identifies six aspects of the teaching act: comprehension, transformation, instruction, evaluation, reflection and new comprehension. One key aspect of their model of pedagogical reasoning (under the transformation process) is representation. According to Shulman (1987),

> representation involves thinking through the key ideas in the text or lesson and identifying the alternative ways of representing them to students. What analogies, metaphors, examples, demonstrations, simulations, and the like can help to build a bridge between the teacher's comprehension and that desired for the students? Multiple forms of representation are desirable. (p. 328)

This model of pedagogical reasoning and action is a good example of a contemporary view of reflective teaching that prioritizes reflection about the content to be taught and how it is to be taught. While this conception of reflective teaching does not ignore general pedagogical knowledge derived from research on teaching, students' understandings and developmental characteristics, and issues of social justice and equity, the standards for assessing the adequacy of the teaching evolve primarily from the academic disciplines.

The Social Efficiency Tradition of Reflective Teaching

The social efficiency tradition of reform in US teacher education, one version of progressivism in American educational thought (Cremin, 1961), has historically emphasized a faith in the scientific study of teaching to provide the basis for building a teacher education curriculum. According to advocates of this view, research on teaching has, in recent years, provided us with a 'knowledge base' that can form the foundation for the curriculum of teacher education programs

(Berliner, 1984). Feiman-Nemser (1990) has identified two different ways in which contemporary teacher educators have interpreted the social efficiency perspective. First, she describes a technological version in which the intent is to teach prospective teachers the skills and competencies that research has shown to be associated with desirable pupil outcomes. This narrow interpretation of the social efficiency view emphasizes 'reflection' by the teacher about how closely their practice conforms to standards provided by some aspect of research on teaching (e.g., Gentile, 1988).

A second and broader interpretation of the social efficiency tradition in US teacher education (the deliberative orientation according to Feiman-Nemser, 1990), is one where the findings of research on teaching are used by teachers as 'principles of procedure' within a wider process of decision making and problem solving. According to the advocates of this deliberative orientation to the use of research on teaching, the crucial task for teacher educators is to foster teachers' capabilities to exercise judgment about the use of various teaching skills suggested by research as well as by other sources:

> Because they view good teaching as good deliberation, their concern is not that teachers follow a set of rules, which could never account for all circumstances anyway, but rather that teachers view teaching as a process of constantly making choices about the means and ends, choices that can be informed by process product research, descriptive research, experience, intuition, and one's own values. (Zumwalt, 1982, p. 226)

A contemporary example of a teacher education program that emphasizes a conception of reflective teaching practice involving the intelligent (rather than mechanical) use of research on teaching is the elementary PROTEACH program at the University of Florida. Dorene Ross and her colleagues have, over a number of years, used the label of reflective teaching to describe an approach to teaching as decision making where research on teaching is one among a number of factors that teachers deliberate about:

> The limits on the appropriate use of teacher effectiveness research must be understood by prospective teachers ... the most important teacher behavior is the flexibility and judgment necessary to select the appropriate strategy for the particular goal and students involved. (Ross and Kyle, 1987, p. 41)

While this conception of reflective teaching does not totally ignore the social contexts of schooling and issues of equity and social justice, student understandings and developmental characteristics, or subject matter, the emphasis is clearly on the intelligent use of 'generic' teaching skills and strategies that have been suggested by research.[12]

The Developmentalist Tradition of Reflective Teaching

The distinguishing characteristic of the developmentalist tradition of reform in twentieth-century US teacher education (another element of progressive thought in US education, Perrone, 1989), is the assumption that the natural development of the learner provides the basis for determining what should be taught to students and how it should be taught. Historically, this natural order of child development was to be determined by research involving the careful observation and description of students' behavior at various stages of development (Mitchell, 1931).

According to Perrone (1989), three central metaphors have been associated with the progressive/developmentalist tradition in US teacher education: teacher as naturalist, teacher as researcher and teacher as artist. The teacher as naturalist dimension has stressed the importance of skill in the observation of children's behavior and in building a curriculum and classroom environment consistent with patterns of child development and children's interests. Classroom practice is to be grounded in close observation and study of children in the classroom either directly by the teacher, or from reflection on a literature based on such study. The teacher as researcher element of this tradition has emphasized the need to foster the teacher's experimental attitude toward practice and to help them initiate and sustain ongoing inquiries in their own classrooms about the learning of specific children to inform their practice. Finally, the teacher as artist element has emphasized the link between creative and fully functioning persons in touch with their own learning and exciting and stimulating classrooms.

One contemporary example of reflective teaching practice within this tradition is the work of Eleanor Duckworth at Harvard University.[13] Duckworth (1987) has elaborated a constructivist view of reflective teaching that emphasizes engaging learners with phenomena and then working to understand the sense they are making of those phenomena (instead of explaining things to students at the onset). According to Duckworth, teachers are both practitioners and researchers and their research is to be focused on their students and their current understandings of the area under study. The teacher then uses this knowledge of students' current understandings to decide the appropriate next steps for their learning and keeps trying to find out what sense the students are making as the instruction continues.

> The essential element of having the students do the explaining is not the withholding of all the teacher's own thoughts. It is, rather, that the teacher not consider herself or himself the final arbiter of what the learner should think, nor the creator of what the learner does think. The important job for the teacher is to keep trying to find out what sense the students are making. (Duckworth, 1987, p. 133)

This developmentalist conception of reflective teaching has become increasingly popular in recent years with the growing influence of cognitive psychology in education (Reilly, 1989). While it doesn't ignore subject matter standards emanating from the disciplines, research on teaching and the social and political context and issues of social justice, the emphasis is clearly on reflecting about students.

The Social Reconstructionist Tradition of Reflective Teaching

In the fourth tradition of reform in twentieth-century US teacher education, social reconstructionism, schooling and teacher education are both viewed as crucial elements in the movement toward a more just and humane society. According to Valli (1989a), proponents of this approach (which draws upon various Neo-Marxist, Critical and feminist perspectives)[14] argue

> that schools as social institutions, help reproduce a society based on unjust class, race, and gender relations and that teachers have a moral obligation to reflect on and change their own practices and school structures when these perpetuate such arrangements. (p. 46)

In a social reconstructionist conception of reflective teaching, the teacher's attention is focused both inwardly at their own practice (and the collective practices of a group of colleagues) *and* outwardly at the social conditions in which these practices are situated (Kemmis, 1985). How teachers' actions maintain and/or disrupt the status quo in schooling and society is of central concern. The reflection is aimed in part, at the elimination of the social conditions that distort the self-understandings of teachers and undermine the educative potential and moral basis of schooling. According to John Elliott (1990), institutional and social critique are a natural part of the process of reflection.

> Reflective practice implies reflexivity: self-awareness. But such an aware-ness brings with it insights into the ways in which the self in action is shared and constrained by institutional structures. Self-awareness and the awareness of the institutional context of one's work as a teacher are not developed by separate cognitive processes, reflexive and objective analy-sis. They are qualities of the same reflexive process. Reflexive practice necessarily implies both self-critique and institutional critique. One can-not have one without the other. (p. 23)

A second characteristic of a social reconstructionist conception of reflective teaching is its democratic and emancipatory impulse and the focus of the teacher's deliberations upon substantive issues that raise instances of inequality and injustice within schooling and society for close scrutiny. Recognizing the fundamentally political character of all schooling, the teacher's reflections center upon such issues as the gendered nature of schooling and of teachers' work, the relationships between race and social class on the one hand and access to school knowledge and school achievement on the other, and the influence of external interests on the process of curriculum production. These and other similar issues are addressed in concrete form as they arise within the context of the teacher's classroom and school.

For example, an issue that is confronted fairly frequently by student teachers at the University of Wisconsin-Madison is disproportionate assignment of pupils of color to the lower tracks of school programs and to such remedial categories as 'learning disabled'. In the Madison area, pupils of color also have higher than average school suspension rates and lower than average high school graduation rates (Ptak, 1988). All of this is fairly common across the US (Goodlad, 1990). In a social reconstructionist conception of reflective teaching these so-called 'facts' about the context of the teacher's work which highlight racial and class differ-

Figure 1   *Traditions of reflective teaching*

Tradition	The Focus of the Reflection is on
Academic	The representations of subject matter to students to promote understanding
Social Efficiency	The intelligent use of generic teaching strategies suggested by research on teaching
Developmentalist	The learning, development and understanding of students
Social Reconstructionist	The social conditions of schooling and issues of equity and justice

ences in educational outcomes would be made problematic and examined as part of the teacher's deliberations about teaching. These reflections would then stimulate an exploration of alternative possibilities through which the painful effects of these practices could be lessened. The more usual scenario is for these and similar issues to serve as background during teachers' reflections.

The third distinguishing characteristic of a social reconstructionist conception of reflective teaching is its commitment to reflection as a communal activity. Social reconstructionist oriented teacher educators seek to create 'communities of learning' where teachers can support and sustain each others growth. This commitment to collaborative modes of learning indicates a dual commitment by teacher educators to an ethic where justice and equity on the one hand, and care and compassion on the other, are valued. This commitment is also thought to be of strategic value in the transformation of unjust and inhumane institutional and social structures. Specifically, it is felt that the empowerment of individual teachers as individuals is inadequate, and that the potential for institutional and social change is greater, if teachers see their individual situations as linked to those of their colleagues (Freedman, Jackson and Boles, 1986).

These four traditions of reflective teaching (see Figure 1) can be used to interpret various aspects of proposals for teacher education reform and descriptions of existing practices. For example, the distinguishing characteristic of many of the chapters that follow is the explicit commitment of the authors to social reconstructionist values. While they differ in terms of the emphasis given to issues of gender, race and social class and in the specific strategies that are used to support and sustain the reflections of student teachers, the chapters reflect (unlike the vast majority of work on reflective teaching in the US) an emancipatory intent in their attention to both self-critique and social/institutional critique. Several of the chapters in this volume (particularly 12 and 13) reflect a very strong emphasis on developmentalist values. In the final analysis, each of these chapters reflects some pattern of resonance with *each* of the four reform traditions. The reform traditions framework represents one way to unpack the assumptions and goals underlying the reforms represented in these chapters. Whether one uses this particular lens or not, however, it is important to attempt to understand the particular quality of reflection that is being advocated by each author. In the final part of this chapter, we will address the important issue of the way in which reflective teaching can take on different meanings within the classroom.

Reflective Teaching — How do we know it when we see it?

In describing the classroom lives of teachers, some twenty or more years ago, Phillip Jackson presented a vision of a social environment whose intensity, complexity and insistent demands for rapid response, seemed to leave little room for deliberation, weighing and choosing alternatives, or anything our common experience would label reflection (Jackson, 1968). That might come later, looking back at what happened and forward to what might be encouraged to happen next and would be desirable in the teacher's view, if it did happen next. Recently, Donald Schon has teased our interest in defining teaching to be a thoughtful enterprise by suggesting the possibility that teachers reflect-in-action (Schon, 1983, 1987), so that even the rapidly unfolding texture of classroom events is partly shaped by the teacher's intellectual intuitions, not merely by routinized or uncritical responses to instructional demands. It is appealing to find that teachers can be reflective, but it is not altogether clear what reflectiveness looks like in action or if it is something that lives in abstractions but is not recognizable as teacher behavior.

If we want to prepare university students to become reflective teachers, it would be useful to know what reflective teaching looks like. Why should it be difficult to recognize reflective teaching when we see it?

One reason for the difficulty is that reflection is commonly considered to be a private activity, while reflective teaching, like any kind of teaching, is expected to be a public activity. Reflection, even when it is conceived to be a private activity, may have public consequences as people say or do things we can observe and that we guess are the result of reflection. In this view, thought and action are connected but separate from one another. If we want to act wisely, we think first, then deliberately do what we have decided is the best way to act.

In an alternative view (Mead, 1938), thinking and doing are inseparable parts of an act. It is not only thinking that leads to and shapes the behavior of the wise actor, but that person's behavior, within a particular social context, also can lead to and shape thinking. Thought and behavior become a duality, interdependent and interactive. For this duality of thought and behavior, it is not only language that identifies what someone believes or intends, but also the person's behavior, within a particular social context, that expresses belief and intention.

In a study of teacher responses to contradictions between their statements of belief and their teaching behavior, we found that two teachers, each in their first year of teaching, resolved contradictions in quite different ways (Tabachnick and Zeichner, 1986). Both teachers, Hannah and Beth, said that they intended to encourage active learning by pupils, respond to pupil interests in order to create more intrinsic motivation to learn, and to connect the school work to the lives and experiences of their pupils. As they began the school year, both were observed teaching in rather routine ways, with almost no pupil initiatives being encouraged in Beth's room and very few in Hannah's.

As the year progressed, Hannah tried continually to change her teaching to make it more consistent with her stated intentions and by the end of the year there were noticeable differences in the way learning activities were planned, organized and implemented. As Beth's year progressed, the few instances of an open and easy approach to teaching (her term) seemed to disappear. Her teaching became more controlling and routinized. What changed noticeably were her statements of belief and commitment; by the end of the year she rejected the value of pupil participation in planning for learning and affirmed the virtues of worksheets and practice exercises that prepared pupils for tests of information transmitted by Beth or by various teaching materials. Beth and Hannah were both thinking about teaching. Are they both reflective teachers?

This question identifies a second reason for difficulty in recognizing reflective teaching that was discussed earlier: that educators from a broad range of ideological persuasions embrace the term 'reflective teaching'. The message in the reform traditions framework presented earlier in this chapter is that we must be interested in more complex questions than whether teaching is reflective or not. We need to ask questions about the nature and purpose of teachers' reflections; that is, what are teachers being reflective about, and why?

Reflective teaching, like any teaching, is a social activity. Either reflective teaching looks back at social interactions and tries to make sense of them in order to plan for future teaching, or it looks forward to social interactions of teaching and learning that have not yet taken place and attempts to shape these, or reflective teaching is within the process of teaching and learning, in which ideas and behavior interact to shape one another. Meanings for the results of teaching and learning are grounded in and confirmed by social relations within a particular social context.

Kemmis (1985), in examining the social character of reflection as a part of teaching, moves beyond its orientation to action within a social context. Kemmis identifies reflection as value-laden, expressing and serving

> particular human, social, cultural and political interests ... it actively reproduces or transforms the ideological practices which are the basis of the social order ... (and) expresses our power to reconstitute social life by the way we participate in communication, decision-making and social action. (p. 149)

In this activist view, thinking about teaching has consequences. Teaching itself always has some effect in terms of enhancing the life chances of students or of maintaining existing constraints to students' access to opportunity. We can see this in action when we look at reports of teaching and learning. The classroom descriptions that follow are taken from a variety of sources, all of them published and readily available, all focusing on the teaching of social studies.

Classroom Vignettes

Anyon (1980) described the teaching of social studies in fifth grade classrooms in five different schools. The schools are located in communities labelled 'working class' (two schools), 'middle class', 'affluent professional' and 'elite executive'. The different designations refer to the range of income and to the occupations of parents. The communities are described as being from 85 per cent to 90 per cent white. Anyon (1980) described teaching in the 'working-class' schools as follows:

> Social studies in the working-class schools is ... largely mechanical, rote work that was given little explanation or connection to larger

contexts. In one school, for example, although there was a book available, social studies work was to copy the teacher's notes from the board.... The fifth grades in the district were to study US history. The teacher used a booklet she had purchased called 'The Fabulous Fifty States.' Each day she put information from the booklet in outline form on the board and the children copied it.... As the children finished copying the sentences, the teacher erased them and wrote more. Children would occasionally go to the front to pull down the wall map in order to locate the states they were copying, and the teacher did not dissuade them. But the observer never saw her refer to the map; nor did the observer ever hear her make other than perfunctory remarks concerning the information the children were copying. Occasionally the children colored in a ditto and cut it out to make a stand-up figure.... These were referred to by the teacher as their social studies 'projects'. (pp. 75–6)

Teaching in Anyon's 'middle-class' school is similarly controlled toward goals that are rarely identified or explained to the pupils. The emphasis is also on information transmitted directly from the textbook and the teacher, but somewhat more explanation or elaboration by the teacher is reported:

In social studies the daily work is to read the assigned pages in the textbook and to read the teacher's questions. The questions are almost always designed to check on whether the students have read the assignment and understood it. The answers are in the book and in one's understanding of the book; the teacher's hints when one doesn't know the answer are to 'read it again', or to look at the picture or the rest of the paragraph.... A critical perspective in social studies is perceived as dangerous by these teachers because it may lead to controversial topics; the parents might complain; what has happened in the past, and what exists now may not be equitable or fair but (shrug) that is the way things are, and one does not confront such matters in school. For example, in social studies, after a child is called on to read a passage about the pilgrims, the teacher summarizes the paragraph and then says, 'So you can see how strict they were about everything'. A child asks, 'Why?' 'Well, because they felt that if you weren't busy you'd get into trouble'. Another child asks, 'Is it true that they burned women at the stake?' The teacher says, 'Yes, if a woman did anything strange, they hanged them [*sic*] What would a woman do, do you think, to make them burn them [*sic*] See if you can come up with better answers than my other [social studies] class'. Several children offer suggestions, to which the teacher nods but does not comment. Then she says, 'Ok, good', and calls on the next child to read. (pp. 77–8)

The teacher-pupil interaction in the 'elite-executive' school is very different in form and substance from the two preceding segments:

Occasionally the children are asked to make up sample questions for their social studies tests. On an occasion when the investigator was present the social studies teacher rejected a child's question by saying, 'That's just fact. If I asked you that question on a test, you'd complain it was just memory! Good questions ask for concepts'. The teachers initiate classroom discussions of current social issues and problems. These questions occurred on every one of the investigator's visits, and a teacher told me, 'These children's opinions are important — it's important that they learn to reason things through'. The classroom discussions always struck the observer as quite realistic and analytical, dealing with concrete social issues like the following: 'Why do workers strike?' ... 'Why do companies put chemicals in food when the natural ingredients are available?' Usually the children did not have to be prodded to give their opinions.... Occasionally the teachers would prod with statements such as, 'Even if you don't know [the answers], if you think logically about it, you can figure it out'. And, 'I'm asking you [these] questions to help you think this through'. (pp. 84–5)

In this brief excerpt, the emphasis is on the connections among concepts and between academic knowledge and pupil experience. Pupils are encouraged, even goaded to think for themselves, to be analytic and possibly even critical, forming meanings together and challenging one another's understanding, with the potential for searching out competing social interests. (We don't know if this potential is realized since the substance of pupil responses to the questions about strikes and chemical additives is not reported.)

Anyon follows these descriptions of classroom behavior with a social class analysis that links the meanings of work in each school to what she perceives to be the present and likely future social class locations of the pupils. While the distinctions between 'working-class' and 'middle-class' schools and between 'affluent-professional' and 'elite-executive' schools may not be as sharp as Anyon concludes, there are remarkable differences in the teaching presented in the least and most affluent schools.

Similar experiences are in the literature elsewhere. For example, Beth's teaching, referred to above, takes place in a community somewhat more affluent than Anyon's middle-class community but there are many similarities in the teaching. The differences follow from the precise and controlling character of the lists of behavioral objectives that form the curriculum of Beth's school. Beth's focus is on *how* to have her pupils ahieve the lists of 'competencies' which a committee of teachers identified some years before Beth joined the school district. Beth says that influences on what happens in her classroom are:

the school curriculum in that they say what should be taught ... us pod teachers in deciding who teaches what ... and then me, myself as a teacher, as in how I'm going to teach it. (Tabachnick and Zeichner, 1986, p. 89)

Selecting or identifying goals is not an important effort. Beth says her goals are

real sketchy ... I don't really have any big ones set out ... I'd like them to understand what I'm talking about, sure ... and to retain some of the things that I've taught, definitely. But that would be it for goals. (She comments that she can generally teach the kind of curriculum that she thinks is important), 'as long as it includes what has been set out for me to teach'. (Tabachnick and Zeichner, 1986, p. 89)

In a community containing elements of Anyon's two affluent communities, Smith describes teaching that is equally challenging intellectually, and which has pupils develop skills that are useful for exercising power in a community. In a senior high school lesson about the Magna Carta,

The lecture/discussion continues, contrasts to American history are raised re the constitution, Lincoln and the Civil War, and Nixon and Watergate. Then he's back to King John. At 10:35 he shifts to 'right of rebellion'. 'Is it in the constitution?' One of the youngsters vacillates. And he's back at Washington, Jefferson, Madison, and 'Did you take American history? Did you study the constitution?' The observer commented in the notes after these self evident rhetorical questions: (... he crowds individuals and class intellectually, e.g., what happened to your rights of rebellion? ...)

Later as one of the students made a point about 'limited orderly rebellion' and another 'might makes right', and the discussion on the point moves toward closure, the teacher comments, 'Fascinating'.

The observer notes: (he backs off). And one of the kids gets in a last lick, 'Don't you ever answer your questions?'; and the teacher, not to be bested, comments, 'No, they're too difficult'.

... So the hour went. It was exciting. It was stimulating. The teacher commented that the kids bounce back and come at him again and again. He perceives them learning independent critical thought (Smith, 1978).

Interpreting the Vignettes

There are different ways to react to these glimpses into various classrooms. There are clear differences represented. For example, some of the teaching aimed to transmit the belief that knowledge is outside of people; that knowledge is most valuable when it is most certain, and that it can be passed from those who have it to those who don't without essentially altering its substance. Instruction was answer oriented. Most activities were routinized, that is activities took place without questions or explanations about goals being necessary and few questions were needed about what to do next because it was decided by the textbook or by a sequence of activities treated as universally appropriate to all learners in all social contexts. Some of the other teachers seemed to invite their pupils to help form concepts together, to think things out for themselves and to illuminate their understanding by testing it against or enriching it with their own experience. There was an effort in these classrooms to help pupils recognize and accept teacher goals for learning, but there is also some teacher concern for pupils coming to direct their own learning, as seen in the question-orientation (as contrasted to an answer-orientation) in these classrooms, the probes for pupil opinions, pupil judgments and pupil choices.

The brevity of the descriptions tends to form them into easy dichotomies and categories that are unlike the reality of most teaching. For those teachers who identify their goals to their pupils or who describe their reasoning in asides to an observer, we can recognize interconnections among ideas and teaching behaviors and we can begin to speculate about the traditions that influence their reflection and the interaction of behavior and idea as each helps form the other.

Observations of teaching do not by themselves tell us what kind of reflective teaching we are seeing, although they might suggest that very little reflection is going on, that a decision, once made, is applied without further question, with activities seeming to be indifferent to the reactions of the pupils for whom they were supposedly designed.

Building on categories of social analysis developed by Jurgen Habermas, Kemmis (1985) explores technical, practical and critical forms of reflection as responses to the question — What do teachers reflect about and why? Technical reflection concerns itself with how goals are to be achieved but does not question the goals. Beth seemed to say that she planned and taught within those parameters. Practical reflection questions and tries to select both appropriate goals and appropriate means to achieve the selected goals. Critical reflection examines goals and means in terms not only of educational consequences but also in terms of the political consequences for creating a more rational, just and fulfilling society. We do not learn enough in these brief vignettes about the processes that led to teacher choices to know the extent to which most of the teachers are technical, practical or critical. We need to hear their interpretations of their work as well as see them carry it out. The likelihood is that few teachers are reflective in the style of only one category or that they are consistently within one category or another.

There is also the probability that teachers who agree about goals will disagree about strategies for achieving them. At odds with many liberal and radical educators, Delpit (1988) argues, for example, that the empowerment of poor children and of children of color is more likely to result when teachers are authoritative and direct, although direct teaching by itself is not enough:

> I do not advocate a simplistic 'basic skills' approach for children outside of the culture of power. It would be (and has been) tragic to operate as if these children were incapable of critical and higher-order thinking and reasoning. Rather, I suggest that schools must provide these children the content that other families from a different cultural orientation provide at home. This does not mean separating children according to family background, but instead, ensuring that each classroom incorporates strategies appropriate for all the children in its confines. (p. 286)

When we studied the development of perspectives toward teaching by student teachers, we found that the students came into student teaching with partly formed perspectives. These tended not to change during the semester but to strengthen as students became more articulate in describing, acting on and justifying their perspectives (Tabachnick and Zeichner, 1984). It is possible that because we kept asking them why they were doing what they did as teachers that they got better at answering that kind of question. Clearly, teachers and student teachers can become interested in probing the purposes of their work and in thinking about its consequences.

Thinking can be a private and individual activity, although it is arguable that it is the anticipation of the critique of potential supporters and opponents that protects us against easy self-delusions. As we have discussed reflective teaching in this chapter, we have developed a concept of reflective teaching as a social activity. It is not merely social in its content, that is, in a concern to interpret the behavior and social interactions of students, teachers, community members, or to anticipate future social behavior. Reflection is itself a form of social interaction; it is carried on through a dialogue of words or actions with other participants in the teaching-learning context or else it is a symbolic dialogue in which the teacher anticipates and invents the reactions of students, colleagues and others, using this symbolic dialogue as test and critique of proposed interpretations and plans for future actions.

In all of the chapters that follow, the authors describe a variety of ways in which teacher educators help students expand their private thoughts and unique personal experiences related to professional concerns of teaching, then encourage students to connect these to the concerns and experiences of colleagues, veteran teachers and school children. To cite a few examples, Maher's students (Chapter 2) search out and share interpretations of gender-related school responses in their own lives. Beyer (Chapter 7) encourages students to discover something of the realities that low-income parents face, by having his students volunteer as workers in community projects where they can encounter at first hand the struggles of low-income people for dignity and survival. White (Chapter 14) leads students to share 'war stories', tales of crises and problem encounters in their classrooms. The unresolved tensions of incidents that ended 'badly' or of teaching problems that remain unsolved, together with their authenticity, makes it very difficult for other students to resist the appeal to join the story-teller's reflective behavior; they all share in interpreting the incidents and thinking toward defensible future action, while the instructor challenges the students' responses to transcend a superficial technical orientation. Richert (Chapter 8) describes student efforts to write and to respond to 'cases' as generating similarly collaborative reflection.

In the social interactions of teachers and student teachers with peers and with mentors/supervisors, and in the social interactions in the classroom, the links between idea and action can be clarified, judgments can be reviewed and re-formed. It is by becoming part of the dialogue of teachers with each other and with pupils — as observers and by joining with them in a search for meanings — that we can learn the dimensions and forms of reflective teaching. We can come to know reflective teaching as 'insiders', that is, when we become a part of the process that produces it. The reflective teacher behavior that takes place while we are uninvolved 'outsiders', for example, as non-participant observers, is something we can guess about. The critique we offer might reveal something about our own theoretical and ethical frames of reference while missing entirely the point of the action we aim to understand. It is through the *shared* experience and perspective of engaged participants in the reflective process, that teacher educators learn what reflection means for themselves and for their students, including some of the meanings of the action that reflection generates.

Notes

1   This growing interest in reflective practice in teacher education does not just exist of course in North America. See Handal and Lauvas (1987, Norway), Martinez (1989, Australia), Pollard (1988, UK) and Wubbels and Korthagen (1990, Netherlands) for examples of non-North American work on reflective practice in teacher education.

2   According to Dewey (1933), reflective action entails 'active, persistent, and careful consideration of any belief or supposed form of knowledge in light of the grounds that support it and the further consequences to which it leads' (p. 9). He distinguishes this from routine action which is guided primarily by tradition and authority.

3   Also see Kirby and Teddlie (1989), Stout (1989) and Osterman (1990).

4   This is not to say that these frameworks have gone without any criticism. See Grimmett and Erickson (1988) for several different kinds of critiques of Schon's work, and Gore (1987) for a critique of Cruickshank's work.

5   The characterization of this distinction between technical rationality and reflective practice as a dichotomy by Schon is challenged by a number of the authors in the Grimmett and Erickson (1988) volume and by Harris (1989). See the chapters by Shulman (1988), Fenstermacher (1988) and Selman (1988) in Grimmett and Erickson (1988).

6   See Grimmett, Erickson, Mackinnon and Riecken (1990) and Valli (1990b) for two additional frameworks for describing varieties of reflective teaching practice. As Valli (1990b) points out, different orientations to preparing reflective teachers frequently use the same instructional strategies, such as journals and action research. They use these strategies, however, in very different ways.

7   Grimmett *et al.* (1990) refer to this tradition of reflection as the 'instrumental mediation of action', see pp. 23–4.

8   See Zeichner (1990) for several examples of how this narrow view of technical competence is sometimes encouraged by practices in teacher education programs.

9   In fact many of the studies which are drawn upon in efforts to promote a social efficiency view of reflective teaching, (Berliner, 1984; Good, 1987) have important implications for realizing social justice and equity.

10   Also see Ball, McDiarmid and Anderson (1989).

11   Shulman (1986b) has argued for example, that 'mere content knowledge is likely to be as useless pedagogically as content-free skill' (p. 8). He has also concluded that 'instruction in the liberal arts and content areas will have to improve dramatically to meet the standards of understanding required for teaching' (p. 13).

12   As is the case in many teacher education programs, different parts of elementary PROTEACH emphasize different traditions of practice. For example, the social efficiency tradition just described is emphasized in the Research in Elementary Education course described by Ross and Kyle. Other parts of this program reflect a very strong emphasis on developmentalist practices which is not surprising given the 'Humanistic' teacher education programs that immediately preceded the development of PROTEACH (Combs, Blume, Newman and Wass, 1974).

13   Also see Fosnot (1989) and Amarel (1988).

14   Each of these labels in turn (e.g., feminist) is also very diverse encompassing a range of different perspectives. See Gore (1990) for a discussion of some of the different perspectives that are included in the categories of 'critical' and 'feminist' pedagogies.

References

AMAREL, M. (1988) 'Developmental teacher education', *Dialogues in Teacher Education* (Issue Paper 88–4), East Lansing, MI: National Center for Research on Teacher Education.

ANYON, J. (1980) 'Social class and the hidden curriculum of work', *Journal of Education*, **162**, pp. 67–92.

BALL, D., McDIARMID, G.W. and ANDERSON, C.W. (1989) 'Why staying one chapter ahead doesn't really work: Subject-specific pedagogy', in REYNOLDS, M. (Ed.) *Knowledge Base for the Beginning Teacher*, (pp. 193–205), New York: Pergamon.

BERLINER, D. (1984) 'The half-full glass: A review of research on teaching', in HOSFORD, P. (Ed.) *Using What We Know about Teaching*, Alexandria, VA: Association of Supervision and Curriculum Development.

BEYER, L. (1988) *Knowing and Acting: Inquiry, Ideology and Educational Studies*, Basingstoke: Falmer Press.

BUCHMANN, M. (1984) 'The priority of knowledge and understanding in teaching', in KATZ, L. and RATHS, J. (Eds) *Advances in Teacher Education*, Vol. 1, (pp. 29–50), Norwood NJ: Ablex.

CALDERHEAD, J. (1989) 'Reflective teaching and teacher education', *Teaching and Teacher Education*, **5**, 1, pp. 43–51.

CLARK, C. (1988) 'Asking the right questions about teacher preparation: Contributions of research on teacher thinking', *Educational Researcher*, **17**, 2, pp. 5–12.

CLIFT, R., HOUSTON, W.R. and PUGACH, M. (1990) *Encouraging Reflective Practice: An Examination of Issues and Exemplars*, New York: Teachers College Press.

COMBS, A., BLUME, R., NEWMAN, A. and WASS, H. (1974) *The Professional Education of Teachers: A Humanistic Approach to Teacher Education*, Boston: Allyn and Bacon.

CREMIN, L. (1961) *The Transformation of the School: Progressivism in American Education, 1876–1957*, New York: Vintage Books.

CRUICKSHANK, D. (1987) *Reflective Teaching*, Reston, VA: Association of Teacher Educators.

DAMERELL, R. (1985) *Education's Smoking Gun: How Teachers' Colleges have Destroyed Education in America*, New York: Freandlich Books.

DELPIT, L. (1988) 'The silenced dialogue: Power and pedagogy in educating other people's children', *Harvard Educational Review*, **58**, 3, pp. 280–98.

DEWEY, J. (1933) *How we Think*, Chicago: Henry Regnery.

DUCKWORTH, E. (1987) *The Having of Wonderful Ideas*, New York: Teachers College Press.

ELLIOTT, J. (1990) 'Teachers as researchers: Implications for supervision and for teacher education', *Teaching and Teacher Education*, **6**, 1, pp. 1–26.

FEIMAN-NEMSER, S. (1990) 'Teacher preparation: Structural and conceptual alternatives', in HOUSTON, W.R. (Ed.) *Handbook of Research on Teacher Education* (pp. 212–33), New York: Macmillan.

FENSTERMACHER, G.D. (1988) 'The place of science and epistemology in Schon's conception of reflective practice', in GRIMMETT, P. and ERICKSON, G. (Eds) *Reflection in Teacher Education*, (pp. 39–46), New York: Teachers College Press.

FLEXNER, A. (1930) *Universities: American, English, German*, Oxford, England: Oxford University Press.

FOSNOT, C.T. (1989) *Enquiring Teachers, Enquiring Learners: A Constructivist Approach to Teaching*, New York: Teachers College Press.

FREEDMAN, S., JACKSON, J. and BOLES, K. (1986) *The Effect of Teaching on Teachers*, Grand Forks, ND: North Dakota Study Group on Evaluation.

GENTILE, J.R. (1988) *Instructional Improvement: Summary and Analysis of Madeline Hun-*

ter's Essential Elements of Instruction and Supervision, Oxford, OH: National Staff Development Council.

GOOD, T. (1987) 'Two decades of research on teacher expectations', *Journal of Teacher Education*, **38**, 4, pp. 32–48.

GOODLAD, J. (1990) *Teachers for Our Nation's Schools*, San Francisco: Jossey-Bass.

GORE, J. (1987) 'Reflecting on reflective teaching', *Journal of Teacher Education*, **38**, 2, pp. 33–9.

GORE, J. (1990) The Struggle for Pedagogies: Critical and Feminist Discourses as 'Regimes of Truth'. Unpublished doctoral dissertation, University of Wisconsin-Madison.

GRIMMETT, P. and ERICKSON, G. (Eds) (1988) *Reflection in Teacher Education*, New York: Teachers College Press.

GRIMMETT, P., MACKINNON, A., ERICKSON, G. and RIECKEN, T. (1990) 'Reflective practice in teacher education', in CLIFT, R., HOUSTON, W.R. and PUGACH, M. (Eds) *Encouraging Reflective Practice in Education*, (pp. 20–38), New York: Teachers College Press.

GROSSMAN, P., WILSON, S. and SHULMAN, L. (1989) 'Teachers of substance: Subject matter knowledge for teaching', in REYNOLDS, M. (Ed.) *Knowledge Base for the Beginning Teacher*, (pp. 23–36), New York: Pergamon Press.

HANDAL, G. and LAUVAS, P. (1987) *Promoting Reflective Teaching: Supervision in Action*, Milton Keynes, UK: Open University Press.

HARRIS, I. (1989) 'A critique of Schon's views on teacher education', *Journal of Curriculum and Supervision*, **5**, 1, pp. 13–18.

JACKSON, P. (1968) *Life in Classrooms*, New York: Holt, Rinehart and Winston.

JOURNAL OF TEACHER EDUCATION (1989) 'Critical reflection in teacher education: Practices and problems', **40**, 2.

KELLY, G. and NIHLEN. (1982) 'Schooling and the reproduction of patriarchy', in APPLE, M. (Ed.) *Cultural and Economic Reproduction in Education* (pp. 162–80), Boston: Routledge and Kegan Paul.

KEMMIS, S. (1985) 'Action research and the politics of reflection', in BOUD, D., KEOGH, R. and WALKER, D. (Eds) *Reflection: Turning Experience into Learning* (pp. 139–64), London: Croom Helm.

KIRBY, P. and TEDDLIE, C. (1989) 'Development of the reflective teaching instrument', *Journal of Educational Research*, **22**, 4, pp. 46–51.

KOERNER, J. (1963) *The Miseducation of American Teachers*, Boston: Houghton Mifflin.

MACKINNON, A. and ERICKSON, G. (1988) 'Taking Schon's ideas to a science teaching practicum', in GRIMMETT, P. and ERICKSON, G. (Eds) *Reflection in Teacher Education*, (pp. 113–38), New York: Teachers College Press.

MARTINEZ, K. (1989) *Critical Reflections on Critical Reflection in Teacher Education*. Paper presented at the Fourth National Conference on the Practicum in Teacher Education, Rockhampton, Australia.

MAHER, F. and RATHBONE, C. (1986) 'Teacher education and feminist theory: Some implications for practice', *American Journal of Education*, **94**, 2, pp. 214–35.

MEAD, G.H. (1938) *The Philosophy of the Act*, Chicago: University of Chicago Press.

MITCHELL, L.S. (1931) 'Cooperative schools for student teachers', *Progressive Education*, **8**, pp. 251–55.

ORNSTEIN, A. and LEVINE, D. (1989) 'Social class, race, and school achievement: Problems and prospects', *Journal of Teacher Education*, **40**, 5, pp. 17–23.

OSTERMAN, K. (1990) 'Reflective practice: A new agenda for education', *Education and Urban Society*, **22**, 2, pp. 133–52.

PERRONE, V. (1989) *Working papers: Reflections on Teachers, Schools, and Communities*, New York: Teachers College Press.

POSNER, G. (1989) *Field Experience: Methods of Reflective Teaching* (2nd edn), New York: Longman.

POLLARD, A. (1988) 'Reflective teaching: The Sociological Contribution', in WOODS, P. and POLLARD, A. (Eds) *Sociology and Teaching*, (pp. 54–75), London: Croom Helm.

PTAK, D. (1988) *Report on the Achievement of Black High School Students in the Madison Metropolitan School District, 1987–1988*, Madison, WI: Urban League.

REILLY, D. (1989) 'A knowledge base for education: Cognitive science', *Journal of Teacher Education*, **40**, 3, pp. 9–13.

RICHARDSON, V. (1990) 'The evolution of reflective teaching and teacher education', in CLIFT, R., HOUSTON, W.R. and PUGACH, M. (Eds) *Encouraging Reflective Practice in Education*, (pp. 3–19), New York: Teachers College Press.

ROSS, D. and KYLE, D. (1987) 'Helping preservice teachers learn to use teacher effectiveness research', *Journal of Teacher Education*, **38**, pp. 40–4.

SCHON, D. (1983) *The Reflective Practitioner*, New York: Basic Books.

SCHON, D. (1987) *Educating the Reflective Practitioner*, San Francisco: Jossey-Bass, Inc.

SCHON, D. (1989) 'Professional knowledge and reflective practice', in SERGIOVANNI, T. and MOORE, J.H. (Eds) *Schooling for Tomorrow*, Boston: Allyn and Bacon.

SELMAN, M. (1988) 'Schon's gate is square. But is it art?' in GRIMMETT, P. and ERICKSON, G. (Eds) *Reflection in Teacher Education*, (pp. 177–192), New York: Teachers College Press.

SHULMAN, L. (1986a) 'Paradigms and research programs in the study of teaching', in WITTROCK, M. (Ed.) *Third Handbook of Research on Teaching*, pp. 3–36, New York: Macmillan.

SHULMAN, L. (1986b) 'Those who understand: Knowledge growth in teaching', *Educational Researcher*, **15**, 2, pp. 4–14.

SHULMAN, L. (1987) 'Knowledge and teaching: Foundations of the new reform', *Harvard Educational Review*, **57**, pp. 1–22.

SHULMAN, L. (1988) 'The dangers of dichotomous thinking in education', in GRIMMETT, P. and ERICKSON, G. (Eds) *Reflection in Teacher Education*, pp. 19–30.

SMITH, L. (1978) 'Science education in the Alte schools: A kind of case study', in STAKE, R. and EASLEY, J. *Case Studies in Science Education*, (Vol. 1), Washington D.C., US Government Printing Office.

STOUT, C.J. (1989) 'Teachers views of the emphasis on reflective teaching skills during their student teaching', *Elementary School Journal*, **89**, 4, pp. 511–27.

TABACHNICK, B.R. and ZEICHNER, K. (1984) 'The impact of the student teaching experience on the development of teacher perspectives', *Journal of Teacher Education*, **35**, pp. 28–36.

TABACHNICK, B.R. and ZEICHNER, K. (1986) 'Teacher beliefs and classroom behaviors: Some teacher responses to inconsistencies', in BEN-PERETZ, M., BROMME, R. and HALKES, R. (Eds) *Advances of Research on Teacher Thinking*, (pp. 84–96), Berwyn PA and Lisse, W. Germany: Swets North America/Swets and Zeitlinger.

VALLI, L. (1990a) 'Moral approaches to reflective practice', in CLIFT, R., HOUSTON, W.R. and PUGACH, M. (Eds) *Encouraging Reflective Practice in Education*, (pp. 39–56), New York: Teachers College Press.

VALLI, L. (1990b) *The Question of Quality and Content in Reflective Teaching*. A paper presented at the annual meeting of the American Educational Research Association, Boston, MA.

WAXMAN, H.J., FREIBERG, J.C., VAUGHN, J. and VEIL, M. (Eds) (1988) *Images of Reflection in Teacher Education*, Peston, VA: Association of Teacher Educators.

WILSON, S., SHULMAN, L. and RICHERT, A. (1987) '150 different ways of knowing: Representations of knowledge in teaching', in CALDERHEAD, J. (Ed.) *Exploring Teachers Thinking* (pp. 104–24), London: Cassell.

WILSON, S. and WINEBURG, S. (1988) 'Peering at American history through different lenses: The role of disciplinary knowledge in teaching', *Teachers College Record*, **89**, pp. 525–39.

WUBBELS, T. and KORTHAGEN, F. (1990) 'The effects of a pre-service teacher education program for the preparation of reflective teachers', *Journal of Education for Teaching*, **16**, 1, pp. 29–44.

ZEICHNER, K. (1990) 'When you've said reflection, you haven't said it all', in STODDARD, T. (Ed.) *Guided Practice in Teacher Education*, East Lansing, MI: National Center for Research on Teacher Education.

ZEICHNER, K. and LISTON, D. (1990) *Traditions of Reform and Reflective Teaching in US Teacher Education* (Issue Paper 90–1) East Lansing, MI: National Center for Research on Teacher Education.

ZUMWALT, K. (1982) 'Research on teaching: Policy implications for teacher education', in LIEBERMAN, A. and MCLAUGHLIN, M. (Eds) *Policymaking in Education*, (pp. 215–48), Chicago: University of Chicago Press.

2 Gender, Reflexivity and Teacher Education: The Wheaton Program

Frances Maher

Introduction

This essay explores some aspects of a reflective, inquiry-based preservice teacher-training program that are particularly rooted in principles of feminist pedagogy. As a member of a two-person education department in a small (1200 students) liberal arts college, I teach most components of the Secondary Program, which prepares undergraduates with liberal arts majors for teacher certification upon graduation. Until 1988, when it became coeducational, Wheaton was an all-women's college, so that my experience of this program has been primarily with women students. The student body is overwhelmingly white (like their teacher), lower-middle to upper-middle class (like their teacher), and either Protestant (like their teacher) or Catholic in background. Most come from suburban New England towns. To overgeneralize, they typically want to be teachers through a combination of a desire for a human service career, a love of children and an uncritical familiarity with the classroom setting. (They all know what teachers do.) For a few, typically the first generation of their family to go to college, teaching represents upward mobility (as does coming to Wheaton), and they are inspired by a teacher as a role model. For others, grandmothers and/or mothers were teachers. Compared to other Wheaton students, I have experienced education minors as on the whole less conventionally ambitious, perhaps slightly less intellectually oriented, and somewhat more liberal or progressive politically.

To introduce this essay by describing my students is to illustrate the experiential and autobiographical emphasis of the courses I teach, an emphasis which is derived from feminist, or *gendered approaches to reflective inquiry*. I will begin by briefly explaining some of these approaches to teaching, commonly defined as feminist pedagogy. Then I will describe the ways in which my own courses enact these approaches, particularly in the construction of a relationship between experience, autobiographical material and critical reflection. Finally, I will use informal anecdotal material to illustrate some ways in which my student teachers have reflected and reacted to these learning experiences in their own early teaching careers.

Feminist Pedagogy

The increasing proliferation in the past twenty years of the new scholarship on women has led to a fundamental transformation of the liberal arts curriculum (Schuster and Van Dyne, 1984). Women's studies scholarship has exposed the traditional curriculum with its goals of scholarly objectivity and universal standards of excellence and truth, as rather the particular and androcentric study of privileged white males. Women's studies courses, and the curriculum transformations which have accompanied them, have emphasized that human experiences must be particularized, framed by variations of gender, race, class and culture. Courses reflecting this variety of human experience are built on the interaction of multiple perspectives in the classroom and elsewhere, rather than imposing one set of experiences as a general norm by which all others must be considered deviant or marginalized.

As discussed in an earlier article (Maher and Rathbone, 1986), teacher education programs rest on and contribute to the academic disciplines. They also train mainly women for a predominantly women's job, half of whose clients — or pupils — are girls. The implications of women's scholarship for teacher education programs are therefore widespread and significant. Schools are central places for producing and enforcing androcentric norms of behavior and achievement in the form of standardized tests, tracking systems and other types of discriminatory and 'compensatory' activities. Feminist scholarship shows how these norms, built on models of societal success based on competitiveness and individual achievement, fail to reflect and attend to the qualities and experiences of many groups of people, including girls. The gendered nature of the school hierarchy, with male administrators and female teachers, reproduces the societal equation of womanhood with nurturing roles, service careers and a consistently lower status. The exploration and revaluation of female careers in this light has been another concern of women's studies scholarship.

Finally, this scholarship has contributed to teacher education in the area of pedagogical theory. As feminist college teachers have looked at the pedagogical (and methodological) implications of including women in the curriculum, we have found ourselves defining feminist pedagogies as similar to and different from both inquiry teaching and critical, or 'liberatory' pedagogy (Maher, 1987a, 1987b). To summarize these approaches, *feminist pedagogies are typically seen as student-centered, interactive and employing more collaborative than competitive forms of classroom discourse. They emphasize personal connection and involvement with learning rather than the cultivation of an impartial, critical stance* (See Belenky, Clinchy, Goldberger and Tarule, 1986). Like the women's consciousness-raising groups of the late 1960s, feminist classrooms are concerned with the *liberatory potential* (for women and minorities especially) *of validating students' own perceptions of the world*, through a curriculum that includes women's lives and contributions and through class discussions which focus on their responses to the issues.

Like critical thinking and inquiry teaching, feminist approaches emphasize a student-centered, problem-solving view of learning. However, traditional inquiry approaches have rested on an adherence to an objective, rational model of knowledge construction, one based on a positivist epistemology and the use of the scientific method to reach a truth which is 'out there'. As summarized in an earlier piece, 'Inquiry teaching is a method of problem-solving which aims for the closest approximation to the most 'rational' solution, (or interpretation) of a given problem, a process in which personal bias and perspective are understood as evils to be transcended. Given the same information, (it is expected that) all reach the same conclusion' (Maher, 1987a, p. 187).

Feminist theorists, on the other hand, reflecting the discovery of women's and minority experiences as alternative and often directly counter to those of privileged men, argue (with other postmodernists), that there can no longer be such a universalized understanding of the world, nor such a unidimensional curriculum. Feminist pedagogies recognize that 'all human experiences are gendered, specific and various'. Therefore, the goals, problems and valid solutions that appear in the classroom must also vary ... 'the process of knowledge construction becomes a tapestry, not an umbrella, in which a range of perspectives and experiences are seen as equally valid, partial, and subject to elucidation by comparison with each other' (*ibid.*). The emphasis on personal, experiential connections to course themes is set in a context of building knowledge through the interaction of these connections. In this context the teacher is not the all-knowing expert but someone whose authority is gendered, specific and also experiential. The goal of feminist teaching approaches is not the discovery or mastery of an objectively verifiable set of standards or answers, but rather an awakening on the students' part of a purposeful, reflective, and particular consciousness, forged in relation to others and to one's specific history, location and goals in the world.

The Wheaton Program

Coming to an all-women's college and encountering women's scholarship and feminist theory for the first time, I began to rethink my previous experience as a inquiry-oriented high school teacher. I wanted to bring consciousness-raising, collaborative modes of discourse and a sense of the varieties of human experience and perspectives to my inquiry approaches to help my students make personal connections to the new materials on women in the curriculum. Rather than providing them with a traditional history of American education, an overview of educational theory, and a set of standards and techniques by which they could become competent teachers, I wanted them to locate themselves, as gendered, 'classed', and 'raced' subjects within these topics, so that they could see themselves as teachers in a particular historical and social context. I wanted my courses to help them compare their experiences to those of others, to see how different groups have constructed and been shaped by the education system and the processes of learning and teaching within it. In 'Schooling in America', the foundations course, I have the students *write educational autobiographies, in which they explicitly place aspects of their own schooling experience in juxtaposition to relevant topics in the course.* In 'Adolescent Development', I have them interview an adolescent they know in terms of some issues raised in developmental theory. In the methods class, I have them design and rationalize lessons according to both feminist and inquiry approaches. I would like now to discuss each of these courses and assignments in turn, paying particular attention to the autobiographical emphasis in the first course by which this process is launched.

Schooling in America

'Schooling in America', the foundations course, introduces Wheaton students to the field of education and helps them decide whether and whom (what age groups) they want to teach. Including observation and field work in local schools, the course is roughly divided into three parts — an introductory section that presents various philosophies of education, from Plato to Dewey to Friere; a section on the history of American education; and finally, several sections on contemporary educational issues. Particularly in the last two sections of the course, the development of American schools is portrayed as affecting different societal groups in a variety of ways. Divisions of gender, race, class and culture have had important interrelated effects on peoples' experience of their education. Contemporary issues discussed under the topic of 'equal educational opportunity' include sexism, racism and multicultural education. Here again the focus is on diversity, and on the effects on women and other oppressed groups of being subjected to universalized, androcentric norms of behavior and achievement.

Assignments for the course include field work journals and a term paper based on issues arising out of their field work experiences. I want here, however, to focus on another ongoing assignment. For many of the above topics the students write short personal essays which are discussed in class and which at the end of the semester constitute a more or less complete 'educational autobiography'. The goals are threefold: first, to help students see themselves as examples of course themes; secondly, to help them define and work through a personal perspective on course issues; and finally, to use that perspective in relation to other perspectives, so that they will become aware of the relations of those stories to those of others, and to a wider context. When they read Plato's *Allegory of the Cave*, they write about a personal 'enlightenment'. When the issues of IQ testing and tracking are discussed, they write about how they felt about being tested in school. During the unit on gender and education, they write on the relation of schooling and gender for themselves, answering the question: 'In what way has it made a difference in your education that you are a girl (or a boy)?' During the history unit they research and write educational family trees, tracing the educational attainments of parents, grandparents and great-grandparents.

In class discussions, particularly of these last two entries, the students have been able to see the powerful ways in which gender, race and class dictate and frame peoples' experiences and choices, including their own, and perhaps come to question the generalized and romantic view of schools, teaching and their own futures that many have initially, The entry about gender and schooling has given rise to stories about girls' limited access to athletic programs, smaller playgrounds, unbalanced math and science classes, and sharply differentiated classroom tasks (such as collecting papers versus moving classroom furniture). Discussions of this entry have nevertheless at times produced firm denials of negative experiences: 'I never felt cheated as a little girl in a dress as opposed to a little boy in pants'.

Students have also reacted differently to the same stories. Several students in one class had male science teachers who were very easy on them and gave them A's for little work. 'They didn't expect us to do well in science; that's ok by me', said one student, whereas another was angry: 'I was completely unprepared for science in college as a result'. In another instance, a student whose experience was that there had been no gender distinctions in her schooling said that she had gone to a very small coeducational prep school. Another, whose classes had been rigidly categorized by both academic track and gender, came from a large urban high school. Through their stories (and others), the class that year was able to elaborate a theory that social class and gender distinctions interact sharply in schooling, particularly in the later grades. The lower the social class and academic track, the more rigid the gender distinctions are, until in the vocational track, with clerical courses and auto mechanics, boys and girls tend to have completely different curricula. In one student's junior high school the issue was very clear: in seventh, eighth and ninth grade tracking began. The 'smart kids' (girls and boys) took French in whatever year they were considered ready; the others took either home economics or shop. Since in home economics they did breakfast in the seventh grade, lunch in the eighth, and dinner in the ninth, my student could easily remember when she started French. All she learned in junior high was breakfast.

Stories like these, combined with readings exploring issues of sexism in schools (see for example, Klein, 1985; Weis, 1988), help students come to a consciousness of gender (and class) issues in their education, and at the same time locate that consciousness in a wider and more explanatory context. The discussions are aimed neither at overall generalizations that will cover every instance nor expressions of individual subjectivity. Rather they are inductive and collaborative; they construct knowledge relationally and interactively. Each story helps to set the others in perspective.

In another example of the autobiography, the students construct educational family trees to parallel their study of the history of American eduction. The history they read emphasizes themes of the tensions between upward mobility and class and ethnic barriers, between standardized norms of achievement and pluralist variety (Nasaw, 1979). They also read about the history and issues around the emergence of teaching as an overwhelmingly female profession (Grumet, 1982; see also Hoffman, 1981; Laird, 1988). When male teachers left rural schools for better jobs in the city, women of the middle class entered teaching in increasing numbers. They were expected to bring to the job a nurturing supportive warmth such as that associated with motherhood, yet as dependent women they were powerless to change the rigid structures of schools (Maher and Rathbone, 1986).

When the students write and then compare the stories of their parents' and grandparents' educations and careers, the differences and commonalities which emerge are illustrative of all these themes as well as provocative of new insights. While some students' stories are of intergenerational upward mobility, others are of long-established (usually white Anglo Saxon Protestant WASP) families who started 'at the top' and stayed there. In one powerful instance, one student's (white Jewish) family left the same town and high school that another's (black) family had entered, both seeking educational upward mobility for their children. Comparing these stories (which happened privately, as I was able to look at the papers before the discussion), the white student felt guilt and the black one anger and bitterness. But as we were able in class to locate some sources of these individual experiences and choices in the structural racism of our society, we were able to contextualize these reactions and begin to move beyond them. The two students became friends, and each wrote journal entries about how much the other had taught her.

Similarly, the discussions of these family tree entries have cast light on structural issues of gender. Every year, the fathers' and grandfathers' occupations run the gamut of possible careers and interests, whereas the mothers and grand-mothers are overwhelmingly housewives, nurses, secretaries and teachers. One year, every grandmother who had worked outside the home was a teacher. As the students discuss and compare their stories, they often come to re-evaluate their own decisions to teach, as I challenge them to reflect how much their impulses are constructed out of an unthinking desire to follow in family foot-steps, to be a nurturer, to accede to women's traditional roles. Later on in the course there are often heated discussions of the degree to which teachers are, or should be, professionals, deserving more money and status, with some students always taking the position that teaching undertaken 'for the money' undermines the purity of a commitment to children. Others will ask why such commitments have to be paid for by material sacrifices, and we discuss the gendered constraints imposed by the concept of teaching as enacting 'women's proper place'. How much is claiming the role of nurturer a trap for women? Should we disclaim it (by, for example, reconsidering teaching as a career choice) or should we avow teaching (and all such nurturing careers) as worthy and socially necessary activi-ties deserving higher respect and remuneration?

In juxtaposing my students' personal stories to a broader structural framework, I want to make them more aware of their choices through an understanding of previously unacknowledged contexts and constraints. The pub-lic discussion of this autobiographical material thus entails some personal risks and conflicts as well as moments of enlightenment. First, students are sometimes angry at the bad news they hear about institutionalized sexism, or about the class-biased nature of the educational system. One wrote in a course evaluation, '*Aren't there any other issues?* (besides gender). I find it difficult to deal with a course which continually makes me feel hostile, oppressed and inferior. A college professor's experience in school and in life is undoubtedly different from ours', she concludes, thereby making of sexism her teacher's personal 'hangup'. Such challenges have made me more sensitive to the role my authority as the teacher plays in shaping these discussions. I try to display my expertise as specific and autobiographical, coming from my experience, my knowledge and my own avowed commitments (to gender, class and race equality). I explain my choices of texts and assignments in this light. But I also seek to contextualize and limit my authority by drawing on the students' expertise and experience. Since the students are thereby learning these stories of gender and class from each other and not just from me, they are more likely to see the themes that emerge as reflective of social realities shared with each other rather than particular preoc-cupations of mine. Another way I use my authority is to bring in the perspectives of those not represented in the classroom, most obviously of course the perspec-tives of Afro-Americans (men and women) and other minorities.

Another issue that arises in the use of autobiographical material is that for some students the comparison of family trees might be embarrassing, particularly for those with unusually low (or high) economic status. I have them compare stories in small groups first to preserve confidentiality, protect individuals and make the general discussion more efficient. Usually, however, the urge to tell one's own story makes it impossible for the small group leaders to summarize — most students want to jump in anyway. No one has ever raised concerns about confidentiality in either journals or evaluations, though such concerns may indeed exist.

A third risk is disagreement and conflict, either over interpretations — It's bad to get an A from your chemistry teacher for no work — or events, such as the coincidence of leaving and entering the same school district referred to earlier. Because these autobiographies and these discussions are about actual experiences, however, it is difficult to resolve or subsume disagreements into a 'right answer' or a consensus — the disagreements represent different perspectives which must be seen and held in relation to each other, enriching and extending each person's particular understanding and particular vantage point. I hope that collaboration in the building of a complex picture of reality replaces competition over the relative overall validity of different viewpoints. And I usually find that the messages conveyed by a messy blackboard full of individual family stories is precisely the one I hope for — namely of a range of choices, sometimes brilliant, often idiosyncratic, within a web of undeniable social and historical constraints. Choices, like the one to be a teacher, which are different for men and women, rich and poor, are neither purely individual nor purely socially determined, but ideally a purposeful (and reflective) mixture of the two.

Student reactions to 'Schooling in America' and to the autobiographies have been generally positive over the years, but they have also reflected a new self-consciousness about the education system and their own location within it that I believe crucial for reflective teaching. Comments include ones like the following (from one year recently):

'It has only been recently that I have become aware of the ways being female has affected me'.

'I learned I have white middle class attitudes'.

'I have gotten a lot out of everyone's educational history'.

'I was being bombarded with the shortcomings of American education in class, and suddenly the entries became increasingly threatening as well. I had to talk about my family's education and see whether or not what I'd heard in class was accurate (for me)'.

'My family's educational history fits in a lot to what we have studied'.

The task for the next courses they take has been to integrate and extend this knowledge of gendered, raced, classed 'self-in-context' to the roles and practices of teaching itself.

Adolescent Development

The students who take 'Adolescent Development' are typically juniors who have determined not only that they want to teach but that they want to be high school teachers. As I see it, their task in this course is to move from seeing themselves within the social contexts of American education to understanding their students within these contexts. Particularly as late adolescents themselves, they initially tend to look at the high school students with whom they work as tutors as being completely unique (and often unclassifiable and unmanageable). They have trouble relating the developmental theories framing the course to the actual adolescents they are and work with. Either a theory is completely true 'about me' and therefore true, or 'not relevant' either to me or my students, and therefore untrue.

To have my students see their pupils (and themselves) as individuals, while at the same time being able to set them in some broader developmental and societal contexts given by gender, race, class and so on, entails three levels of assignments. First, the reading that they do in developmental theory includes materials on women's and other minorities' experiences of adolescence. They read, for example, Joyce Ladner's (1971) *Tomorrow's Tomorrow*, about young working-class black women, and explore some aspects of the work of Gilligan (1982), Chodorow (1978) and Belenky *et al.* (1986) on female morality, development and cognition. In this way, they learn that stages of growth are various rather than immutable and one-dimensional, that norms established by Freud, Erikson and others are based primarily on white male experience, and that differences do not represent deviance but rather alternative patterns of accommodation (and resistance). (See, for example, Prose, 1990, for a description of Gilligan's latest work, with 11-year-old girls.)

Next, my students conduct an in-depth interview with an adolescent of their choice, preferably someone they are tutoring or working with, although siblings and family friends are sometimes chosen as well. The interview topics are derived from protocols in developmental studies, including the 'Heinz' moral dilemma from Kohlberg's and Gilligan's work, a Piagetian reasoning problem, and a series of questions, adapted from *Women's Ways of Knowing* (Belenky *et al.*, 1986), asking about their concepts of self and relationships.

The third step is a collaborative one. After conducting and summarizing their interview data, but before writing up their conclusions, they meet in small groups of four or five with others who have interviewed similarly situated students. That is, all the people with interviews of 14-year-old girls, or 16-year-old boys, will work together. The groups are based on the principle of the closest possible commonalities, with age and gender being the main variable (as the informants usually share common cultural characteristics and are usually, unfortunately, all white). In their small collaborative groups the students compare notes, with the aim of seeing some ways in which their own subjects are unique and atypical as well as noticing some traits that they all seem to (more or less) share.

After the small group meetings, the students are in a position to write up a final analysis in which they set their adolescent in the framework of one or more general themes raised in the readings or in previous discussion. They are able thus to see some ways in which their subjects' views and experiences are both unique and at the same time representative of broader issues. As in the family tree assignment, this one highlights the interactions between individuality and the social (and developmental) context in giving people their sense of themselves, their choices and constraints.

Student reactions to this assignment have included resistance based on its initial difficulty and more or less qualified enthusiasm at its outcome. The first year I tried the collaborative groups, a political science major who had been very skeptical of the ability of 'abstract' psychological theories to explain anything about human behavior was persuaded by her friend, a psychology major, to join her small discussion group. The political science major said later that neither the reading nor her own interview had shown her any connections between theory and practice. In the small group, however, as she compared her younger brother to other boys, some commonalities emerged that startled her into seeing the value of the ideas discussed for making sense of some of his concerns. The psychology major, for her part, invented what she called 'A whole new theory' to explain some aspect of the relation she now saw between social class, gender and developmental stage.

My own experience is that the small group meetings improved the final interview papers, precisely in the area of a better understanding of the links and boundaries between the individual and the theories designed to chart his or her behavior. More generally, if it had not been for the range of studies now available, generated from looking at diverse adolescent experiences, this assignment would not have been possible, as all the interviews would have had to be pressed into the frameworks of traditional male-centered models of growth. I think too that attention to the gendered and classed positions of their subjects has made my students more aware of their own gendered identity in this assignment. They are asked to reflect, in a way also encouraged by the small group discussions, on their own role in the interview and on the nature of their relationships with their informants.

Finally, the small group stage is important, in much the same ways as the autobiography discussions have been, for the construction of knowledge about these adolescents that is both specific and generalizable. The different frameworks of individual and theoretical perspectives are woven together in patterns that emphasize both uniqueness and commonalities, and show the validity as well as the limitations of each singular viewpoint. As examples of collaborative learning, these assignments seek connections and relationships among diverse perspectives, rather than the one best answer or the overall generalization. A richer and more complex view of the many sides of adolescence is made available to the students as a result.

Curriculum and Methods, and Student Teaching

In their 'Curriculum and Methods course' the students are required to write lesson and unit plans as they prepare to student teach. Often, though not always, they can design units and collect materials in knowledge of their student teaching placement the following semester, a placement they may already have begun informally by doing the methods course field work there. One of their assignments, based on reading about techniques of feminist pedagogy (Maher, 1985, 1987) is to design a unit or lesson which reflect different groups' experience of, or reaction to, the same topic. How, for example, did women's contribution to the abolitionist movement differ from men's? One student designed and was later able to teach a unit on World War II in an American history class based on having pupils research and compare different experiences of the war, including those of women workers, pacifists and other groups usually ignored in traditional histories. As part of the unit she had her students interview family members (grandparents) on their memories of the period. Another student designed an English unit (for our methods class) on *The Tell-Tale Heart*, by Edgar Allen Poe, which she introduced by asking us all what our associations were with ideas of being locked up alive (and other phobias). She had us write about our own favorite fears before looking at the literary devices Poe used, thus putting us in a better position, through our feelings and reactions, to analyze the story.

As these students and others have moved into their student teaching semesters, they have had various degrees of success in implementing the philosophies and practices they have experienced in their courses at Wheaton. In one school, a Social Studies department chair teased me whenever I came to visit, calling women's history an oxymoron. The two students in his department ruefully went along with the standardized curriculum offered, while complaining to me about it. Like many student teachers everywhere, they had little choice. Others, however, took advantage of receptive student teaching contexts to continue to explore their own versions of gender-balanced, student-centered teaching. While my examples are necessarily anecdotal, they include the following. The student of *The Tell-Tale Heart* taught *Hamlet* through journals exploring aspects of personal identity. How does it feel to be powerfully at odds with family members, to not know which way to turn, to have a loved one spurn you, as happened to Ophelia? A sociology student teacher had each pupil make a genealogical chart for her unit on the family. The breaks, interruptions and new connections of modern marriage, divorce and remarriage had the class talking animatedly about new concepts of 'family' beyond the nuclear stereotypes. A student teacher in social studies took advantage of the social history emphasis of her American History course to include women's experiences of every historical situation covered, from the settlement of the West to the Depression and World War II.

Operating always within the constraints imposed by their cooperating teachers' and schools' curricula, my students have often used their 'elbow room' to teach about women, to focus on a variety of perspectives as legitimate and to elicit and utilize pupils' own experiences of the topics at hand. Moreover, through our discussions held once a week during the student teaching semester, it is clear to me that they retain a critical and self-reflective eye on their schools and their own positions within them. They discuss what they can and can't do as teachers, the relations between social class and academic standards that they see in their classrooms and schools, and the ways in which boys and girls are treated and behave differently. Like all student teachers they face discipline problems and have special concerns for particularly needy pupils — in class we discuss the social contexts for these issues.

Conclusion

The results of any educational program, particularly one in which the formal coursework is only one factor in the overall experience, are impossible to measure and difficult to describe. As mentioned above, the hospitality of given high school settings to curricular and pedagogical innovation varies greatly. (Wheaton is located in a small town in a largely rural area, so that the available placements are limited and must often be in quite conservative smallish towns.) Therefore, it is hard to gauge the relative weight of Wheaton and the student teaching site in shaping the kinds of teachers my students become, even though I see my university supervisor role as that of standard bearer, translator and mediator. I try to support my student teachers through their required tasks, but also try to keep their creative and reflective skills alive. As I mull over what I know of Wheaton graduates after they go on to their own careers, some commonalities emerge. One is that in the social sciences and English, most continuing teachers report concern with women students and with teaching a curriculum that includes women in some way. The relatively few science and math teachers I have had (who have kept in touch with me), do not discuss these issues, perhaps because they (we) had a much harder time integrating women into their courses and lesson plans (an issue for scientists and mathematicians in the academy as well). Several teachers have become residential advisors at nearby colleges, and they have reported concerns with women students there (but they were Dorm Head Residents at Wheaton as well).

One social studies teacher now takes courses in Women's Studies through the Harvard Graduate School of Education, and has recently done a paper on Wheaton's transition to coeducation. In a particularly satisfying recent letter, an English teacher, now in graduate school in literature, writes the following:

> I didn't realize until I came to this totally 'old boy' department how ingrained in me Wheaton was. I've never been so aware of my feminism before. Now that I have to fight to write about black women that aren't Zora Neale Hurston, or do a paper about sexuality in George Eliot, I'm very aware of what I learned ... truly you (all) had an amazingly powerful and forceful effect on my life.

A second commonality, more subtle than the first, may be that the students who were in the student teaching situations most supportive of reflective approaches tend to be those who have remained committed to both teaching and to a professional (as well as personal) feminist stance. The two teachers just described, for example, were both from such high school departments, as were the two resident advisors mentioned earlier. On the other hand, the two history teachers from the more traditional departments emerged, I think, with a more instrumental view as they approached their first teaching jobs. If they could fit in materials based on women's experiences, and make time for inquiry approaches, my sense was that they would. But they had learned that their choices might be limited in the schools that would hire them.

Finally, if I really ponder the intersections of these students' lives with the Wheaton program, I am led back to the issues with which I started this essay, namely those of personal choices and constraints within contemporary social frameworks of gender and class. The courses in the Wheaton program affected these students variously at least partly in terms of the personal and professsional choices they faced upon graduation. The overt feminists at the Harvard School of Education and in the graduate literature program are upper-middle class women who can afford, in fact, to let their feminisms guide them as they explore career options. In short, after several years of high school teaching, they can take time out for graduate school right now. Many of my other students, including the two resident advisors and the two from the traditional social studies departments, have needed to continue working in the several years since their graduations, and have had to look for teaching jobs in a brutally circumscribed market. Thus, their opportunities for self-conscious and critical reflection in the classroom have been limited, and/or they have enacted their commitments in different (but perhaps more direct) ways. A third English teacher, also from a progressive student teaching context, spent her first year out teaching in a literacy program for adult women, another way of balancing her social commitments and her economic necessities.

In fact, writing this chapter has taught me that from now on, as part of the student teaching semester, I should take my students through a final entry in their two-year long educational autobiography, one concerned with the choices and constraints they now see themselves facing as they enter (or choose not to enter) the field of teaching. While I think my teachers know how to be 'reflective practitioners' as a result of the Wheaton program, I am not sure I have yet fully helped them to see the possibilities and limitations inherent in their own entry into the profound inequalities of the gendered, classed and raced society upon which they have been reflecting for three years. I think that a combination of the Wheaton program with a student teaching situation hospitable to the practice of such reflective teaching is the best basis for creating a sense of committed and conscious choices on the part of my students, but much will continue to depend on their own situational constraints, their own imaginations and their own priorities. It is these intersections of social circumstance and individual possibility that I continue to want to focus on (and broaden) as teacher.

References

BELENKY, M., CLINCHY, B., GOLDBERGER, N. and TARULE, J. (1986) *Women's Ways of Knowing, the Development of Self, Body and Mind*, New York: Basic Books.

BUNCH, C. and POLLACK, S. (1983) *Learning our Way, Essays in Feminist Education*, New York: The Crossing Press, Trumansberg.

CHODOROW, N. (1978) *The Reproduction of Mothering, Psychoanalysis and the Sociology of Gender*, Berkeley, CA: University of California Press.

CULLEY, M. and PORTUGES, C. (Eds) (1985) *Gendered Subjects: The Dynamics of Feminist Teaching*, London: Routledge and Kegan Paul.

DAVIS, B. (Ed.) (1985) *Feminist Education*, Special Topic Edition of *The Journal of Thought, an Interdisciplinary Quarterly*, **20**, 2.

GILLIGAN, C. (1982) *In a Different Voice: Psychological Theory and Women's Development*, Cambridge, MA: Harvard University Press.

GRUMET, M. (1982) 'Pedagogy for patriarchy: The feminization of teaching', *Interchange on Educational Policy*, **12**, 2 and 3, pp. 165–84.

HOFFMAN, N. (1981) *Women's 'True' Profession: Voices from the History of Teaching*, New York: Feminist Press and McGraw-Hill.

KLEIN, S. (Ed.) (1985) *Handbook for Achieving Sex Equity through Education*, Baltimore: Johns Hopkins Press.

LADNER, J. (1971) *Tomorrow's Tomorrow*, New York: Doubleday.

LAIRD, S. (1988) 'Reforming women's true profession: A case for feminist pedagogy in teacher education?' *Harvard Education Review*, **58**, 4, pp. 449–63.

MAHER, F. (1985a) 'Pedagogies for the gender balanced classroom', *Journal of Thought, An Interdisciplinary Quarterly*, pp. 48–64.

MAHER, F. (1985b) 'Classroom pedagogy and the new scholarship on women', in CULLEY, M. and PORTUGES, C. (Eds) *Gendered Subjects, The Dynamics of Feminist Teaching*, London: Routledge and Kegan Paul, 29–48.

MAHER, F. (1987a) 'Inquiry teaching and feminist pedagogy', *Social Education*, **51**, 3, pp. 186–92.

MAHER, F. (1987b) 'Towards a richer theory of feminist pedagogy: An analysis of liberation and gender models for teaching', *Journal of Education* (Boston University), **169**, 3, pp. 100–9.

MAHER, F. and RATHBONE, C. (1986) 'Teacher education and feminist theory: Some implications for practice', *American Journal of Education*, **94**, 2, pp. 214–35.

NASAW, D. (1979) *Schooled to Order*, New York: Oxford University Press.

PROSE, F. (1990) 'Confident at 11, confused at 16', *New York Times Magazines*, Vol. 139, p. 22, col. 1, 7 January.

SCHNIEDEWIND, N. (1985) 'Cooperatively structured learning, implications for feminist pedagogy', *Journal of Thought*, **20**, 3, pp. 74–87.

SCHNIEDEWIND, N. and MAHER, F. (Eds) (1987) 'Feminist pedagogy', Special issue, *Women's Studies Quarterly*.

SCHUSTER, M. and VAN DYNE, S. (1984) 'Placing women in the liberal arts: Stages of curriculum transformation', *Harvard Educational Review*, **54**, 4, pp. 413–28.

WEIS, L. (Ed.) (1988) *Class, Race and Gender in American Education*, Albany, New York: State University of New York Press.

3 Educative Communities and the Development of the Reflective Practitioner*

Robert V. Bullough Jr. and Andrew D. Gitlin

As we head into the 1990s an increasing number of scholars are focusing their attention on teacher reflectivity (Waxman *et al.*, 1988). A movement seems to be forming, and with it the question of what can be done to develop teacher reflectivity in preservice teacher education becomes insistent. In this article we provide a partial response to this question. The significance of the suggestions presented, however, can only be understood by considering them in relation to a larger set of concerns and issues tied to our conception of the appropriate direction for teacher education reform. We begin, therefore, with a brief analysis of what we see as the central problems of teacher education which is followed by a discussion of what we believe to be a promising approach to confronting these problems. We will return then to the question of what can be done to cultivate teacher reflectivity.

What's Wrong With Teacher Education

The problems of teacher education are inextricably linked to the problems of American education and how they are understood. The dominant view of what is wrong with American schools goes something like this: Until very recently standardized test scores in the United States continued a twenty year gradual decline, while at the same time student misconduct and school violence have increased. As a consequence, the schools are not producing a labor force that has the technological skills or the 'proper' character traits and work ethic necessary to maintain our economic position in relation to other industrialized nations (Nation Commission on Excellence in Education, 1983).

When addressing these problems current reform proposals have, for the most part, focused on the teacher. Two solutions to the 'teacher problem' stand out. First, admission standards to teacher education programs need to be raised and a much greater portion of a perspective teacher's time needs to be spent

* A previous draft of this paper was published in *Qualitative Studies in Education*, 1989, vol. 2, no. 4.

working in the content areas, which necessitates extending program length. Second, because of a shortage of talent and the need to recruit and retain more able persons in teaching, the role of the teacher needs to be differentiated so that the less able can be carefully monitored and the more able, functioning as experts, given increased responsibilities along with higher salaries (Holmes Group, 1986).

While much enthusiasm has been generated around these proposals they have serious shortcomings, not the least of which is the devaluation of the strengths teachers bring to the profession. Consider the following: Most teachers are women, and they enter teaching for reasons often tied to their experience of being a woman. Instead of building on these strengths, current reforms attempt to alter the teaching role along lines consistent with the work patterns of other, male-dominated, professions where nurturing is a sign of weakness and theoretical knowledge more valued than practical knowledge (Leach, 1988). Job differentiation in particular tends to undermine the strengths women bring to the profession by undervaluing 'connected' ways of knowing while bolstering competitive and individualistic relations that require a more solitary, separate approach to the pursuit of knowledge (Belenky *et al.*, 1986). Further, by formalizing job descriptions where higher status is associated with being removed from intimate involvement in the lives of young people, these reforms devalue work with children and help reproduce the sexual division of labor that currently leaves women on the bottom rungs of the school hierarchy.

The formalization of job descriptions has other serious potential negative consequences as well. Formalization will most assuredly speed up the trend toward the proletarianization of teachers. The effects of proletarianization already have been dramatic: because teachers are viewed as deficient and intellectually passive, school structures and training programs are in place that limit the teacher role to the consumption and then transfer of knowledge (Gitlin, 1987). Teachers are not encouraged to pose questions, critically examine issues and engage in research. Instead, as consumers of knowledge, their responsibility is to pass information along and down to students, and thereby to fill up their heads. Moreover, teacher decision making increasingly is confined to 'how to' questions, thereby silencing teachers in debates about the aims schooling (Apple, 1986; Bullough and Gitlin, 1985; Bullough, Goldstein and Holt, 1984). Rather than confront these role boundaries, a differentiated profession is likely to strengthen them.

The effects of creating teacher roles based on narrow views of intellect, that constrain rather than enhance the strengths teachers bring to the profession generally, will be profound not only for teachers but also for students. Clearly, most teaching will be done by those at the lower rungs of the hierarchy with the result that increasingly students who struggle within the current school framework and who need both a nurturing and a creative approach to learning — the same students who have in good measure prompted the current reform movement — will find themselves interacting with teachers who have the least control over the curriculum, are most vulnerable politically, least rewarded for expressions of intellectual independence and most responsive to the value of standardized test score results. These students, as a consequence, are likely to slip through the system uneducated while most others will find the school to be less and less about intellectual and personal development and more and more about sorting and labeling.

For the majority of teachers, the constraints of teaching will likely result in increasing alienation. As teachers spend inordinate amounts of energy focusing on test score results and obtaining good behavior, they will find less less time, and fewer outlets, for connecting with students in caring ways which is often the one source of pleasure sufficient to soften the hurt that comes from seemingly endless criticism and the exhaustion that comes from having to carrying ever heavier social responsibilities (Bullough, 1988a). Furthermore, while teachers may know their subject matter better as a result of these reforms, there is little reason to believe that this will challenge the dominant teaching orientation that leaves students docile and cynical and teachers unable to express and develop their intellect (Grumet, 1989).

In sum, these proposals offer false hope for school reform primarily because they do not challenge basic assumptions about teachers and teaching. What is wrong with teacher education in our view, then, is that it is based upon the same set of assumptions that inform current reform efforts which ultimately devalue the strengths teachers bring to the profession and, despite seemingly contradictory moves to increase content area background, devalue and constrict intellectual involvement of the vast majority of teachers in education. These assumptions are embedded in the tradition of teacher *education* as *training*, a tradition that has successfully contained reform efforts of this century and may very well drain whatever radical potential the current effort has to forge a different teacher role around reflectivity.

Teacher Training

Some of the implications of the training tradition of teacher education are the following: in the spirit of training, emphasis first and foremost is placed on obtaining technical competence, mastering the skills of teaching; it is the means of education, in a very narrow sense, and not the aims of education, that matter most for teachers regardless of their subject matter expertise or intellectual ability. Like the blacksmith, the good teacher is the one who through a set of skills can make the 'shoe fit'. The training emphasis also supports an extreme form of individualism quite consistent with job differentiation proposals where preservice teachers view themselves (like other students) in competition for grades, supervisor recognition, teaching resources and ideas, and eventually jobs. This competition leaves common interests unacknowledged and, importantly, masks the need for and potential of collective teacher action as a means for educational improvement.

The training orientation also assumes an established teacher role into which all potential teachers must fit and against which they will be evaluated. Part of that role centers on the assumption that teachers are consumers, not producers, of knowledge (Smyth, 1987). As consumers of knowledge, the history and experience of those being trained may be discounted. As trainees, teachers are treated as though they are shapeless raw material to be molded into teachers. As raw material, little need be done to help the beginning teacher articulate a teaching philosophy, consider how teacher histories shape practice or examine educational aims; instead they are encouraged to be dependent on experts. Additionally, dependence on experts limits the potential for a more democratic school organization and also legitimates and strengthens constrained and institutionalized gender roles (Belenky *et al.*, 1986).

Assumptions about the nature of teaching and learning are also embedded deeply in the training tradition. These also need to be challenged. Teaching is understood essentially as a process of 'banking' bits of information into the heads of the apprentice or student (Friere, 1985). It should not be totally surprising, therefore, that when these students become teachers it seems only natural to them to think of learning as the consumption of information. Moreover, the training orientation brings with it a tendency to think of clear cut beginnings and endings: once training is over, teachers are ready to teach just as when schooling is completed a person is presumed to be educated. It is assumed, for example, that the university's responsibility for the teacher ends with certification and so the beginning teacher, upon assuming a position, frequently faces alone the pressures of institutional socialization (Blase, 1988; Darling-Hammond, 1985).

The training orientation to teacher education maintains a set of structures and embodies a cluster of ideologies which encourage the following: a constricted view of teacher intellect through emphasis on teaching as technique, an extreme form of individualism, teacher dependence on experts, acceptance of hierarchy, a consumer or 'banking' view of teaching and learning (teacher is 'banker'; learning is consuming), a limited commitment to the betterment of the educational community and a conservative survivalist mentality among novice teachers (Bullough, 1989a).

Teacher Reflectivity

If reform efforts emphasizing reflectivity are to result in any changes of substance they must not be contained by notions of training, but rather confront them. On first glance, this would appear to be an easy task but on closer inspection it becomes apparent that many of the conceptions of reflectivity currently being championed fit quite nicely within a training orientation to teacher education.

For purposes of analysis reflectivity can be organized without too much violence to our understanding under three general headings: technical, interpretive and critical (Gore, 1987). The technical approach is well represented by Cruickshank (1985). This conception of reflectivity emphasizes the careful consideration of means rather than the aims of education which are assumed. Within this context, reflectivity is often seen as a way for teachers to assess how well they are employing teaching techniques and the related concern of how their performance compares to that of others teaching the same or similar lessons (Cruickshank and Applegate, 1981). This conception of reflection is contained ny the training orientation, reproducing a limited teacher role which focuses intellect narrowly on the development of teaching techniques, and encourages a strong sense of individualism.

For those within the interpretative camp, reflectivity essentially finds its purpose in exposing and clarifying personal meaning. Connelly and Clandinin (1988) represent this view:

Through reflection it is possible to reconstruct, to rebuild a narrative that 'remakes' the taken-for-granted, habitual ways we all have of responding to our curriculum situations. (p. 81)

While giving an important place to the individual's experience and an expanded arena for the expression of teacher intellect, thereby confronting the notion that teachers are simply consumers of knowledge, the interpretive orientation too often fails to reach out beyond the individual. The danger is that reflection may become nothing more than therapy, a form of disconnected but interesting indwelling which assumes schooling aims and fails to confront the hierarchical and alienating structures currently found in most schools (Apple, 1982; Bullough and Gitlin, 1985). Indeed, reflection may become merely a means of personal adjustment. Further, the interpretative view of reflectivity, as was true of the technical, appears to do little to challenge the competitive individualism which is so much a part of the training orientation to teacher education. Reflectivity of this sort may well serve only the interests of the status quo.

The critical orientation to reflectivity, in contrast to the other two conceptions, seems to hold the most promise for confronting the structures and ideologies that underpin the training orientation to teacher education. This is so because reflectivity, as a particular kind of expression of intellect, not only aims at *clarifying* educational means and ends, but importantly, holds them up to *critical scrutiny* in the belief that teachers have the potential to recognize and then confront unquestioned teaching roles, internalized values, and the structures and power relations which foster narrow and oppressive school relations. Further, this view of reflectivity escapes the relativism often associated with the interpretative position by viewing reflectivity as part of a larger project that is explicitly political, being based on the values of social justice and equity (Zeichner and Liston, 1987). With this said, however, it is also clear that a few aspects of the critical view also reside comfortably within the training orientation.

Because reflectivity, even from the critical view, is often seen as an individual undertaking, the extreme form of individualism found in the training orientation may not be confronted. Moreover, in the quest to escape liberalism — which does not confront underlying structures of inequality — in the hands of enthusiasts this conception of reflection becomes, at times, expert driven and impositional in that the problems to be reflected on are determined *for* rather than *with* prospective teachers. A somewhat hierarchical relation may thereby develop that actually silences preservice teachers and strengthens their dependance on experts. Under these circumstances, teachers are treated as only consumers of knowledge as attempts are made to 'correct' their view of teaching and schooling, their 'false consciousness'.

To varying degrees each of these three views of reflectivity are or may easily be contained within a training orientation to teacher education. To help avoid cooptation, reflectivity needs to be grounded in a project, and an alternative ideal that powerfully challenges the training orientation. This ideal, in our view, centers around the creation of communities of a particular kind, what we are calling 'educative communities'. We turn now to a brief discussion of what we mean by an educative community and how such an ideal informs the discourses about teacher reflectivity. Before doing so, a word of caution is in order: we are speaking about an ideal community the attainment of which is unlikely. What is important, in our view, is that programs of preservice teacher education move in the direction of the ideal.

Reflectivity and the Educative Community

A community is a group that has certain characteristics: first 'membership is valued as an end in itself, not merely as a means to other ends'; second, it 'concerns itself with the many and significant aspects of the lives of members'; third, it 'allows competing factions'; fourth, its 'members share a commitment to common purpose and to procedures for handling conflict within the group'; fifth, its 'members share responsibility for the actions of the group'; and sixth, its 'members have enduring and extensive personal contact with each other' (Newman and Oliver, 1972, pp. 207–8). What distinguishes an educative community from others is two fold. First, an educative community involves not just any group of people but rather those who take an active interest in schooling. This ethic not only carries with it a general concern for others but also honors what others know and aims at enhancing that knowing in what Belenky and her colleagues (1986) call 'connected' ways, ways that do not separate argued positions from personal concerns. When in place this ethic provides the foundation for a type of school change that is grounded in an evolving and articulated form of community knowledge. Second, an educative community seeks to establish a particular kind and quality of relationship among its members. In contrast to communities where privilege and decision-making power are strongly tied to the accumulation of wealth, or the attainment of a status position, the educative community seeks to establish relations, and institutional structures, where decisions are based on dialogue that seeks to develop and extend mutual understanding (Habermas, 1976). Within such relations reason carries the day, not imposition, status or the ability to control resources. Because dialogue is such a central part of the establishment of educative relations, a brief consideration of the meaning of dialogue and how it differs from everyday conversation follows.

People talk to each other all the time, but the talk is often not important to the participants. A good example of this is when two individuals greet each other in the hall and one asks 'how are you doing?' and the other replies 'fine'. And even when the talk is important to one of the participants it may not be to the other. Dialogue, on the other hand, is entered into because it presupposes a 'tacit sense of relevance' (Bernstein, 1983, p. 2). A precondition for dialogue is, therefore, that both participants think the discourse important, in part by virtue of having a say in determining its course.[1] Talk also differs from dialogue in its purpose; generally it is only intended to be a pleasant time filler. At other times its purpose shifts and it becomes debate where the purpose is to sway someone to a particular point of view, to win an argument. In contrast, the purpose of dialogue is to enable the participants to come to a shared understanding of the subject being discussed. It implies a respectful relationship among equals. Thus, dialogue requires that even if one person understands a situation or subject more completely than the other, 'the person with understanding does not know and judge as one who stands apart unaffected, but as one [who] thinks with the other and undergoes the situation with [her/] him' (Gadamer, 1975, p. 288). Finally, while dialogue can and should lead to mutual understanding, this intention does not require that all prejudices or prejudgments be removed for certainly this is impossible. It does, however, necessitate that effort be directed to making pre-judgments — blocks to mutual understanding — apparent and to 'test them critically in the course of inquiry' (Bernstein, 1983, p. 128). Hence, the reasons for or against a particular understanding of an event or situation ought not be viewed as objective facts possessing universal character but rather as intersubjec-tive agreements embedded in a particular historical and cultural context. It is through the continuing examination of these agreements and their underlying prejudgments that actors are empowered to rethink the way they see the world and judge their practice.

By emphasizing the value of dialogue, an educative community is democra-tic in intent in that all members have access to decision-making processes. Futher, it is liberative in that the emphasis on dialogue requires that actors consider how history, prejudgments and material conditions influence meaning and meaning making, and thereby shape their actions. And finally, it is through dialogue that caring and reason are bound together as necessary characteristics of educative communities.

At present those groups that have a strong interest in schooling are often adversarial; we know of no educative communities. Teachers, who are 'sensitive to criticism and attacks from parents in a wide range of areas', limit the involve-ment of parents in schools (Blase, 1988, p. 134). But more than this, not only are parents — especially those in working-class schools — given limited opportuni-ties to be involved in shaping school decisions, they are also frequently blamed for their children's lack of classroom success (Connell, 1985). While teachers appear somewhat united against parents, they too clearly represent a group divided. Often teachers see themselves as being in competition with other teachers and are loath to share materials and ideas; collegiality is all too rare among teachers. On their part, administrators and parents often share a deep distrust of teachers, particularly female teachers, and blame them for educational failure. And university faculty find status and comfort by distancing themselves from all the other groups. The situation, in short, appears to be one of all for none, and none for all.

In contrast to this situation, a commitment to creating an educative com-munity would seek to establish means for breaking down barriers and for identifying common interests in the name of education. Indeed, all groups, including students, would necessarily have a say in school matters; democratic, caring, relations would replace those based exclusively on privilege and position where some groups determine for all others the nature of schooling. As conflicts arise between community members, as they inevitably must, when seeking resolution emphasis would be placed on the exercise of reason within the context of caring relations, and the common good, rather than on power and authority. Moreover, an educative community is one in which there would be continuous and constant examination of aims and means, an examination necessitated by shifting member relations and the need to insure equality of membership, and a shifting political and school context which challenges group identity.

A genuine commitment to creating educative communities would present a significant challenge to training views of teacher education. Teacher education tied to the educative community ideal disallows the sharp distinctions between preservice and inservice work, and between theory and practice, that characterize the training orientation. As members of the community, the university faculties' responsibilities do not end with certification. Nor are university faculty allowed a privileged position in either program design, development or even research; indeed, they are among many other groups with a responsibility to understand and improve schooling. To not embrace these responsibilities is to ignore one's role as a community member.

In the creation of educative communities, reflectivity as a certain kind of expression of intellect has an extremely important part to play (Bullough, 1989b). This kind of reflectivity honors the interpretative orientation by insisting that careful attention be given to individual experience and meaning making, and the critical orientation by focusing on the analysis of the politics of human relations in context. It avoids the weaknesses to which these orientations are prone by grounding reflectivity in community and binding it to the aim of community development through establishing dialogic relations. From this view reflectivity becomes a form of community participation; a means for community enhancement and redirection; and an aim. As a form of community participation, reflectivity is not something limited to several individuals but part of a larger group activity, an intellectual exercise grounded in the ethic of caring. Further, as means for community enhancement and redirection, reflectivity aims at uncovering oppressive and alienating conditions by critically examining educational practices and purposes within their historical context. In this regard, special attention must be paid to students who are often the least privileged of community members. As an aim, reflectivity represents a set of qualities to be enhanced that are essential to community vitality: among them the willingness to tolerate differences, suspend judgment, compromise, and to openly and honestly share opinions in the quest for shared understanding.

Cultivating Reflectivity in Practice

We can now return to the original question, 'What can be done within preservice teacher education programs to cultivate teacher reflectivity?' Given our normative framework, this question can be divided into three parts, each focusing attention on essential elements of a program that is attempting to further teacher reflectivity as part of a larger project to build educative communities. These elements are: the *context* of teacher education programs; the *texts* that serve as program content, and; the intellectual *processes* used for text analysis. Each element is inextricably interrelated with the others; and each must be attended to and in relation to the others — ends must not be separated from means, nor content separated from methods or from program structure or form. To separate program elements or to attend to one without considering carefully its relationship to the others is to fall victim to the assumptions underpinning a training orientation to teacher education and thereby to drain from reflectivity any potential it has to facilitate genuine educational reform. The first question to be considered is, 'What program structures are most likely to encourage a type of reflectivity based on dialogue, reason and the ethic of caring that also confronts competitive individualism?'

Context

From the vantage point of this question, the context of teacher education must meet the following standards:

1   Technical questions and issues should not be separated from questions of value and meaning;
2   preservice teachers must have ample time to engage in reflection and act on insights gained; and
3   they must have extended periods of time together engaged in challenging and shared activities, essential to building caring dialogical relations.

Linking value and meaning to the technical

It is commonplace within programs of teacher education to separate content and foundations courses from methods courses. Within such programs the effect is to strengthen the assumption that teacher education is training; teaching is assumed to be 'a delivery system ... and knowledge [the] accumulation of cherished things, like a coin collection carefully labeled and ordered' (Grumet, 1989, p. 16). To overcome the training orientation, methods courses emphasizing teaching skills must be carefully linked to foundations and theory courses so that the politics of method and technology, and the social construction of knowledge are seen as related concerns that shape the meaning of teaching.

Efforts to link content, foundations and methods courses, however, will do little to challenge a training orientation if student teaching remains a three month, intensive, apprenticeship emphasizing the development of survival skills and technical teaching competence alone. At best this approach limits reflectivity to the first of the three orientations discussed earlier, the technical, where ends are forgotten in the quest for means 'that work'. At worst, it makes certain that questions of value and meaning, that many foundations and theory courses seek to develop, are washed out leaving many student teachers with the impression that university work is irrelevant to the legitimate demands of teaching.

Transforming the narrow technical emphasis of student teaching is no easy task. In this regard, one area of special concern is student teacher evaluation which plays such a prominent role in shaping the nature of the experience. Most approaches to evaluation are based upon a deficit model of teacher performance and utilize a list of desired teaching behaviors against which the novice is rated (Gitlin and Smyth, 1989). Such approaches encourage conformity, intellectual passivity and conservatism (Bullough, 1987, 1988b, 1989; Gitlin, 1987) as appropriate student teacher responses to the threatening and often ambiguous position within which they find themselves. Where the development of educative communities is the aim, alternative evaluation processes must be created that place value on what students teachers know and who they are; that encourage dialogue as opposed to the unidirectional message sending of supervisor to novice, and; that acknowledge the importance of the political aspects of teaching, including those values embedded in technical understandings of teaching.[2]

Another structure that fosters a technical orientation is the separation of the student teaching experience from formal, planned opportunities for reflection. As we will emphasize in the next section, the sheer intensity of student teaching puts a premium on 'doing' but not on examining practice. If student teaching is to be more than an apprenticeship in training, student teachers must be put in situations within which they are expected and encouraged to engage in reflection on more than just technical problems and issues. To this end, a student teaching seminar, while no panacea, is promising (Goodman, 1983). When properly organized and taught, such a seminar can be a means for identifying and extending common interests and concerns, and accessing and illuminating the theories embedded in practice, which expose the ethical and political implications of teaching and schooling.

Time to reflect

It is not unusual to hear teacher educators lament that despite all their good work helping novices become more reflective, in some sense, that once student teaching begins there is little evidence of transferral. It may be true that student teachers are not at first creative, innovative or experimental in their teaching, but it is also most certainly true that the student teaching experience is organized to make activity of this kind difficult if not impossible.

The short duration and extreme intensity of student teaching are important culprits in preventing novices from thinking about their practice in reflective ways. By having student teaching be a full-time activity that occurs over a relatively short period of time, survival becomes the main concern of the novice teacher (Bullough, 1989b). Clearly it is unreasonable to expect to see more than an occasional example of teacher reflectivity when the novice is trying to keep up with as many as four preparations and adjust in only a few weeks to an unfamiliar and in some ways threatening and complicated bureaucratic organization. Even within internship programs which lengthen the experience — and thereby offer the possibility of internalizing the values of reflectivity and of engaging in its practice — frequently nothing is done to lessen intensity, with unfortunate results. If reflectivity is to be a teacher education program aim, then student teaching needs to be lengthened and the intensity lessened. Less daily teaching time and less intensity means more time and energy for novices to think about their practice richly and deeply, and more time to observe other teachers and peers to gain insights useful for thinking about future practice.

Unfortunately, just freeing up more time in itself may not encourage reflectivity if supervisors and cooperating teachers discourage or undervalue this type of activity. As mentioned previously, supervisors rarely encourage reflectivity in part because their attention is focused on the summative rating scales that they must fill out. Given the intensity of cooperating teachers' work (Apple, 1986) and the limited opportunities they have to reflect on practice, they too frequently see such activities as being of little value when learning to teach. If reflectivity is to be cultivated among novices, then clearly it must be valued by both supervisors and by cooperating teachers. From our perspective, supervisors and cooperating teachers need to become part of the educative community; they too need opportunities to engage in reflection on their practice and particularly upon their relations with the novices with whom they work and the assumptions informing those relations that so often are tied to training.

Confronting individualism

Individualism is one of the strongest features of preservice teacher education programs grounded in the training orientation. This is a particular and peculiar kind of individualism, one that simultaneously ignores the value of individual experience while rewarding individual competiveness. If reflection is to play a part in the larger project of fostering educative communities then clearly we must begin to establish structures which encourage more collective relations and action.

A modest step in this direction is to organize programs around a cohort ideal where groups of students are formed and remain intact thoughout their teacher education program. Within a cohort it becomes possible for participants to establish the level of trust — part of an ethic of caring — needed to explore openly and critically the prejudgments about teaching and learning participants bring with them into the program. Preservice teachers cannot be expected to possess this level of trust if they are thrown together for the first time in a seminar, for example, just prior to student teaching.

The establishment of group identity, and the building of dialogical relations, can also be furthered by concentrating field experiences in a few schools. Through sharing a placement, group members have increased opportunities to interact with one another but more than this they have the opportunity to explore meanings and differences in meanings based upon very similar experiences. Sharing school placements, and perhaps even sharing some students, also enables student teachers to locate problems and resources useful for resolution that reside outside a particular classroom context thus encouraging a more communal perspective and weakening the extreme form of individualism common to training approaches to teacher education.

Sharing placements has additional advantages as well. Although seldom considered, teacher educators, as members of the educational community, can and should play an important role in the school. Instead of just dropping the student teacher off at the doorstep, teacher educators are able to concentrate their efforts and begin working with cooperating teachers and student teachers in seeking better and closer links between university coursework and school practicum experience. Furthermore, by concentrating field placements in a few carefully selected schools, teacher educators are able get to know the student teachers intimately, and establish more collegial relations with cooperating teachers generally as they seek to build a wider professional community. Such relations hold the potential for decreasing the isolation and the individualism of practising teachers that bolster training views of teacher education just as they hold the potential for enriching the practice of university and college teacher educators.

Text and Text Analysis

Thus far we have described in broad strokes a program structure that holds promise for developing reflectivity as we conceive of it. While going a long way toward confronting training views of teacher preparation, the structure itself is no guarantee that such views will not remain dominant. The content and processes of teacher education are also in need of change. Specifically, we need to ask, 'What ought to be the content of a teacher education program that seeks to form educative communities and how should students engage this content?'

Our response to these questions draws on insights gained from both the interpretative and critical orientations to reflectivity. The interpretative speaks directly to our concern for developing an ethic of caring which honors who novices are and what they know while tempering the tendency of the critical to ignore the value of individual experience. Similarly, the critical tempers the tendency of the interpretative to restrict analysis only to the individual's experience as it reaches out into the wider material and ideological context within which meaning is made. Taken together they form a significant challenge to training views of teacher education and suggest a radically different kind of teacher education program.

We need to be very clear here: in the discussion that follows we will not be focusing our attention on the development of technical teaching skills *per se*. However, this does not mean that we do not believe strongly that the study and practice of teaching skills has no place in teacher education. Indeed, such study and practice is of great importance but only when linked to a larger set of questions and issues. Once again, means must always been considered in relationship to ends and in context. Our ends are tied to the challenge of training assumptions about teacher development and to building educative communities.

This said, teacher education programs ought include content and emphasize processes that meet the following standards:

1   The experience of the preservice teacher should be honored and serve as a central focus of study;
2   attempts should be made to examine the meaning of experience by seeing its relation to material conditions, issues of power and cultural traditions and norms;
3   the content and processes used should encourage the view that novice teachers are creators, not merely consumers, of legitimate knowledge, and;
4   the content and processes used should encourage the development of collegial and communal links among participants.

What follows are two brief and partial case studies drawn from our work at the University of Utah in a three-quarter sequence of professional education courses leading to certification that present some of the ways in which we attempt to meet the above standards. Neither case study describes the entire preservice program but rather focuses on the central threads and activities that hold the respective programs together. While pointing to a direction for teacher education reform, the cases also will underscore some of the difficulties involved in attempts to foster educative communities.

Case Study #1

Teacher education students come to their programs with long histories as students and generally with strongly held views about teachers and teaching (Crow, 1987). To pretend that they do not bring with them 'implicit theories' (Clark, 1988) about teaching and about the purposes of education is to ignore their personal histories and to dishonor the individual. Starting the preservice program with the writing of personal histories, therefore, provided a teacher produced text that articulated what they know about teaching and schooling. Each prospective teacher was asked to write on three questions: Why did I choose teaching?; What factors have influenced my views of myself as teacher?; and, What is my philosophy of teaching? The instructor also answered these difficult questions. Through answering these questions it was clear that the prospective teachers did not enter the program as 'blank slates'; and neither did the instructor. The personal histories — contrary to texts reflecting a 'banking' view of teaching and learning — provided a point of desparture for building a dialogue starting with the sharing of prejudgments and knowledge brought by the cohort members to the program. While sharing such information is of value in and of itself, more than sharing is required if pedagogical practices are to confront weaknesses of the interpretive orientation to the development of teacher reflectivity. To avoid these weaknesses other experiences were structured around and built upon the personal histories. ·

One such experience was the writing of a school history. Specifically, preservice teachers were asked to identify the dominant structures of the school (e.g., school-wide management programs, required curriculum, physical organization of the school), the relations of power and the culture of teachers and students. In each of these areas the prospective teachers were asked to describe the current school context and then try to situate the current pattern in its historical context to see if and how the school had changed over time. To gather such information extensive interviews were conducted, questionnaires passed out and long hours were spent observing the everyday life of the school.

Once written, insights gained from the school histories were linked to those found in the personal histories. By asking the students to carefully consider the relationships between their philosophies and the structures, power relations and cultural groups found in the schools, a first attempt was made to go beyond the interpretative orientation. Through comparison and analysis, these prospective teachers began to consider in an informed way how their own experience influenced and shaped their teaching philosophy and values, the relationship between personal values and the values and experiences that certain groups of students bring with them to school, and the way the culture of teaching influences and is influenced by gender issues. Additional readings and research related to these student-generated areas of interest were identified and became part of the growing text.

An example will help clarify how this process worked. One student, in her personal history, noted that:

> Having grown up in a very traditional, and conservative family, teaching, or any other 'public service' position, was in my parents' eyes, a suitable, but no doubt temporary, career for me. Of the women in my family who had careers five were teachers and one a nurse. I believe it was partially these familial expectations that ... later induced me to become a teacher.

This prospective teacher's school history revealed that many of the women teachers in the school studied also entered teaching for similar reasons. Through analysis it became apparent that issues related to gender and to the value of public service played a significant role in shaping the culture of teaching. With this theme identified, the students and the instructor identified articles and research

47

that would enrich and further the discourse on the topic. The educational theories and research were then related to the insights derived from the teacher produced texts. In making comparisons, neither practitioner knowledge nor educational theory and research were assumed to be beyond reproach or of a higher status. Instead, the prejudgments found in both forms of knowledge were debated as a basis for reconsidering the interpretations presented in the school and personal histories.

While the process described meets most of our standards — e.g., prospective teachers were viewed as producers of knowledge and what they knew was honored — it may not necessarily challenge individualism. Indeed, it may represent nothing more than typical group work. To challenge individualism more directly and to continue building a dialogue about teaching and schooling, the students were asked to extend their personal and school histories by writing collective personal and school histories. Specifically, students were asked to get into groups of their own choosing and share the dominant themes that were articulated in their personal histories. The group looked across these themes to identify areas of shared perspective and difference. Then, the group was asked to analyze why these shared perspectives and differences occurred and their implications for the practice of teaching and for understanding schooling. Much the same process occurred with the school history. Because one of the schools was a junior high and the other a high school the analysis centered on what was common and different about those schools. This type of experience not only deepened the analysis of the school and personal histories but pointed to shared interests and encouraged the identification of and debate about ideological differences. While we cannot claim that an individualistic perspective disappeared, the teachers did begin to develop a common terrain within which they honored, but openly explored and sometimes challenged, differences.

To this point, the program focused primarily on political and ethical questions related to teaching and schooling. The next challenge was to connect the insights gained to the beginning teachers' own practices. To do so the teachers were introduced to Horizontal Evaluation, a model of evaluation based upon structured dialogue and peer observation (Gitlin and Goldstein, 1987). The model begins with the identification and analysis of the relationship between what a participant wants to do — the intentions — and what actually occurs — the teaching practice. In thinking through this relationship, the previous exploration of personal and school histories proved to be a rich source of insights and understandings when thinking through intentions and when debating the interests served by teaching practices.

To begin this process, the preservice teachers were asked to develop a lesson plan that stated their aims and described in some detail what they would do in the classroom. Even before teaching the lesson, groups of two or three teachers used Horizontal Evaluation to dialogue about the relation between intentions and the proposed practices as well as to examine the intentions themselves. In many cases this led to a number of questions about the legitimacy of what was intended and about the kinds of teaching practices that would most likely serve the articulated ends. These questions were shared with the larger group and used as a basis for setting the agenda for future meetings within which teaching methods would be discussed in relation to desired ends. Many of the preservice teachers, for example, wanted to take into account the cultural capital particular minority groups brought to the classroom (Apple, 1979). They realized this meant individualizing the classroom but were unsure how this could be done. To fill this void we worked together to investigate ways of individualizing the curriculum. Thus, individualization was understood in relation to an explicit set of political aims arising from the students themselves.

Following this activity, the preservice teachers had the opportunity to try these plans in a classroom setting. To assess the relation between what they wanted to do, their theories of schooling and practice, Horizontal Evaluation was again utilized. Groups of two or three students — who over the course of the year had developed a level of trust and openness — observed each other teaching, and used the observations and stated intentions as a text for analysis. Through dialogue about the text, students were able to identify problems previously hidden and to consider and examine the political implications of the instructional means employed. One teacher, for example, had assumed that the central problem in his biology class was how to get more lab experiences into the curriculum: a technical problem. After the dialogue with a peer he understood the issue differently: the primary concern was no longer how many but what kind of experiences would best serve his articulated aim of having a student-centered classroom, one that confronted the problem of the high failure rate especially of female students. For this student, and others, theory and practice had been linked in ways that represented a growing critical and ethical understanding of teaching and of schooling.

Case Study #2

The second program began much as the first by prospective teachers writing personal histories but added an additional assignment, that of identifying for analysis and discussion a central or 'root' teaching metaphor. The assignment to write a personal history differed somewhat from that presented in the first case study, emphasizing the identification and analysis of critical school-related instances (Measor, 1985), but the process was roughly similar and the intention the same: to enable the students to begin exploring how previous schooling shaped their understanding of teaching and schooling, and to begin building a text for analysis.

The identification and exploration of personal teaching metaphors is a promising means for accessing and exploring teacher values and assumptions, an approach consistent with the interpretative orientation to reflection and grounded in the ethic of caring. Metaphors, as Lakoff and Johnson (1980) argue, give coherence to experience and function like private theories through which the individual makes situations meaningful. The identification and analysis of metaphors provide a short-hand means for accessing fundamental values and, as such, are a rich focus for analysis. Moreover, changes in teaching metaphors signal changes in self-understanding and therefore provide a means for beginning teachers to think about, and perhaps even redirect, their own development. The potential for metaphor analysis as a means for helping beginning teachers to make some of their assumptions about teaching explicit, and as a way for thinking about how they are changing while teaching, is well illustrated by one of our students who wrote:

The whole idea of ... teaching metaphor [analysis] has really been ... powerful ... for me. It comes at a time when I am experiencing a personal crisis over the age old question of 'who am I?' Just when I thought that my identity was fairly secure and well established, I am being subjected to yet another identity crisis. For the last few weeks I have been plagued by the question of 'Who am I as a teacher?' ... [Analyzing my] metaphor has really helped me to sort out my thoughts and come to realize what my intentions are as a teacher ...

There are a variety of approaches to identifying teaching metaphors. With this group we approached the task directly by asking the students to identify, based upon their personal histories, a metaphor that 'caught the essence of their views of themselves as teachers'. Once identified, the metaphors were explored in writing and then compared and analyzed within the group for their theoretical and practical implications. Questions were posed about the ethical implications of some metaphors, as well as about their appropriateness given various teaching contexts (of this more will be said shortly); and questions were asked about what holding to one or another metaphor meant practically.

Throughout the year, we periodically returned to our metaphors and explored whether or not they had changed and what the educational and personal significance of the changes were. For example, one student discovered half-way through student teaching that his metaphor had shifted from 'teacher is mentor' to 'teacher is benevolent father'. When exploring the shift he realized that a significant change had taken place in how he understood himself as teacher and in his understanding of the teacher role: caring for children had become more important than the teaching of mathematics. For him, personally, this was an important discovery that affected how he thought about planning as well as about discipline and management. When planning, he thought more carefully about how the students would react and about how they would feel about his assignments; he cared about them as people: 'I care about them and their lives.... I have become possessive. These are *My kids*'.

By returning to consider the metaphors over the course of the program, the novice teachers were encouraged and helped to attend to the ways in which they were developing, to consider the factors influencing their development, particularly those associated with the structure of schooling and the culture of teaching, and to analyze, critically, the directions in which they seemed to be heading in the light of their values and goals. Occasionally this was a painful process. Through analysis, one of our students was forced to confront a significant mismatch between his metaphor and the public school teaching context and in the process he faced the question of whether or not he should become a teacher.

To go beyond the interpretative, personal understandings of self-as-teacher needed to be grounded contextually. To begin to accomplish this aim prior to student teaching, students conducted ethnographies of the classrooms within which they would eventually be student teaching. The initial charge was to describe how students and teachers experienced the classroom, the roles, relationships and informal rules that operated within it and gave it order, and how they seemed to be interrelated, influencing and reinforcing one another. To help them with this assignment a variety of readings were provided. Next, based upon insights gained through the personal history and through their first metaphor analysis, the students carefully considered the environment in the light of the teaching role they hoped to develop, seeking to identify constraining and enabling influences. The ethnographies were shared and discussed and common themes, sometimes school-specific themes, were identified for further study. These themes centered on those aspects of the teaching environment that enabled teacher development and student learning and those that stood as impediments. Taken together, they represented a powerful critique of schooling and of its effects. The themes were linked with appropriate readings to deepen and enrich the analysis and to connect it with a wider set of issues and concerns. It should also be noted that not all the themes were negative; a few represented messages of hope embedded in the creative efforts of some teachers to stay alive intellectually and to provide classroom settings within which students could and did learn.

Among the themes identified, a few related to the kind and quality of the curriculum presented in the school and to the methods used which were seen by many of the students as seriously flawed and occasionally deadening. Many of the observed teachers emphasized the use of textbooks while others used state and district materials. Honoring this theme, the group engaged in an analysis of the materials used seeking to identify the assumptions about teaching, teachers and learning embedded in them and any biases they might have contained. Recognizing the weaknesses in the materials, as well as some of their more positive aspects, the novice teachers then wrote lesson and unit plans that would later be used in student teaching. These plans were critiqued by group members not only in terms of their aims and the relationship between aims and means but also in terms of the relationship between the plans and the teaching values earlier articulated in the metaphor analysis and personal histories.

Once student teaching began, the emphasis shifted to the critical study of practice with the intention of linking practice to theory (theorizing practice) and of extending the group's shared understanding of teaching and of schooling while continuing to build a teaching text for study. To this end, within the student teaching seminar the beginning teachers continued to participate in the analysis of teaching units and lesson plans. In addition, throughout student teaching, the novices engaged in action research. We think of action research in rather straightforward ways: It is the gathering of data on practice, the identification of problems or concerns arising from the data, and the development and testing of alternative courses of action (Carr and Kemmis, 1986). Given our aim to build educative communities, we expected both the process and the results of action research to be openly and critically explored not only to understand precisely what transpired in the lessons under review and the problem being considered, but also to help one another think through alternative conceptions of the problem or issue and alternative responses to it. Moreover, the majority of the issues identified were shared by members of the group. Analysis of these issues clearly helped strengthen community bonds and understanding.

With this group, given time and other constraints, a single class that was considered to be most interesting or troubling was selected for study by each student. The action research project was divided into three phases, each involving either audio- or video-taping of three class sessions for a total of nine. During the first phase the novice teachers taped the classes and then reviewed the tapes seeking to identify surprises, and strengths and weaknesses apparent in their teaching. In this phase some students identified problems and began generating with the group ideas for adjusting their teaching in response to the problems. For these students, the purpose of subsequent audio- and/or video-taping sessions was to gather data useful for assessing the changes they had implemented. Others used phase two as an opportunity to more clearly define a problem in the light of the feedback given by group members on the write up from their first tape analysis and the subsequent discussion. For these students, phase three involved the testing of alternative solutions. At the conclusion of each phase and in anticipation of the next, the beginning teachers sharing a student teaching school met to discuss their work, explore options or other questions and to identify further directions for study. In the group analyses, special attention was given to the relationship of ends to means and to personal values in the light of the earlier work on metaphor, personal history and teaching context.

Conclusion

Our aim has been to set forth a view of reflectivity and an approach to its development that we believe holds promise for challenging training views of teacher education that have thus far blunted attempts at genuine educational reform. Although much of our work is preliminary in nature (it will always be experimental) our view is that teacher education programs can start with what teachers know and through the process of text building and reflection on the text enable them to articulate and enhance that knowledge in ways that expose the political aspects of schooling, challenge individualism, extend the ethic of caring and build community.

This said, however, our arguments and case studies leave unanswered many important questions just a few of which we shall mention. While we have made modest attempts to develop more collective and collegial relations among teachers and in small ways among teachers and university teacher educators, we have ignored the role that other university professors, school administrators and perhaps even parents and students could play in preservice teacher education programs. If we are to move in the direction of building educative communities based on reason and caring then surely the groups involved in teacher education must be expanded in some ways, particularly as we think through the larger question of educational reform. How this can can done is a question we need to explore as we continue to think about the structure, content and processes of the preservice programs in which we work.

Another question concerns the relation between honoring what teachers know and the processes involved in enhancing that knowledge. While procedures such as Horizontal Evaluation, metaphor analysis and action research can help teachers identify and rethink taken-for-granted views of teaching and learning, and point to political and ethical implications of schooling that require careful attention, it is likely that once they leave our programs given current school structures, much of what we do will be set aside in the quest for institutional survival. No matter how hard we work in preservice settings, it is clear that some kind of significant support must be given into the first years of teaching. In the quest for the reflective practitioner a fundamental rethinking of the relation between preservice and inservice programs must take place; this is a relationship we have yet to think through carefully.

Finally, while we have suggested some structural changes that would culti-vate educative communities, we have not talked about the relation between current structures and those we propose. For example, while it is possible to imagine that evaluation procedures could be implemented that value reflection as we describe it, it is unlikely that the more traditional procedures based on training views of teacher education will disappear. If this is the case, what will be the relationship between these procedures? Will more reflective types of assess-ment be added on to the other procedures and thereby further intensify teachers' work? Will these new procedures be looked upon as merely something one does after engaging in real evaluation, the one that counts for certification?

While these questions are more than a little troubling, they, and others suggested in this article, need to be raised as part of challenging the training orientation to teacher education. It is not easy to escape the influence of training; training assumptions are deeply embedded in our thinking. As we have reflected on the two brief cases presented it has become clear to us that regardless of our explicit attempts to escape such a tradition, our practice has within it a number of contradictions where we have stumbled into a trainer's role. In particular, we have found ourselves being seduced by the language of training that is all pervasive. The challenge, then, is to keep asking questions while continuously seeking ways to uncover and move beyond the assumptions of training. Ultimately, the future of teacher reflectivity and of teacher education reform is dependent upon the ability and willingness of teacher educators to enter into dialogical relations with other members of the wider education community in order to begin the long and complex process of peeling from our eyes the training assumptions that blind us. This is a first step toward creating a new vision of teacher education, one based upon the possibilities of developing educative communities.

Notes

1 Given that both participants must view the dialogue as important, it is clear that this type of discourse cannot be imposed and may be inappropriate in certain situations for particular individuals or groups.
2 Currently there are several approaches to teacher evaluation that place value on what teachers know, encourage dialogue and acknowledge the importance of politics. See, for example, Gitlin, A. and Smyth, J. (1989) *Teacher Evaluation: Educative Alernatives.*

References

APPLE, M. (1979) *Ideology and Curriculum,* Boston: Routledge and Kegan Paul.
APPLE, M. (1982) *Education and Power,* Boston: Routledge and Kegan Paul.
APPLE, M. (1986) *Teachers and Text: A Political Economy of Class and Gender Relations in Education,* New York: Routledge and Kegan Paul.
BLASE, J. (1988) 'The everyday political perspective of teachers: Vulnerability and conservatism', *Qualitative Studies Journal,* 1, pp. 125–42.
BELENKY, M.F., CLINCHY, B.M., GOLDBERGER, N.R. and TARULE, J.M. (1986) *Women's Ways of Knowing: The Development of Self, Voice, and Mind,* New York: Basic Books.

BERNSTEIN, R. (1983) *Beyond Objectivism and Relativism: Science, Hermeneutics and Praxis*, Philadelphia: University of Pennsylvania Press.

BULLOUGH, R.V. JR. (1987) 'Accomodation and tension: Teachers, teacher role, and the culture of teaching', in SMYTH, J. (Ed.) *Educating Teachers: Changing the Nature of Pedagogical Knowledge*, Basingstoke: Falmer Press, pp. 83–94.

BULLOUGH, R.V. JR. (1988a) *The Forgotten Dream of American Public Education*, Ames, Iowa: Iowa State University Press.

BULLOUGH, R.V. JR. (1988b) 'Evaluation and the beginning teacher: A case study', *Education and Society*, 6, pp. 71–8.

BULLOUGH, R.V. JR. (1989a) *First Year Teacher: A Case Study*, New York: Teachers College Press.

BULLOUGH, R.V. JR. (1989b) 'Teacher education and teacher reflectivity', *Journal of Teacher Education*, 40, pp. 15–21.

BULLOUGH, R.V. JR. and GITLIN, A. (1985) 'Schooling and change: A view from the lower rungs', *Teachers College Record*, 87, pp. 219–37.

BULLOUGH, R.V. JR., GOLDSTEIN, S. and HOLT, L. (1984) *Human Interests in the Curriculum: Teaching and Learning in a Technological Society*, New York: Teachers College Press.

CARR, W. and KEMMIS, S. (1986) *Becoming Critical: Education, Knowledge, and Action Research*, Basingstoke: Falmer Press.

CLARK, C. (1988) 'Asking the right questions about teacher preparation: Contributions of research on teacher thinking', *Educational Researcher*, March, pp. 5–12.

CONNELL, R.W. (1985) *Teachers' Work*, London: Allen and Unwin.

CONNELLY, F.M. and CLANDININ, D.J. (1988) *Teachers as Curriculum Planners: Narratives of Experience*, New York: Teachers College Press.

CROW, N. (1987) Socialization within a teacher education program: A case study. Unpublished doctoral dissertation, University of Utah, Salt Lake City, Utah.

CRUICKSHANK, D.R. (1985) 'Reflecting on reflective teaching', *Journal of Teacher Education*, 38, pp. 33–9.

CRUICKSHANK, D.R. and APPLEGATE, J.N. (1981) 'Reflective teaching as a strategy for teacher growth', *Educational Leadership*, 38, pp. 553–4.

DARLING-HAMMOND, L. (1985) 'Valuing teachers: The making of a profession', *Teachers College Record*, 87, pp. 205–18.

FREIRE, P. (1985) *The Politics of Education: Culture, Power and Liberation*, South Hadley, Mass.: Bergin and Garvey Publishers.

GADAMER, H. (1975) *Truth and Method*, New York: Seabury Press.

GITLIN, A. (1987) 'Common school structures and teacher behavior', in SMYTH, J. (Ed.) *Educating Teachers: Changing the Nature of Pedagogical Knowledge*, Basingstoke: Falmer Press, pp. 107–20.

GITLIN, A. and GOLDSTEIN, S. (1987) 'A dialogical approach to understanding: Horizontal evaluation', *Educational Theory*, 37, pp. 17–27.

GITLIN, A. and SMYTH, J. (1989) *Teacher Evaluation: Educative Alternatives*, Basingstoke: Falmer Press.

GOODMAN, J. (1983) 'The seminar's role in the education of student teachers: A case study', *Journal of Teacher Education*, 34, pp. 44–9.

GORE, J.M. (1987) 'Reflecting on reflective teaching', *Journal of Teacher Education*, 38, pp. 33–9.

GRUMET, M. (1989) 'Generations: Reconceptualist curriculum theory and teacher education', *Journal of Teacher Education*, 40, pp. 13–17.

HABERMAS, J. (1976) *Communication and the Evolution of Society*, Boston: Beacon Press.

HOLMES GROUP (1986) *Tomorrow's Teachers: A Report of the Holmes Group*, East Lansing, Michigan: Michigan State University.

LAKOFF, G. and JOHNSON, M. (1980) *Metaphors We Live By*, Chicago: University of Chicago Press.

LEACH, M. (1988) 'Teacher education and reform: What's sex got to do with it?' *Educational Foundations*, 2, pp. 4–14.

MEASOR, L. (1985) 'Critical incidents in the classroom: Identities, choices and careers', in BALL, S.J. and GOODSON, I.F. (Eds) *Teachers' Lives and Careers*, Basingstoke: Falmer Press, pp. 61–77.

NATIONAL COMMISSION ON EXCELLENCE IN EDUCATION (1983) *A Nation at Risk: The Imperative for Educational Reform*, Washington, D.C.: Government Printing Office.

NEWMAN, F. and OLIVER, D. (1972) 'Education and community', in PURPEL, D. and BELANGER, M. (Eds) *Curriculum and the Cultural Revolution*, Berkeley, California: McCutchan Publishing Corp., pp. 205–52.

SMYTH, J. (1987) 'Introduction: Educating teachers: Changing the nature of pedagogical knowledge', in SMYTH, J. (Ed.) *Educating Teachers: Changing the Nature of Pedagogical Knowledge*, Basingstoke: Falmer Press, pp. 1–9.

WAXMAN, H.C., FREIBERG, H.J., VAUGHAN, J.C. and WEIL, M. (Eds) (1988) *Images of Reflection in Teacher Education*, Reston, Virginia: Association of Teacher Educators.

ZEICHNER, K.M. and LISTON, D.P. (1987) 'Teaching student teachers to reflect', *Harvard Educational Review*, 57, pp. 23–48.

4 Using a Methods Course to Promote Reflection and Inquiry Among Preservice Teachers*

Jesse Goodman

During the last decade, there has been growing criticism of teacher education programs that merely emphasize the technical proficiency of their graduates. Critics suggest that this orientation often results in the development of passive preservice teachers who take the relatively routine and mechanistic instruction found in most traditional schools for granted. In response, there has been growing interest in creating teacher preparation programs that (in addition to teaching specific techniques) encourage preservice teachers to thoughtfully inquire into the merits of various teaching strategies, learning theories, instructional resources, children and the role of schools in a democratic society. Most of these inquiry approaches to teacher education have centered primarily around the field experiences of preservice teachers (e.g., Boud, Keogh and Walker, 1985; Goodman, 1986a; Gitlin and Teitelbaum, 1983; Salzillo and Van Fleet, 1977; Zeichner, 1981; Zeichner and Liston, 1987). Using avenues such as seminar groups, supervisory conferences and action research assignments, preservice teachers are encouraged to seriously reflect upon their practicum experiences. Although these accounts have been illuminating, if inquiry and reflection are to have a significant impact upon future teachers, then this orientation needs to be a central aspect of each component within teacher education programs. From this perspective, methods courses (which traditionally emphasize the teaching of technical skills) provide a unique opportunity to help preservice teachers understand the valuable relationship between reflection and classroom practice. After all, if this relationship cannot be established, then one must question the value of this inquiry orientation as a basis for teacher preparation.

In an effort to address the above concern, this chapter will describe the way in which an elementary social studies methods course promotes inquiry and reflection among preservice teachers. First, a discussion of reflection and its

* This chapter was based upon and further develops the ideas that were originally published in a number of articles in *Curriculum Inquiry, Interchange* and *Journal of Teacher Education.*

relationship to teacher education will be presented to provide a context within which this course can be presented. Second, avenues for promoting reflection and inquiry in this course will be discussed. Finally, a detailed portrait of the course's major assignment will be presented to illustrate the link between reflective inquiry and classroom practice. Representative examples from preservice teachers' work, excerpts from class records (kept by the author/instructor) and course evaluations (filled out by preservice teachers at the end of the semester) are used to further illuminate the lived experience of this course.

Reflection and Teacher Education

The first step in promoting reflection among preservice teachers is to develop a comprehensive understanding of this concept. Drawing upon the work of Dewey (1933) and others, three areas of concern must be examined:

1 the focus of reflection,
2 the process of reflective thinking; and
3 the attitudes necessary to be a reflective teacher.

The Focus of Reflection

Perhaps the most important task in developing a concept of reflection is that of examining what preservice teachers reflect upon. Van Manen's (1977) analysis of reflection and teaching is helpful in this regard. Van Manen identifies three levels of reflection, each one emphasizing a different focus. The first level is concerned with specific techniques needed to reach stated objectives. The worth of these objectives is taken for granted, and the criteria for reflection are limited to technological issues (e.g., accountability, efficiency and effectiveness). At this level of reflection, preservice teachers are concerned with 'what works' in meeting institutional expectations (e.g., keeping their pupils quiet and on task).

At the second level, preservice teachers focus on the relationship between educational principles and practice. However, as Dewey (1933) emphasizes, it is not enough merely to give an educational rationale for certain practices. This level of reflection also implies the need to assess the educational implications and consequences of both actions and beliefs. As a result, there is serious consideration of principles and goals that may or may not be reflective of a given school's or society's values.

The third level addresses both ethical and political concerns as part of educational discourse. Principles such as justice, equality, caring and emancipation are used as criteria in deliberations over the value of educational goals, curriculum content and teaching practices. At this level of reflection, preservice teachers begin to identify the connection between classroom life and broader societal forces and structures. Although reflecting upon specific techniques to preservice teachers is necessary, it is equally important to incorporate Van Manen's second and third levels of reflection into teacher education programs.

The Process of Reflection

Along with understanding the importance of one's focus for reflection, it is also necessary to examine the process of reflective thinking. Dewey (1933) clearly states that the process of reflection does not merely refer to a method of problem solving but to a way of thinking or being. 'Not the thing done, but the quality of mind that goes into the doing, settles what is utilitarian and what is unconstrained and creative' (Dewey, 1933, p. 215). In developing a conception of reflection, three different 'ways of thinking' are examined.

The first way of thinking is in direct opposition to that of reflection. Dewey (1933) refers to this process as *routine thought*. Schools, like other institutions, influence individuals by setting up predefined patterns of behavior, attitudes and ideas (Berger and Luckmann, 1967). An individual who thinks routinely is guided by tradition, authority and official definitions of social reality within a given setting. Preservice teachers who think in this way consider the means to reach a given goal, but they take for granted the official ends toward which they are directed.

While routine thought is clearly distinguishable from reflection, most individuals equate reflective inquiry with *rational thought*. The view that often comes to mind is of a teacher who processes information logically, sequentially and orderly. She or he does not automatically accept commonplace views of reality but researches relevant information and makes decisions based upon careful deductive reasoning. However, this commonly accepted notion is severely limited in scope.

Unfortunately, many teacher educators who encourage reflection fail to recognize the importance of *intuitive thought*. While rational thinking involves dissection of the whole into parts, the sequential organization of information, judgments of correctness and explanatory language systems; intuitive thought involves imagination, humor, emotions, integration and synthesis, tacit understanding, and non-verbal expression of ideas (De Bono, 1970; Garrett, 1976; Guilford, 1967; Maslow, 1977). Intuitive thought is often associated with the spark of creative ideas, insight and empathy.

Intuitive thinking allows one to be spontaneous and to avoid overdependency upon pre-established plans, time schedules and standardized curriculum. This style of thinking provides the basis for 'mental play' among teachers in which they generate novel topics for study, develop new ways to conceptualize ideas and visualize pupils acting in fresh situations. Rather than only depending upon 'official procedures' to determine teacher practices, intuitive thinking enables teachers to respond thoughtfully in the midst of ongoing activity when there does not seem to be any time to reflect (Schon, 1983). As Dewey (1933, p. 124) notes, intuition marks the difference between the artistic thinker and the intellectual bungler.

It is the position of this author that reflective thinking occurs with the integration of both rational and intuitive thought processes. In legitimating intuition, one should not discount the importance of rationality. It is one thing to have flashes of inspiration and creative insights, but it requires careful planning and rational decision making to put most novel ideas into practice. As Ornstein (1972, p. 80) suggests, 'It is ... the complementary workings of the intellect (rational thought) and the intuitive which underlie our highest achievements'.

While routine thought is the antithesis of reflection, the most promising teachers are able to blend rational and intuitive modes of thinking into one dynamic thought process. Teacher education programs need to provide opportunities for preservice teachers to work on original projects that challenge them to 'be both secondary (rational) and primary (intuitive); both childish and mature ... to regress and then come back to reality, becoming more controlled and critical in his (her) responses' (Maslow, 1977, p. 90).

Reflective Attitudes

Finally, in developing a conception of reflection, it is necessary to examine the underlying attitudes of teachers. Dewey (1933) identifies three attitudes as prerequisites for reflective teaching. The first is *openmindedness* — an 'active desire to listen to more sides than one; to give heed to the facts from whatever source they come; to give full attention to alternative possibilities; and to recognize the possibility of error even in the beliefs that are dearest to us' (p. 29). Human beings tend to order and label their world in a consistent fashion. Because our sense organs simultaneously receive thousands of 'messages' from the external world each moment, our brains perform the useful function of sorting all this information in a way that is consistent with past perceptions. Therefore, the interaction between the individual and his or her sensory stimulation, along with the filtering process which is consistent with past experience, potentially creates a narrow and limited view of reality. As several educators have suggested (e.g., Lortie, 1975), teachers go through an 'apprenticeship of observation' while they attend school as children, and this apprenticeship often contributes to their willingness to take ongoing practices in the school for granted. However, openminded preservice teachers examine the rationales that underlie what they may initially take for granted as right and natural in the schools. They realize that traditional perceptions of education may or may not be valid, and they are willing to question their own views of and reactions to the school culture.

The second attitude is *responsibility*. It is not enough to be open to a variety of ideas. There must also be a desire to synthesize diverse ideas and apply information in an aspired direction. As mentioned in the discussion of Van Manen's work and as suggested by Zeichner (1981), responsible preservice teachers ask why they are doing what they are doing in classrooms in a manner that goes beyond questions of immediate utility. They do not automatically assume that the goals of a given school district reflect the best interests of their pupils or for the development of a democratic society (i.e., an active and critically informed population).

The final attitude described by Dewey (1933) is *wholeheartedness*. This attitude gives individuals the strength to move beyond abstract notions and put their ideals into practice. Many preservice teachers express fears of making mistakes, being criticized, disturbing traditions and making changes. These fears often prevent them from acting within a given classroom or school. However, as previously mentioned, one cannot be truly reflective unless she or he is willing to take risks and act. Wholeheartedness enables preservice teachers to work through their fears and insecurities, and thus provide a basis for action.

Teacher education programs need to be sensitive to these attitudes. First, preservice teachers need to be exposed to ideas that run counter to the premises that underlaid their own elementary education in order to stimulate the process of openmindedness. Second, they should be encouraged to consider and possibly assume the responsibilities of teachers committed to social justice and democracy. Third, preservice teachers need encouragement to experiment and create without fear of being condemned if their efforts do not work out as planned. Preservice teachers can best develop the attitude of wholeheartedness from proposing original ideas and being given opportunities to act upon those ideas.

Summary

Reflection suggests much more than taking a few minutes to think about how to keep pupils quiet and on task. As used in this chapter, reflection implies a dynamic 'way of being' in the classroom. This conception of reflection suggests that teacher preparation will focus on substantive, rather than only utilitarian issues. Second, teacher education needs to provide opportunities for both rational and intuitive thinking among preservice teachers. Finally, preservice teachers need exposure to ideas and assignments that will help them develop the attitudes of openmindedness, responsibility and wholeheartedness.

The Course: Avenues for Reflection and Inquiry

Keeping the previous discussion of reflection and teacher education in mind, 'Social Studies in the Elementary School' was developed to foster three general goals: 1) to empower future teachers as creators of curriculum, 2) to strengthen the link between critical viewpoints of education and teaching practice, and 3) to encourage thoughtful analysis as an integral aspect of teaching and learning. Although space does not allow for a complete portrayal of this course (see Adler and Goodman, 1986; Goodman, 1986a; Goodman, 1986b for additional analysis of this course), two avenues for promoting reflection and inquiry can be presented. The way in which substantive issues are integrated into classroom discourse will be illustrated, and a description of the course's major assignment which links reflection and teaching practice will be described.

Classroom Discourse

As Taxel (1982) notes, certain courses, as a result of their natural context, easily lend themselves to an examination of substantive educational issues (e.g., graduate level curriculum theory courses, undergraduate 'foundation' courses). Although methods courses traditionally have a technical orientation, it would be a mistake to assume that these courses cannot be used to examine the 'foundations' of education (Beyer and Zeichner, 1982). For example, the beginning of this course is designed to help preservice teachers explore several basic questions of teaching and learning. Following an adaptation of Pinar and Grumet's (1976) method of 'currere', over the course of several class periods preservice teachers examine their past experiences in schools; project what social studies and education in general might or could become in the future; examine the present situation in schools (through interviews with teachers, analysis of textbooks and reflection upon previous early field experiences); and compare these three 'pictures' for similarities, differences and common themes among them. During this process, a number of analytical frameworks (historical, psychological, political and social) are employed through class readings and discussions. Questions such as: 'What is the purpose of education?' 'Who should (does) control and develop the curriculum used in a given classroom?' 'What is the 'hidden curriculum', and how does it affect children and teachers?' are typically addressed. As these questions are explored, the preservice teachers synthesize their own knowledge with the ideas gathered from the readings and other members of the class:

> The class was given an exam compiled from recent fourth grade social studies tests. This exam contained numerous rote-answer questions about the European explorers, the industrial revolution, and immigration. After taking the exam, we explored the relationship between this test, their own experiences of elementary curriculum, and the 'hidden messages' of traditional schooling as discussed in *Teaching As a Subversive Activity* (Postman and Weingartner, 1969, pp. 20–21). One student (preservice teacher) said that school often seems like a game of *Trivial Pursuit*. Several issues were then discussed such as: what is covertly learned when rote memorization is emphasized in schools, speculations about why rote memorization continues to be dominant in our schools, validity questions about the 'correct' answers as defined in the teacher's manual, the worthiness of the information in this exam given the goals of a democratic society, the legitimacy of textbook writers as curriculum decision makers, the use of knowledge as a stimulus for learning rather than a product to consume, and alternatives to depending upon mass produced textbooks for determining curriculum content and instructional procedures. Students were then asked to identify something they knew that they would consider worthwhile enough to be included in an elementary curriculum. Most had a very difficult time thinking of anything. One student made this observation, 'I've always gotten really good grades in schools, but I still feel like I don't know anything. I think the reason is because no matter what grade I got on an exam, as soon as it was over, I completely forgot about it (the content). In other words, anything I learned from studying for that exam became totally unimportant. As a result, I think I've received a hidden message from school that no matter what I know, it can't be very important. The only important information is stuff I don't know yet. So naturally, I can't imagine that I know anything worth teaching'. Another student said, 'It always seems that, in school, it's what you don't know that's seen as valuable; not what you do know'. (excerpt from class notes)

These initial dialogues lay the groundwork for the rest of the course in that most preservice teachers become openminded to the view that alternative approaches to education are at least worthy of serious consideration.

In addition to raising general questions of education within the context of a methods course, it is also important for preservice teachers to examine substantive issues related to a given subject area. Most of the time in this social studies methods course is spent exposing preservice teachers to alternative resources for and methods of teaching history, sociology and anthropology in elementary schools. However, substantive questions are also explored as they relate to each of the above-mentioned subject areas. For example, during the study of history the class is asked to explore whose history we have traditionally emphasized in schools and why (Alder and Goodman, 1986). The class examines the way in which history often reflects the values and achievements of only the most powerful groups of people within a given society. In studying sociology, preservice teachers are asked if teachers should raise controversial issues in schools and investigate the role controversy plays in a democratic society. While studying anthropology in the classroom, the class examines issues of ethnocentrism and cross-cultural oppression (Goodman and Melcher, 1984). In this manner, preservice teachers recognize the need to be aware that substantive issues will always underlie the teaching of specific subject matter to pupils.

Integrating Reflection and Practice

While involving preservice teachers in substantive dialogue is a central aspect of this methods course, the more difficult task is that of involving them in assignments that also help them experience the relationship between reflection and teaching practice. This challenge is primarily met through the major assignment of the course. Contrary to the view that teachers should be trained to be efficient technicians and managers of pre-packaged instructional programs, this course advocates the view that teachers should be the primary decision-making force behind the content, resources and activities needed to stimulate learning among a given group of children (Carson, 1984). The central assignment of the course asks preservice teachers to develop and implement (in their early field experience) an original social studies unit that encourages inquiry and reflective action for themselves and their pupils. The effort to integrate reflection and classroom practice can be most effectively conveyed by a description of the five phases that make up this approach to curriculum development. As will be illustrated, within each phase, preservice teachers are asked to engage in particular types of activities and to consider various viewpoints that present an alternative to Tyler's (1950) 'objectives first' model of curriculum development and to traditional approaches toward teaching and learning. For the purpose of this analysis, the phases of developing and implementing curriculum that are taught to these preservice teachers are presented separately, and in numbering each phase a linear sequence may be inferred. However, developing curriculum involves the complex, simultaneous juggling of different considerations: past experiences of the teacher and pupils; subject matter; educational and social goals; teachers' and pupils' personalities, interests and talents; materials and resources available; and ongoing feedback as the unit progresses (McCutcheon, 1981). It is important to emphasize that in the actual process of creating units of study these phases overlap, are worked on simultaneously, and do not follow a predetermined sequence.

Phase I: Generating curriculum themes

As creators of curriculum, preservice teachers must first choose a topic of study. In preparation for this work, they are asked to reflect seriously upon their own intellectual interests, and upon what knowledge is worth exploring with the pupils in their practicum sites (Postman and Weingartner, 1969, pp. 59–81). They are asked not only to consider what information is necessary for adulthood, but more importantly, what topics would enrich the children's lives and broaden their horizons (Bode, 1927; Dewey, 1929, p. 292). Egan (1985) describes the way in which developing curriculum can be viewed as a process of story-telling. As in any good literature, the crucial aspect of a given body of content is that it be meaningful to the readers, or in this case the pupils. Egan (1985, p. 398) suggests asking a number of questions as one selects content for a given unit of study:

1 'What is most important about this topic?'
2 'Why does it matter?'
3 'What is affectively engaging about it?'
4 'What binary opposites best express and articulate the importance of this topic?'

Preservice teachers are asked to consider these types of questions as they develop the content for their units. As part of this process, they are also encouraged to examine the social/political implications of their unit's content. As previously mentioned, they are asked to consider substantive questions of content as they examine different 'fields' of social science. In this manner, there is a conscious effort made to select thoughtful content as a basis for their units of study.

Since most preservice teachers have little prior experience in selecting curriculum content, a number of strategies are employed to assist them. At first, they are asked to engage in 'mental play' by day-dreaming about possible topics. In class, they are taught brainstorming strategies and how these strategies can be used to generate ideas as a basis for creating units. Negotiating techniques also are examined in preparation for discussing possible topics with their cooperating teachers. In addition, each preservice teacher meets with the course instructor and university supervisor shortly after being placed in his/her practicum site to discuss possible topics. During class discussions, subsequent individual meetings with the instructor, supervisory conferences and seminar meetings, issues of curriculum content are addressed. In addition, the content of the unit is also an important aspect of evaluating the quality of the preservice teachers' efforts in developing curriculum (see Phase V).

Once a topic has been chosen, units are developed around broad issues, concepts or themes. As Dewey (1929, p. 223) proposed, knowledge is seen as a means rather than an end product of education. Specific information is viewed as a catalyst for stimulating or reinforcing a child's curiosity, rather than an object for intellectual consumption. Perhaps the most essential characteristic of knowledge is its ambiguity and constant change. Rather than focusing on predetermined objectives (e.g., facts, skills and 'right answers'), themes contain questions, theories and mysteries, as well as specific information. For example, instead of emphasizing the names, dates and places associated with European explorers, one preservice teacher's fifth grade unit studied the topic of *exploration*.

Pupils investigated what characteristics are found in explorers, why individuals seek new horizons and the diverse foci for exploration (e.g., one's self, a field of knowledge, new landscapes, life). In addition to learning about European explorers, pupils discovered that many individuals have investigated the unknown, including Native Americans, scholars and themselves. While the pupils acquired specific information, the emphasis was on their analysis concerning the above themes.

Using the techniques of brainstorming, preservice teachers construct web diagrams to develop the topic's themes (Kohl, 1976, pp. 37–54; Rachelson and Copeland, 1983). For example, the first draft of a web for a unit on the pre-colonial Ashanti culture of West Africa (see figure 2) illustrates the possibilities that can arise from a single idea. As illustrated on the web, initially many of the themes or sub-themes have question marks after them due to their speculative nature. It is only as the preservice teacher and his or her pupils begin to study a given topic that these questions are answered and speculations are either supported or discarded. In fact, one of the common, concluding activities for a given unit is to re-examine the initial web in light of what the preservice teacher and his/her pupils have discovered about the topic. For example, in the unit of the pre-colonial Ashanti culture, the preservice teacher and her pupils discovered that while these people did live in villages, they also built cities and used a variety of materials in the construction of their homes that were far more complex than simple 'huts'. That is, they uncovered for themselves several stereotypical images they had of these African people's traditional culture and way of life.

After a topic is initially developed, preservice teachers often reduce or expand the number of themes and/or sub-themes to be studied, taking into consideration the knowledge base and interests of themselves and their pupils, the amount of time they have to teach their unit and the resources available. For example, the unit on the Ashanti culture eventually explored themes such as: entertainment, education, occupations, economy, relations with other cultural groups and medicine. Since each situation is unique, units on the same topic usually contain different themes and/or sub-themes. Rather than standardizing the curriculum, this course emphasizes the need for curriculum to respond to the specific learning milieu in which preservice teachers are placed (Berman, 1984). Teaching preservice teachers to *generate ideas* is central to developing these units of study.

Finally, an important epistemological implication of generating curriculum themes through the use of webbing is that it demonstrates the holistic nature of knowledge. Preservice teachers learn to integrate traditionally separated subject areas. For example, units on ecology often combined social studies and science. Pupils would explore the science of the life cycle along with the social issues of pollution, energy use and conservation. Skills such as reading and writing were not taught as segregated subjects but were integrated into the study of content. Many preservice teachers developed a literary/individualized reading program as part of their units (Rudman, 1976). Classroom libraries were established that reflected the themes being studied. For example, in a unit entitled *People's Changing Roles* pupils read children's literature that explored the woman's suffrage movement; portrayed men/boys as sensitive and nurturing and girls who were dare-devilish, determined and active; and pictured boys and girls who were close friends. By having children use literature to study social topics, they not

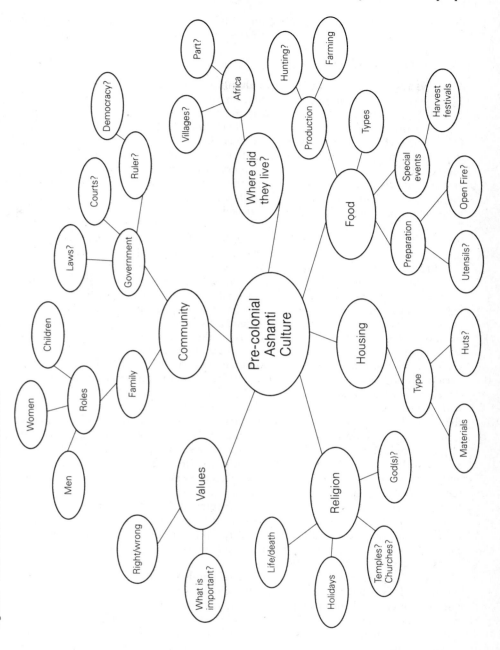

Figure 2 Initial web of Pre-colonial Ashanti Culture

only learned to read, but more significantly, they read to learn. An integrated perspective of knowledge is central to this approach to designing curriculum.

Phase II: Exploring resources

The second phase in developing curriculum involves the exploration of resources. This phase requires significant inquiry on the part of the preservice teachers. There are two types of resources that must be investigated. The first is adult resources that increase the preservice teacher's knowledge on a particular subject. Prior to this course, most preservice teachers knew little about the topic for their unit and considerable research was often necessary in developing the unit's themes. They read books and articles, interviewed professors and, if appropriate, watched television programs to enlarge their own knowledge base. For example, one individual researched the psychological principles of transactional analysis in preparation for a seventh grade unit entitled *Human Beings: What Makes Us Tick?* For a sixth grade unit on the USSR, a preservice teacher read some of the writings of Marx, Lenin and Trotsky. Individuals often summarized what they discovered to their pupils as one of the unit's learning activities (see Phase III).

Preservice teachers must also discover resources that their pupils can use to explore the themes of a given unit. Instead of viewing textbooks and other pre-packaged instructional programs as infallible and exclusive sources of knowledge, this course emphasizes the perspective that knowledge emerges from many different spheres of life: people, art, legends, nature. The list of potential sources of knowledge is endless. A major focus of this course is to expose preservice teachers to a wide variety of potential resources that can be used to study a given topic (Adler and Goodman, 1986; Goodman and Melcher, 1984). For example, a variety of local, community resources were used by preservice teachers who developed history units (Weitzman, 1975). One fifth grade unit, *The Nifty Fifties*, had pupils explore what life was like during this period of history within the United States to determine how 'nifty' it really was. In this unit, parents, grandparents and other adults became the major source of knowledge through pupil-created interviews and questionnaires. 1950s magazines, comic books (from a local dealer who also spoke to the class), music (from parents' record collections and a history of rock and roll program played weekly on a local radio station), television shows (played on cable TV) and a film on the Army-McCarthy hearings were some of the other sources employed in this unit. In using various resources, preservice teachers are encouraged to present knowledge as tentative, open to questioning and tide to its source (i.e., according to this document, picture, author, etc.); thereby reducing the mystifying authority that external knowledge often has over children.

In addition, the personal knowledge of pupils is also considered a legitimate resource. Too often the knowledge that children bring with them to school is ignored. In contrast, most preservice teachers involved their pupils in developing the themes for their units. They often did webbings with their pupils as part of their units' introductory lessons in which they specifically drew upon their pupils' knowledge and interests. A few preservice teachers developed units primarily organized around their pupils' knowledge base. For example, one fourth grade classroom contained children from many different cultural backgrounds. The preservice teacher decided to create a unit, *Americans: Who Are We?* that had the pupils research and share their ethnic traditons, customs and beliefs with other members of the class.

Eventually, most preservice teachers sharpened their powers of observation and developed the talent to discover resources as they participated in their daily life activities. For example, just prior to the start of his unit on the USSR, this individual noticed a poster on a university bulletin board that announced the coming arrival of a Russian dance troupe which was being sponsored by the US-USSR Friendship Association. He contacted this organization and arranged for a few of the dancers to come to his class for a presentation. Perhaps the most important aspect of this alternative approach to designing curriculum is that teachers develop the ability to discover innovative, stimulating resources from which they and their pupils can learn. In this manner, the activity of inquiry becomes an habitual component of teaching.

Phase III: Developing learning activities

After increasing one's knowledge base on a topic and gathering potential re-sources, preservice teachers generate and organize learning activities for their units. Brainstorming techniques are again used during this phase as they consider a wide spectrum of possible activities through which pupils can learn. For a brief period of time, they suspend all judgment of appropriateness, practicality, legality or usefulness when generating a list of possible activities. They are also encouraged to employ visual thinking techniques when considering learning activities. That is, they are asked to *imagine* their pupils involved in potential classroom situations while engaged in various types of actions.

In making their final choice of activities, preservice teachers are asked to consider two goals. First, learning activities should illuminate the topic of the unit and, second, they should promote thematic inquiry. Thematic inquiry rests somewhere between the two extremes of closed inquiry in which both the content and procedures are rigidly predetermined and open inquiry which implies no predeterminism of information and process. Rather than basing instructional activities on prespecified objectives (i.e., information and behavior), thematic inquiry promotes the notion of 'soft determinism'. The teacher, as leader of the class, has educational aims and knows the direction that the unit will take (as reflected in its themes), but not necessarily every detail that the pupils will learn from a given activity or resource. Eisner (1979, pp. 93–107) refers to this form of goal setting as 'expressive outcomes', and it implies a search into the unknown within broadly defined thematic boundaries. For example, a number of pre-service teachers had pupils explore, though a variety of activities, the relationship between the literature in their class libraries and the themes in their units. Exactly what individual pupils were expected to learn from this literature was not predetermined, but emerged from the activities and books read.

Contrary to passive drilling and testing for memorization, thematic inquiry suggests that learning is dynamic and active. A child is 'not simply passive material that, like moist clay, receives the impress of the empirical world, but is an active agent that selects and organizes aspects of that world for cognition' (Eisner, 1982, p. 32). At various times children learn more from reading and writing; at other times from discussions, art work, visual or audio stimulation, or working with concrete materials. In planning their units, preservice teachers diversified their activities in an effort to capitalize on different modes of learning and thinking. Most preservice teachers integrated music, art, literary reading, writing and/or creative dramatics into their units. These activities were used either to study the content of their topic or served as a means by which pupils could express their ideas. In many units, pupils did not participate in the same activities, read the same books or complete the same assignments. Often pupils chose from a list of possible projects in which to get involved. A few preservice teachers encouraged pupils to develop their own projects and activities. For example, in a unit on European immigration, the pupils created role plays to portray various aspects of life in Europe, the boat trip over and early experiences upon arrival. Two pupils who were interested in clothes and sewing developed their own project by making costumes for the plays. They researched old photographs for the styles of clothing worn and got help in designing from the school's home economics teacher. Connelly (1970) suggests that instruction should help pupils take responsibility for their learning, and preservice teachers are asked to seriously consider the type of responsibilities their learning activities foster.

It is important to stress that just getting pupils 'involved' or having 'hands on' experience is not enough. Preservice teachers are exposed to Dewey's (1938) view that to be educative, experiences must stimulate and challenge a child's mind and encourage pupils to use their powers of imagination, speculation and analysis. Preservice teachers are urged to ask themselves, 'What do I want pupils to be *thinking about* as a result of this activity?' For example, in a sixth grade unit on the Civil War the thematic focus was on being a slave, a slave owner and a common soldier from the North and South. The class explored why individuals fought in this war, what it was like for the people who lived through it and what was gained and lost at its conclusion. The unit's resources and activities were oriented towards helping pupils understand that there are no simple answers to questions of war and peace, right and wrong, or justice and injustice. When pupils conduct research and write reports, it is not enough simply to give an opinion. While personal knowledge is important, this knowledge must be grounded in reason and intuitive insight that is obtained from exploring other sources and ideas (Connelly, 1970). As Matthews (1980) concisely illustrates in his book, *Philosophy and the Young Child*, even small children have the ability to confront meaningful questions regarding themselves, human experiences and the social world around them. Preservice teachers are asked to consider this level of intellectual involvement as a criteria for choosing the unit's learning activities.

Finally, although objectives are not specifically predetermined and stated in behavioral terms, one should not assume that instruction becomes aimless. On the contrary, to help in the planning of their units, preservice teachers are encouraged to place their ideas into two categories: teacher activities and pupil activities. Teacher activities are those which the teacher assumes primary responsibility for producing (e.g., planning a field trip, leading a discussion, telling a folktale). Pupil activities often involve reading, writing or speaking. However, as previously mentioned, these activities are not considered more important than art, music or other forms of expression. Using the concepts of soft determinism and thematic inquiry, preservice teachers are encouraged to organize their units' activities into three sections:

The Introduction	These activities introduce pupils to and stimulate interest in the topic of study. Introductory activities also solicit pupils' previous knowledge about a given topic.
The Body	These activities are organized into a series of lessons (or learning centers) that illuminate the themes of a given topic and stimulate the children's thinking.
The Conclusion	These activities summarize the main points of the unit. Concluding activities also give the pupils a chance to appreciate and share what they have learned and produced.

This organization is important. Children need a distinct period of time to think about what they want to study and to build anticipation for the coming investigation. A period of time is also needed to explore diverse resources, participate in various activities and formulate ideas about the chosen topic. Finally, children should have an opportunity to appreciate and reflect upon what they have learned and formulate ideas about the chosen topic. Finally, children should have an opportunity to appreciate and reflect upon what they have learned and created before moving onto another topic. Without a beginning, middle and end to a given unit of study, instruction often becomes an endless series of tasks that eventually grinds down the children's spirit and interest in learning. However, the structure of a unit must remain flexible and spontaneous. Preservice teachers often altered the initial organization of their units' themes or activities depending upon what happened in their practicum sites, what resources became available and what interests the pupils developed as topics were studied. Most preservice teachers' units reflected careful research, thoughtful planning, flexibility and a willingness to actively guide pupils in their search for knowledge and understanding.

Phase IV: Evaluation of pupils

Perhaps the most difficult aspect of using this approach to curriculum design is that preservice teachers are asked to consider alternative methods of evaluating pupils' work. Rather than relying heavily upon quantitative measures (e.g., workbooks, worksheets and tests of memorization), learning activities such as informal reading and discussions, art work or research projects require more comprehensive evaluation procedures. While an occasional objective test or worksheet is appropriate, quantitative proof of learning is usually not emphasized. However, one important goal of the teacher should be *to discover what pupils are learning* as they participate in a unit's activities. Through observation of and dialogue with their pupils (in this manner the children are involved in the evaluation process) and careful examination of their pupils' work, teachers can make substantive assessments regarding the quality of the children's efforts. From this perspective, evaluation is an ongoing process and not an event that happens at the end of a chapter. There are numerous methods for subjective, interactive evaluation (e.g., Almy and Cunningham, 1959; Hull, 1984). Several preservice teachers kept a file folder on each of their pupils. After an activity or at the end of the day, the preservice teacher would write his/her assessments of the children's work. Entries often addressed work completed by the pupils or at times just an observation of an individual child as she or he interacted within a given context. One representative example stated,

> Noticed Bill was looking at the bulletin board (on the history of farming in the state) this afternoon. This is the first time he has shown some independent interest in shcool work since I started the practicum. I'll have to remember to find out his reaction tomorrow and try to get a sense of what he got out of it. (excerpt from preservice teacher's folder)

If nothing was added to a given child's folder for a few days, the preservice teacher would give careful attention to that child's work the next day, thus maintaining individual attention. Although these assessments were not quantitative, by keeping systematic, written records, pupil evaluation was given careful attention and was comprehensive.

Phase V: Evaluation of the unit

The final phase in designing curriculum involves the evaluation of the unit. Rather than focusing solely on whether pupils meet prespecified performance objectives, the evaluation of a unit's content and activities should focus on the qualitative human experience of both teachers and pupils (e.g., Eisner, 1985; MacDonald, 1976; Parlett and Hamilton, 1972). In evaluating their units, pre-service teachers are encouraged to ask themselves: What conception(s) of knowledge is presented to the children? What type(s) of learning is emphasized through the unit's activities? What 'hidden messages' are given to the pupils through this unit? What are the pupils' intellectual and affective reactions to the unit? What are your (the teacher's) reactions to the unit? Preservice teachers are asked to consider these questions in light of the issues raised in the course and their own common sense, beliefs and experiences. Rather than waiting until the end of a unit to evaluate it, preservice teachers evaluate their units on a weekly basis during their seminar meetings. In this way, they recognize the value of ongoing feedback and reflection.

In addition to carefully evaluating the educational significance of their units, these individuals are also encouraged to consider the social implications of what they teach. Many educators suggest that there is no such thing as 'value free' or neutral education (e.g., Apple, 1979, 1982; Cagan, 1978; Elshtain, 1978; Giroux and Penna, 1977). Preservice teachers are asked to analyze critically the social values, beliefs and attitudes embedded in the content of their units.

This critical awareness was manifested in a several ways. As some educators have illustrated, children's literature, textbooks and other resources may reinforce unhealthy social perceptions and attitudes (e.g., sexism, racism, classism) among children if not critically examined (e.g., Banfield and Wilson, 1983; Hall, 1978; Taxel, 1978–79; Wolf-Wasserman and Hutchinson, 1978). As previously mentioned, through class discussions and individual conferences, most preservice teachers became sensitive to these issues and raised them with their pupils when using materials that reflected non-humanitarian views. Units on other cultures or minority cultures within the United States often raised issues of ethnocentrism or prejudice. Preservice teachers who developed historical units made efforts to emphasize the role that all people play in the creation of history, rather than overemphasize the role of famous white men. A number of individuals developed units on contemporary social, political issues such as ecology, human rights and nuclear arms. Other individuals integrated social issues into more traditional units. For example, a third grade unit on 'careers' included themes such as: the changing role of women in the workforce, the notion of class conflict and the problems of unemployment. These units exposed children to many viewpoints on a given issue and encouraged their participation in society. As Apple (1971) implies, preservice teachers are encouraged to view conflicting ideologies as a central concern in the study of social life. Preservice teachers' criteria for evaluating their units did not only include the quality of their pupils' work, but also the type of educational experiences that children were asked to participate in and the social implications of their units' content.

Conclusion

This chapter has detailed the way in which a methods course can promote reflection and inquiry among preservice teachers. In particular, it illustrated an assignment through which preservice teachers could *experience* the relationship between serious reflection and teaching practice. This connection was more firmly cemented through a follow-up assignment that asks preservice teachers to write term papers in which they create 'an approach' to social studies elementary teaching. Preservice teachers title their approach to reflect its general focus. Some recent titles have been: 'An Active Learning Approach', 'An Integrated Approach', 'A Cognitive-Stimulant Approach'. More important than the title of the approach is the fact that in this assignment preservice teachers develop a social and educational rationale for using this approach, discuss the essential characteristics and perspectives of their approach and, finally, describe their unit as an example of this approach in action. Throughout the paper, preservice teachers use readings from this and other courses they have taken to support their ideas. During the last few days of the semester, they present their approach and unit to the rest of the class, thus helping them learn how to articulate their ideas. A few individuals recently presented their papers to a state social studies conference in an effort to more fully develop their reflective and expressive abilities. This assignment seems to help preservice teachers recognize the value of relating abstract ideas to teaching practices:

> Developing my approach helped me begin to develop a philosophy of teaching and to back my ideas up with reasons. The paper was difficult but worthwhile in that I now feel I can contribute some of my own ideas to the field of education. (excerpt from preservice teacher's course evaluation)

After listening to each other's presentations, several preservice teachers have mentioned that they could now 'see' how progressive concepts of education could (if given institutional support) be put into practice. The two most repeated comments found on written evaluations were that this course encouraged individuals 'to think' (consider critical viewpoints), and that it was 'practical'.

Once the connection between reflection and teaching is made, preservice teachers often begin to reconsider their notions of what it means to be a teacher.

By having these individuals choose a topic, generate its themes, discover resources, develop learning activities and organize this work into a comprehensive
unit of study, their conception of teaching is broadened. Rather than seeing
themselves as educational technicians and managers of instructional programs,
they begin to view themselves as moral craftspeople (Tom, 1984). At the center
of this craft is their talent to develop and implement original units of study and to
reflect upon the educational and social implications of their work. As these
preservice teachers develop their units, they gain confidence in their ability to
make important curricular and instructional decisions:

> The most exciting concept I got from this [course] was that my students
> and I have the power to 'create knowledge'. I no longer feel that
> I, as a teacher, have to know everything before I teach it to kids. I realize
> that I could teach just about any topic to kids because now I know how
> to research and find resources for us to learn from. (excerpt from
> preservice teacher's course evaluation)

Since most of the children in the practicum sites get interested in and excited
about their unit, preservice teachers recognize that they can develop more
thoughtful and challenging learning experiences than those found in many standardized, instructional programs. This work tends to facilitate within these preservice teachers what Eisner (1979) calls 'educational connoisseurship', the ability
to discover 'what is educationally significant'.

Instead of seeing their main goal as 'fitting into' the pre-existing patterns
found in their practicum sites, these individuals take an active role in creating
their own field experience.

> The most important thing I learned from this experience was to assert
> myself and ask questions to see if I could try things. I'm the kind of
> person who has real difficulty in confronting authority figures, but with
> your [the supervisor's] help, I've overcome a lot of my fears. (excerpt
> from preservice teacher's practicum evaluation)

As their sense of autonomy grows, preservice teachers are asked to consider the
importance of being change agents in the schools (Kohl, 1976, pp. 119–63). They
consider problems of initiating substantive change within a given school in ways
that do not needlessly alienate administrators, other staff or parents. Planning for
short-term and long-term changes, developing a support system among other
progressive individuals within the school and community, writing proposals for
curriculum change and presenting ideas at local and state conferences, are some of
the strategies examined.

A number of preservice teachers got to practice some of these strategies in
their practicum sites. While some were given the freedom to teach anything they
wanted, most had to negotiate with their cooperating teacher in order to teach
their unit. Others had to follow the school's curriculum guide, but significantly
altered it. For example, several individuals had to teach units on state history, but
beyond this directive they negotiated the freedom to develop their own content,
materials and activities. In this manner, these preservice teachers got practical

experience, to some degree, at being change agents in their practicum sites. Helping preservice teachers assume this more expanded role of teaching did not come easy. In addition to class meetings, it was necessary to work with each individual at least once (and up to four times) to help him or her get started, discuss the unit's content, share ideas and resources, and provide support and encouragement.

It is important to note that not all preservice teachers value the focus of this course. Each semester there are a couple of individuals who only marginally complete their unit assignment due to a lack of interest, motivation or intellectual ability.

> I didn't do very well this semester because I thought it [the course] was basically worthless. As teachers, we are going to be expected to teach out of a textbook. Instead of wasting our time developing units, I think you should teach us the best way to use these textbooks. (excerpt from preservice teacher's course evaluation)

While these individuals would most likely be viewed as competent, their reaction to this course suggest that they would not assume the role of moral craftsperson in the future.

Although most preservice teachers express satisfaction with the course, more than the good intentions of a few individuals and the existence of viable alternatives are needed to change school practices (Stake and Easley, 1978). What happens in this course hardly constitutes a panacea for the ills found within teacher preparation or schools in general. The relationship between school practice and the sociocultural context within which it exists is complex, and no one strategy can be expected to fundamentally alter the present system. Obviously, this course cannot alter the stratification of labor and distribution of resources in our society that greatly contributes to our present, weak educational system. Nor can it do much about the power that some (e.g., testing agencies, textbook publishers, state legislators) have to determine teachers' work (Cohen, 1978; Wise, 1979). In addition, as Zeichner and Liston (1987) point out, it is important not to assume an overly romantic view of giving teachers more control over their work. Several studies indicate that efforts to promote teacher professionalism, autonomy and democratic decision making do not necessarily result in a significantly improved education (e.g., Buswell, 1980; Duke, Showers and Imber, 1980; Larson, 1977; Mohrman, Cooke and Mohrman, 1978). However, in spite of these limitations, this course has helped many preservice teachers look critically at the process of educating children, at realistic alernatives for progressive change within public schools and at their role as future teachers. In addition, the primary course assignment gave these preservice teachers an opportunity to engage in both rational and intuitive thinking; to develop the attitudes of open-mindedness, responsibility and wholeheartedness; and to experience the relationship between reflection and teaching practice. Given the narrow technical tradition of methods courses, this accomplishment is noteworthy.

Promoting reflection and inquiry among preservice teachers is a difficult goal to attain. Many preservice teachers have not had any experience at seriously reflecting upon school knowledge or life experiences. Initiating them to this process during their professional preparation can be extremely challenging. In addition, there are many contextual factors that inhibit the success of inquiry-based teacher education programs (Zeichner and Liston, 1987). As a result, our work must be comprehensive and not restricted to field experience settings alone. In order to have a more meaningful impact upon future teachers, this orientation needs to be the focus of seminars, supervision, foundation courses, field experiences and methods courses. Without a coordinated effort among each component of a given teacher preparation program, our efforts to prepare more thoughtful and active teachers will be severely limited.

References

ADLER, S. and GOODMAN, J. (1986) 'Critical theory as a foundation for methods courses', *Journal of Teacher Education*, **37**, 4, pp. 2–8.

ALMY, M. and CUNNINGHAM, R. (1959) *Ways of Studying Children: A Manual for Teachers*, New York: Bureau of Publications, Teachers' College.

APPLE, M. (1971) 'The hidden curriculum and the nature of conflict', *Interchange*, **2**, 4, pp. 27–40.

APPLE, M. (1979) *Ideology and Curriculum*, London: Routledge and Kegan Paul.

BANFIELD, B. and WILSON, G. (1983) 'The black experience through white eyes: The same old story once again', *Interracial Books for Children Bulletin*, **14**, 5, pp. 4–13.

BERGER, P. and LUCKMANN, T. (1967) *The Social Construction of Reality: A Treatise in the Sociology of Knowledge*, Garden City, NJ: Doubleday.

BERMAN, L. (1984) 'Beyond Measured Curriculum', Paper presented at the annual American Educational Research Association meeting, New Orleans.

BEYER, L. and ZEICHNER, K. (1982) 'Teacher training and educational foundations: A plea for discontent', *Journal of Teacher Education*, **33**, 3, pp. 18–23.

BODE, B. (1927) *Modern Educational Theories*, New York: Macmillan.

BOUD, D., KEOGH, R. and WALKER, D. (1985) *Reflection: Turning Experience into Learning*, London: Kogan Page.

BUSWELL, C. (1980) 'Pedagogic change and social change', *British Journal of Sociology of Education*, **1**, 3, pp. 293–306.

CAGAN, E. (1978) 'Individualism, collectivism and radical educational reform', *Harvard Educational Review*, **48**, 2, pp. 227–66.

CARSON, A.S. (1984) 'Control of the curriculum: A case for teachers', *Journal of Curriculum Studies*, **16**, 1, pp. 19–28.

COHEN, D. (1978) 'Reforming schools politics', *Harvard Educational Review*, **48**, 4, pp. 429–47.

CONNELLY, M. (1970) 'The right to responsibility', *Curriculum Theory Network*, 6 (winter), pp. 75–9.

DE BONO, E. (1970) *Lateral Thinking*, New York: Harper and Row.

DEWEY, J. (1929) 'My pedagogic creed', *Journal of the National Educational Association*, **18**, 9, pp. 291–5.

DEWEY, J. (1933) *How We Think: A Restatement of the Relation of Reflective Thinking to the Educative Process*, Chicago: Henry Regnery.

DEWEY, J. (1938) *Experience and Education*, New York: Macmillan.

DUKE, D., SHOWERS, B. and IMBER, M. (1980) 'Teachers and shared decision making: The constraints and benefits of involvement', *Educational Administration Quarterly*, **16**, 1, pp. 93–106.

EGAN, K. (1985) 'Teaching as story-telling: A non-mechanistic approach to planning teaching', *Journal of Curriculum Studies*, **17**, 4, pp. 397–406.

ELSHTAIN, J. (1978) 'The social relations of the classroom: A moral and political perspective', in NORTON, T. and OLLMAN, B. (Eds) *Studies in Socialist Pedagogy*, pp. 291–313, New York: Monthly Review Press.

EISNER, E. (1979) *The Educational Imagination*, New York: Macmillan.

EISNER, E. (1982) *Cognition and Curriculum: A Basis for Deciding What to Teach*, London: Harlow.

EISNER, E. (1985) *The Art of Educational Evaluation*, Basingstoke and Philadelphia: Falmer Press.

GARRETT, S. (1976) 'Putting our whole brain to use: A fresh look at the creative process', *Journal of Creative Behavior*, **10**, 5, pp. 239–49.

GIROUX, H. and PENNA, A. (1977) 'Social relations in the classroom: The dialectic of the hidden curriculum', *Edcentric*, 40–41, pp. 39–46.

GITLIN, A. and TEITELBAUM, K. (1983) 'Linking theory and practice: The use of ethnographic methodology by prospective teachers', *Journal of Education for Teaching*, **9**, 3, pp. 225–34.

GOODMAN, J. (1986a) 'Making early field experience meaningful: A critical approach', *Journal of Education for Teaching*, **12**, 2, pp. 109–25.

GOODMAN, J. (1986b) 'Teaching preservice teachers a critical approach to curriculum design: A descriptive account', *Curriculum Inquiry*, **16**, 2, pp. 179–201.

GOODMAN, J. and MELCHER, K. (1984) 'Culture at a distance: An anthroliterary approach to cross cultural education', *Journal of Reading*, **28**, 3, pp. 200–7.

GUILFORD, J.P. (1967) 'Factors that aid and hinder creativity', in GOWAN, J., DEMOS, G. and TORRANCE, E. (Eds) *Creativity: Its Educational Implications*, New York: Wiley and Sons.

HALL, S. (1978) 'What do textbooks teach our children about Africa?' *Interracial Books for Children Bulletin*, **9**, 3, pp. 3–10.

HULL, C. (1984) 'Marking: A critical alternative', *Journal of Curriculum Studies*, **16**, 2, pp. 155–64.

KOHL, H. (1976) *On Teaching*, New York: Schocken.

LARSON, M. (1977) *The Rise of Professionalism: A Sociological Analysis*, Berkeley: University of California Press.

LORTIE, D. (1975) *Schoolteacher*, Chicago: University of Chicago Press.

MACDONALD, B. (1976) 'The portrayal of persons as evaluation data', Paper presented at the annual American Educational Research Association meeting.

MASLOW, A. (1977) *The Farther Reaches of Human Nature*, Middlesex, England: Penguin.

MATTHEWS, G. (1980) *Philosophy and the Young Child*, Cambridge, MA: Harvard University Press.

McCUTCHEON, G. (1981) 'Elementary school teachers' planning for social studies and other subjects', *Theory and Research in Social Education*, **9**, 1, pp. 45–66.

MOHRMAN, A., COOKE, R. and MOHRMAN, S. (1978) 'Participation in decision making: A multidimensional perspective', *Educational Administration Quarterly*, **14**, 1, pp. 13–29.

ORNSTEIN, R. (1972) *The Psychology of Consciousness*, New York: Penguin.

PARLETT, M. and HAMILTON, D. (1972) 'Evaluation as illumination', in TAWNEY, D., (Ed.) *Curriculum Evaluation Today: Trends and Implications*, New York: Macmillan.

PINAR, W. and GRUMET, M. (1976) *Toward a Poor Curriculum*, Dubuque, IA: Kendall/Hunt.

POSTMAN, N. and WEINGARTNER, C. (1969) *Teaching as a Subversive Activity*, New York: Delta.

RACHELSON, S. and COPELAND, G. (1983) 'Webbing: A humanistic approach to curriculum development', *Journal of Humanistic Education*, **7**, 1, pp. 6–8.

RUDMAN, M. (1976) *Children's Literature: An Issues Approach*, Lexington, MA: Heath.

SALZILLO, F. and VAN FLEET, A. (1977) 'Student teaching and teacher education: A sociological model for change', *Journal of Teacher Education*, **28**, 1, pp. 27–31.

SCHON, D. (1983) *The Reflective Practitioner*, New York: Basic Books.

STAKE, R. and EASLEY, J. (1978) *Case Studies in Science Education*, Urbana, IL: Center for Instructional Research and Curriculum Evaluation.

TAXEL, J. (1978–79) 'Justice and cultural conflict: Racism, Sexism, and instructional materials', *Interchange*, **9**, 1, pp. 56–84.

TAXEL, J. (1982) 'Sensitizing students to the selective tradition in children's literature'. Paper presented at the annual American Educational Research Association meeting, New York.

TOM, A. (1984) *Teaching as a Moral Craft*, New York: Longman.

TYLER, R. (1950) *Basic Principles of Curriculum and Instruction*, Chicago: University of Chicago Press.

VAN MANEN, M. (1977) 'Linking ways of knowing with ways of being practical', *Curriculum Inquiry*, **6**, 3, pp. 205–28.

WEITZMAN, D. (1975) *My Backyard History Book*, Boston: Little, Brown,

WISE, A. (1979) *Legislated Learning: The Bureaucratization of the American Classroom*, Berkeley: University of California Press.

WOLF-WASSERMAN, M. and HUTCHINSON, L. (1978) *Teaching Human Dignity: Social Change Lessons for Every Teacher*, Minneapolis, MN: Education Exploration Center.

ZEICHNER, K. (1981) 'Reflective teaching and field-based experience in teacher education', *Interchange*, **12**, 4, pp. 1–22.

ZEICHNER, K. and LISTON, D. (1987) 'Teaching student teachers to reflect', *Harvard Educational Review*, **57**, 1, pp. 23–48.

5   Forming a Critical Pedagogy in the Social Studies Methods Class: The Use of Imaginative Literature

Susan Adler

'I was really looking forward to this class', said Rodney as he entered his elementary methods class for the first meeting. 'Then I went to the bookstore; we have to read a novel!' he continued with disdain. Rodney, like most other elementary education students, was anxious to learn *how* to teach. He could not understand how Chinua Achebe's *Things Fall Apart* could possibly help him in that endeavor and, besides, as he was quick to point out, he hated to read novels. Most of the other students argued that reading novels is fine — for entertainment. But since they were coming to class for the serious business of learning how to teach, *Things Fall Apart* seemed to be an imposition and entirely irrelevant. However, Rodney and the others were 'good' students: comfortable enough with their instructor to complain a bit, but willing, in the end, to do what the teacher assigned.

The students' unhappiness increased as they began to read the book. Set in what is now Nigeria, the novel tells the story of Ibo villagers confronting the arrival of European missionaries and British colonial administration. The characters' names are unfamiliar to American students; it was difficult for them, at first, to keep track of the personalities. Achebe uses an occasional Ibo word to convey a sense of a non-Western culture. But even with the glossary provided, the students struggled with the strange language that would suddenly appear.

My students had confronted another of my strategies to encourage them to engage in critical inquiry — in this case inquiry into the nature of social studies, of teaching social studies and into their personal knowledge and assumptions about social studies related subjects.

Teacher educators concerned about issues of justice and equity in schooling in the United States face an inherent tension between preparing teachers who can work in schools as they are and preparing teachers who can work in schools for things as they might be. This tension is exacerbated by the felt need of many preservice teachers to be instructed in ways that will enable them to survive and thrive in existing school climates. Stimulating prospective teachers to see their social worlds, including the world of schooling, from a new perspective is no simple task for teacher education.

This essay is an argument for the use of imaginative literature as a stimulus for moving preservice teachers to new angles of vision. It is premised on the assumption that a major goal of teacher education is that of enabling preservice teachers to develop a critical, reflective stance toward schooling and toward knowledge. Examples of the use of literature in the social studies methods class are included in order to illuminate the possibilities for and problems involved in using works of fiction in teacher preparation courses.

Teaching as Critical Inquiry

Preservice teachers have been students of teaching for most of their lives; they begin their teacher preparation programs with many preconceptions about teaching and learning, and with many clear images which seem to confirm those conceptions. Teaching, for many prospective teachers, is a technical problem and they are anxious for information and techniques which will help them solve such problems. They carry with them, for the most part, images of schools as they are and few of them question these images or consider, to any great extent, alternative possibilities. They expect that teacher education will prepare them for success in existing school structures.

Teaching as critical inquiry, however, presents both students of teaching and teacher educators with very different images of the nature of teaching. While technical questions are addressed, the teacher as critical inquirer is concerned with situating such questions within normative and political contexts (Berlak and Berlak, 1981; Zeichner, 1983). Thinking about one's teaching as a critical inquirer means thinking about schooling practices within ethical, cultural and political frameworks. It means, as well, examining the ways in which teaching generally, and one's own teaching specifically, contributes, or does not contribute, to a just and humane society. It means considering the ways in which current schooling practices contribute to the perpetuation of social inequalities (Smyth, 1989; Giroux, 1981).

To engage students in critical reflection is to stimulate them to question the taken-for-granted, to probe hidden assumptions, to see from new perspectives. It means asking students to consider, not only questions of 'how', but 'what' and 'to what end'. It means helping them develop the ability to make decisions about teaching and learning which demonstrate awareness of ethical and political consequences and of the possibilities of alternatives.

Teacher educators who hold to this image of the teacher's role take on the task of helping their students to step away from the preconceptions of schooling and of teacher education they are likely to carry with them. These preconceptions, rooted as they are in personal experience, are often reflections of the *status quo*, schooling as it is (Lortie, 1975). In order to consider alternative possibilities, preservice teachers should be helped to develop new images of teaching, learning and knowledge. Facilitating the break from unquestioned assumptions requires a critical pedagogy which will allow students to see the ordinary and the taken-for-granted in new and unusual ways (Shor, 1980, p. 93). The pedagogy utilized in teacher education courses can be aimed at expanding students' visions of what is desirable and what is possible. One challenge to teacher educators is, then, to develop teaching practices in their own classrooms which encourage students to question, analyze and consider alternatives within an ethical, political framework.

Critical inquiry is not easy, even for those eager to engage in it. Many college students have become accustomed to a passive student role which requires little more than completing assignments promptly and passing exams which demonstrate an ability to memorize given information. Even more significantly, beginning teachers are generally anxious about taking on a new role, the role of teacher. For many preservice teachers, becoming a teacher coincides with becoming an adult, taking on new responsibilities surrounded by uncertainty. They *want* to know the 'one best way' — never mind moral questions and social issues.

Their resistance is often exacerbated by the conditions they confront in their field experiences. Many states have responded to the public criticism of education which emerged during the 1980s (e.g., National Commission on Excellence in Education, 1983) by mandating changes which emphasize external standards and accountability, making good teaching appear to be the implementation of ideas developed elsewhere (see, for example, Apple, 1982, 1986).

The pedagogical problem presented to the teacher educator is that of finding the stimuli which will open students to asking questions, to taking new perspectives, to examining alternatives. This problem of teacher education is the problem of liberal education generally: how can we emancipate students from mindlessness; how can we free them for the difficult task of making choices.

The Role of Imaginative Literature

One way to stimulate students toward what Maxine Greene (1978) called 'wide awakeness' is through imaginative literature. While works of literature can be used effectively throughout a teacher education program, using works of literature in the social studies methods class can provide preservice teachers with alternative perspectives toward human history and social interaction. To many students in an elementary teacher education program, social studies is boring and lifeless. The images they too often hold are those of memorizing lists of names and dates for tests (Goodlad, 1984). This image of social studies has little to do with interpretation, perspective or point of view. History and the social sciences are not seen as constructions of human beings working within accepted boundaries of a discipline. Through the use of imaginative literature, the methods instructor can raise questions about the nature and learned content of history and the social sciences, as well as create images of alternative ways to approach the study of social studies. Many students come to the social studies methods course with a narrow image of social studies, but, at the same time, their memories of an unpleasant subject provide an opening for new considerations.

Imaginative literature, like other art forms, provides an alternative way of knowing, an approach to knowledge that is unlike the textbook and other declarative forms of knowledge. It can present another way of 'seeing', a new vision or viewpoint on that which previously was taken for granted, given little thought or question. Imaginative literature can stimulate the reader beyond habitual ways of knowing, to new angles of vision and new insights, to alternative views of the world (Bruner, 1967).

An important role for imaginative literature in teacher education is that of illuminating the problematic. To create, the artist must stand outside the ordinary, unquestioned world. Through art forms, the artist can present new ways of seeing, can tap into the human psyche, can move us, in small steps, beyond the objectification of our rational society. As Greene (1978) noted, '. . . aesthetic experiences provide a ground for questioning that launches sense making and the understanding of what it is to exist in the world' (p. 166).

While literature can serve as a stimulus to raise questions not otherwise seen, it also can engage the reader on an empathetic and emotive level. A work of fine literature allows the reader to walk in another's shoes, to experience, in some form, the existence of others. It allows the reader, as Bronowski (1965) wrote, to 'stretch the skin inside which each of us lives . . .' (p. 72). In the social studies classroom, and in the social studies methods class, imaginative literature can connect the public knowledge of history and the social sciences, the names and dates, the charts and graphs, to inner personal meanings which include feelings and images, as well as cognitive knowledge. Children, particularly, often respond to the subjective nature of history (Levstik, 1986). In this way, the use of imaginative literature in a social studies methods class can serve to present an alternative way of knowing and understanding social studies which renders problematic both the nature of knowledge and ways of teaching and learning.

Using works of literature in the social studies methods class not only facilitates discussion of social, cultural and historical issues, but facilitates, as well, discussions about the nature of knowledge and scholarship. Preservice teachers are prompted to consider ways in which fictional accounts differ from factual, ways in which they illuminate the factual, and the ways works of fiction might be used to teach social studies.

Fictional accounts are the personal renderings of public life, not subject to the standards of reliability and accuracy of historians and social scientists. But the line between fact and fiction is less clear than might first appear. The 'facts', the data of the historian or the social scientist, do not, after all speak for themselves. It is not enough to simply know the facts; rather, it is necessary to know what to make of the facts. The process of interpretation, although subject to standards of the community of a discipline, is ultimately a personal one. The historian uses his or her skills of analysis; the conclusions drawn must meet standards of evidence and verifiability. Ultimately, however, the historian's interpretations, the conclusions of the social scientist, are creative, personal acts and, if well crafted, are creatively rendered. The writer of fiction, meanwhile, uses imagination, but to be accepted the work must meet standards of plausibility, of appearing to derive logically and emotionally from what precedes it and from some reality of the social world.

Social science and literature are not, of course, interchangeable; the standards and expectations from which the creation and judgment of each form spring differ. However, they do share a foundation in imagination and insight. And they complement each other as scholarship strives to resolve ambiguities and draw conclusions, and art strives to present the contradictions and tensions of human existence (Bronowski, 1965). Preservice teachers can come to see fact and fiction less as opposites than as different sets of lenses, one meeting the standards of scholarly community, the other seeking personal meanings in the social world. Truth is many faceted; no one tradition has a monopoly (Borenstein, 1978).

Finally, works of literature may be used to introduce a moral consciousness to social and historical issues and to teaching itself (Borenstein, 1978). As noted above, critical inquiry rests within a normative context; questions of equity and social justice are part of the decision-making process of teaching. Such questions can be asked about the process of schooling and about the nature of curriculum. Works of literature, approached mindfully and openly, can present students with new perspectives and extend their conceptualization of 'what ought to be' (Barone, 1988, p. 154). For the prospective social studies teacher, imaginative literature can raise new issues about the social world, about history and about the interaction of human beings. The social studies methods class can provide a context for raising such issues — about the knowledge taught as well as about the processes of schooling.

Literature can be used to raise questions concerning moral commitment and ethical action. Most social studies textbooks convey seemingly objective facts, with little sense of personal choices or decisions. The personal, emotive, empathetic response to literary works, can facilitate the discussion of ethical and political issues as they relate to issues and topics in social studies. Students can thus be shown a perspective on social studies knowledge and curriculum which includes questions of what is right and good, and why. Such questions can be brought to bear, as well, on issues of teaching and schooling.

Literary Examples

There are many works of literature which can illuminate issues appropriate to a course dealing with the teaching of social studies. Two possibilities are Arthur Miller's drama *The Crucible* (1953) and Chinua Achebe's novel *Things Fall Apart* (1959). Each work serves to illuminate questions and concerns relevant to social education and to give these concerns a human form which can touch the reader's feelings as well as the reader's mind.

Although ostensibly set in Puritan New England, Miller's *The Crucible* raises questions about individual freedom, law and authority, and social conscience which are relevant to a consideration of citizenship in a democracy. *The Crucible*, first produced in 1953, is the story of the Salem witchcraft trials of 1692; however, Miller also intended it as a not very veiled attack on McCarthyism.[1] In his stage notes, he makes clear his analogy between witch hunting in 1692 and witch hunting in 1953:

> Since 1692 a great but superficial change has wiped out God's beard and the Devil's horns, but the world is still gripped between two diametrically opposed opposites (Miller, p. 30)

> A political policy is equated with moral right, and opposition to it with diabolical malevolence. Once such an equation is effectively made, society becomes a congerie of plots and counter plots, and the main role of government changes from that of the arbiter to that of the scourge of God. (Miller, p. 32)

At the same time, there is a timelessness to Miller's work. This is a play which must be understood in the context in which it was written; but it raises questions for today, as well.

John Proctor, Miller's protagonist, faces a double dilemma. First, though seen as a virtuous man in the community, he knows he has sinned, sinned against both his own standards and those of the community. He is a man who abhors hypocrisy, but he must live with his own in order to hide sin. Second, he is a man who prefers not to get involved; he disdains the witch trials but will not speak publicly against them. However, when his wife, Elizabeth, is accused, he can no longer maintain his detachment. He must get involved and finally must not only acknowledge his own wrong doing, his sin, but also face his responsibility as a public as well as a private person.

Through Proctor, as well as other characters Miller creates for us, we confront questions of social commitment. Should Proctor remain silent although he believes the witch trials to be wrong? Can an individual truly keep apart from public affairs? John Proctor is forced to take a stand; has he become somehow a better, more admirable person because of it? What does citizenship, membership in a community, mean for the private self?

Other questions may be probed as well. What is the meaning of freedom and what are the tensions between protecting individual freedom and preserving the social order? Where is the balance between freedom and social responsibility? 'The balance has yet to be struck between order and freedom,' wrote Miller (p. 5). Authority, the secular manifestation of God, was important to the Puritans: 'A minister is not to be so likely crossed and contradicted' (Miller, p. 27). Is authority any less powerful to modern Americans?

By the end of the play, Reverend Hale, brought to Salem as an expert on witchcraft, has come to doubt his work and is appalled by the ruin the trials have brought to Salem.

> I came into this village like a bridegroom to his beloved, bearing gifts of high religion; the very crowns of the holy law I brought, and what I touched with my bright confidence, it died; and where I turned the eye of my great faith, blood flowed up. (Miller, p. 126)

He urges those who have been accused, but not yet hanged, to confess to witchcraft in order to be saved; he counsels them to lie in order that they might live:

> It is a mistaken law that leads you to sacrifice. Life, woman, life is God's most precious gift; no principle, however glorious, may justify the taking of it. (Miller, p. 127)

John Proctor is now among the accused, as are other members of the community who previously had been regarded as upright. Authority, rule of law, has failed them; they must act upon their own consciences, look to their own beliefs about what it means to be an honest, godly person. Should they be dishonest in order to protect themselves from the law and the authority which has been unjust, or should they maintain what they see as their personal integrity even when that means certain death?

Miller answers these questions on the side of personal integrity and death. Rebecca Nurse, whom Miller has described as godfearing and honest, accused of witchcraft because of border disputes and jealousies, refuses to save herself by confessing: 'Why, it is a lie, it is a lie; how may I damn myself? I cannot, I cannot?' (Miller, p. 134). Proctor, tormented by the decision, first agrees to a confession: 'I want my life', he tells one of the judges (Miller, p. 132). But when a confession means turning against others, he will not.

> I speak my own sins; I cannot judge another. I have no tongue for it. (Miller, p. 135)

Nor will he make a signed confession:

> You will not use me! I am no Sarah Good or Tituba, I am John Proctor! You will not use me! It is no part of salvation that you should use me!
> . . .
>
> I have three children — how may I teach them to walk like men in the world, and I sold my friends! (Miller, p. 139)

The readers' sympathies are, in the end, with the honesty of the men and women who refused to accuse others in order to save themselves, and who maintained their sense of personal integrity in the face of political pressure and even death.

For preservice teachers, as for the rest of us, the questions Miller raises are not easy ones. While attacking a social order which promotes witch hunts, his characters must still act as public persons, persons with an obligation to the community and to themselves. By not turning on others, they acknowledge their social responsibility; by not giving in to political pressure, they preserve their personal identities.

Probing these issues while reading the text, each student must consider his or her personal reaction to the choices made by Rebecca Nurse and John Proctor. A class discussion focusing on the tensions and dilemmas faced by Miller's characters, prods students to examine their underlying assumptions about private self, personal integrity and public action, issues which are likely to undergird their conceptions of social studies education. They consider their own assumptions in the light of both the play and the responses of others in the class. They are questioning the taken-for-granted and exploring their own belief systems.

There are a number of other social issues embedded in Miller's work. Social class discrimination, as well as discrimination against those who don't fit the acceptable social mold, was an issue in Salem and is an issue today. No one is terribly alarmed by the witch trials, for example, until the respected and respectable members of the community are among the accused. 'I am no Goody Good that sleeps in ditches, nor Osburn, drunk and half-witted', Elizabeth cries out when she sees that she will be accused (Miller, p. 59). Students may be challenged to consider modern day parallels.

Another possible issue for discussion is that of the psychology of political acts. The witch trials at Salem occurred at a time when the community perceived a breakdown of established ways and threats to the social order. Again, a discussion of modern day parallels can help students to gain insights into political behavior.

Chinua Achebe's novel *Things Fall Apart* (1959) raises a different set of issues for prospective social studies teachers. Achebe's novel is set in an Ibo village in his native country of Nigeria around the turn of the century. Much of the action takes place before the influence of British colonization has begun to be felt. The reader learns about traditional cultural patterns, and only toward the end of the novel is the reader confronted with the impact of the coming of European civilization.

Prospective social studies teachers enter a pre-European African culture which is rich in history and traditions. Throughout the novel, the reader encounters some of the myths and legends of the people and the educational function of these myths. Readers are introduced to the governing structures and social order of the village. We learn, through the experiences of the protagonist, that these are people who admire individual achievement, and whose governing Elders are men of distinction, not simply inheritors of title.

> Fortunately, among these people a man was judged according to his worth and not according to the worth of his father. (Achebe, p. 11)

Achebe makes clear the traditional value of living in harmony with nature. Land, and working the land, are the basis of this civilization. Natural rhythms dictate the patterns of ordinary life and of special days and extraordinary behavior.

> You know as well as I do that our forefathers ordained that before we plant any crops in the earth we should observe a week in which a man does not say a harsh word to his neighbor. (Achebe, p. 117)

Achebe's novel allows us to sympathetically experience another culture. Prospective social studies teachers can contrast these experiences with the stereotypes of pre-European Africa which they are still likely to encounter, and with stereotypic thinking about pre-industrial society generally. Students read about a civilization which is stable, harmonious and rich — and is also very different from the industrial world we know today.

The novel introduces preservice teachers to another way of seeing the people who inhabit the social studies textbooks. The people of Umuofia are encountered, not as abstractions, but as personalities with passions, fears and ambitions. Although these personalities are fictionalized, they nonetheless bring the reader into a culture and allow vicarious participation in a way of life that, for the most part, no longer exists. Readers can explore the effects of change from within the psyche, albeit imagined, of those who resisted change and of those who embraced it (although the latter is a minor theme).

As the title of the novel suggests, Achebe is not sympathetic with the imposition of Western ways on African culture. He describes, not a violent conquest, but an insidious one in which European missionaries, and later government, quietly establish their ways over the village. The reader sees the old ways slip into disarray:

> The white man is very clever. He came quietly and peaceably with his religion. We were amused at his foolishness and allowed him to stay. Now he has won our brothers and the clan can no longer act like one.

He has put a knife on the things that held us together, and we have fallen apart. (Achebe, p. 162)

At the same time, Achebe does not romanticize traditional ways. He tells his readers of those who do not fit in, and the reader is helped to understand the appeal of Christianity as well as its disruption. The protagonist's son, Nwoye, is gentle and kind, with none of the drive that possesses his father. The father, in turn, disdains Nwoye's gentle ways. The reader understands that, much to his father's disappointment, Nwoye will not be a great man in his village. In the traditional society of the family and village, Nwoye feels himself to be a misfit and hungers for a place where he can find peace and acceptance. He becomes one of the first who is not an actual outcast in his own society to join the white man's church:

He felt a relief within as the hymn poured into his parched soul. The words of the hymn were like drops of frozen rain melting on the dry palate of the panting earth. (Achebe, p. 137)

As we learn about Nwoye and his father, Okonkwo, readers can also consider the question of how an individual comes to adapt, or fails to adapt, to cultural norms and expectations. Even in traditional societies in which, to the modern mind, the way seems less complex, roles more clear and choices less open, individuals may encounter more or less difficulty in finding their place, in knowing their way. Okonwo's drive to succeed made him a great man in the village, but alienated him from his family. Nwoye's gentle soul found no place in the family of Okonkwo and was able to easily embrace the new was brought by Christianity.

Thus Achebe, like Miller, raises questions that are appropriate to social education and does so in a reflective aesthetic sense, rather than through the expository discourse of the textbook. Readers are asked to become involved with places and times far from their own, and there they confront enduring questions about what it means to live in the social world. Readers are not confronted with givens, but with human experiences with which they can identify and through which they can broaden their own perspectives on the social world.

A Case Example

My students, although somewhat intimidated by Achebe's novel and not entirely convinced that it was relevant to their needs, were nonetheless willing to go along with the task of reading. They were assigned to begin reading the book with particular questions in mind. Some questions directed them to focus on understanding the Ibo culture as described by Achebe. The students were directed to look for and note passages and descriptions that would give them evidence about Ibo beliefs, attitudes and practices in domains such as government, economic livelihood, nature and family. Other questions directed them to concentrate on the development of key characters, particularly Okonkwo and Nwoye. They were to try to develop an understanding of these two characters.

85

What kind of men were they? What does Achebe tell us about them that helps us understand their behavior? How do they respond to the arrival of the missionaries and the administrators and why? Finally, the students were directed to consider what Achebe might have meant by the title he chose for the book the book: *Things Fall Apart*.

Two class sessions were used for discussion of the book. The first session, for which the students were to have read at least half the book, focused on a discussion of Ibo culture as Achebe presented it and on questions that students had from their reading. The students, many of whom had found the book difficult at first, indicated that they had become quite interested in it. The more they read, the less confused they were by the characters' names and the more interested they had become in the people Achebe created. They were developing a sense of the 'life of the place', as one student put it. They were enjoying the book. During both the class sessions, students first worked in small groups; each group was given the task of focusing their discussion on one of the questions posed to guide their reading. One group, for example, was to talk about, and be prepared to talk to the class about, the government of the Ibo village. Another group focused on relationships with nature, and so forth. The small groups were then asked to share their conclusions with the whole class.

The first class session ended with a discussion of the stereotype of nineteenth-century Africa as 'uncivilized' and 'primitive'. What do these terms connote? Was the village protrayed by Achebe uncivilized? The students noted that the social structures, the political organization, the religion and traditions all suggested a civilization. While primitive, by Western standards, in their use of technology, the Ibo maintained a balance with nature. There was much in their belief system and attitudes that well may be superior, many students argued, to those of technological societies which pollute and destroy.

The second class session focused on the effects of European culture on Nwoye, and Okonkwo and on the village generally. During this session, the groups were directed to talk about the coming of the white man, the responses of Okonkwo and Nwoye, and the ways in which 'things fell apart'.

During the class meeting following the discussion of the novel, the students were asked to consider what literature has to do with social studies. 'I really liked this book,' Rodney said, 'It brought the people to life.' The students talked about how the novel helped them understand, from a different perspective, an era in history as well as some geographical concepts they had learned. They all agreed that the novel was much more interesting than any social studies textbook they had ever read and a discussion of ways to supplement textbooks ensued. They concluded that at the elementary level, it's very important to help students see the human connection to social studies, that social studies is, after all, the study of people, their history, their interactions, their problems and their struggles. That understanding, they felt, was a most important foundation for further study of social studies topics in middle and high school. Some students noted that while fact and fiction are different, textbooks weren't as objective as they had previously seemed. More importantly, fiction and other art forms could bring a real dimension to the study of human history and human life. One student noted that the subjective experience of history might well be more important than the textbook rendering. Questions of point of view, perspective and objectivity were explored with some enthusiasm. Students were directed to find works of literature and/or other art forms which they could incorporate into the units they were writing as a major course project. 'I'm glad we read this', Rodney said with a smile as the students left class.

During student teaching, almost all of these students incorporated some work of art in their social studies teaching. One student was very enthusiastic about helping students learn about the past through the music of a time period. Other students found children's books they were able to use in both language arts and social studies. Several student teachers in primary grade classrooms were able to teach social studies concepts through the stories their classes read during reading time; they felt pleased that they had made a little more space for social studies in the teaching day. When asked their thoughts about using literature, and other art forms, in their social studies teaching, all the student teachers reponded with enthusiasm:

It made social studies more interesting.

Using the story really stimulated good discussions about decision making.

By using the book, we were able to talk about the values people had.

I used the story to get my students started on a research project about American Indians; they wanted to know what it was really like.

My students started bringing in stories of their own to share with the class.

No student teacher from this group had a negative response to her or his experience from this group had a negative response to her or his experience with novels, short stories, poetry, music or the visual arts in teaching social studies.

Humanizing or personalizing the subject matter had become a key to enabling my students, and later their students, to consider the subject called social studies from new vantage points, to question what for many was the taken-for-granted assumption that social studies is rather tedious stuff. The content of social studies not only took on a human form, but the students' conceptions of sources of knowledge were expanded. They found the non-expository, non-textbook source to be a compelling and legitimate text. For many, this called into question reliance on textbooks and expert knowledge and expanded their conceptions of sources of knowledge.

Using literature in the social studies methods class not only raised issues about the content of social studies and about sources of information, but about classroom practices as well. The methods class students found that the literature they read helped them to understand concepts and form generalizations which could then be tested against their background knowledge or against new knowledge gained. Furthermore, they learned about 'what is' from a different angle, while at the same time, ethical questions were raised and students began to consider questions about 'what ought to be'. In this way, my preservice teachers came to experience the very processes in which their own students might potentially be engaged.

While there has been no systematic follow-up with these students specifically regarding their use of literature in teaching social studies, graduates who have returned for a visit have indicated that they continue to seek ways to integrate literature into their teaching of social studies and that, in fact, some are finding encouragement for that from their administrators. They feel they can better accomplish both the development of language skills and the teaching of social studies concepts by integrating literature and social studies. As they gain teaching experience, the work of integration becomes easier. Social studies maintains its integrity, while language arts skills are enhanced.

The methods class just described, was part of a small teacher education program at a Jesuit college in a midwestern metropolitan area. As products of a Jesuit education, these preservice teachers were well-grounded in the liberal arts. As preservice teachers in a troubled urban school system, they were well aware of the need to somehow alter their conceptions of teaching as telling and directing, to do something, somehow different. The experience of discussing a novel in a social studies context had given them an image of a possible alternative. The use of that alternative was reinforced by their own students who found the books and stories interesting, if not always 'real' social studies which is 'boring'. And for some the experience was reinforced by administrators who wanted to develop language skills, to capture the interests of their students and who were not opposed to a greater emphasis on social studies.

No one talked to me about failures when they tried to use literature in their social studies classrooms, although there may well have been failures. And some preservice teachers, less steeped in the liberal arts, might be less responsive to reading a novel in a methods class, or less perceptive about its uses. But there are at least some preservice teachers who can carry an alternate image of teaching, of social studies and of knowledge into their classrooms, who can themselves read critically and help their students read critically, who are aware of alternatives and consequences and can bring this awareness to their own teaching experiences.

In sum, using works of literature in the social studies methods class can facilitate several course goals. Preservice teachers may begin to see the school curriculum and the possibilities of social studies in new ways. Literary works provide these prospective teachers with text they can react to and interact with and this suggests many possibilities. Social studies becomes something which can engage students. Prospective teachers begin to see that there are diverse sources of knowledge and that learning can involve interaction with texts and can involve, as well, students' own background knowledge. The students' experience with literature in a method class has the potential for being what Dewey (1938) termed an educational experience. That is, through encouraging reflection on alternatives for the classroom curriculum and teaching practices, engagement with literature fosters a sense of potential control over one's teaching experience.

Of course, the use of a novel or a play in a social studies methods course is no panacea for improving the teaching of social studies in the elementary school. There will be students who resist the discourse of imaginative literature. They take little pleasure in reading a novel or a play and have difficulty with making the connections to a school subject called social studies. This appears, however, not to be a problem which affects many students. As described above, many of those students who approach a work of literature with reluctance catch the enthusiasm of their peers and at least begin to see the possibilities.

The more compelling concern addresses the impact of any experience in a methods class. In the university classroom, engaging a work of literature seems to stimulate students to question their background assumptions and to consider new possibilities. However, when they begin teaching, their experiences may be quite different than the experiences of those of my graduates who have returned and reported success in using literary works. For other beginning teachers, the socializing processes of the school culture may well push the questions and the alternatives into the background of the new teachers' conceptions (see, for example, Tabachnick and Zeichner, 1984).

Encouraging reflective teaching is not a process that can end in the methods class. But we cannot sit by and wait for school structures and habits of thought and action to change before we begin preparing teachers to be reflective practitioners. There are spaces now where teachers find opportunities and ways to teach as minded practitioners. If our students don't at least have some image of possibilities, their chances for professional development will be further diminished. To the extent that literature opens doors of possibility, it becomes a significant piece of the preparation of teachers.

Note

1 A reading of *The crucible* illustrates a point that may be made about artistic works generally. In *The Crucible*, Miller tells his readers more about the period in which he was writing than about the period in which he set the action. History is always viewed through the eyes of the time in which it is written, and that is no less true for works of historical fiction. Good literature however, also has a timeless quality, raising issues and concerns about what it means to be human, as well as about life in a particular time and place.

References

ACHEBE, C. (1959) *Thing Fall Apart*, New York: Random House.
APPLE, M.W. (1979) *Ideology and Curriculum*, Boston: Routledge and Kegan Paul.
APPLE, M.W. (1982) *Education and Power*, Boston: Routledge and Kegan Paul.
APPLE, M.W. (1986) *Teachers and Texts*, New York: Routledge and Kegan Paul.
ARONOWITZ, S. and GIROUX, H. (1985) *Education Under Seige*, Hadley, MA: Bergin and Garvey.
BARONE, T.E. (1988) 'Curriculum platforms and literature', in BEYER, L.E. and APPLE, M.W. (Eds) *The Curriculum: Problems, Politics and Possibilities*, pp. 140–65, Albany: State University of New York Press.
BERLAK, A. and BERLAK, H. (1981) *The Dilemmas of Schooling*, New York: Metheun and Co.
BORENSTEIN, A. (1978) *Redeeming the Sin: Social Science and Literature*, New York: Columbia University Press.
BRONOWSKI, J. (1965) *The Identity of Man*, Garden City, New York: The Natural History Press.
BRUNER, J.S. (1967) *On Knowing: Essays for the Left Hand*, New York: Atheneum.
DEWEY, J. (1938) *Experience and Education*, New York: Macmillan.
GOODLAD, J. (1984) *A Place called School*, New York: McGraw-Hill
GIROUX, H.A. (1981) *Ideology, Culture and the Process of Schooling*, Basingstoke: Falmer Press.
GREENE, M. (1973) *Teacher as Stranger*, CA: Wadsworth Publishing.

GREENE, M. (1978) *Landscapes of Learning*, New York: Teachers College Press.

LEVSTIK, L. (1986) 'The relationship between historical response and narrative in a sixth-grade classroom', *Theory and Research in Social Education*, **14**, 1, pp. 1–19.

LORTIE, D. (1975) *Schoolteacher: A Sociological Study*, Chicago: University of Chicago Press.

MILLER, A. (1952) *The Crucible*, New York: Bantam Books.

NATIONAL COMMISSION ON EXCELLENCE IN EDUCATION (1983) *A Nation at Risk: The Imperative for Educational Reform*, Washington D.C.: US Government Printing Office.

SHOR, I. (1980) *Critical Teaching in Everyday Life*, Chicago: University of Chicago Press.

SMYTH, J. (1989) 'Developing and sustaining critical reflection in teacher education', *Journal of Teacher Education*, **40**, 2, pp. 2–9.

TABACHNICK, R.B. and ZEICHNER, K.M. (1984) 'The impact of the student teaching experience on the development of teacher perspectives', *Journal of Teacher Education*, **35**, 6, pp. 28–36.

TOM, A. (1984) *Teaching as a Moral Craft*, New York: Longman.

ZEICHNER, K.M. (1983) 'Alternative paradigms of teacher education', *Theory and Research in Social Education*, **34**, 3, pp. 3–9.

6 Teaching a Language of Opportunity in a Language Arts Methods Course: Teaching for David, Albert and Darlene

Mary Louise Gomez

Why Teach about Diversity?[1]

Nearly twenty years ago in a small Vermont milltown where the looms had long been silent, I learned firsthand about the diversity of opportunity for learning and achievement by elementary school children.[2] As a student teacher working for three semesters in the town's one elementary school, I taught the offspring of local attorneys and shopkeepers as well as the children of those struggling in poverty caused by the decades earlier closing of the factories. Faces from my first grade class at Black River School[3] haunt me still: tiny and sickly Albert whose father was jailed throughout the child's primary school years; David, a Canadian Indian who was often looked after by neighbors while his impoverished, alcoholic mother was hospitalized; and 6½-year-old Darlene, tall and slender, wise beyond her years, daily recounting tales of the 'uncles' who had slept at her apartment the prior night and of the challenges of dressing and feeding her younger siblings.

David, I recall, struggled the entire year to recognize and reproduce the alphabet and numerals zero to ten; Albert and Darlene were placed in the next to lowest reading group where their frequently empty bellies and sleepy eyes contributed to their slow progress. The children's poverty was not, however, solely responsible for their low achievement (as measured by standardized tests) and slow progress in learning to read, write and do mathematics. David, Albert, and Darlene did not see themselves, their experiences or their skills reflected in the first grade curriculum; they did not see themselves in the pages of their basal readers, in their mathematics texts or in the story books their teacher read.

While the children brought many skills and experiences to school — skills of household organization, child care, food preparation and creative play as well as experiences, some unpleasant, others simply foreign to middle-class teachers — those were not skills and experiences valued in Vermont classrooms in the 1970s or in most US classrooms today. Rather, their kind-hearted teacher, Ms Paterson, labored for hours over lesson plans which combined fun with practice in phonics, counting and word recognition skills. She filled her classroom with colorful decorations, plants, games and books. She worried constantly about the children's health and safety, and regularly phoned the appropriate social services agencies to obtain medical and dental care and warm clothing for her students. She planned delightful holiday parties; in all of this I helped her. Together, Ms Paterson and I tried to make her classroom a refuge from the children's other worlds. We saw the deficits of the children's lives and tried to fill these with different sets of knowledge, skills and experiences valued by us and by schools.

I think often of Ms Paterson and the first graders in her classroom. Over the years I have come to understand what was missing in her classroom and others in which I worked at Black River School. Missing were essential ingredients to all children's school success, the critical links which bind home and school, including recognition that *all* children come to school with skills and experiences upon which we can draw, build and expand. Further, Ms Paterson and I failed to extend an invitation to the children's families to make *this* school *their* school.

As middle-class female teachers, we deplored the conditions in which many of our children lived; we felt sorry for them and sometimes disdainful of their families. We wished the children's lives might have been different and more like our own. We failed, however, to build links of skills and understandings between their homes and school. Rather, we wanted to replace the knowledge, skills and dispositions which the children brought to school with others, a set with which we felt more comfortable, one which *we* knew. Ms Paterson and I failed to do what Chambers Erasmus (1989) and others (Dean, 1989; Heath, 1983; Jordan, 1988; Taylor and Dorsey-Gaines, 1988) advocate; we did not listen carefully to the stories the children brought to school other than to confirm our own vision of their families' pathology. We did not listen to learn ourselves. Therefore, we could not, in Chambers Erasmus' words, '. . . extend, rather than limit, the possibilities these children [brought] to school' (1989, p. 274).

David, who became my foster son for many months that year, should now be twenty-three years old. I do not know where, or if, he lives. I am certain, however, that his socioeconomic status, his lived experiences, combined with our responses as teachers, handicapped his opportunities to engage in and profit from school activities. I fear also that years of such reponses by teachers limited his and his classmates' social and economic choices for a lifetime.

It has not been easy to understand or accept my complicity in these children's school failure. From these early teaching experiences, however, has come the determination that those new teachers whom I help to prepare will come ready to listen, to learn from their students and their families and to build with them links between home and school as we build the children's enjoyment and skills of literacy. I hope to prepare new teachers who speak what Henry Giroux (McLaren, 1988) has called 'a language of opportunity' and Mike Rose (1989) has termed 'a discourse of possibility', ways of talking and working with children which foster hope, see beyond failure to expectation and value diversity.

Changing Demographics in the US Population

While my own early encounters with classrom diversity were primarily with poor White children, the sorts of diversity facing new teachers in the decades of the twenty-first century are more varied. US classrooms are increasingly filled not only with children who are poor (Kennedy, Jung and Orland, 1986), but with children who have limited English proficiency (Hispanic Policy Development Project, 1988) and those who are children of color (Center for Education Statistics, 1987a, 1987b). Estimates of the growth of the non-White school population include a rise from 24 per cent in 1976 to 30–40 per cent in the year 2000 (Center for Education Statistics, 1987a, 1987b). Many children in the US also come from non-English background (NELB) homes. Currently, 30 million school age children speak a language other than English or come from homes where English is not spoken (Romero, Mercado and Vazquez-Faria, 1987) and those numbers will increase as the total NELB population is expected to grow to 39.5 million by the year 2000. While the largest percentages of these children speak Spanish or Chinese, there are increasing numbers of children entering US schools who speak different languages than English.

Many of these children also live in poverty. While data show that one in four children in the US lives in poverty, a breakdown of these figures for race shows a much higher rate of poverty for Blacks — 50 per cent — and for Hispanics, 40 per cent. Of the 80 million school age children in the US in 1988, nearly 10 million came from homes headed by a single, female parent (Strong, 1989). For children living in female-headed households, rates of poverty are high, rising to 47.6 per cent, 68.5 per cent and 70.5 per cent for Whites, Blacks and Hispanics (Kennedy *et al.*, 1986). In 1988, only 4 per cent (in contrast to 60 per cent in 1955) of US families represented our traditional image of one mother, one father and two children (Strong, 1989).

What are the implications of these figures? Poverty, living within a single-parent family and limited English proficiency are key variables contributing to the high secondary school dropout rates of US students of color. Of students who were enrolled as sophomores in public secondary schools in 1980, 12.2 per cent of Whites had dropped out by the autumn of 1982 while 17 per cent of Blacks had dropped out, 18 per cent of Hispanics and 29.2 per cent of American Indians had left school (Wheelock and Dorman, 1989). These students' failures cannot solely be attributed to classroom experiences as complex cultural and economic webs bind people and their life chances and choices. Yet, the opportunities to learn and achieve in US schools must be changed and expanded if schooling is to play a role in increasing all children's social and economic chances and choices in the US.

We cannot expect, however, that school change for children of color will be conducted by teachers of color, for the majority of US teachers are White females (Center for Education Statistics, 1987a, 1987b; Georgiades, 1988). Gil (1989, p. 83) estimates that 29 per cent of US children are children of color (16.2 per cent African American, 9.1 per cent Hispanic, 2.5 per cent Asian American, and 0.9 per cent American Indian) while only 10 per cent of their teachers are persons of color (6.9 per cent African American, 1.9 per cent Hispanic, 0.9 per cent Asian American, and 0.6 per cent American Indian). The existing mismatch between numbers of students of color and teachers of color will only increase as employment opportunities outside of teaching grow for non-Whites, and as testing initiatives for entry, certification and tenure purposes block the candidacy, certification and tenure of teachers of color (Darling-Hammond, 1988). Numbers of teachers of color are expected to drop to 5 per cent by the year 2000 (Association for Supervision and Curriculum Development, 1989).

Further, data from surveys conducted by the American Association of Colleges of Teacher Education (AACTE) indicate students enrolled in teacher preparation programs hope to return to the suburban or rural areas from which they came. These prospective teachers do not anticipate teaching in our cities, nor do they anticipate teaching children unlike themselves (AACTE, 1987). Finally, while many teacher education programs contain components of attention to education that is multicultural, in most cases issues of race, class, gender or handicap are peripheral to the central concerns of programs' learning-to-teach curricula (Grant and Secada, 1990).

Simply increasing the numbers of teachers of color is not suggested here as a solution to the lower rates of achievement and higher rates of dropping out of students of color and those of low socioeconomic status. Yet, the combination of three forces: the paucity of successful classroom models of students' own race, culture or language group; the lack of systematic attention to education that is multicultural in teacher education programs; and the lack of dispositions of White teachers to work in urban areas impacted by large numbers of poor students of color creates a bleak outlook for changing the life chances of many students. Those whom we are currently preparing to be teachers neither have the life experiences, the education nor the dispositions which would assist them in preparing to teach the children coming to our schoolhouse doors.

Recruitment into teaching of persons of color and Whites with the life experiences, disposition and education necessary to meet the challenges of the classrooms of the 1990s is a long-term solution to creating schools which welcome the diversity of US children. (See Haberman, 1989, for suggestions for recruiting more persons of color into teaching.) A second, also needed approach, is to work to create dispositions for and skills of working with diverse learners for those already enrolled in teacher education and for those who currently teach.

I view the role of teacher educators and classroom teachers as central to the enterprise of school reform required in the US today. Therefore, I view methods courses for prospective teachers as critical places to lay the foundation for developing teachers who listen, learn and respond to the diversity present in their classrooms. The content of professional coursework must move beyond attending to issues of diversity to making issues of race, class and gender central concerns of US teacher preparation.

The Course and the Students

The language arts methods course for prospective elementary school teachers which I teach at the University of Wisconsin-Madison occurs in the second semester of a four-semester sequence of professional coursework, practica and student teaching. Prospective teachers are juniors when they enter this series of activities. When they begin the 'reading and language arts semester', students have completed an introductory course to the profession which includes eight visits to different local schools. While enrolled in one of the three class sections (taught by different faculty and staff) of the 3-credit course 'Teaching Language Arts in the Elementary School', prospective teachers are also enrolled in a companion 3-credit course 'Teaching Reading in the Elementary School'. They also engage in a 3-credit, 9-week long practicum in one of the elementary schools of the county. Each 'methods' course is held either on a Monday or a Tuesday for a 2 hour and 40 minute block for the 15 weeks of the semester. The practicum is held Wednesday through Friday mornings from the fifth through the thirteenth weeks of the semester. Students are supervised by both a cooperating teacher in the school and by experienced teachers who are full-time graduate students at the university.

I first taught this course eight years ago as a doctoral student at a time when our elementary education program enrollment at Wisconsin was shrinking. The National Writing Project[4] was less than a decade old; Janet Emig's and Donald Graves' groundbreaking research on the teaching and learning of writing had only recently been published; multicultural education was not yet a byword and few had predicted that the term 'minority' would become an oxymoron. As the years have passed, as my own understandings about teaching and learning and diverse learners have deepened and as the challenges to US schooling have shifted, the course has changed. It will continue to change as my thinking and other needs require it.

At the beginning of a new decade, those enrolled in the Wisconsin elementary education program have also changed. Many of our students are returning to the university to complete a long abandoned degree, others hope to change careers; many are parents; a few are persons of color. Yet, our enrollment of prospective teachers was eight years ago, and remains today, primarily composed of single White females in their twenties who are natives of Wisconsin or neighboring Minnesota. Other than summer camp or teenaged babysitting jobs, they have had few contacts with elementary-aged children since their own early classroom experiences. They enter teacher education, they say, because they love children, have always wanted to be teachers or have a parent in whose career path they are following. My perception of these prospective teachers is that, for the most part, they are earnest, thoughtful people, eager to 'do a good job'. While they come to teacher education with few experiences with persons unlike themselves, most seem disposed to be kind and caring with all children.

Like me two decades ago, they are also full of pity, puzzlement and anger for the children and families they encounter. Like their counterpart Stephanie,[5] a prospective secondary teacher whom I recently interviewed, they believe one has to consider the social class of one's students because '. . . maybe someone from a lower class has not been exposed to as many outside experiences during the course of their lifetime' or they may '. . . not have been exposed to good literature, what a piece of good writing looks like', as 'they haven't seen their parents reading in the home as much because their parents have to spend more time at work'. Stephanie shared her views concerning diversity as part of a structured interview in a large research project, yet her words echo those spoken by students at Wisconsin as they begin their program of teacher preparation.

Stephanie and her counterparts at Wisconsin often fail to take into account that children of different cultural, language and economic backgrounds bring *valuable* as well as *varied* experiences to school. Rather, many of these young teachers believe that there is one preferred way of living for which all people should strive. A recent Wisconsin student named Natalie told me, for example, that she was shocked at the numbers of children in her practicum classroom who did not eat breakfast. When I explained that my own preschool daughter often refused to eat breakfast or chose to eat a piece of bread in the car on the way to school, Natalie was shocked. She awakened her own two children at six every morning so they could, she said, have a 'hearty, nourishing start to the day'. The implication of Natalie's words was that I, like the parents of the children in her practicum classroom, was neglectful of my daughter's health and well-being.

As teachers who care about their students' futures, Natalie and many of her prospective teacher peers believe that their job is to engage students in the behavior and knowledge of that group of which they are a part — the White middle class. While such dispositions may be altruistic, they often deny the positive, yet different rituals and activities of other racial, cultural or language groups. Among the goals for the courses I teach, then, must be to move prospective teachers' thinking beyond that which labels others' behaviors or experiences as deficient and pathological to thinking which focuses on questioning their notions about teaching, teachers, learners and learning. In the language arts methods course, I ask the following framing questions as one means of engaging prospective teachers in alternate ways of thinking:

1   What are the different ways in which we think about literacy? What, then, does it mean to be a literate person?
2   How are the various ways in which we think about literacy reflected in schools' curricula and methods for teaching language arts?
3   What are the ways in which we define diverse populations of learners? How are language arts curricula differentiated for various groups of learners? What curricula and what methods best serve diverse learners?
4   What should be the role of varied constituencies — students, teachers, parents and community members — in determining the goals, means and materials used to teach language arts to diverse learners?
5   What should be the role of varied constituencies — students, teachers, parents and community members — in determining the purposes and procedures of assessment in the language arts? How should the results of such assessment be used?

Each of these questions is designed to help prospective teachers examine closely the concepts of literacy and diversity. The questions serve as guideposts for our reading, thinking and talking so that prospective teachers enrolled in the course begin to view literacy and diversity as problematic, as historically and culturally defined, and as concepts which, transformed into school practices, have profound consequences for *who*, which learners, receive *what* instruction. Course readings, written assignments and classroom discussions are the vehicles for examining these questions.

The Course Readings

The course readings, which change from time to time as new work becomes available, currently include three core texts: (1) the autobiographical chronicle, *Hunger of Memory: The Education of Richard Rodriguez* (1982), Mexican American scholar Richard Rodriguez' account of cultural alienation as he and his family are encouraged to 'practice' English at home by his elementary school teachers; (2) Denny Taylor's and Catherine Dorsey-Gaines' *Growing Up Literate: The Lives of Inner City Families* (1988), an ethnographic account of the lives of low socioeconomic status Black first graders who demonstrated school success (accompanied by the authors' critique of US schooling in literacy); and (3) Donald Graves' seminal text on teaching a process approach to writing titled *Writing: Teachers and Children At Work* (1983). Previously, students read Anne Haas Dyson's articles concerning the ways in which young children learn to write, but in the future I will use her *Multiple Worlds of Child Writers: Friends Learning to Write* (1989). Here, Dyson follows a multi-ethnic group of young children as they learn to write over a two-year period. Another recently published volume which will become a core text is Mike Rose's *Lives on the Boundary* (1989). Rose uses his own life in a poor urban neighborhood, as well as the lives of others he has encountered in his many years of teaching, to explore how and why some students remain consigned to the boundaries of US life. He also discusses the sort of teaching it takes to offer hopes and expectations rather than despair to these students.

The texts I have chosen to use have in common this idea — that the acquisition of English literacy is a series of challenges shared by all peoples in the US and that these challenges are linked across occasions of time, from early childhood to adulthood, and across places — home, school and work. For some of these authors or their subjects, the acquisition of literacy in English is painful, alienating and unlinked in meaningful ways across time and places. For others, the children in Dyson's stories, for example, language learning is most often a joyful encounter which bridges home and school. Through the reading and discussion of these authors' words, I hope to awaken in my students what psychiatrist and teacher Robert Coles refers to as *The Call of Stories* (1989).

In his latest book, Coles tells of his early training as a psychiatrist and the powerful role one of his mentors played in shaping his thinking. This mentor, Dr Ludwig, continually admonished Coles to listen to the stories of his patients' lives and become reluctant to make judgments and label their problems with medical jargon. Among the wisdom Ludwig imparted is the following, 'Remember what you are hearing [from the patient] is to some considerable extent a function of you, hearing' (p. 15). Coles also recalls the message passed to him by his friend, physician and writer, Dr William Carlos Williams, who admonished, 'Their story, yours, mine — it's what we all carry with us on this trip we take, and we owe it to each other to respect our stories and learn from them' (p. 30). Both of Coles' teachers reminded him of the central role of the listener in filtering and understanding the stories of others and of the worthy character of all persons' stories/lives.

While I do not suggest that teachers are therapists, I do believe that Coles' message is as critical for prospective teachers as it is for new physicians. Prospective teachers must also listen carefully to the stories their students tell, trying not to judge or label their students' lives. Rather, I hope that through reading and talking about well-told stories, like those of Rodriguez, Taylor and Dorsey-Gaines, Dyson, Graves, and Rose, new teachers can explode the cultural and class ties which bind our viewpoints and can learn, like Robert Coles, that we must constantly re-check our lenses and their filtered perceptions. In this way, we work towards respect and careful response to all of our students' stories.

Students' initial encounters with writing by and about people unlike themselves can be unsettling, especially when the authors do not confirm students' prior knowledge or beliefs about the subjects of the texts. With this in mind, I have purposefully chosen to begin the course with the reading of Richard Rodriguez' autobiographical tale of his schooling and its consequences. Rodriguez, the child of Mexican immigrants, began his schooling in a Catholic elementary school in Sacramento, California, and completed it in London, funded by a Rhodes scholarship. Along the way, he writes, he became alienated from his family. Well-meaning teachers who ran his school had suggested to the family that shy Richard and his siblings would benefit from the speaking of English in their home. As English became the means of private as well as public discourse, Rodriguez' family life was changed in profound and unanticipated ways. The texture and rhythm of their household changed, never to be retrieved.

When White, middle-class students in my course read Rodriguez' bitter and angry words, they become confused and angry as they imagine themselves in the role of the teachers suggesting to the Rodgriguez family that they abandon their native language at home. Carla, a Wisconsin student enrolled in the course two years ago, represented the feelings of many her peers when she cried, 'I just don't get it, what's he complaining about anyway? He learned English, got scholarships, now he's a famous writer! My dad's still driving a truck in Milwaukee!'

Carla's comments touched off a torrent of lively debate that day. To many students, Rodriguez had little about which to complain. He had risen beyond others' expectations, by his own admission now attended fashionable parties in places exotic to Wisconsin — New York Park Avenue apartments, Beverly Hills, Paris. So what, his family had to practice English at home and that helped him acquire later privileges. That was good, some students say. He got what lots of people want, didn't he? Still others ask: What choices could the teachers have made other than to recommend the replacement of Spanish with English in the Rodriguez home? What choices or options would they or their peers recommend today to Rodriguez family? How might these other choices have affected the Rodriguez family? Finally, a few students ask: What other choices might Rodriguez have made in his life, how might these choices have affected his feelings of alienation? What responsibility did he have for the alienation from language, family and culture that he experienced?

Weeks later, the reaction to Rodriguez' story is varied. A few students retain their anger at the author as they, like Carla, feel he has risen beyond his and their dreams to a high status position and should not complain about that which he has lost. Other students struggle with his ideals, yet do not appear, over the course of a semester either to fully understand Rodriguez' pain regarding his cultural alienation nor his arguments concerning the inseparability of language and culture. Richard Rodriguez' story does, however, cause many prospective teachers to question their assumptions about the superiority of English over other languages, about the bonds between language, customs, family life and culture and to question their prior notions regarding teachers' rights to prescribe what is 'good' for their students.

In recent semesters, I have deliberately juxtaposed the reading of *Hunger of Memory* with that of Taylor's and Dorsey-Gaines' account of the poor, urban Black families of Shay Avenue and their successful struggles to prepare their children for school literacy tasks. Still puzzled and a bit irritated with Rodriguez, students are at first soothed by the 'winning despite all odds' quality of the opening pages of these stories. Yet, as the lives of the Shay Avenue families unfold, and then unravel from the weight of social and economic forces beyond their control, students alternate between 'blaming the victim', the poor protagonists of the stories, and railing at the government and welfare system which they view as partially responsible for these families' plights.

Early discussions of the text do not surface the role of school or schooling in the families' problems. The Black male adolescents in the families who eagerly began school and succeeded at school tasks succumb to problems familiar to poor, urban youth. Discouraged and disillusioned as they mature, the young men of Shay Avenue frequently encounter the juvenile court system in a series of escalating conflicts. Some student-readers begin at this point to invoke their prior knowledge and beliefs about Black, urban male youths, e.g., they all use drugs and belong to gangs, therefore, they are justly punished for their transgressions.

However, three forces work to assist students in rethinking these assumptions and enable them to see the complexity of the forces responsible for these youths' problems, including the role of schooling, in their downward spiral. The first is Taylor's and Dorsey-Gaines' richly textured narrative of the Shay Avenue families' lives, showing the complexity of forces at work spinning the families into the vortex of the legal and welfare systems. Second, the authors provide, in the latter half of the text, a searing critique of American schooling that isolates literacy activities to unlinked and often meaningless, trivial skills. A third force causing students to rethink their assumptions about the protagonists of the Shay Avenue families is their extended discussion with peers and teacher educator. In the third week of the course when students read this material, they already acknowledge the high value we place on questioning, on looking beyond one's own experiences to understand others and they begin to challenge one another.

Establishing such a climate for debate has been essential to the success of the course in encouraging the development of prospective teachers who are thinking hard about their ability to listen to and understand others. From the first week of the course, we acknowledge that scholars have been grappling for many years with the same questions we are addressing and without a single, unified conclusion. Therefore, there are few 'correct' answers or recipe-type responses to many of the questions we ask; rather, we are making our way together and relying on the published debates and other resources available to us. I ask students to read the words of excellent story-tellers to awaken passionate responses and to raise questions as well as confusions which will help prospective teachers challenge their beliefs about teachers and teaching, learners and learning, about themselves, and about people unlike themselves. I hope also to encourage beginning teachers to seek and tell what Thomas Barone (1988) has termed 'likely stories' about teaching diverse learners. Barone writes:

> A likely story is a carefully (if nonmethodologically) researched story that throbs with vivid, contextually detailed, dramatically fashioned aesthetic content. This content is comprised of observations that lay bare the meaning and significance of selected educational events from the characters — and of course, the author's point of view.... Indeed, likely stories are premised on the openness of the horizon, on Gadamer's fundamental notion that we cannot entirely escape our own ontologic situation, we do indeed seek to understand landscapes other than our own view. A story that lends itself to this process of understanding is more likely to render the horizons of others more accessible to the reader (1988, pp. 154–5).

One of the ways I hope to encourage prospective teachers to tell and learn from likely stories is through the six assignments of the course.

The Assignments

Students enrolled in the course are required to complete the following assignments:

1 a research paper
2 a parent interview
3 a series of observations of one child's school performance in language arts
4 a critique of one piece of computer software
5 a critique of one selection of children's literature, and
6 the construction of one teaching plan which is to include diverse persons' experiences and voices in the chosen instructional materials.

Each of these assignments relates to one or more questions of the course and is designed, like the readings, to cause students to question their beliefs and assumptions about literacy, about themselves, and about others like and unlike themselves. All assignments for the semester are explained briefly on the first day of class so that students may see the links between the various pieces of work they are to conduct over the semester. Later, we spend greater amounts of time discussing the individual assignments; for some, like the parent interview, we brainstorm questions, role play an interviewing situation, etc. On the day each assignment is due, we talk about what students learned from the work, about what remains puzzling, troubling, etc.

An early start for the research paper is especially important as the goal of this assignment is to allow students enrolled in the course to explore in depth one topic in the language arts as it relates to their personal interests and to one of the five central questions of the course. Early in the semester students are required to turn in an abstract of their planned paper, including a list of bibliographic resources which they have located. The design of such a project is a difficult task as few students have given prior thought to an area within the language arts of particular interest to them. While I offer possible topics to illustrate the breadth of possibilities for the paper, I primarily offer encouragement for students to follow their interests in answering one of the course questions. When at all possible, students are to link their library investigations of a topic with interviews of teachers, children, community members and also to the daily life of their practicum classroom.

An example of the sorts of investigation students choose to conduct is the project selected by a Mexican American student. Ana-Luz was returning to the university to complete an undergraduate degree relinquished ten years earlier for childrearing and clerical employment. As the mother of two young daughters, she was increasingly concerned that her children were not meeting images of people like themselves in the media or in school. Her dark-haired and dark-eyed kindergartner, Mariana, spent a great deal of time wishing for hair as blonde as that of many of her classmates. Ana-Luz was troubled as she wished Mariana to have a strong, positive self-image as a Mexican American. Therefore, she conducted a research project which brought her to both her daughter's elementary school classroom and to the research libraries on campus to investigate the school images of persons of color and those print and media publications available to schools.

The outcomes of this project were three-fold: Ana-Luz was chagrinned at the lack of available materials representing Mexican Americans, both in her daughter's room and in the marketplace at large. Yet, as a result of her investigations, she gathered titles of children's literature featuring positive images of Mexican American protagonists and distributed these lists to her classmates and to her daughter's kindergarten teacher and the librarian at her daughter's school. She included with these lists the names of local libraries and bookstores where the books could be found. She added a note to the teacher's and librarian's copy of the book lists, explaining that these were the outcome of a project for one of her courses and that she hoped the list would help the school locate resources which were in scarce supply. Second, Ana-Luz vowed to make her own future classrooms places where children of color and those of non-English language backgrounds saw themselves positively reflected. Last, Ana-Luz shared her work with her peers in the course. In a voice breaking with anger and frustration, she told her classmates of her pride in her native language and culture and of her desire to instill that pride in a youngster already suspicious that dark hair and dark eyes were not the hallmarks of success.

In Ana-Luz's presentation, she shared with her classmates the questions which had guided her actions with Mariana's teacher and school librarian. She asked: What consequences would result from a confrontation with the teacher or school principal if she were to challenge them about the paucity of multicultural images in their kindergarten? How could she, despite drawbacks of lack of time and money, provide resources for Mariana and her kindergarten classmates? How could she avoid encouraging what she called the 'pinata and taco syndrome'; — the frequent elementary school practice of devoting a single day or week to the foods and celebrations of a particular culture? As the other students considered her questions, one woman asked why Ana-Luz had not volunteered to read the books she had found in a story time in her daughter's room. Ana-Luz replied that while she had considered this activity, she wanted the teacher herself to own the responsibility of providing more multicultural resources to the classroom. Further, she feared that she, too, like tacos and pinatas, would be viewed by the children as a cultural oddity. Ana-Luz remarked, 'I can see it now — today, a Mexican lady, Mariana's mother, will be here to read to us about her country. End of Mexico. Next week, Africa!'

When Ana-Luz opened her questions for consideration by her classmates, everyone could benefit from as well as enhance her deliberations regarding school change. Many of the students in the class had not previously encountered anyone who personally brought such passion to her concerns for school change and were initially startled by the anger and bitterness evident in Ana-Luz's voice. Over time, however, their interactions with someone for whom our readings and discussion had daily, personal impact increased several students' interest and commitment to learn how to develop classrooms where all people were honored. Ana-Luz had long before begun to question the role of schooling in parceling out the economic and social capital of US culture and this assignment offered her the opportunity to follow a hunch about the environment of her daughter's class-room and school, to share her feelings about the inequities present in the school and to consider, with concerned peers, practical strategies for change. The project offered Ana-Luz's classmates the opportunity to share her reflections-in-action as well as develop their own personal investigations. The discussions the student teachers held moved beyond procedure, moved beyond dilemmas of 'how to' effect some teaching strategy to consideration of the questions which underlie teachers' actions.

Students begin the semester-long project in the first weeks of the term and continue to investigate the problem they have chosen for the remainder of the course. After determining their project topics, each student is asked to begin a second assignment, the interview of a parent of a school-age child. The parent should differ from the student on a minimum of one dimension of race, social class or gender. The three goals for the project include:

1 to help prospective teachers see the universals of caring for children which cross different races, social classes and gender;
2 to assist prospective teachers in viewing parents' different understandings of the expectations of schools in relation to learning literacy, and;
3 to assist prospective teachers in valuing communication with parents concerning children's needs, skills and achievements.

Over the years, this assisgnment has helped students develop a small win-dow on someone else's world. They find that while all parents care about their children, the parents' own past school and cultural experiences influence their views about school and their perceptions of how best to prepare their children for school. Many students choose to interview the parent of a child in their practi-cum clasroom; others are more comfortable in interviewing a neighbor or some-one whom they know as a co-worker from part-time or summer jobs. While those who interview the parent of a child in their classroom see most directly the links between parental expectations and preparation for school with a child's performance, all students profess a clearer understanding of one person's hopes, dreams and plans for a child following the assignment's completion.

The third assignment of the course requires students to conduct a series of observations and an analysis of one child's school performance in the language arts. The goal of this assignment is to understand the encouragements and constraints of one child's learning and to assist the child's teacher in planning for the child's greater school success and achievement in the language arts. Students interview the child and the teacher and closely observe the child in both formal and informal occasions of teaching and learning. Among the outcomes of this assignment are the surprise of students that a teacher has underestimated or misidentified a child's potential or skills. In this way, prospective teachers learn to develop a healthy skepticism for the labeling of learners and for the ready acceptance of others' diagnoses. They learn the value of withholding their judg-ments regarding learners until they personally have looked closely and weighed the evidence. They learn that the judgments of teachers have long-term conse-quences for children's lives.

The final three assignments of the semester are designed to orient students to choosing and using instructional materials. They are asked to critique literature for children and adolescents, to critique computer software and to construct an instructional plan that includes the experiences and voices of diverse persons. These assignments are designed to help prospective teachers think about building connections between home and school which will foster enjoyment and skills of reading and writing, listening and speaking, for all learners. Students are encouraged to revisit and critique favorite books and poetry from their own childhood as well as explore the array of new instructional materials which reflects the experiences of persons from a broad range of backgrounds.

The Teaching of Writing

These assignments, combined with the course readings and discussions, are designed to help prospective teachers become sensitive to the culture and lives of their pupils and to help them learn effective strategies for teaching skills of literacy — primarily the teaching of writing. Prospective teachers first need to hear their students' voices, then decide on instruction which weds effective practices of teaching writing to the knowledge, skills and needs of their diverse learners. Effective practices of teaching writing have been labeled by Hillocks as 'environmental' in nature, characterized by:

> (1) clear and specific objectives, such as to increase the use of specific detail and figurative language; (2) materials and problems selected to engage students with each other in specifiable processes important to some particular aspects of writing; and (3) activities such as small group problem-centered discussions, conducive to high levels of peer interaction concerning specific tasks. (1986, p. 144)

Hillocks contrasts this mode of instruction with those he calls 'presentational', the traditional school model of lecture followed by practice exercises graded by the teacher, and the 'natural process' model, in which writing is student-centered and the teacher offers little structure or direction to students.

Donovan (1978) notes the work of good writing teachers is demonstrated by the opportunities they create for tentative and searching discourse by their students, opportunities to establish perspectives on people, objects and ideas, opportunities to act as writers. In a recent paper, Nystrand (1990) also focuses on the significance of the actvity of learners of writing. He concludes:

> Perhaps the most important insight from recent research on composition is that effective writing instruction is less a matter of teaching knowledge about composition, rhetoric, or grammar to students and more a matter of promoting and refining the process of writing. English teachers need to think of writing as a verb, not a noun. In any case, information about writing (e.g., parts of speech, principles of rhetoric, types of paragraphs, etc.) makes best sense only in the context of the activity itself. That is why writing teachers' primary responsibility concerns initiating and sustaining appropriate writing activities and arranging for effective feedback.

Florio-Ruane and Dunn (1987) argue, however, that traditional school practices of teaching writing do not conform to Hillocks' 'environmental' model, do not reflect Nystrand's metaphor of teaching writing as a 'verb', nor do school practices allow students to generate meaning. Florio-Ruane and Dunn describe current clasroom models of teaching writing as follows:

1   Students generally write in response to teacher initiations.
2   Teachers tend to select the purposes and format of student writing.
3   Teacher response to student writing tends to be limited to product evaluation.
4   Product evaluation tends to focus on surface features of language rather than on meaning.
5   Little or no technical support is offered students during actual writing time.
6   Writing time is limited and considered a private time when peer interaction is discouraged.
7   Little time is spent writing first drafts, and revision is rarely undertaken by student writers.
8   Most school writing never leaves the school or classroom to be read by a wider audience. (p. 53)

Nystrand and Gamoran (1988) argue that those students placed in low ability groups are more likely to receive instruction of the type noted by Florio-Ruane and Dunn with heightened emphasis on 'clerical' — editing and fill-in-the blank type tasks — rather than on 'compositional' activities of writing. Others (e.g., Cole and Griffin, 1987) argue that students of color and those of low socioeconomic status are more likely to receive skill- and drill-type instruction than their schoolmates. Such decontextualized instruction in pieces of language does not provide the sorts of teaching researchers have found to be effective practice, nor does it engage writers in becoming what Delpit (1988, p. 297) cites as a critical factor in engaging low socioeconomic status students of color in writing, the power of becoming 'authentic chroniclers of their own experience'.

Therefore as we read, observe, and talk over the course of the semester, three guiding principles for the teaching of writing to diverse learners emerge:

1   that *all* learners require opportunities to write multiple drafts, engage in peer response groups, and edit their work while writing for real purposes and genuine audiences;
2   that writing instruction should focus on the lives of the students as a source of topics and materials for instruction; and
3   that a powerful theme that can tie together the writing curriculum and the learners' lives is the investigation of language, its variety of forms and uses.

Developing these principles in class and using their teaching experiences to both challenge and elaborate upon them allows prospective teachers who do not share the cultural, language, race or socioeconomic backgrounds of their students to be effective teachers of writing. However, such teaching requires that individual teachers relinquish ideals of *transferring* their subject matter knowledge to students and replace these with *transforming* themselves and their students into inquiry-oriented partners working together for understanding and the creation of effective texts. Such teaching allows children to fulfill their needs, in Taylor's and Dorsey-Gaines' (1988) words to 'create public and private text worlds with continual opportunities to use their expressive abilities to generate new meanings and maintain personal and shared interpretations of the social, technical, and aesthetic types and uses of literacy' (p. 201).

As we read, in mid-semester, Donald Graves' stories of White New Hampshire children daily writing stories, journals and observations, we test these principles against our imagined classrooms filled with the children of Taylor's and Dorsey-Gaines' and Rodriguez' stories. We ask — can the model of teaching and learning that works in rural New England also be viable in urban centres or with children of color, or poor children? We speculate — what are the potential challenges to these ideas working in other settings? Would urban children be as cooperative in peer editing groups — the students ask — as the rural children of whom Graves' writes? We take risks of practice — students with practicum placements in diverse settings use these three principles to shape their practice; they share their victories and defeats and as a group, we ponder the reasons for the outcomes of their lessons. We also read the work of teachers who have successfully conducted this sort of teaching with diverse populations of students at varied levels of schooling.

The stories of four such teachers stand out as being especially helpful to students in envisioning how to enact principles of transformation in a writing classroom. Reading the stories of teachers who have stretched themselves to learn with their students gives prospective teachers courage to try such activities for themselves. While the particular stories we read change as new work becomes available, this section of the course always begins with the reading of excerpts from the stories of Sylvia Ashton-Warner, a New Zealander who taught reading and writing to Maori youngsters by building a key sight word vocabulary based upon concepts which were meaningful in the children's home and community lives. Second, students read selections from Shirley Brice Heath's *Ways With Words* (1983), her inquiry into the habits and patterns of language use in the Carolina Piedmont which led to her engagement of teachers (enrolled in her graduate courses) in similar language investigations. Teachers working with Heath learned that they could look closely at the rituals, patterns and habits of language students brought to school and use these as a basis for teacher and student inquiry.

One selection from Heath's book which is particularly helpful for students trying to understand new ways of teaching and learning is the story of one elementary teacher's work with a small group of Black boys working together on a science project. The teacher led the children in a collaborative investigation of the gardening practices of community members. Following their interviews with good local gardeners, the children analyzed both the different activities of gardening which adults used, and the varied ways in which the gardeners used language to explain their endeavors. The children effectively used writing and speaking in different forms and for genuine and useful purposes, described and analyzed the language of community members, shared the work with interested others, as well as scored, for the first time, passing grades on tests regarding knowledge of science concepts.

A third story we read is that of Terry Dean (1989), a teacher of English as a Second Language and Basic Writing courses at the University of California-Davis. Dean provides another example of teaching that draws on effective, research-based practices of teaching writing and honors the knowledge and culture of learners while engaging students in inquiry about language and culture. Dean's classes, enrolled by students often bridging alien worlds of home and university, purposefully honor the diverse cultures of the student body and link them with the culture of the university via activities of learning to write — drafting, peer revising and publishing. Dean structures topics for writing focused on issues of language learning and use, provides opportunities for students to share their work in culturally diverse peer response groups and asks students to write class newsletters focused on generating knowledge about multicultural experiences. Dean explains the importance of structuring writing experiences around topics focused on issues of language learning and culture in this way:

> These topics and assignments not only help students mediate between home and school cultures, they provide windows for the teacher into the diversity within each of the cultures that students bring with them. They can serve as a base for ongoing teacher research into the ways in which home and university cultures interact. There simply is no training program for teachers and can be no definitive research study that will ever account for the realities our students bring with them. Change is constant. Each generation is different. Given the lack of homogeneity in our classes, given the incredible diversity of culture we are being exposed to, who better to learn from than our students? (1989, p. 36)

A fourth set of stories we have lately read come from African American scholar and poet June Jordan's writing about her teaching. Like Terry Dean, June Jordan has taught students who were bridging very different worlds of home and university campus life. Jordan's work seems especially important to read as White students can be surprised that while Jordan shared common racial ties with her students, she, too, was challenged by her students' understandings and skills of literacy. In Jordan's case, Black students in her English literature course, 'In Search of the Invisible Black Woman', were embarassed and disturbed by Alice Walker's use of Black English Vernacular (BEV) in her novel *The Color Purple*. Rather than choosing to transfer her understandings of Walker's purposes to her students, Jordan chose instead to transform herself in a learning partnership with her class. Together, they translated Walker's characters' conversation from Black English Vernacular to 'standard' English. This led to inquiry into the rules which govern BEV and requests from the students for Jordan to teach another course with a focus on language. The result was Jordan's commitment to teach 'The Art of Black English'. Of her decision, she writes:

> Most of the students had never before seen a written facsimile of the way they talk. None of the students had ever learned how to read and write their own verbal system of communication: Black English. Alternatively, this fact began to baffle or bemuse and then infuriate my students. Why not? Was it too late? Could they learn how to do it now? And ultimately, the final test question, the one testing my sincerity:

Could I teach them? Because I had never taught anyone Black English and, as far as I knew, no one, anywhere in the United States, had ever offered such a course, the best I could say was 'I'll try' (1988, p. 365).

In the following weeks, Jordan joined her students in investigation of how written BEV encodes its spoken form as well as how BEV differs from 'standard' English. In so doing, Jordan and the class learned the rules by which BEV is governed and wrote nineteen 'Guidelines for Black English'. The students gained an appreciation for differences between speaking and writing as well as discovered a pride and pleasure in language they had learned was 'incorrect'. As they worked, they discovered '. . . three qualities of Black English — the presence of life, voice, and clarity — that intensify to a distinctive Black value system' about which the class 'became excited' and 'consciously tried to maintain' (p. 367). Further, the class drew on their collectively discovered voice to write newspaper editorials (in BEV) decrying the murder of a Black classmate's brother by White policemen. They coupled their new understandings about language with their rage at the police, writing for real purposes and genuine audiences which lay beyond teachers' gradebooks and classroom walls.

The sort of teaching conducted by Heath, Dean, Jordan and others is difficult for many students to conceptualize as their own classroom experiences of learning to write have been largely of the worksheet, fill-in-the-blank type teaching in elementary school followed by practice in writing five paragraph themes in secondary school. Writing has also been confined, for many students, to language arts or English classes where themes were produced on an irregular basis. Thinking about teaching in these new ways, then, requires more than taking good class notes on 'activities to conduct with children'.

The opportunity to read and think about the teaching of writing conducted by Heath, Dean, Jordan and others offers prospective teachers new ways to think about their own teaching. Prospective teachers draw on the activities which these teachers and authors have conducted and try to enact these activities with their own practicum classes. For example, the prospective teachers attempt to use interviews and oral histories to engage their students in learning about language and about subject matter.

Prospective teachers also use the work of those they have read to generate questions about their teaching of writing. Recently, for example, several prospective teachers were placed in the same elementary school with cooperating teachers who wished them to celebrate the anniversary of the publication of a text by a noted children's author. The teachers asked that their student teachers adapt the text into a play format with children from their classrooms. At the time of this request, the prospective teachers had read the work of Shirley Brice Heath and June Jordan and were about to discuss Terry Dean's article. Three of the five prospective teachers working in the building raised questions concerning the wisdom of pursuing a project in which a text with a White male protagonist and his various 'monster friends' were the focus of learning. These three student teachers brought the following discussion to their peers: Was it wise to pursue the project of adapting the book to a play?

Children around the world had, for generations, enjoyed the book to be featured. Yet, nearly half of the children in the building were African Americans and a smaller percentage were children of Hispanic and Asian descent. Such a project, due to its size and scope, would supercede many other classroom-based writing projects for the semester. In light of Heath's, Dean's and Jordan's messages about linking literacy to the culture, language background and interests of learners, the project appeared flawed. How, the student teachers asked, were the backgrounds of half of the school population honored by the choice of this work for a school-wide writing project?

The prospective teachers at this school asked peers in their coursework and practicum to help them think through their dilemmas: Did student teachers have a 'right' to object to what was, on the surface, an innocuous and potentially exciting project for children? Given their hesitancy to endorse the project, how could they share their objections with their cooperating teachers? Finally, the student teachers asked, what, if any, projects should replace the one the teachers had promulgated?

Given their hesitancy to endorse the project, how could some students best share their objections to the project with their cooperating teachers? Finally, the student teachers asked if any project they supported should replace the one the cooperating teachers had promulgated. Lengthy in-class discussions were followed by meetings of the class members (outside of regularly scheduled class time) to determine whether they should endorse a project which did not more closely link the home lives, experiences and backgrounds of the building's children.

As a result of the student teachers' deliberations, each spoke individually with her cooperating teacher about the dilemma she believed was posed by participation in the play development. Nearly all of the cooperating teachers were receptive to the student teachers' questions about the links between the proposed writing and literature project. For a complex set of reasons, including those put forth by the student teachers, enthusiasm for the play adaptation project waned over the spring semester. In the long run, no play was written, nor was any school-wide writing project initiated. The student teachers continued to enthusiastically lead individual projects which incorporated aspects of the writing Heath, Dean, Jordan and others endorsed. As a result of their reflection-in-action, the students were pleased; they had deliberated as a group about a significant issue of curriculum and instruction and had positively affected the curriculum of the building in which they worked. They also learned about the power of working with one's teacher peers for school change.

In addition to the challenges faced by student teachers questioning the curriculum of the schools in which they work, students also face challenges related to the willingness of cooperating teachers and graduate student supervisors to enable them to enact the ideas *they* bring to the classrooms. While there exist varying formal and informal mechanisms for sharing with supervisors the goals of individual faculty and staff courses, there are far less systematic means for similarly sharing course goals with individual cooperating teachers. While supervisors carry syllabi to individual teachers, neither busy cooperating teachers nor supervisors with as many as eighteen to twenty practicum students to supervise have adequate time for extended discussion of the coursework in which students are enrolled at the time of their practicum. Some students meet resistance on the part of cooperating teachers in enacting their plans; others are told they can create lessons of their choosing, yet must complete the spelling workbook, basal reader and language arts/grammar book lessons, as well. Clearly, as a teacher education program, we require better mechanisms in which to articulate the goals of particular courses and/or semesters of the program to the individual teachers with whom we work.

A further constraint to articulating such goals with cooperating teachers in various school districts is the autonomy enjoyed by faculty teaching courses of the same name and assumed similar purposes. While the faculty and staff teaching in the 'language arts semester' share some common goals and perspectives, e.g., teaching a processs approach to writing and an emphasis on 'whole language' approaches to teaching, all do not use the education of diverse learners as a central theme of their courses. So, too, do the schools in which our students practice their teaching vary. While some buildings and indeed, entire nearby communities in which our students teach are composed of white, lower- and middle-class persons, others like Madison, have a population of persons of color which has doubled to nearly 18 per cent in the last decade. In Madison, some elementary buildings enroll as many as 40 per cent children of color, many of whom live in poverty. Attending these same schools are the children of university faculty, business people, etc. Prospective teachers placed in these buildings do have the opportunity to teach diverse learners; others, peers who teach in other nearby suburban areas, will teach children whose lives vary by socioeconomic status, but vary little by race, language background or ethnicity. Prospective teachers, then, have varying opportunities to think through the intentions of the course in relation to children in their classrooms.

While these constraints do exist, the students are remarkably responsive to ideas they meet in the work of the course. Naturally, not all are convinced that teachers need to stretch themselves in ways suggested here; a few openly resist the ideas of the course throughout the semester. Stephen, for example, spoke out throughout the course and also visited with me a few weeks after the semester's conclusion. 'I just don't know', he said, 'these people [people unlike himself] you talk about, they need to work harder, they need to try harder. Life isn't going to work out unless you really try'. Stephen, married and the parent of a young child, worked as a janitor every day after class in the rural school district in which he lived. His spouse, a practical nurse, also drove a long distance to her job every day and took responsibility for their daughter's daycare arrangements. Stephen could not understand why other people could not also make these arrangements and sacrifices to meet their goals. His prior life experiences and years as a classroom participant did not prepare him for the students about whom he read in his books nor those who sat in his practicum classroom. Experiences in one course were insufficient to change his views.

Other students quietly conduct the work of the course and appear to struggle with its ideas, yet also fail to integrate these into their existing world view. Like a recent student named Bonnie, they continue to rely on their personal experiences to guide their understandings of teaching and learning. As she listened to her classmates' research presentations, Bonnie responded to ideas about teaching a 'whole language' approach to primary grade children. She said, 'It [integrating the teaching of reading and writing] all sounds good, but I still am going to use basal readers. Kerry [her daughter] loves those little stories; she is so proud when she finishes reading them; she loves those stars, too' (rewards for correctly answered workbook pages). Clearly, their knowledge and dispositions about learners and learning, as well as their orientations towards challenging prior beliefs and practices, were left largely unchanged by Stephen's and Bonnie's fifteen weeks of work in my course.

The impact of the course is less clear on most students. It is often not until nearly one year later when they are completing their student teaching that many students return to share the ways in which they have challenged their own taken-for-granted and conventional beliefs about learners, learning and teaching. A few students write or phone from Milwaukee, Minneapolis or suburban Wisconsin years after they have left the program to tell about times they have challenged their immediate understandings of a student or her skills or family life and have subsequently found a way to enhance a child's life. At the present time we lack, yet are collecting, data concerning the impact of our teacher education program on our students' dispositions for and skills of teaching diverse learners and their ability to daily re-examine their classroom practices. I am hopeful that a research project in which I currently work (studying a cohort group of our students) will yield information regarding work yet to be done on developing teachers who are skillful at thinking hard about their classroom life and about teaching diverse learners.

Our nation already faces schooling dilemmas which are made more urgent by the rapidly increasing numbers of diverse learners in our population. The failure to educate nearly half of our children in the next decades foretells disaster for us all. We must meet the social and economic challenges of the next decades with citizens who are skilled as thinkers as well as skilled as workers. This requires a population of teachers who speak *and* enact a language of opportunity, a discourse of possibility, for *all* children. Failure to enact such a promise for our youth is our collective failed creative and intellectual, social and economic harvest.

Afterword

As I wrote this story, I challenged my perspectives with the responses of friends and colleagues. One memorable response came from a Mexican American colleague who teaches third grade in a local elementary school. Pilar is a talented teacher often requested by parents disparate in race, language and socioeconomic background. As we talked of the urgency of recruiting and educating teachers worthy of the challenges that lay before them in the next decades, she shared a story of her own youth which underscores the critical difference a single teacher can make in a lifetime for one child:

> Mike Rose is right, you know, children do work and connect with one teacher and it makes all the difference. I will never forget my second grade teacher; he is the reason I am here today. We were a family of farmworkers, we moved, we couldn't count on knowing the curriculum taught in the fall. Yet, when my brothers and sisters and I showed up (in January in a Texas classroom), he taught us material we had missed. He cared; he made time; he pushed himself to understand my family's ways; he shared his knowledge and skills. I will never forget him. I'd like to think there is at least one teacher like mine in every child's life.

So, too, would I; better yet, I hope for a succession of teachers reaching out beyond their immediate understandings to respond to someone else's story, linking home and community with schooling, using their knowledge and skills to enhance all learners' lives.

Notes

1   I use the term diverse learners in this paper to highlight attention to the children populating US classrooms who are of low socioeconomic status, are children of color, and those of non-English language backgrounds.
2   My thinking about the education of diverse learners has been greatly influenced by listening to four decades of powerful storytelling by my father, Manuel Gomez, whose own education and opportunities have been irrevocably marked by racism. In the past decade, my thinking on this subject in relation to teacher education has been influenced by conversations with Elizabeth Ellsworth, Maureen Gillette, Carl Grant, Julie Kailin, Walter Secada, Bob Tabachnick and Ken Zeichner.
3   The names of children, prospective teachers, teachers and, in the case of Black River School, a building and community, have been given pseudonyms.
4   The National Writing Project is a staff development effort founded by Professor James Gray of the University of California, Berkeley, aimed at educating class-room teachers in the teaching of writing.
5   Stephanie is the pseudonym of a teacher whom I followed through her graduate program of teacher education and first year of teaching in a project funded by the National Center for Research on Teacher Education, Michigan State University.

References

AACTE (1987) Teacher education enrollment survey, Fall 1987. Washington, D.C.: Author.

ASCD (1989, May) 'Equity expert faults "choice" plan', *ASCD Update*, **31**, 3, p. 2.

BARONE, T.E. (1988) 'Curriculum platforms and literature', in BEYER, L.E. and APPLE, M.W. (Eds) *The Curriculum: Problems, Politics, and Possibilities*, pp. 140–65, Albany, NY: State University of New York Press.

CENTER FOR EDUCATION STATISTICS (1987a) *The Condition of Education*, Washington, D.C.: Government Printing Office.

CENTER FOR EDUCATION STATISTICS (1987b) *Digest of Education Statistics*, Washington, D.C.: Government Printing Office.

CHAMBERS ERASMUS, C. (1989) 'Ways with stories: Listening to the stories Aboriginal peoples tell', *Language Arts*, **66**, 3, pp. 267–75.

COLE, M. and GRIFFIN, P. (1987) *Contextual Factors in Education: Improving Science and Mathematics Education for Minorities and Women*, Madison, WI: Wisconsin Center for Education Research, University of Wisconsin-Madison.

COLES, R. (1989) *The Call of Stories*, Boston, MA: Houghton Mifflin Company.

DARLING-HAMMOND, L. (1988) *The Evolution of Teacher Policy*, Santa Monica, Ca.: Center for Policy Research In Education, Rand Corporation.

DEAN, T. (1989) 'Multicultural classrooms, monocultural teachers', *College Composition and Communication*, **40**, 11, pp. 23–7.

DELPIT, L. (1988) 'The silenced dialogue: Power and pedagogy in educating other people's children', *Harvard Educational Review*, **58**, 3, pp. 280–98.

DONOVAN, T. (1978) 'Seeing students as writers', *Composition and Teaching*, **1**, pp. 13–16.

DYSON, A.H. (1989) *Multiple Worlds of Child Writers: Friends Learning to Write*, New York, NY: Teacher's College Press.

FLORIO-RUANE, S. and DUNN, S. (1987) 'Teaching writing: Some perennial questions and some possible answers', in RICHARDSON-KOEHLER, V. (Ed.) *Educator's Handbook: A Research Perspective*, pp. 50–83, White Plains, N.Y.: Longman.

GEORGIADES, W. (1988) 'The new America for the third millenium', in ORLOSKY, D.E. (Ed.) *Society, Schools, and Teacher Preparation*, pp. 25–30, A Report of the Commission on the Future Education of Teachers. (Teacher Education Monograph No. 9). Washington, D.C.: ERIC Clearinghouse on Teacher Education.

GIL, W. (1989) 'Who will teach minority youth?' *Educational Leadership*, **46**, 8, p. 83.

GRANT, C. and SECADA, W. (1990) 'Preparing teachers for diversity', in HOUSTON, R.W., HABERMAN, M. and SIKULA, J. (Eds) *Handbook of Research on Teacher Education*, New York: Macmillan.

GRAVES, D.H. (1983) *Writers: Teachers and Children at Work*, Portsmouth, NH: Heinemann Educational Books.

HABERMAN, M. (1989) 'More minority teachers', *Kappan*, **70**, 10, pp. 771–6.

HEATH, S.B. (1983) *Ways with Words: Language, Life, and Work in Communities and Classrooms*, Cambridge: Cambridge University Press.

HILLOCKS, G. (1986) *Research in Written Composition: New Directions for Teaching*, Urbana, Ill.: Conference on Research in English and ERIC Clearinghouse on Reading and Communication Skills, National Institute of Education.

HISPANIC POLICY DEVELOPMENT PROJECT (1988) *Closing the Gap for US Hispanic Youth: Public/Private Strategies*, Washington, D.C.: Author.

JORDAN, J. (1988) 'Nobody mean more to me than you and the future life of Willie Jordan', *Harvard Educational Review*, **58**, 3, pp. 363–74.

KENNEDY, M.M., JUNG, R.K. and ORLAND, M.S. (1986) *Poverty, Achievement, and the Distribution of Compensatory Education Services*, (An interim report from the National Assessment of Chapter I, OERI), Washington, D.C.: Government Printing Office.

MCLAREN, P. (1989) *Life in Schools: An Introduction to Critical Pedagogy in the Foundations of Education*, White Plains, NY: Longman.

NYSTRAND, M. (1990) 'On teaching writing as a verb rather than as a noun: Research on writing for high school English teachers', in HAWISHER, G. and SOTER, A. (Eds) *On Literacy and its Teaching: Issues in English Education*, Albany, N.Y.: State University of New York Press.

NYSTRAND, M. and GAMORAN, A. (1988) *A Study of Instruction as Discourse*, Madison, WI: National Center for Research on Effective Secondary Schools.

RODRIGUEZ, R. (1982) *Hunger of Memory: An Autobiography, the Education of Richard Rodriguez*. Toronto, Canada: Bantam Books.

ROMERO, M., MERCADO, M. and VAZQUEZ-FARIA, J.A. (1987) 'Students of limited English proficiency', in RICHARDSON-KOEHLER, V. (Ed.) *Educator's Handbook: A Research Perspective*, pp. 348–69, White Plains, N.Y.: Longman.

ROSE, M. (1989) *Lives on the Boundary*, New York, NY: Penguin Books.

STRONG, L.A. (1989) 'The best kids they have', *Educational Leadership* **46**, (5), p. 2.

TAYLOR, D. and DORSEY-GAINES, C. (1988) *Growing up Literate: Learning from Inner-City Families*, Portsmouth, N.H.: Heinemann Educational Books.

WHEELOCK, A. and DORMAN, G. (1989) *Before It's Too Late*, Boston, MA: Massachusetts Advocacy Council.

7   Teacher Education, Reflective Inquiry and Moral Action

Landon E. Beyer

In an essay that sparked a great deal of interest at the time of its publication, and one that may still enjoy fairly wide theoretical appeal, William Heard Kilpatrick (1918) asks two preliminary questions about 'the project method':

> First, is there behind the proposed term ['project'] and waiting even now to be christened a valid notion or concept which promises to render appreciable service in educational thinking? Second, if we grant the foregoing, does the term 'project' fitly designate the waiting concept? (p. 319)

Now I find myself thinking about both these questions with respect to 'reflective teaching' and associated terms that have become reasonably popular in the teacher education literature in the last ten to fifteen years. A concern for developing professional teachers who are reflective, able to engage in ongoing, classroom-based inquiry, and who are academically and emotionally sensitive practitioners has become an increasingly common one (see, for example, Popkewitz, 1987; Smyth, 1987; Liston and Zeichner, 1987). Especially in contrast to an educational vision dedicated to the training of prospective teachers as managers or technicians, able to efficiently transmit, orchestrate and evaluate the acquisition of forms of knowledge, skills and attitudes through a predefined set of activities and objectives handed down by others; there is a growing emphasis on reconceptualizing teaching so that the creative, autonomous, committed nature of teachers' work is recognized, thereby reconstructing what it means to be a professional (Beyer, Feinberg, Pagano and Whitson, 1989). In short, 'reflective teaching' as at least some sort of ideal seems to have attracted a sizeable number of adherents in the recent past, promising an alternative that moves beyond the mainstream of teacher preparation. Yet I am reminded of Kilpatrick's questions: is there a valid concept here that promises to provide significant service, and does 'reflective teaching' name this concept? There are at two related areas of difficulty addressed in this chapter.

First, it is not always clear that people who use the term 'reflective teaching' have the same idea or concept in mind, share an understanding of how reflective teaching is to proceed, or agree on how teaching or teacher education would change, in substance and in practice, if this idea were made central to the preparation of teachers. On the one hand, it is fairly easy (perhaps too easy) to contrast the dominant patterns of education in the US with some conception of reflective teaching. The tendency for routinized, habitual, deskilled activities to dominate within classrooms is well documented, both historically and in the contemporary literature on teaching (see, for instance, Apple, 1982; Cuban, 1984; Sizer, 1984; Sirotnik, 1988; Beyer and Apple, 1988). Such routinization of teaching is an important fact of school life for students and teachers alike. On the other hand, I take it as nearly axiomatic that all teachers 'reflect' on *something*, along certain lines, using particular frames of reference, etc., during the course of their teaching day, even those teaching within the most deskilled of teaching environments. The absence of any sort of reflection (regarding students, various classroom activities aimed at pupil socialization, the results of spelling tests, the phone call from an irate parent, the latest directive from the administration, school board, or state department official, and so on) seems unlikely if not counter intuitive. The nature of this reflection, of course, is quite variable, and may have little to do with the kind of systematic analysis and inquiry coveted in the academy. And here lies a central issue. Without a theoretical framework that addresses the sort of reflection that is being sponsored by any particular approach to 'reflective teaching', we will be at a loss to make judgments about its attainment and value within the context of public school classrooms, and how this approach is to become manifest in programs of teacher preparation. So while it is well and good to emphasize reflective teaching as a central aspect of what it means to be a practitioner, a careful analysis of reflection — one that helps us understand the nature, aim and process of the activities associated with a particular view of reflection — is needed if this alternative to technical training is to be viable.

Second, models of what reflective practice might imply for teaching and teacher education that have their origins in other professions (e.g., Schon, 1983) or in a theoretical analysis — even one that is more conceptually rigorous in the ways suggested in the preceding paragraph — can help illuminate the contours of critical reflection for teachers. Yet what these models and analyses concretely mean for the practices of teacher preparation is not always so clear. That is, a theoretical framework for reflective teaching must not only be worked out and clarified, but the particular configurations of teacher education programs, courses and policies that will help enact this framework must also be addressed. This is perhaps a more difficult, and more pressing, problem than the theoretical issue already addressed; better, it is clear that these problems must be seen as conjoined, as we work toward a view of teacher preparation founded upon a conception of teaching as moral action (Beyer, 1988a).

The Possibilities for Reflection and 'Reflective Teaching'

Deterrents to reflective inquiry can come in many shapes: for example, in the guise of bureaucratic and other structures that are used to impose a regularity, given-ness and an apparently self-evident commonsense; such regularities make routine action seem like the only kind possible. Or, given a situation where physical actions within an occupation are routine, requiring only a small portion of our conscious attention, we are apt to reflect on activities or possibilities that lie outside the situation in which we are immersed. Given the repetitive and uninteresting nature of work on an assembly line, for example, we may well engage in prolonged reflection, but on some person or event outside the immediate set of circumstances, thereby providing a kind of escape from current drudgery. We may call this 'escapist reflection'. This can include activities that range from the relatively common day dreaming that we all exhibit from time to time, to the more cultivated forms of feigned attention we give to tasks that have little or no inherent meaning or apparent value. Such reflection, while common, adds nothing to an expanded awareness of or sensitivity to the work in which we are involved, and is thus of little relevance (aside from indicating something of possible personal and social consequence about the nature of the work itself) in understanding the meaning of reflective teaching.

At a different level, we may use the non-directed time we have to ourselves to reflect on our own situations and predicaments. Such reflection leads us to an inward-looking perspective, variously described as 'getting in touch with ourselves', becoming introspective, creating opportunities for self-analysis, and other forms of psychological reflection. Such situations create the possibility for what I shall call 'therapeutic reflection', and can be distinguished from escapist reflection by its focus and aim. Instead of a situation in which a loss of personal meaning becomes a catalyst for escape from that sort of alienation, we may use it as an opportunity to self-consciously analyze our emotional or psychological states — even as an opportunity to think through a pressing personal problem, say. In any case, such reflection is not so much given over to sheer entertainment or amusement, but to a sort of self-analysis that may produce some measure of personal understanding.

Yet such therapeutic reflection, drawing us exclusively (obsessively?) inward, misses the socially and professionally emancipatory possibilities of reflection — as, of course, does escapist reflection. Both miss the important aspect of experience as integrating the personal and collective, the psychological and the social (Dewey, 1916; Greene, 1978). This is not to deny that there are important emotional and psychological aspects to all experience, nor that these may be quite profound. Rather, it is to claim that since people cannot be islands unto themselves, any psychological reflection that does not lead us outward, into the world, and that does not help connect 'inner' states with 'outer' realities, is at best partial, at worst narcissistic (see Lasch, 1978). Therapeutic reflection, even if from time to time personally insightful, cannot be the basis for the kind of socially contextualized reflection on concrete practice that is the concern of teachers. Like escapist reflection that uses an imaginary state as its point of departure, as it were, therapeutic reflection seems ill suited to the professional contexts of teaching.

A third possibility for reflection, one that I believe dominates (for good reasons) within the practices of many teachers, involves 'commonsense' reflection on a particular classroom situation or problem. In general, this sort of reflection utilizes the themes, categories and frames of reference that have developed within the mainstream codes of a particular profession. For virtually any setting or occupation, categories, values, perspectives and ways of thinking are developed that constitute a way of seeing and making sense of that situation. This is not to suggest that some individual or small group of people is able to define a situation in a way that allows them to manipulate those who find themselves within it; rather, a dominant culture develops which helps practitioners understand their situations, how they are to evaluate those situations and their own successes and failures within them, and even what alternatives exist to the status quo. In other words, reflection in this sense entails using the accepted definitions, categories and ways of thinking and feeling that have been developed historically within the context of that practice.

Within the confines of teaching and teacher education in the US the development of a mainstream culture has had a long and important history, which can only be summarized here. We have inherited a system of teacher preparation that in the nineteenth century consciously sought to avoid social and political controversy as it fought for professional acceptance within local communities (Cremin, 1957; Mattingly, 1975; Beyer, Feinberg, Pagano and Whitson, 1989). This desire for social acceptance within the community and intellectual consensus within the school served to keep hidden the broader social and ideological purposes served by the inclusion of values, dispositions and attitudes within the 'commonsensical' mores and norms of the institution (Nasaw, 1979; Tyack, 1974). Within normal schools and other teacher training institutions, the sort of liberal education found in colleges and universities was seen as impractical, so that the stress tended to be placed on vocational preparation for a trade — one dominated by social class, gender and racial/ethnic determinants that themselves became a part of the 'definition of the situation' that was embedded within the dominant culture of teaching. Being a professional within the context of the public schools meant avoiding controversial political and moral issues even as the 'proper' values and habits were taught so as to socialize troublesome immigrant, working-class and poor children; treating knowledge as something objective and trans-historical (as revealed through Protestant teachings and the Bible, say); being careful to follow the wishes of the local community-even when women teachers were, as a result, made subservient to the wishes of the local community and its male leaders (Kaufman, 1984); and, within normal schools, especially later in the nineteenth century, the development of a technical, pragmatic, largely vocational training where subject matters and activities were often directly tied to the perceived requirements of common school teaching.

The subsequent emphasis on making teaching and teacher training more scientific, predictable and capable of predetermined, socially useful outcomes had several consequences. It resulted in an attention to the scientific management of curriculum in which waste would be eliminated and socioeconomic 'needs' met (Kliebard, 1986, especially chapter 4), a variety of mental and other standardized tests via the emerging field of eductional psychology that would measure ability, and the inculcation of 'necessary' traits and dispositions for the new industrial age. Like the earlier traditions of teaching and teacher preparation, the modern approach to these fields tended to emphasize the presumably asocial, non-ideological, 'neutral' perspectives from which to judge students' academic achievements and socialization.

It should be clear that the type of reflection countenanced by the mainstream culture of schooling and teacher preparation has been dominated by an allegedly non-political, instrumental, socially functional perspective that tended more and more, as the twentieth-century progressed, to be enamored with the search for a science of education that would result in predictable, certain results. While this is not the whole story of the American educational system, of course, and while there were always counter-cultural groups that attempted to shape the teaching profession in alternative ways, the dominant culture of the profession continues to play an important role in shaping teachers' possibilities for reflection. As Sirotnik (1988) concludes, on the basis of the research conducted in *A Study of Schooling*, there is an apparent contradiction between what we say we want schools to do and what they actually have done and continue to do. If goal statements were written for schools that reflect the contemporary realities of schooling, they would include:

> ... to develop in students the abilities to think linearly, depend upon authority, speak when spoken to, work alone, become socially apathetic, learn passively and nonexperientially, recall information, follow instructions, compartmentalize knowledge, and so on. (p. 62)

Such deduced goal statements tell us much about the quality of life for students within the institution of schooling, and provide a glimpse of the cultural context of teaching. Another indicator of the current culture of the school, and its more specific effects on the treatment of teachers, is provided by the Boston Women's Teachers' Group (n.d.):

> ... the debate over seniority versus merit [in deciding upon layoffs] is never discussed within the context of teaching as an occupation requiring less and less critical thinking, originality, and creativity. As more and more administrative decisions are made for the teacher by the school or the school system, the teacher's role is returned to that of dispenser of various prepackaged curriculum systems. 'Merit' in such situations can only mean adherence to pre-established dicta. (p. 19)

As the context within which education takes place is increasingly taken for granted — with its gender, social class, racial and ideological characteristics increasingly taken for granted — the tendency for technical language, instrumental/rationalized procedures, apolitical forms of analysis and individualistic frames of reference to become integrated into a common cultural code becomes manifest. As these ways of thinking and acting within the institution become accepted as part of the 'definition of the situation', they foster what I will call a pattern of 'procedural/technical reflection'.

Within this sort of reflection, emphasis may be placed upon such things as judgments regarding the success of curricula in raising student test scores, the degree to which students acquire the 'appropriate' work and study habits, whether students are achieving up to 'grade level' in the various subject matters, whether social relationships are formed within the accepted parameters of the institution, and so on. Such reflection is procedural or technical in the sense that it uncritically incorporates the dominant characteristics of the culture of the profession, and then attempts to measure the results of instruction to ascertain whether the appropriate procedures have been utilized. In so doing, procedural/technical reflection leaves unchallenged the accepted traditions and conventions of the profession, the ways of thinking and feeling that have characterized what it means to teach and be schooled.

In pointing to some of the shortcomings of procedural/technical reflection, I am not suggesting that there is some inherent limitation in teachers' judgment or sensitivity that leads them to limit reflection to the frames of reference and perspectives that have been dominant in teacher education and the practice of teaching. I am not, in other words, positing some sort of personal or psychological flaw in teachers that results in this rather limited reflection. Instead, I am suggesting that the way teachers are often prepared — the ways in which we treat questions of knowledge and social structure, and those dealing with normative issues and political interests within teacher preparation — plus the culture that tends to dominate in public educational institutions in the US, together constitute a powerful set of professional and institutional values that shape teachers' ways of thinking in particular ways. Nor is the preponderance of procedural/technical reflection exclusively traceable to developing mental states of mind in prospective teachers that are reinforced by compatible expectations in schools. For just as ideological presuppositions built into school practice extend ways of thinking acquired in teacher preparation, the very material and physical contexts of schooling reinforce ways of acting that are consistent with these dominant presuppositions. That elementary school classrooms often contain twenty five or thirty children, with quite diverse backgrounds, needs and interests, leads teachers to make decisions almost constantly, with little time for anything but procedural reflection; again, that teaching tends to be an isolated activity, done without benefit of collegial exchange and cooperative planning, and without support for alternative practices and directions, leads to a sort of reification, where 'what is' becomes a substitute for 'what ought to be'; that technical models for planning, enacting and evaluating curricula tend to dominate more and more has a corrosive effect on the possibility of locally produced projects and activities; and that evaluation of teaching tends to be along bureaucratic and technical lines — are Ms Allen's second graders scoring at or above the norm in reading, is Ms Brown keeping her pupils 'on task', why aren't the fourth grade teachers better able to control their students during recess, and the like — diminishes the likelihood of risk-taking among teachers. It is not that teachers are generally lacking in personal qualities or in intellectual capabilities, but that the context within which they work reinforces the parameters, often acquired earlier, within which reflection takes place.

The existence of these impediments within the workplace of teaching gives rise to a fourth possibility for reflection, what I shall call 'ameliorative reflection'. Basically, teachers who practice this sort of reflection recognize the physical, psychological and bureaucratic constraints with which they must deal, and critique those constraints, because of their effects on both students and teachers. Many teachers dislike and actively resist the contemporary push for goals, as we saw in Sirotnik's (1988) study, that foster in students linear thinking, dependence upon authority, obedience and the passive learning of knowledge that is highly compartmentalized. In response, teachers may try to emphasize more active and cooperative learning, lessen dependence upon authoritarian social relations and institute at least some non-didactic teaching. In embodying such alternative approaches to teaching, they strive mightily to alter the ways of thinking, seeing and valuing that accompany the dominant culture of the school and of teaching, and the procedural/technical reflection that accompanies them. Thus, ameliorative reflection that seeks to create a more humane, creative, interactive context for teaching has much to recommend it, as it attempts to move away from the more traditional practices in schooling.

Yet even this ameliorative reflection on teaching does not, in my view, go far enough in altering the status quo. While such reflection may be the best that we can do at any given time in many school contexts, teacher educators must strive to foster a deeper, more complex mode of reflection with students, if reflective teaching is to truly aid in the reconstruction of schooling and the society from which many of its values and ways of thinking are derived.

Critical Reflection and Teacher Education

What is missing from ameliorative reflection in classrooms is a connection between school practice and the interrelated contexts within which it takes place and which provide a substantial part of its meaning. That is, the procedural/technical nature of teaching and teacher reflection isolates school phenomena; in an attempt to be 'scientific' or 'professional' or socially accepted, we have defined our jobs in predominantly apolitical, non-ideological terms, isolating in the process the school, our classroom and our students. Similarly, teachers who embody an ameliorative perspective try to alleviate some of the more immediately constraining influences on classroom life, without connecting these to ideas, values and actions that are not especially visible within the immediate confines of educational institutions, as perceived through the frames of reference sanctioned by the dominant culture of schooling.

Part of the problem here is that we usually posit two separate 'spheres' or areas of influence, the school and the wider society; then, even within a good deal of literature that wants to make the latter a subject of discussion and critique, connections or bridges must be built that connnect these spheres, allowing us to discuss possible overlaps or linkages between them. Critical reflection, on the other hand, must begin with a more integrated, synthetic vision of education — one that is of a piece with some social, political and ideological set of commitments — even if these differ from those which now exist. Instead of conceptualizing 'education' and 'society' as two distinct entities which are perhaps related in some causal or even dialectical way, we do better to see education and society as coextensive. Further, this entails thinking carefully and imaginatively about why things happen as they do in schools, and what alternatives we might build together.

Such an emphasis places a premium on critical inquiry into present predicaments without becoming cynical or defeatist, and thinking through alternative ideas and practices without becoming naively utopian. It requires a teacher education program based on praxis. Instead of escapist, therapeutic, procedural/technical or ameliorative reflection, teaching is seen as a field of moral action in which critical reflection on the schools of society is valued.

Central to this mode of reflection, as enacted in the programs within the Department of Education at Knox College, is the following. First, the development of a historical consciousness. Rather than regarding schools, educational policies and practices, and teacher preparation as somehow 'natural' or given, we discuss the various groups that have vied for control of schooling, and the values, interests and perspectives schools have served. This does several things. It undermines the assumption that schools were designed 'for the benefit of all', and that their workings are disconnected from more general social, political and ideological realities. For instance, we discuss at length the meaning of teaching as it was filtered through gender, class and racial categories that shaped the nature of schooling. At the same time, seeing the constructed nature of schooling and teaching makes at least potentially possible its reconstruction, along alternative lines. Examining both historical continuities and discontinuities, we may together conceive of an alternative future. Seeing that the world of schooling is a *constructed* one, rather than a *discovered* or 'naturally generated' one, we may help make possible a different world.

Second, this approach to reflective teaching emphasizes the relationship between the hidden and overt curriculum, forms of evaluation, pedagogical approaches and social relations within the classroom as allied with the dynamics of social power. Not only must certain forms of knowledge be excluded from the classroom because of a finite amount of time, for example, but particular forms of knowledge (either some group's knowledge that lacks social power, or an approach to a subject matter that resists 'official' interpretations of events and people, alternative ways of thinking about a subject matter, non-mainstream interpretations of significant events, and so on) are rejected for political and ideological reasons. Thus a central question becomes how to take a moral stand on the issue of 'which knowledge is of most worth', and the politics of this process of deliberation.

Third, much of the reflection that takes place is related to developing options, alternatives and possibilities with students that require the creation of autonomous, creative, independent and critical inquirers. For example, instead of relying on prepackaged curriculum at the elementary level, these become the object of pedagogical and ideological critique. Questions then arise, such as: What are the visions of the student and the teacher contained in these materials? How much autonomy do they require or permit? What sort of social relations do they support or require? What sort of people will be judged to be 'successful' as a result of undergoing this curriculum? and, What sort of world am I helping to build through this process? Again, instead of emphasizing the technical procedures associated with much curriculum development, students are asked to develop their own platforms which, together with more concrete subject matter and social interaction preferences, can result in their own curricular materials and activities.

Fourth, running through the entire program is a commitment to praxis. This refers to a commitment to critical reflection — for example, on the origins of what we regard as social and educational commonsense, whose interests it serves, what alternatives exist or can be created, and how this is related to our own moral and political positions. Rather than accepting uncritically notions of what is 'given' and 'commonsensical', and regarding these as beyond the purview of programs for preparing future teachers, such reflection on commonsense is a crucial aspect of virtually all courses in our program. A concern for praxis, thus, also entails a consideration of alternative ideas and practices. In addition to considering critiques and criticisms of 'what is', students are involved in creating both alternative perspectives and divergent practices within schools that can bring to life 'what ought to be'. Praxis also includes a sensitivity to the dynamics of power within educational institutions and within the array of social, political, economic and ideological constraints in which schools are embedded. In taking a relational perspective on schooling, this commitment to praxis entails a view of the social relations, values and habits of mind and heart that occur in schools that recognizes how these 'internal' dynamics of schools are related to the dynamics of power in society. One central concern in fostering this commitment to praxis is to help students develop an understanding and awareness of current realities (in classrooms and other settings) without reifying them; just as we hope to foster the development of alternative ways of thinking, seeing and valuing without romanticizing their plausibility within the current context. To deny the authenticity of current realities or to suppose that they can be overcome simply with the development of 'better ideas' is to engage in a form of Idealism antithetical to praxis; similarly, to focus only on the current predicaments of schooling, without struggling to develop other possible ideas and strategies for intervention, is to regard the current reality as the only viable one. Neither course of action is tenable. Praxis entails a familiarity with current reality without being overcome by it, and a commitment to reflection on alternatives that is based in part in concrete action. This requires that we see reflection and action as mutually reinforcing, and that we walk a sort of intellectual and ideological tightrope, giving in neither to cynicism about 'what is' nor to idealism about how to create 'what might yet be'.

A central theme of our program involves the dynamics and consequences of social inequality. Both historically and currently, the inequalities inherent in American society have had profound consequences for teachers, students and citizens — ones that call into question our apparent commitment to democratic participation (Beyer, 1988b). An important aspect of helping students come to grips with the realities of social inequality involves helping them not only intellectually understand, but actively experience, the predicaments of those who have had to bear the brunt of social inequality. It is not enough to simply see this as an academic problem requiring analysis, reflection and discussion, as important as these things are. If we are to really understand the meaning of social inequality, and recognize its face within our classrooms, we must experience it, as best we can, directly. This is a fundamental aim of the first course normally taken by education students (and many other, non-education students), 'School and Society'. It also raises an especially pointed issue given the social class and racial backgrounds of many (but by no means all) students who attend Knox College. By looking in depth at this course, and some recent students' reflections on their experiences within it, an example of the kind of critical reflection advocated in this chapter will be provided. We will, as a result, be in a better position to evaluate the meaning of reflective teaching as critical reflection, and its role within teacher preparation.

Critical Reflection, Personal Meaning and Moral Action

'School and Society' is normally the initial course taken by students interested in either elementary or secondary certification. In addition to being required for all education students, about one-third of the students who enroll in it are non-education majors. Thirty to forty students take part in this course each time it is offered, and range from freshmen to seniors, with a few continuing education students typically enrolled.

There are several themes woven into the fabric that constitutes this course.[1] First, as already noted, the internal characteristics of the school do not arise out of thin air or even entirely of their own accord, independent of other institutions, social groups or societal values. Educational institutions do have their own history and perhaps even their own 'logic'. Yet a purely internal perspective on schooling misses something of vital importance about the nature of educational institutions and processes. Second, since their founding, public schools have been pointed to as a social institution that will help eliminate poverty, raise our general standard of living, provide for democratic values and policies, help prevent drug abuse and the spread of AIDS, and even assure a safer world as they contribute to our economic, political and military well-being. Clearly schools in US society have had placed on them the responsibility for a wide variety of social purposes and values. Such expectations have affected both the social outcomes of schooling and the nature of their internal dynamics. Third, in order to really understand schools, then, we must understand how they have been, and continue to be, a constitutive element of the social, political, cultural, economic and ideological forces that typify American society. Fourth, a central concern of this course, and one that recurs in subsequent courses, concerns the dynamics of social inequality and their instantiation in the public schools. As a society in which inequality by gender, race, social class, ethnicity, age and cultural affinity is perpetuated, some institutional means must be found for the reproduction of those inequalities. While this is not all they do, the schools occupy a central place in helping reproduce such patterns of inequality. A major question in examining the process of reproduction involves the sources of social inequality and possible avenues for its transformation.

Beyond academic inquiry into the dynamics of social inequality in American society, this course aims at a more personally meaningful, 'close up' encounter with an individual or small group of people who have been subject to the forces of inequality. The basic premise here is that 'social inequality' is not only a concept discussed by academics; nor is it a distant, unfortunate fact about which we merely need to read and formulate positions, important as these things are. 'Social inequality' names a condition that has significant, often dramatic, consequences for people's day-to-day lives–in schools and other settings. It affects what people can and cannot do, what (and whether) they eat, what kind of medical care, if any, they will receive, what kind of housing they can or cannot locate and, in some cases, whether they live or die. To see the dynamics of social inequality as only a theoretical issue is to deny its real life consequences and problems.

To help students obtain a more comprehensive perspective on inequality in American society, the final assignment for this course is to undertake a 'human service project' that involves individuals or groups that have been the victims of social inequality.[2] This project must involve a minimum of twenty-five hours of volunteer work in some social service agency in the community surrounding Knox College or in some more informal, socially or economically disadvantaged setting (e.g., the home of a local person or family) of which students are aware from their own experience. Among the former choices from which students may choose are: a local community action agency, serving predominantly African-American and poor people, including an after-school center; a local agency that furnishes food and other necessities to families with no other source of support; a local rescue mission and battered women's shelter; a nearby Headstart preschool; a day care center for senior citizens; a local chapter of the Salvation Army; and a regional literacy project.

While students are undertaking this human service project in the local community they are also reading about and discussing a number of books dealing with social and educational issues, all of which deal in one way or another with the dynamics of social inequality in American life. Most recently these included: Michael W. Apple and Lois Weis (1983) *Ideology and Practice in Schooling*; George S. Counts (1978) *Dare the School Build a New Social Order?*; Peter McLaren (1989) *Life in Schools*; David Nasaw (1979) *Schooled to Order*; Caroline Hodges Persell (1977) *Education and Inequality*; and Lillian Breslow Rubin (1976) *Worlds of Pain: Life in the Working-Class Family*. The intent here is in part to deal with issues of social inequality as these have affected the historical development of public schooling in the US, the form and content of contemporary school curricula, the family and educational policies; an equally important aim is to discuss the possible role of educational and other institutions in reversing the dynamics of social inequality — including the role that teachers might play in this regard.

But, again, the issues addressed and discussed in these readings need to be seen within the real contexts of flesh and blood people if they are to become personally meaningful to students; thus the need for a human service project of the kind sketched above. In addition to the social service agencies already mentioned, students have become involved with local individuals and families that had been especially disadvantaged — some through the economic crisis of the 1980s that devalued and undermined agricultural activities in the region especially significantly, some through the inequalities of race, class and gender that we read about in class. All students keep a journal in which they record observations, feelings about the experiences they are undergoing, and thoughts about the linkages between their human service project and the course materials.

Three recent examples of student involvement in such projects illustrate the meaning they typically have for members of this course. One woman became heavily involved with a single parent family through a part-time job in a local place of business. While the student, whom I shall call Judy,[3] had worked there for some time before class began, she became much more involved with her co-worker, Donna, and her children as a result of her involvement in this project. She interviewed Donna on several occasions, and ended up with a brief but interesting oral history of Donna and her extended family, traveling with her to a nearby town one weekend to talk with Donna's relatives, especially concerning their experiences with racism. Judy also volunteered to baby-sit for Donna's children so that she might have a rare night out with her fiance. At one point in their meetings, Judy brought up the fact that we were reading Rubin's (1976) *Worlds of Pain* in class. They discussed some issues from the reading and Judy subsequently loaned her copy of the book to Donna, who recognized in her own life many of the experiences documented in this study; this book became one more source of connection between Donna and Judy. After the conclusion of the class in November of 1989, Judy continued her friendship with Donna and her children; other students report similar lasting, fulfilling friendships.

A second student, Heidi, worked at the Salvation Army facility within the community. During the day Heidi assembled and distributed food boxes for adults who came in to purchase items with food stamps. During some evenings she volunteered to assist with 'Youth Night', attended primarily by poor and single parent children from the surrounding area. Coming from an affluent suburban area in the northeastern US, the experiences in which Heidi became involved during the term were quite moving and often startling. Toward the end of the term I showed the class an important film, 'The Women of Summer'. Writing in her journal, Heidi says:[4]

> Saw *Women of Summer* and couldn't believe it. The entire time I was in complete awe.... These women did things because they *felt it*, not because it was the proper or socially acceptable things to do.... I sat through the movie with my textbooks and notepads, wearing nice clothes and feeling relatively secure in my life. All the time I'm wondering what does this all mean. Everything I have and all my material possessions don't add up to much when compared to the action that these women took. Then I think ok. I'm volunteering at the Salvation Army and I'll go every day and really make an effort and so on and so on but then we all leave class for the day and go back to our dorms and watch tv and eat lunch and forget about everything.

Later, reflecting on her experiences at the Salvation Army, Heidi comments,

> These teen boys don't have the troubles that I'm used to seeing. Like in the private high school that I came from, the toughest problem was whether to spend $200 or $500 on cocaine of which the quality is unknown. I mean get real. I feel much more down to earth at the Salvation Army, where the toughest problem for the boys, and other people as well, is where will their next meal come from and is their family income low enough to qualify them for aid. Because even if their family income figure gets just a little bit above the cut-off, they don't get any aid. [note to me at end of entry]: Sorry that this is so sloppy and strange. I just have all these thoughts running wild and want to get them down on paper.

Again, Heidi writes in her journal,

> It's interesting to talk to the parents too. One young, single mother sometimes drops her kids off on the way to her night job. She and her kids wear old, out of style clothes, they just have that 'run-down' look.... The real animal instincts of people come out when they are in dire circumstances. Like food, a warm coat, and enough money for the holidays are the most important things. No luxuries. It's funny because we sit in class at college and talk abstractly about education systems and various problems etc., while these families have no time/luxury to philosophize. It's like I'm on the outside, while they are really *living* the problems that face our nation's poor. Another girl told me that her mom works at Kentucky Fried Chicken. Geez! If I said that to someone at home, no one would believe me. They would think that is was a joke. But, hey, this is reality.

Like many students in this course, Heidi was actively wrestling with a situation that was unlike any other in which she had been immersed. What she saw frightened, angered and frustrated her, and often, as she put it, she felt like she had 'all these thoughts running wild' that she wanted to get down on paper.

It is difficult to assess the long-term impact this human service project will have on Heidi, and I am not naive about the power of one experience in a single course to alter students' perceptions of social inequality and what to do about it. On the other hand, as is clear in the above excerpts, Heidi not only was struck by the situations in which she found herself at the Salvation Army, but also by the contrast between the predicaments of the men, women and children with which she came into contact there and the family and school environment in which she had grown up and the college community in which she was living at the time. Such connections at least provide a beginning for thinking through the personal meanings of social inequality and our individual and collective responses to it.

Jane is the third student whose human service experiences will be considered in the context of 'School and Society'. She choose to become involved with a local rescue mission that included a battered women's shelter. She worked most closely with one woman who was trying to find ways to 'struggle against an abusive husband'. Jane's project for this course included entries in her journal (similar to the ones completed by Judy and Heidi), a collection of essays and poetry, and the beginning of a book by Chris, the woman with whom Jane worked and, eventually, became close friends. Among Jane's writings for the course were the following comments and reflections on her experiences at the battered women's shelter:

All of the institutions that are made to deal with society's problems, which they wrongly see as the person's, are set up in such a way as to blame the victim. It is wrong to say these people are 'misfits' or not yet 'fit for society'. They *are* society. They are products of the same system that produced 'mainstream' society. They do not need to fit back into society. Saying they don't fit only proves that society has *marginalized* these people. . . .

These institutions fail to recognize that the long tern goal is not to change the individual. Rather, to change the forces that create the individual. . . . BLAMING THE VICTIM ONLY RELEASES THE OFFENDERS FROM THE RESPONSIBILITY OF WHAT THEY HAVE DONE. . . . The people in these [social or community service] institutions expect the victim to conform to standards that are hierarchical and patriarchal.

There is no way to remain detached. To remain apart is not to experience truth. If the wish of the participant in the Human Service Project [for 'School and Society'] is to be anesthetized into feeling that society is dealing adequately with social ills, then by all means remain detached. . . . The idea is to become *allies*, companeros, understanding people in the struggle. Until this happens the victim will be victimized. . . . We [must] ally ourselves, consider ourselves equally valuable, and understand the problem is not that which belongs to the individual. . . .

Besides such social criticism and anger at a system that deals insultingly with social injustices generally, Jane was often personally and visibly moved by her experiences and friendship with Chris and her children. In a characteristic example of self-reflection, Jane writes,

> Can I handle this? Am I going to be a wreck everytime? Am I qualified to do this? If not me — then who?
>
> I couldn't justify my project, or my qualifications for my project, to myself, Chris, or my friends. I feel that I am not qualified. I feel guilty for my class, my background, my college education, my clothes, my jewelry, my small diamond earring, and myself. How can I possibly understand how someone can possibly think I can understand. How can I understand these problems that are so far removed from my life experience. I want to become untied from my malt-o-meal, Polly Flinders, oldsmobile, suburban childhood. I have no right to claim that I can really counsel or give advice. I guess I can just listen. You don't have to be qualified to listen.

Jane did much more than listen to Chris and her children, however. One specific episode that represents Jane's work for this project is especially telling, as taken from Janes's journal notes:

> Spent the day with Chris's very sick son John. John's eyes were glazed, he was murmuring unintelligible answers to Chris's simple questions. He was twitching and it seemed as if he was shaking as if he were cold though his temp. was 104°. We didn't know exactly what to do. Chris asked me to draw her a map to the hospital. John had fallen asleep. Not knowing what else to do, only having $5 and ¼ tank of gas, Chris had wanted to buy 7-Up and co-tylenol to get the fever down and settle his cramping stomach. There was no fruit juice at the rescue mission. Chris borrowed medicine from another woman at the shelter. We left with the kids, John sitting on my lap in the front seat. Chris thought, perhaps, if we stopped by [the state agency] and picked up her green card then things would be easier at the hospital. The kids and I waited in the car. Chris returned to tell us that they couldn't give her this card because they were mailing it to her permanent address, even though she informed them she didn't even have an address. I told her John had thrown up all over me and the front seat. It wasn't much, but it was the medicine. . . .
>
> We went to the hospital. Chris was apologizing the whole way for me spending my afternoon and apologizing for John throwing up. When we arrived, there were no available beds and we ended up in the waiting room where Chris had to fill out a bunch of forms and answer a bunch of questions . . . questions met with bad feelings, feelings of inadequacy. I guess when you have to say out loud you have no home, job, husband, money, food, medicine, address, it makes it seem all the more real and hurt all the more.
>
> Aside from John not being able to hold down any liquid, he was dehydrated so they gave him an IV to get his fever down. John is

deathly afraid of needles. Marsha [Chris's daughter] and I left the room. We returned and John had relaxed and all was going better.

What a feeling of helplessness and defeat, not being able to help and protect your own children. How can one be so poor that they can't buy tylenol for a sick child?

As with many other students who have been involved in a human service project for 'School and Society' over the years, Jane's experiences affected her deeply and personally. Many students report that such projects are among the most important experiences they have while at Knox College. While not all students conclude, as Jane did, that together we must realize inequality exists and begin working for the welfare of the human race, together', students do make connections between the theoretical issues surrounding social inequality and the real plight of people caught in situations not only 'unfortunate' but related to structural constraints that exist in contemporary society.

Conclusions

As is the case in all teaching situations, each of the three students whose experiences in a human service project are excerpted above had quite different backgrounds. An important dimension of this difference involves the previous commitments and consciousness of political, economic and social issues that students bring with them. While Judy, Heidi and Jane all grew up in situations markedly different from the ones in which their projects took place, they had significantly different levels of political and theoretical commitments well before enrolling in 'School and Society'. Of the three, Jane had an articulate, well thought out theoretical framework that provided her experiences with meanings that would not otherwise have been evident; this framework had been responsible, in part, for social and political activities in which Jane had previously been involved. This was less the case with Judy and Heidi. While their experiences in the project were no less significant for them than Jane's were for her, the extent to which such experiences have or will become a part of a larger political and social commitment is less clear for Judy and Heidi.

A central question here is how moral commitments are formed, and how teacher preparation programs can help students generate such commitments as a key part of what it means to be a professional. We may too often rely on theoretical analysis that, while of course crucial and essential, misses something of the affective, existential quality of moral engagement and commitment. Especially for students like Judy and Heidi, then, the experiences of which they movingly wrote can become one important route to such commitment.

Yet if the sort of issues raised and the experiences gained through this initial course in the department represent merely an isolated attempt to integrate social and pedagogical concerns, they will probably be of limited value in the long run. Such issues cannot be raised in a 'social foundations' course, to be dropped in subsequent ones dealing more specifically with curriculum and teaching (Beyer and Zeichner, 1982). On the other hand, if critical reflection can become a central part of the ethos of a teacher education program — as I think it is becoming at Knox College — and if the insightful and personally moving qualities of the experiences documented here can be incorporated into that process of reflection, students will be in a much better position to see teaching as a field of moral action.

If 'reflective teaching' is to avoid becoming simply another in a long line of slogans within educational theory and practice, the kind of personally empowering and morally engaging experiences undertaken during these projects must be included. They do not simply 'illustrate' issues of social inequality, they bring them to life and give them a dimension not otherwise obtainable. At the same time, as evidenced by Jane's experiences and reflections, it is clear that an equally compelling need exists to help prospective teachers develop a theoretical framework that will draw them outward, uncovering the political, moral and social issues with which teachers necessarily deal. Based upon a view of teaching as a socially sensitive, personally committed, politically self-conscious praxis, teacher preparation can be furthered by a commitment to reflective teaching in which critical reflection is practiced.

Without the sort of invigoration which results when a critically reflective theoretical framework illuminates and is partially shaped by profound experience, 'social inequality' will remain simply one more unfortunate fact of social life, not something to be redressed. If critical reflection as the key to reflective teaching is to make a difference, it must help us not only to see and understand the dynamics of social inequality, but to overcome them.

Notes

1 The description which follows is taken directly from the syllabus for the most recent term in which 'School and Society' was taught, the fall term of the 1989–90 academic year.
2 For logistical reasons only, this final project is from time to time made an option, along with a more traditional research paper. Even when presenting these options becomes necessary, though, my experience has been that about three-fourths of the students select the sort of human service projects that are discussed below.
3 To protect their anonymity, the actual names of all the people included in this section have not been used.
4 To provide something of the flavor of their experiences, quotations from student journals are taken verbatim — without correcting occasional grammatical and other errors — as they were written and felt.

References

APPLE, M.W. (1982) *Education and Power*, New York: Routledge and Kegan Paul.
APPLE, M.W. and WEIS, L. (1983) *Ideology and Practice in Schooling*, Philadelphia: Temple University Press.
BEYER, L.E. (1988a) *Knowing and Acting: Inquiry, Ideology, and Educational Studies*, Basingstoke: Falmer Press.
BEYER, L.E. (1988b) 'Can schools further democratic practices?' *Theory Into Practice*, **27**, 4, Autumn, pp. 262–9.
BEYER, L.E. and APPLE, M.W. (1988) *The Curriculum: Problems, Politics and Possibilities*, Albany: State University of New York Press.
BEYER, L.E., FEINBERG, W., PAGANO, J.A. and WHITSON, J.A. (1989) *Preparing*

Teachers as Professionals: The Role of Educational Studies and Other Liberal Disciplines, New York: Teachers College Press.

BEYER, L.E. and ZEICHNER, K.M. (1982) 'Teacher training and educational foundations: A plea for discontent', *Journal of Teacher Education*, **33**, 3, May–June, pp. 18–23.

BOSTON WOMEN'S TEACHERS' GROUP (n.d.) 'The other end of the corridor: The effect of teaching on teachers', Boston: Boston Women's Teachers' Group.

COUNTS, G.S. (1978) *Dare the School Build a New Social Order?* Carbondale: Southern Illinois University Press.

CREMIN, L. (1957) *Horace Mann on the Education of Free Men*, New York: Teachers College Press.

CUBAN, L. (1984) *How Teachers Taught: Constancy and Change in American Classrooms 1890–1980*, New York: Longman.

DEWEY, J. (1916) *Democracy and Education: An Introduction to the Philosophy of Education*, New York: The Free Press.

GREENE, M. (1978) *Landscapes of Learning*, New York: Teachers College Press.

KAUFMAN, P.W. (1984) *Women Teachers on the Frontier*, New Haven: Yale University Press.

KILPATRICK, W.H. (1918) 'The project method', *Teachers College Record*, **19**, 4, pp. 319–35.

KLIEBARD, H.M. (1986) *The Struggle for the American Curriculum 1893–1958*, London: Routledge and Kegan Paul.

LASCH, C. (1978) *The Culture of Narcissism: American Life in an Age of Diminishing Expectations*, New York: W.W. Norton.

LISTON, D.P. and ZEICHNER, K.M. (1987) 'Reflective teacher education and moral deliberation', *Journal of Teacher Education*, **38**, 6, pp. 2–8.

MATTINGLY, P. (1975) *The Classless Profession: American Schoolmen in the Nineteenth Century*, New Yok: New York University Press.

MCLAREN, P. (1989) *Life in Schools*, New York: Longman.

NASAW, D. (1979) *Schooled to Order: A Social History of Public Schooling in the United States*, Oxford: Oxford University Press.

PERSELL, C.H. (1977) *Education and Inequality*, New York: The Free Press.

POPKEWITZ, T.S. (1987) *Critical Studies in Teacher Education: Its Folklore, Theory and Practice*, Basingstoke: Falmer Press.

RUBIN, L.B. (1976) *Worlds of Pain: Life in the Working-Class Family*, New York: Basic Books.

SCHON, D. (1983) *The Reflective Practitioner: How Professionals Think in Action*, New York: Basic Books.

SIROTNIK, K.A. (1988) 'What goes on in classrooms? Is this the way we want it?' in BEYER, L.E. and APPLE, M.W. (Eds) *The Curriculum: Problems, Politics, and Possibilities*, pp. 56–74 Albany: State University of New York Press.

SIZER, T. (1984) *Horace's Compromise: The Dilemma of the American High School*, Boston: Houghton Mifflin.

SMYTH, J. (1987) *Educating Teachers: Changing the Nature of Pedagogical Knowledge*, Basingstoke: The Falmer Press.

TYACK, D. (1974) *The One Best System: A History of American Urban Education*, Cambridge: Harvard University Press.

8 Case Methods and Teacher Education: Using Cases to Teach Teacher Reflection

Anna E. Richert

Happenings we perceive to be strange or unusual cause us to stop and think. If we were to see an ancient tribal ritual, for example, assuming we knew little or nothing about the culture of which the ritual were a part, we would probably ask ourselves a number of questions: What is going on? Who are the people and what are their relationships with one another? What meanings are embedded in the actions and for whom? What occurred before the ritual and what would occur after? and so on.

Happenings that are familiar, on the other hand, often go unnoticed and receive much less scrutiny. Schooling falls into that category of the familiar. Schools are familiar places. In this country almost everyone has spent many hours in school. That means we hold some common notions about how they operate — who does what, when, how often. We know, for example, that most students and teachers arrive at school before the morning bell rings. We also know that when the bell rings students find their seats somewhere, usually somewhere that the teacher tells them to sit. We know that most teachers talk a lot because we have seen lots of teachers stand in front of lots of students and talk. We know that some of what teachers talk about is interesting, and some is not-so-interesting. We may have noticed that occasionally students talk with one another about school matters, or about whatever else matters. In fact, we may believe that school matters and whatever else matters are one and the same. People beginning a career in teaching, therefore, enter the field knowing and believing a great deal about the work they intend to do, and about the *milieu* in which that work takes place.

The familiarity of teaching presents both a dilemma and a challenge for teacher education. If teacher education students perceive that they know much of what there is to know about the context and process of the work they are being prepared to do, they are less likely to stop and think about their work than if they were entering an arena about which they knew little or nothing. Even the promise of change holds little weight for creating an illusion of the unknown for most teacher education students. In spite of the demographic and societal shifts that permeate almost every aspect of our technological culture, and in spite of the progressive waves of school reform that stretch the agendas of Boards of Education Meetings and district level politics, schools function much the same now as they have for the past century (Cuban, 1984; Goodlad, 1983).

Preparing novice teachers to be reflective in this context of apparent stasis is problematic at best. The process involves convincing teachers to question what they know and believe to be true, and preparing them to reframe as 'problematic' that which they see as 'given'. Both the teacher and the teacher educator in this model are called upon to engage in an authentic conversation that challenges what *is* in schooling, and consider what *might* be, or what *ought* to be, instead.

This chapter presents case methods as one strategy for preparing such a reflective practitioner. In the first section of the chapter I consider the question, 'Why reflection; given the state of schools as we know them, why is it important for teachers to be reflective about their work?' In this first section I attempt to do exactly what I require of my students which is to justify my pedagogical decisions. I present my rationale based on what I believe my students need to know, how they might come to know it, and what I believe I can do to create the environment for that learning to occur.

The discussion in the second section of the chapter focuses on the relationship between program structure and the intended outcome of preparing reflective practitioners. My current work on case methods follows from a body of research in which I have explored the relationship of various teacher education strategies and the reflection novice teachers employed as a result of engaging with those strategies (Richert, 1987, 1989a, 1989b). In that work I found that the novice teachers I studied reflected about different things and in different ways when they reflected about their teaching under different circumstances. In the second section of this chapter I discuss the relationship between case methods and teacher reflection.

In the third section I discuss my current experiences using case methods in my own teaching. The discussion includes what case methods are in this context, and why and how I use them given my goals as expressed in earlier sections of the chapter. I include what I find to be the successes of the method and conclude the section with the difficulties I have encountered.

In this chapter I consider the potential of case methods for preparing reflective teachers. The strategies in this volume are instances of a larger category or a set of principles that guide teacher education practice. They assume a fundamental connection between teaching, inquiry and reflection. The question that guides this chapter is similar to the one I pose to my students as we move our case discussions from a consideration of the particular, to an understanding that is theoretical: 'What are case methods a case of?' As a pedagogical strategy, what do case methods represent for teaching and teacher education?

Why Prepare Reflective Teachers?

Reflection is at the heart of good teaching. As Dewey (1933) reminds us, reflection is what allows teachers to act with intent. It is what makes teaching an intellectual rather than a routine task. I will assume reflection as a central goal in preparing teachers and begin by noting briefly several teacher education concerns that underscore its critical importance.

First, is the infinite complexity of teachers' work. To do their work well teachers must know vast amounts of information about a vast numbers of things. They must also know how to pull this information together often under strained and changing circumstances. And, they must know how to act given what they believe about the goals, purposes and potential consequences of their work with children.

Let's think about what teachers need to know. In addition to knowing about oneself when one teaches, for example, it is imperative that a teacher know her students — who they are, what they know, what they believe, where they come from. Additionally, she must know her subject matter including the ideas, themes and concepts in her field (or in multiple fields for the elementary school teacher) and how these ideas and concepts are related to one another as well as how they relate to the ideas and concepts in other fields. In addition to knowing the subject matter, a teacher must know how to *teach* the subject matter which involves, among other things, knowledge of curriculum. Knowing about the context in which one teaches is essential, as is knowing the legal, moral and ethical dimensions of the work. All of what the teacher knows to do her work well she must know in relation to the goals and purposes she holds for teaching and learning in her classroom.

Since teaching is situational, furthermore, it is imperative that teachers know how to 'read' particular situations to learn from their experiences in ways that allow them to respond thoughtfully to changing circumstances. Each situation in which a teacher finds herself occurs at a different moment in time, with different students and a different purpose. In each case the teacher draws on her store of knowledge in a way that responds to the particularities of the circumstance. She must know how to think about that experience, how to learn from it and how to help her students learn how to learn from it. She must know what knowledge to bring to bear.

Given the limits of both her own rationality and that of the technical world of which she is a part,[1] the teacher must know how to reflect on her work in ways that allow her to make sense of it. As a teacher makes sense of her own experience in the classroom, she models an inquiring and critical approach to teaching which is at the heart of reflective practice. A reflective teacher is able to deal with the complexity of the task by drawing on what she knows to direct and illuminate her classroom work. Using what she knows, she is able to both inform her actions, and learn from them as well.

Knowing what to do and how to do it require prior consideration of one's purposes in teaching. Considering the purposes and consequences of their work is probably the most important reason for preparing teachers to be reflective. It is also probably the most difficult teacher education goal to achieve as teachers typically enter the field assuming what is 'given' in schools is given. What could be, or might be, or ought to be, are seldom taken into account, especially in this time of high accountability when both teachers and students are held to externally imposed standards of performance.

Currently teachers operate in a framework that defines progress in education as improving student skills that will contribute to the economic and technological well being of our 'nation at risk'. In this system teachers have little time and no support for questioning what they do and why. They are rewarded not for thoughtful deliberation about what it means to teach in the twentieth century, or for what might be a changing definition of the purposes of their work, or how we might reconceptualize schooling to better meet the needs of greater numbers of people, but rather for the efficient and effective accomplishment of externally imposed standards for student work. Learning to be reflective given this context requires not only learning the knowledge and skills of reflective practice, therefore, but acquiring the disposition for it as well. As Maxine Greene (1986) suggests in her provocative essay on passion and reflection in teaching, our hope for change and a new vision for our nation is predicated on teachers and students alike having a safe and open space for questioning what they are doing and towards what end.

Reflective teaching suggests both challenge and commitment. The task is intellectual rather than routine, expansive rather than singularly focused. Reconceptualizing teaching to be based on the ideas of reflective practice, and thus re-emphasizing the intellectual demands of the work, require a teacher education curriculum that goes well beyond the creation of opportunities for the acquisition of technical skill. Teaching thus conceptualized — and teacher education thus mirrored — promise to attract and retain people capable of visioning and revisioning both schools and schooling. It is towards that end that my work with case methods is directed.

Program Structure and Reflective Teaching

Current reform efforts in teacher education have taken us back to the drawing board as we consider and reconsider the form our programs of teacher education take (Holmes Group, 1986; Carnegie Forum, 1986). In the processes of self-study, research and evaluation, we ask ourselves, 'What program structures will bring about learning in the direction we hope for our student teachers? What do we want our graduates to know? and How can we help them come to know?' The number of specific questions is endless: should students student teach from the time they enter teacher education, is one example. If the different components of the teacher education curriculum offer different occasions for learning, as Sharon Feiman-Nemser (1983) suggests, where in our programs should we emphasize what ideas? What can students learn from their field experiences? What is better learned in the university courses? Within either of these settings — the college classroom or the school-site classroom — how should the experience be organized? And, as the chapters in this volume ask, what program structures house methods that best promote reflective practice in novice professionals?

Though it is widely accepted that program structure and the pedagogical strategies housed in those structures are important in determining learning outcomes, teacher educators have been slow to consider systematically how successful, and in what ways, particular program structures prepare teachers for their complex work in classrooms. In a recent study on reflective teacher education (Richert, 1987), I considered the relationship between program structure and teacher reflection as it was perceived by twelve student teachers during their preservice teacher education year. Drawing on the professional education literature in teaching, architecture, law and medicine, I isolated two variables typically used to facilitate a reflective approach to professional practice. The two variables represent two different ways the professional education community attempts to help novices think about their work and learn from their experiences.

The first set of structures was *social* in nature. All four professions incorporate a number of ways for novices, during their preservice preparation, to interact with one another and with their faculty in consideration and deliberation of the central questions, ideas, issues and dilemmas of the field. The assumption seems to be that people learn better when they work together. Current literature in social learning theory provides ample evidence that this is so (Hertz-Lazarowitz, Sharan and Steinberg, 1980; Cohen, 1984; Shulman and Carey, 1984). Teacher education programs typically provide several opportunities for a social or community deliberation of ideas — partnerships, small group work, seminars, the supervisor-student teacher relationship. Though not all occasions of social interaction result in enhanced reflection, a social exchange seems to be one way professional educators attempt to facilitate and extend the careful deliberation of professional issues by the newcomers to their fields.

The second set of structures used to promote the capability for reflective practice in the professions were *artifactual* in nature. Artifacts are tangible representations of one kind or another. Artifactual facilitators to reflection include the use or creation of artifacts that represent some aspect of the given working situation. The assumption in using artifacts to enhance reflection seems to be that people learn best from experience when they have help in remembering that experience. Like the other professions in this small cluster, teaching as work is 'active'.[2] Occurrences in the work setting happen in rapid-fire succession. Little time is available for deliberation 'on the spot'. Consequently, the details of any given experience are lost almost as quickly as they are gained.

Artifacts of clasroom experience are needed to help teachers remember what occurred in the classroom if they want to think about and learn from their work with children. Artifactual aids to reflection, then, are mechanisms practitioners employ to record in some way a given aspect of a professional situation about which they need, or want, to think. Physicians keep charts, for example, which serve as a running record of their decisions and their patients' progress. The charts are available not only to the attending physician, but also to interns and residents associated with the case. Similarly, architects record the development of ideas through annotated schematic drawings. The drawings are used for presentation purposes, frequently. They are also used for the ongoing deliberation by the architect and her colleagues — both novice and expert — about the project.

In teaching, a number of mechanisms for artifactual representation of classroom activity is also employed. Some teachers keep journals which help them remember what has occurred in the classroom. Other teachers make quick notes at the end of the period — or even during the period as is the case with one teacher with whom I spoke recently (Alban, 1989). Often teachers have lesson plan books or other record keeping systems that allow them to record their plans and their reactions to those plans. Videotapes are another strategy used from time to time by teachers who want to note classroom activity for later analysis. Artifactual aids to reflection provide the practitioner with an 'audit-trail' of sorts that helps in the recollection, and consequent reflection about that work. With a tangible representation to help them focus their thinking, furthermore, teachers are able to assess their experiences not only to determine the success or lack of success, but also to consider if these activities are consonant with their aims and purposes.

In considering the relationship between these social and artifactual aids and the reflection that occurred when the student teachers engaged in using them, I found a difference in both the *content* and the *process* of the student teacher reflection. I looked at teacher reflection under four conditions which I created by crossing the social and artifactual variables. I operationalized social to be working with a partner and artifactual to be working with a portfolio of materials representing one week of teaching. The four program structures under which the student teachers reflected, then, were: 1) no partner and no portfolio; 2) no partner and a portfolio; 3) a partner but no portfolio; and 4) a partner *and* a portfolio.[3]

The findings of this research suggest that depending on the conditions we create for student teachers to think about their work, they think about different things and they think about them in different ways. For example, when teachers think about their work with the assistance of an artifact of some sort, in this instance a portfolio, they focus their thinking on whatever is represented by that artifact. In this study, the novice teachers working with portfolios reflected about the content of instruction, and the teaching of that content as represented by the lesson and unit plans included in the artifactual collection. Working with a partner, the research showed, focused the reflection on the social or interactive aspects of the teaching-learning enterprise — asking questions, motivating students, classroom management. The teachers who reflected with the assistance of both a portfolio and a partner focused on the interactive aspects of teaching the particular content or lessons in the portfolio representations. In this latter group, for example, the reflective conversations included discussions of how to help students understand the processes involved in 'completing the square', what language and examples worked best for teaching about electrostatic fields, and whether or not the logic of a mathematical explanation was presented too quickly or not quickly enough for student understanding. Structure matters, according to the results of this project. If we want to teach teachers to think about a broad cross-section of teaching issues and concerns, we need to find a variety of ways to help them do so. The teacher education curriculum must be structured with the expectation that student teachers will deliberate the complexities of classroom practice if we help them learn how to do so, and if we provide adequate support for them to do so as well. Time and safety, an opportunity to talk, support in learning how to generate and ask questions, how to frame and solve problems, a professional atmosphere that encourages divergent thinking and risk-taking, are all aspects of the kinds of structures that are needed in teacher education to promote and facilitate reflective practice. Creating a norm of reflection that is supported within the system of socialization that occurs in teacher education is a first step in preparing a cohort of teachers who have the capability for reflective practice including a disposition that tolerates ambiguity, a capability for asking questions and a propensity for identifying, analyzing and hopefully solving problems, in the forever changing and often unjust world of schools and schooling.

The Case for Case Methods

Case methods, or the use of cases for teacher education, is one way to structure into the teacher education curriculum an opportunity to enhance reflective thinking (Richert 1989a, 1989b). The methodology combines the artifactual and social elements just described. The artifactual component is the case itself, which is typically a description of an actual teaching situation. Cases draw on data collected in school settings and are therefore artifactual representations of various aspects of teachers' work. The social component of case methods is the discussion of the case by colleagues. After studying the case alone, teachers convene to study the case together. The 'studying together' usually takes the form of a case discussion (often referred to as a 'case conference'). Another aspect of the social component of case methods involves the preparation of the case. Often, cases are prepared by teachers. There is a social dimension in putting together a case: the person creating the case necessarily interacts with various members of the school setting during both the data gathering and the analysis processes.

As a program structure, then, case methods offer great potential for enhancing reflection. The case is a gathering point around which teachers come together to think about teaching and learning, and to think about the schools where this teaching and learning are meant to occur. Since the number of ways this coming-together can happen are many, and the number of ways one might conceptualize what constitutes a case is complex, it is important to clarify meanings. Let me proceed with a discussion of how I think about, and use, cases and case methods in my own teacher education classes.

What is a Case?

Teaching cases describe teaching practice. In a richly descriptive form, cases tell stories that typically include the actions, thoughts, beliefs and feelings of both teachers and students. The length and comprehensiveness of a case depends on its purpose. Some cases are short and describe brief teaching episodes. Others are long and include thick descriptions (Geertz, 1973) of many aspects of a teaching situation, including the context, the events leading to the situation and those that follow, the actions of people involved as well as their thoughts and feelings.

The descriptive nature of cases provides an opportunity for presenting teachers' work in all of its complexity. Teaching tradeoffs and dilemmas emerge in the text[4] as do the strategies teachers use, the frustrations they experience, the brilliant and less-brilliant decisions they make, the actions they take, the knowledge they bring to bear, and so on. Additionally, cases present teachers' work as relational. Ideas, actions and feelings are not isolated from one another; rather, one idea leads to another which leads to a feeling and possibly another idea, an action, a set of feelings, a different action, and so forth. A well crafted case reveals in narrative form the work of schools and of those who inhabit them.

Another feature of cases is that they are situational;[5] they present specific situations — a particular teacher with particular students teaching a particular content for a particular purpose. The situational nature of cases is significant for teacher education. It reflects what we know from learning theory, that learning is neither context nor content independent. Factors of the context — who the teacher is, who the students are, what both students and teacher know and hope to accomplish, what the content of instruction is — are important for understanding the case presented. It matters, for example, if the school is rural, suburban or urban. A white teacher with Hispanic kids faces a different situation from a black teacher with the same group, or an Hispanic teaching children from his own community. Teaching mathematics is different from teaching English, just as teaching social studies to fourth graders in one context is different from teaching it to fourth graders in another.

In their description of a particular situation, cases present the information needed to make sense of that situation.[6] The first focus of case writing and case analysis, therefore, is on the particulars of the case. Using cases to understand teaching, teachers are able to contemplate what occurs in the situation described. In addition to reflecting on the particular learning situation, they can grapple with what could be, or what ought to be given the case's contextual frame.

While it is always important to understanding teaching and learning, the issue of context is especially relevant and increasingly problematic today considering the demographic changes that face our schools. Teachers preparing to teach in the twenty-first century will likely face classrooms characterized by diversity rather than homegeneity. Dealing with differences among children has always been part of teaching. However, teachers today face diversity that is increasingly complex and wide-spread. Cultural diversity provides an example — an especially challenging example for teaching and teacher education. Increasing numbers of kids enter classrooms today with cultural backgrounds different from one another and different from their teacher.[7] These children bring with them not only different languages, but different expectations, behaviors, norms and dreams for their futures.

Diversity caused by a changing family structure provides a second example. The structure of families today is different from the two-parent, two-child model we have associated with American culture until recently. In her disscussion of child and family trends of the 1970s and 1980s, Ann Rosewater (1989) explains a number of economic and social changes that have affected American life and the caring, including schooling, of children. Many families are headed by one adult rather than two; this adult is typically a woman (23 per cent) with a below-the-poverty line, disproportionately low income. Income for all young families is lower, she explains, which is created by a decrease in the availability of jobs relative to those seeking employment, and lower wages. Young parents, especially young minority parents, suffer most and are often without adequate income to support themselves and their children; in 1986, 20 per cent of American children lived in poverty, she reports. Parents typically have to work so children are left on their own, and often precariously on their own, more frequently than in the past.

In contemplating such contextual factors therefore, it becomes clear that the situational nature of cases is not incidental to the case, but rather centrally important to it. The particulars of any given situation are presented in the case, and are understood as an integral and essential part of the story. As descriptors of actual situations, cases provide a way of documenting what teachers do, as well as what they know and how they feel. They present school life in particular situations as it is in those situations. Furthermore, since cases are textual in some form or another, they 'freeze' time and thus allow for a sense-making about school life that is otherwise difficult to attain without this moment of time and space held still for analysis.

One additional feature of cases as we think of them for teacher education purposes is that they can, and do, describe many aspects of teachers' work, not only acts of instruction. While each case focuses on one event or aspect, there are a variety of types of cases about a broad set of teacher-related concerns. There are cases of teacher planning, for example, and cases of content instruction.[8] There are cases describing problems or dilemmas associated with the contextual factors of schooling as perceived by teachers; this was the focus of one project I did with one of my classes.[9] There are also cases focusing on multicultural dilemmas, such as the dilemmas encountered by novice teachers entering rural Alaskan schools that Kleinfeld (1989) and her colleagues at the University of Alaska prepare and use. Since cases are available to describe any of the many dimensions of teachers' work, they offer infinite possibilities for teacher reflection and consequently for teacher learning. Additionally, cases written about teachers' work provide a potential for documentation about teaching that is different in kind from what has been available up until now. A library of cases such as those described here offers tremendous potential for teacher education curricular reform.

Where Do Cases Come From: Creating the Artifact

Teaching cases come from practice that is observed, documented, synthesized and reproduced in some form. Often teachers prepare cases about their work or the work of others. Sometimes teaching cases are prepared by others such as researchers or teacher educators looking for ways to teach particular content in the teacher education context.[10] Whether constructed by teachers, teacher educators or researchers, cases are drawn from data collected in actual school settings. Descriptions of what occurs, including what teachers and students say, as well as what these same actors feel (as interpreted by the case writer from observation and interview data) are part of the case write-up.

In my own teacher education classes I use cases from a number of sources depending on the purpose of the case method I am using. In some classes I use cases relatively infrequently and only to illustrate in practical terms the theoretical constructs under consideration. In those instances I use cases from one of the sources I cited above, or cases prepared by students of mine in previous years. As my own case library grows, I am able to find cases that illustrate the broad principles of the course, which also take into account both the contextual and content factors that stretch (or challenge) the applicability of the principles for certain settings. Cases having to do with diversity provide good examples. The changing demographics illustrated by these cases, as well as the consequences for school lives as presented in the case, challenge our conceptions of how schools do, and ought to, function.

The second source of cases for my classes comes from the written work of student teachers in the class. My students write cases based on observations, interviews and various participatory experiences in the situation about which they are writing. In the next section of the chapter I will discuss how these cases, once written, are used in class. However, the *use* of these cases constitutes only one aspect of my intended outcome in employing a student-prepared case strategy. An equally critical piece of the assignment concerns the learning opportunity embedded in case construction.

Case construction involves studying a situation and learning enough about it to describe it accurately in a way that others can understand. If the case is presented in a written form, for example, and it is done well, the reader will vicariously experience the described situation. In a research project in which I compared the effect of various case methods on teacher learning (Richert, 1989b), I found a consistent set of reactions to the case methods as described by the students in my classes. Preparing cases involves developing skills central to reflective practice, according to this cohort of student teachers. For example, to prepare a good case the case writer must watch and listen carefully — skills essential to good teaching in general, and to good reflective teaching in particular. One student teacher with whom I spoke said this about writing cases:

> It taught me to listen. I mean, you really had to listen. And I think writing it out, that made you listen at a much deeper level. (TE)[11]

In choosing *what* to write about, the case writer needs to determine a focus and a reason for choosing that focus, another essential skill of reflective practice. She must also decide what is relevant to the story and what is not — what background factors to include, what actors and actions are essential, what contextual information is necessary for understanding the case, what part of the dialogue should be included. Finding that focus and developing the story around it is both knowledge and skill building for novice teachers. Knowing what to attend to amid the cacophony of school life is what separates novices from experts, recent research suggests (Berliner, 1986). Schools are very busy places; a lot goes on at all times. What noise is important to hear and what noise can be considered background quickly becomes important information as one learns to manage classrooms. Similarly, learning what to attend to as students talk is important as well. A teacher quickly learns that words a ninth grader chooses to describe 'freedom', for example, become essential as that same student's inability to comprehend *Huck Finn*, or *To Kill a Mockingbird*, becomes apparent.[12]

Learning to listen and to focus, then, are two outcomes of constructing cases according to my students. A related skill is learning to analyze a situation; choosing the focus and determining what is relevant to the story that the casewriter aims to tell involves carefully analyzing the classroom event as it is observed and experienced. 'Writing the case makes me think more clearly in having to delineate it', one student explained, 'And again to organize it I guess' (TN). And another said,

> [Writing the case] helps you zero in. It helps you focus in on one thing at one moment in time, and what you want out of it. (TI)

First you must 'focus in on one thing at one moment in time', according to this teacher, and then you need to determine 'what you want out of it'. Both require analysis and judgment. 'I felt the experience was very helpful', one teacher said. 'It helped me focus, analyze, and re-evaluate one current problem' (TK).

Another outcome of having student teachers write cases is that the process helps them think more clearly about what teachers know and need to know. By focusing in on one specific situation the novice teachers found themselves grappling with the complexity inherent in teaching. Each situation, while similar in some ways to others experienced in school, is different along dimensions the student teachers came to identify and understand. In contemplating with close scrutiny what happens in one situation and why, novices find that they are able to think about what they might do in a similar situation, and about what they would need to know to be able to function under changed circumstances. One teacher explained,

> Since the case studies were about issues that concerned me, I also learned how these topics related to what I am doing. So, for example, I learned a great deal about styles of teaching and how I think about which style of teaching I can use in my own work.... (TD)

Moving from the case to a more theoretical understanding of the principle embedded in the case happen as a matter of course during the case construction phase of the assignment. The cases 'help us focus on the specific and at the same time give us a method to link our work to broader issues', one teacher said (TA). And another concluded:

> The cases helped me to think about what I'm doing and why. Also to think about what's going on in education as a whole — not just my room. I'm definitely giving much more thought to what I'm doing, and I think, understanding it more. (TC)

Using Cases in Teacher Education

Two factors guide my thinking about the *use* of cases as a teacher education methodology. The first is that cases represent teaching practice, which is ultimately the subject matter of teacher education. Since the form is narrative, furthermore, teacher knowledge is represented in a way that unifies practice and theory. The second is that studying cases is social in nature and thus the methodology underscores the essence of teaching as a collective endeavor and knowledge as socially constructed. Let's take a look at each of these factors and consequently what they suggest for the methodology as actualized in teacher education practice.

Cases as Content in Narrative Form

First, cases represent teaching practice, which is the subject matter of teacher education. Cases present teachers' work as it is. Therefore, students can study cases and think about the actual happenings of classroom life. Once they have studied the case itself, and deliberated the elements of practice thus described, teachers can also consider the *principles* of practice embedded in the case — ideas about learning, for example, or pedagogical content, or the social imperatives of a multicultural setting, or the notion of ethical decision making in teaching.

The narrative form of cases suggests a consideration of practice that is both practical and theoretical. Studying cases actually relies on a dialectic between events and meanings, practice and theory. We learn from the narrative as we reflect on the content and make sense of it based on what we know and believe.

In studying the particular, we consider the general; similarly, we challenge the general by studying the particular. I am reminded of Carolyn Heilbrun's (1988) discusssion of biography as a narrative tool for learning about one's life:

> What matters is that lives do not serve as models; only stories do that. And it is a hard thing to make up stories to live by. We can only retell and live by the stories we have read or heard. We live our lives through texts. They may be read or chanted, or experienced electronically, or come to us, like the murmurings of our mothers, telling us what conventions demand. Whatever their form or medium, these stories have formed us all; they are what we must use to make new fictions, new narratives. (p. 37)

Cases are stories that help us learn about classroom life. Drawn from actual classroom practice, they describe real situations and therefore are powerful as learning tools. The problems and dilemmas of the case are believable because they are parts of the stories of real lives such as Heilbrun notes above. This tie to reality is not incidental; it is critical to the power that cases offer for teaching teachers. One student teacher captured the sentiment expressed by many of her colleagues:

> I think the valuable part for me was that I really had to clarify my thoughts because it was a real problem and it was a problem that was nagging me and bugging me. (TE)

The irony of studying cases is that the problems of episodes thus represented are real, but the opportunity case methods offer for studying them is not. Unlike the real world of schools, the case method format provides the time, safety and opportunity for consideration of issues presented; additionally it provides the expectation that the material of the case is important, and in need of deliberation. The content of cases — school practice — is seen, therefore, as problematic rather than given. It is this content, and this content construed as problematic, that is at the heart of teaching and teacher education. Finding ways to document teaching practice, think about it, and make sense of it in line with what we believe about the aims and purposes of teaching, is the hope of reflective teaching and reflective teacher education as well.

Coming to understand the cases as they encounter them in the teacher education setting prepares novices to become scholars of their practice and therefore creators of knowledge, not solely dispensers of it. Preparing students to be scholars of practice is a common goal of teacher education, even if the language used to describe that goal varies. We all want our graduates to know how to think about their work and the work of others in the field in order to understand it, to learn from it and eventually contribute to new conceptions of it. How to accomplish that goal, however, is problematic given the inherent complexity of teachers' work, and the strained circumstances of schools where that work takes place.

Historically, teacher educators, as with their colleagues in other professions, have relied on the fieldwork component of their programs to accomplish the learning about, and from, practice. A decade of research in teacher education, however, has demonstrated the pitfalls and problems of learning from experience in teaching (Feiman-Nemser and Buchmann, 1985). Learning from experience is difficult for everyone; nowhere is this more so than in teaching where the task is infinitely complex, constantly changing and uncertain along almost every dimension (Buchmann and Schwille, 1983). Schools are not good learning environments for teachers (Shulman, 1988), even student teachers (Zeichner, 1981; Richert, 1987). Rather than encouraging novices to reflectively question the goals and actualities of what they see and experience, school people and school systems encourage newcomers to assimilate into an existing way of being and way of knowing. The result limits rather than liberates the novice teacher as he or she learns to think about school practice (Borrowman, 1956; Conant, 1963; Wehlage, 1988; Tabachnick *et al.*, 1979; Zeichner, 1981; Zeichner and Liston, 1987).

Cases offer teacher educators a viable alternative. Rather than bringing fledgling novices into classrooms for a single source of information about practice, cases bring practice to teachers in a form that can be studied, understood and challenged. The presentation of cases for study suggests a view of practice that requires contemplation and analysis. In my experience, the typical student teacher views the problems, dilemmas and complexities of practice as something to survive rather than something to deliberate. Not that survival is unimportant; it is especially important to the novice. However, what cases allow is several levels of analysis which results in a process that moves the novice beyond immediate survival responses. The basic level of analysis may be how to 'live through' a particular situation. From that basic level, cases allow the novice to advance to a consideration of what is happening in the situation, and why. And, she can then consider the purposes and consequences of the teacher's decisions in that particular situation. Before the case deliberation is complete, a set of questions that is more theoretical can also be introduced: What is this a case of? What, if anything, does this example from practice teach us about teaching in general? What principle of practice is this case an instance of?

By using cases, I present the content of teacher education — the issues and dilemmas of teaching practice — when I use case methods in my classes. I am concerned with both what my students think about, and how they think about it. When teachers think, they think about something, and they think about it in particular ways. Our task in teacher education is to help our students (and ourselves in the process of reflective teacher education) know what to think about, and how to think about it; what to attend to, and how to attend to it; what is important, and what is less so; what questions to ask, and why. Cases are representations of teachers' work. As objects of study, they provide a vehicle for us to move ourselves and our students towards this goal of reflective practice.

The Social Aspect of Case Methods

The second factor that guides my thinking about cases in teacher education is that the methodology is social in nature. Cases bring teachers together for deliberation about their work. At least two teachers are always involved in the process — the teacher in the case, and the one reading it. Two is the minimum number; typically cases are studied by groups of teachers numbering three or four, up to twenty or more. In my larger classes where I use short cases to illustrate theoretical constructs, as many as thirty of us work together to make sense of the circumstances the case describes. Whatever the number, the fact that more than one person is present challenges the norm of isolation that pervades teaching and teacher education.

There are several reasons why I believe working with colleagues is essential to good teaching. One reason is that working together requires a conversation, and a conversation is a necessary piece of the process of reflection. The authors of *Women's Ways of Knowing* emphasize the conversation aspect of reflection in a way that corresponds with my belief. They say:

> In order for reflection to occur, the oral and written forms of language must pass back and forth between persons who both speak and listen or read and write — sharing, expanding, and reflecting on each other's experiences. Such interchanges lead to ways of knowing that enable individuals to enter into the social and intellectual life of their community. Without them, individuals remain isolated from others; and without the tools for representing their experiences, people also remain isolated from the self. (Belenky *et al.*, 1986, p. 26)

In my classes the students read or study cases alone before they come together to discuss them with their colleagues. Sometimes I ask them to read the case with a set of questions in mind: eg. What does the case suggest about appropriate methods for urban settings? What contextual factors contribute to the situation described in this case? As you think through this situation, what do you think were the motivations of the teacher? Does Hawkin's notion of 'critical barriers' help in understanding this case? If you were to use this case as the example, how would you end the sentence 'Teaching is most like ____'?

Frequently, I do not ask guiding questions before the students study the case on their own. Instead, I instruct students to read and respond to the case, determine what occurs and why, and come to class knowing the case well. The first step of the process, then, is the reflective conversation one has with oneself about teaching practice. As the semester moves along, students become more adept at having this conversation on their own. They know what to ask, how to isolate critical aspects of the text for consideration (a mode of problem 'framing' in Donald Schon's, 1983, terms), what practical or theoretical knowledge they might bring to bear and, finally, how to formulate and articulate their own conception of what is important to them about the case. The reflective conversation allows them to assess what they know, understand old knowledge in new ways and construct new knowledge as part of the process of growth. One student teacher explained a combination of those outcomes when she said:

> Besides the general benefits which just doing the cases have brought to me, each case has helped me learn more about the topic we were studying at the time. Since the case studies were about issues that concerned me, I also learned how these topics related to what I am doing. So, for example, I learned a great deal about styles of teaching and how I think about which style of teaching I can use in my own work in teaching computers. (TD)

In reflecting further on her experience she added:

> What is interesting to me about this was that I had never understood the value of these principles — why they are good for the learner — until I did this case study. This, even though I was a psychology major, and went through teacher education courses. It's not that I never heard these principles explained. It was just that the case study helped me understand how and why they work. (TD)

This process of studying the case and preparing for the case discussion with colleagues gives teachers 'voice' — a second reason for emphasizing the social aspect of case methods for teacher education. The requirements of the assignment require that the teachers learn to articulate what they know about teaching and learning. In the process of coming to know, they grapple with the real dilemmas of practice as presented in the case. Eventually they come to a personal understanding of the situation which they subsequently 'name' in preparation for presenting their ideas to their colleagues. Talking about what they know empowers teachers. They find that they know more than they thought they did, what they don't know they can learn and that they can contribute to a professional conversation. In fact, they come to believe that such a process is part of their professional responsibility. One student expressed her reaction to hearing her own voice as part of the professional conversation in this way:

> You have your time [to contribute] and you put down your ideas and then you have the discussion. It was like [a colleague would say] 'Oh wow, that's a real good idea. I'd like to add that to my reaction'. You know, it really let's you see and it gives [joint] ownership to the discussion afterwards. (TI)

The process of knowledge construction is demonstrated powerfully as cases are examined and discussed in the case methods format. 'The process helps unleash ideas that might not surface if one isolated individual is trying to solve the problem alone', one student teacher commented (TP). Teachers working together, contemplating the dilemmas of practice and building on each other's ideas, are at the core of the method. New ideas are generated and new ways of thinking explored. Occasionally I have students analyze a case alone, discuss it with colleagues, rethink the case alone and re-examine it with colleagues the next week. In that format the building of ideas is especially clear. One student teacher remarked:

> The second case I had heard the week before and I soon realized something incredible was going on. A whole new bunch of ideas were emerging — we were truly breaking new ground. Last week's discussion, I believe, was valuable to the presenter because I saw the results of our discussion implemented.... [but] this discussion, which included different people — I was the only one who had heard it before — was just amazing. She has a whole new set of really valuable ideas to think about and follow-up on. I changed my mind. Maybe something more is to be gotten in presenting the case a second time. (TH)

As students put ideas together, choose language to describe their sense-making and finally bring that construction to the public forum for re-examination among colleagues, they engage in an intellectual pursuit that honors both their knowledge and their contribution, as well as the knowledge and contribution of their peers. The process builds a sense of self, a sense of self as teacher and a sense of self and community. This community connection suggests an enhancement of professional identity which is another outcome of the social exchange dimension of case methods. One student teacher described it this way:

> The biggest benefit to me in doing case studies has been the chance to examine issues with other people in the teaching profession. What the case studies do is give us a context in which to have a conversation, which I have found to be very powerful. My perception of myself and other teachers as professionals and as researchers has been enhanced through this process. (TD)

Part of associating with one's professsional colleagues in a shared delibera-tion such as that of a case conference discussion, involves listening to other voices, and acknowledging the importance of multiple perspectives. Diversity is honored by a process that requires sharing perceptions, exchanging ideas and building on one another's notions. While there are thorough and less thorough ways of considering any given teaching situation, accurate and less-accurate ways of recalling the facts of the case, and perhaps even insightful and less insightful ways of making sense of the circumstances, there is no right or wrong anwer. The group deliberation celebrates different perspectives on the one hand, and checks for myopic misunderstanding on the other. In both ways (celebrating diversity and challenging myopia), the bounds of one's personal rationality are taken into account as professional colleagues use the case conference format to join both heads and hearts in the process of deliberating the dilemmas of practice in their field.

Cautions to Consider

While my experience using case methods in my classes has been well received by my students, and successful in moving my teaching towards the goals I have outlined in this chapter, the process has not been without its difficulties nor its disappointments. Important to understanding the difficulties is to consider the teacher education context. The assumptions underlying case methodology and the goals of the method as I have presented them in this chapter, contrast with a performance-based model of teacher education that serves an ideology of extern-ally defined accountability. My hope is for current programs of teacher educa-tion to prepare a generation of teachers who themselves can define the knowledge base of teaching and the conditions of their own work. Rather than seeing teaching as a set of skills requiring technical mastery that are clearly identifiable and easily measured, my view is that teaching is an intellectual task requiring an ability to ask questions, search for answers, tolerate ambiguity, take risks and proceed in a thoughtful and caring way towards goals that are multiple, complex and constantly shifting to meet new and changing imperatives. In this model a good question holds high value. But good questions are hard to come by (and hard to measure); they require time to formulate and a safe environment in which to be asked.

Another difficulty of case methods is that it is labor intensive. First there is finding a case that is appropriate for the intended outcome. Since the methodology is relative new, cases are not yet abundant.[13] Those cases that are available are uneven in quality. Case selection is difficult, furthermore, since experience is limited and selection criteria are not available. The teacher educator is thus establishing criteria and choosing cases at the same time.

Second, once a case is located, preparing to teach it and actually teaching it are labor intensive as well. Teaching a case is teaching using discussion. To do it well, it is essential to know the case thoroughly which includes having the details of the case at hand, enumerating the principles demonstrated by the case and identifying questions for guiding the discussion towards a consideration of those principles.

Moving case discussions towards a consideration of principles is also difficult. The descriptive character of the case is a blessing and a liability both, in this regard. While as a text for deliberation the descriptive case is powerful for all of the reasons cited earlier, its narrative form presents difficulties for moving a discussion from the level of the story, to that of the principles embedded in the story. 'Story swapping' is a favorite pastime of teachers, myself included. In studying cases, however, it is imperative to move the discussion well beyond the sharing of tales. It is my experience that a carefully prepared plan for teaching the case mitigates against a one-level consideration of its content. Modeling the processes of professional deliberation and thoughtful reflection is part of the task of teaching cases. As in the classes I teach that I have discussed in this chapter, this modeling becomes particularly critical when the curriculum calls for students to lead themselves in case discussions as the semester moves ahead.

Because the culture of schooling does not prepare students to take responsibility for their learning the way case method requires, there is a socialization element involved in teaching cases as well. Students must come to the case discussions carefully prepared. This involves their knowing the case, and being ready and willing to articulate their views on it. For my students, taking the responsibility to know the case well, and being ready to talk about it, are both learned skills sometimes met with initial resistance. Also difficult for students is the complexity that diversity brings to the process. Working with cases requires learning to manage multiple perspectives and diverse points of view. Conflicts arise. People silence themselves or are silenced by others. Preparing students to responsibly participate in a group process and manage these complex group dynamics requires making explicit the processes of collegiality, reflection, professional deliberation. Ultimately these factors and their relationship to good teaching must be made explicit as well.

So, while cases offer great promise for teacher education, they present some important-to-consider difficulties at the same time. We have much to learn about cases and case methods for teacher education. In a recent paper discussing similarities between case methods for law education and teacher education, Carter and Unklesbay (1989) caution against embracing case methods without careful reflection ourselves about the potentials and pitfalls they bring to the endeavor of preparing novice professionals. In the spirit of inquiry, then, and with the same standard of scrutiny we ask of our student teachers as they select strategies for their teaching, we must scrutinize ourselves. We are at an important crossroads in teacher education. It is incumbent upon us at this juncture when the eyes of the nation are on teachers and how they are prepared, that we conduct research on our own teacher education methods. It is time for us to determine when, and under what conditions, particular program structures and the methodologies associated with them, are most likely to contribute to the preparation of reflective novice teachers. For it is with these novice professionals whom we send off to schools in desperate need of their best capabilities, that we offer hope for a new vision and a better human condition.

Notes

1   The notion of limited or 'bounded' rationality as it affects teacher's capability for reasoned decision making is discussed by Lee Shulman and Neil Carey (1984) in their provocative essay, 'Psychology and the limitations of individual rationality: Implications for the study of reasoning and civility'. Donald Schon (1983) discusses the limits of technological rationality which also affect teachers in their ability to rely on purely technical strategies for solving complex problems.

2   'Active' professions, according to Dornbusch and Scott (1975), are ones that are characterized by uncertainty. In addition to being fast-paced, they have multiple and shifting goals which result in a consequent complexity in the work tasks at any given time.

3   See Richert, 1987, for a complete discussion of the research.

4   By using the term 'text' here, I do not mean to imply written text only. While cases are most frequently presented in written format, this is not always so. I have had students create and present cases that are primarily video- or audio-based rather than written. See Richert (1989b) for a discussion of case methods using video cases.

5   In conceptualizing cases as 'situational' I am drawing on the work of Brown, Collins and Duguid. See, for example, their article, 'Situated cognition and the culture of learning', *Educational Researcher*, 18, 1, pp. 32–42.

6   In thinking about how 'cases present information needed to make sense of the situation' it is important to keep in mind that the case is presented as the writer of the case, who, in the cases I use in class, is typically a teacher. By including some information and not other, the case writer is highlighting the relative significance of particular contextual information as he or she sees it. Not all of the available data are presented in the case. Therefore, as teachers study cases, part of the process is to consider the contextual information presented to determine its potential bias and its adequacy for understanding the case. The case can be studied and interpreted as it is presented, and again as it might be understood given a different perspective with additional (or other) information highlighted.

7   The complexity of increased heterogeneity in American classrooms is intensified when considering the shortage of teachers representing the growing populations of non-white, and non-US born children. Minority (soon to be non-minority) populations of school children are rapidly increasing, while people from those same groups are entering teaching is fewer numbers. With a growing non-white student population and a growing predominantly-white teaching population, the

significance of improving cultural sensitivity and awareness becomes increasingly important for teacher education.

8   One source of case studies from which teaching cases focusing on *content* have been created is the 'Knowledge Growth in a Profession' research project which was sponsored by the Spencer Foundation and directed by Lee Shulman at Stanford University. For a description of this research see Shulman, L.S. (1987) 'Knowledge and teaching: Foundations of the new reform', *Harvard Educational Review*, 57, 1, pp. 1–22.

9   A description of this class assignment and the cases that resulted from it can be found in two places. The first is a chapter written for a book in press. The chapter and book titles are: 'Writing cases: A vechicle for inquiry into the teaching process', in Shulman, J. (Ed.) *Case Methods in Teacher Education*, Teachers College Press. In the second paper, I again describe this case assignment and include some perceptions of effect from the student/teachers who wrote and presented the cases. The second paper, 'Cases written by teachers: A case for case methods in teacher education', was presented at the Annual Meeting of the American Education Research Association Meeting in San Francisco in April, 1989.

10   The writing of teaching cases is happening all across the country. At Harvard, for example, cases are prepared for both the teaching of teachers and the teaching of teacher educators (see Lyons, 1989). Far West Lab for Educational Research in San Francisco has published two books of cases and they are working on several others (Shulman and Colbert, 1988, provides an example). The Kleinfeld cases at the University of Alaska are another set of cases prepared for teacher education (Kleinfeld, 1988). Silverman and Welty (in press) at Pace University are also writing cases which they use in their teacher education classes. Books of cases that focus on different dimensions of teachers work — classroom management, the teaching of science, teaching in urban settings — are beginning to appear in the literature as well.

11   This quote comes from data gathered for a study I conducted comparing two forms of case methods in teacher education (Richert, 1989a, 1989b). The student-teachers in the study were enrolled in a masters class I teach entitled 'Inquiry into the Teaching Process'. The notation at the end of the quote indicates the teacher's assigned project initials (TE, in this instance). All quotations included in this chapter are taken verbatim from the interview and/or questionnaire data.

12   A potential tension exists between the writing of the case and the studying of it for teacher learning. In order to write a case, the teacher must make decisions about what details of the event to include. The teacher's judgment, therefore, frames the story that the case tells. In good cases the writers present the details as they determine their significance. Since cases are used for teacher learning, a good case also includes some of the additional cacophony of school life so that the teacher-learners can practice sorting through the 'real' distractions of school life as they work to make sense of the situation described.

13   While case methods as it is being explored and articulated currently in the teacher education literature, is relatively new, the notion of studying incidents of practice such as those described in the current case form has a long historical precedent in teacher education. On an informal basis teachers have always learned from shared stories of practice visited and revisited by teachers and their colleagues. There are more formal teacher education strategies described in the literature that also provide a basis to understand the potential power of cases for teacher learning. Two recent examples include classroom simulations and teaching protocols. See Cruickshank's (1984) discussion of both of these strategies and others like them in his Phi Delta Kappa book on teacher education models.

References

ALBAN, J. (December, 1989) Personal conversation.

BELENKY, M., CLINCHY, B., GOLDBERGER, N. and TARULE, J. (1986) *Women's Ways of Knowing: The Development of Self, Voice and Mind*, New York: Basic Books Inc.

BERLINER, D.C. (1986) 'In pursuit of the expert pedagogue', *Educational Researcher*, **15**, pp. 5–13.

BORROWMAN, M. (1956) *The Liberal and Technical in Teacher Education*, New York: Teachers College Bureau of Publications, Columbia University.

BROWN, J.S., COLLINS, A. and DUGUID, P. (1989) 'Situated cognition and the culture of learning', *Educational Researcher*, **18**, 1, pp. 32–42.

BUCHMANN, M. and SCHWILLE, J. (1983) 'Education: The overcoming of experience', *Journal of American Education*, November, pp. 30–51.

CARNEGIE FORUM (1986) *A Nation Prepared: Teachers for the 21st Century*. The report of the Carnegie Forum on education and the economy's task force on teaching as a profession. Washington, D.C.: The Forum.

CARTER, K. and UNKLESBAY, R. (1989) 'Cases in teaching and law', *Journal of Curriculum Studies*, **21**, pp. 527–36.

COHEN, E.G. (1984) 'Talking and working together: Status, interaction and learning', in PETERSON, P., WILKINSON, L.C. and HALLINAN, M. (Eds) *The Social Context of Instruction: Group Organization and Group Processes*, New York: Academic Press.

CONANT, J. (1963) *The Education of American Teachers*, New York: McGraw Hill.

CRUICKSHANK, D. (1984) *Models for the Preparation of Teachers*, Bloominton IN: Phi Delta Kappa.

CUBAN, L. (1984) *How Teachers Taught: Constancy and Change in American Classrooms 1890–1980*, New York: Longman.

DEWEY, J. (1933) *How We Think: A Restatement of the Relation of Reflective Thinking to the Educative Process*, Chicago: Henry Regnery Co.

DORNBUSCH, S.M. and SCOTT, W.R. (1975) *Evaluation and the Exercise of Authority*, San Francisco: Jossey-Bass.

FEIMAN-NEMSER, S. (1983) 'Learning to teach', in SHULMAN, L.S. and SYKES, G. (Eds) *Handbook of Teaching and Policy*, pp. 150–70, New York: Longman.

FEIMAN-NEMSER, S. and BUCHMANN, M. (1985) 'Pitfalls of experience in teacher preparation', *Teachers College Record*, **87**, 1, pp. 53–65.

FLODEN, R.E., BUCHMANN, M. and SCHWILLE, J. (1987) 'Breaking with everyday experience', *Teachers College Record*, **88**, 4, pp. 485–506.

GEERTZ, C. (1973) *The Interpretation of Cultures*, New York: Basic Books.

GOODLAD, J.I. (1983) *A Place Called School*, New York: McGraw Hill.

GREENE, M. (1986) 'Reflection and passion in teaching', *Journal of Curriculum and Supervision*, **2**, 1, pp. 68–81.

HEILBRUN, C.G. (1988) *Writing a Woman's Life*, New York: Ballantine Books.

HERTZ-LAZAROWITZ, R., SHARAN, S. and STEINBERG, R. (1980) 'Classroom learning style and cooperative behavior of elementary school children', *Journal of Educational Psychology*, 72, pp. 97–104.

HOLMES GROUP (1986) *Tomorrow's Teachers: A Report of the Holmes Group*, East Lansing, Michigan: The Holmes Group.

KLEINFELD, J. (1988) Learning to think like a teacher. Unpublished manuscript, Center for Cross-Cultural Studies Rural College, University of Alaska, Fairbanks.

KLEINFELD, J. (1989) The special virtues of the case method in preparing teachers for minority schools. Unpublished manuscript, Center for Cross-Cultural Studies Rural College, University of Alaska, Fairbanks.

KLEINFELD, J. and NORDHOFF, K. (1989) Getting it together in teacher education: A

'Problem-centered' curriculum. Unpublished manuscript, University of Alaska, Fairbanks.

LYONS, N. (1989) 'Teaching by the case method: One teacher's beginnings', *On Teaching and Learning*, The Journal of the Harvard-Danforth Center, April.

NORDHOFF, K. and KLEINFELD, J. (1990) 'Shaping the rhetoric of reflection for multicultural settings', in CLIFT, R., HOUSTON, W. and PUGACH, M. (Eds) *Encouraging Reflective Practice: An Examination of Issues and Exemplars*, New York: Teachers College Press.

RICHERT, A.E. (1987) Reflex to reflection: Facilitating reflection in novice teachers. Unpublished doctoral dissertation, Stanford University.

RICHERT, A.E. (1989a) Cases written by teachers: Case method and inquiry in teacher education. Paper presented at the Annual Meeting of the American Education Research Association, San Francisco.

RICHERT, A.E. (1989b) Preparing cases, promoting reflection: A case for case methods in teacher education. Paper presented at the Annual Meeting of the American Education Research Association Meeting, San Francisco.

ROSEWATER, A. (1989) 'Child and family trends: Beyond the numbers', in MACCHIAROLA, F. and GARTNER, A. (Eds) *Caring for America's Children*, New York: Academy of Political Science.

SCHON, D.A. (1983) *The Reflective Practitioner*, New York: Basic Books, Inc.

SHULMAN, L.S. (1984) 'The practical and the eclectic: A deliberation on teaching and educational research', *Curriculum Inquiry*, **14**, 22, pp. 183–200.

SHULMAN, L.S. (1987) 'Knowledge and teaching: Foundations of the new reform', *Harvard Educational Review*, **57**, 1, pp. 1–22.

SHULMAN, L.S. (1988) 'Teaching alone, learning together: Needed agendas for the new reform', in SERGIOVANNI, T.J. and MOORE, J.H. (Eds) *Schooling for Tomorrow: Directing Reform to Issues that Count*, Boston: Allyn and Bacon.

SHULMAN, J. and COLBERT, J. (1988) *The Intern Teacher Casebook*, Eugene, Oregon: ERIC Clearinghouse on Educational Management, Educational Research and Development; Washington, D.C.: ERIC Clearinghouse on Teacher Education.

SHULMAN, L.S. and CAREY, N.B. (1984) 'Psychology and the limitations of individual rationality for the study of reasoning and civility', *Review of Educational Research*, 54 (Winter), pp. 501–24.

TABACHNICK B., POPKEWITZ, T. and ZEICHNER, K. (1979) 'Teacher education and the professional perspectives of student teachers', *Interchange*, 10, pp. 12–29.

WELTY, W. and SILVERMAN, R. (in press) *Cases in Teacher Education*, New York: McGraw Hill.

WEHLAGE, G. (1981) 'Can teachers be more reflective about their work: A commentary on some research about teachers', in TABACHNICK, B.R., POPKEWITZ, T.S. and SZEKELY, B.B. (Eds) *Studying Teaching and Learning*, New York: Praeger.

ZEICHNER, K.M. (1981) 'Reflective teaching and field-based experience in teacher education', *Interchange*, **12**, 4, pp. 1–22.

ZEICHNER, K.M. and LISTON, D. (1987) 'Teaching student teachers to reflect', *Harvard Educational Review*, **57**, 1, pp. 23–48.

9 But Is It 'Teaching'?
The Use of Collaborative Learning in Teacher Education

Michelle Comeaux

Early last semester, I was observed by a member of my review committee, Ann, as I taught one of my 'Social Foundations of Education' classes. During that particular fifty minute class period, students heard some of their peers read their book reviews of Patrick Welsh's *Tales Out of School* (1986). The rest of the time they spent in collaborative learning groups, discussing a chapter from Jeannie Oakes' *Keeping Track* (1985). During our post-observation conference over lunch, Ann relayed to me a comment one of my students had made to her as class was ending, 'Too bad, you observed her today. She didn't do any teaching.' The comment jolted me — did my students really think that the only time teaching occurred was when there was a lecture or a teacher-led discussion? Was their only vision of teaching a didactic, mimetic or authoritarian one? Such seemed to be the case.

The next day, I used the above student's comment as a springboard for a class discussion on metaphors of teaching, such as the 'empty vessel' metaphor, and what it means to 'teach' and to 'learn'. It was an exciting discussion and I realized that, perhaps, I needed to make clearer to them the connection between my philosophy of teaching and the collaborative group learning I frequently use in my classroom. The discussion also reaffirmed my conviction that one of the best ways to teach them alternative methods of classroom instruction is to model them myself.

The context in which I use collaborative learning is that of my 'Social Foundations of Education' class,[1] a required course for all education majors at Gustavus Adolphus College, a small liberal arts college with an enrollment of 2300. 'Social Foundations' usually is the first course taken by both secondary and elementary education majors at Gustavus, and is composed of primarily sophomores. Class size is limited to thirty students. The purposes of the course are to 'explore some of the past and current debates that have shaped and continue to shape American education' (Course syllabus, 1990) and to address such questions as: What are/should be the purpose(s) of schooling? What forces shape a school's curriculum? What are the history, assumptions and effects of tracking? What is multi-cultural education, why is it desirable to have a multi-cultural curriculum and how does a teacher create one? In addition, a goal of the course is to help students 'think about political and ethical aspects regarding schools and teaching in a thoughtful and knowledgeable way' (Course syllabus, 1990). The course orientation, methods and materials reflect the education department's desire to develop students with the following dispositions:

> They are reflective teachers who consistently examine their beliefs and judge the moral and ethical implications of their actions. [They] view themselves as life-long learners ... [and] are humanistic in their approach to education, valuing cultural and ethnic diversity. They see themselves as partners, both with their colleagues and their students. They are concerned citizens of the world, recognizing the interdepend-ence of all life forms ... [and] are open to new ideas, are willing to change, value learning for its own sake, and want their students to be successful at learning. (Teacher Education Report to NCATE, 1989)

The purpose of this chapter is to describe what collaborative learning is, provide a rationale for using it and give some guidelines/suggestions for its use. I will share some of my students' reactions to the method, based on an analysis of end-of-the semester surveys completed by them. As I hope to show, collabora-tive group learning has much to offer those of us who seek to foster reflective practice in our prospective teachers.

Collaborative Group Learning: What It Is and Isn't

Collaborative group learning is not a 'new' method in any sense. Its philosophical roots of how knowledge is constructed can be traced to the writings and in-fluence of such philosophers/psychologists as John Dewey, George Kelly, George Herbert Mead, Thomas Kuhn, Jean Piaget, L.S. Vygotsky, and others. While collaborative group learning has only recently received much attention in college classrooms in the United States, it had been developed and explored in the 1950s and 1960s by a group of British secondary school teachers and by a British biologist, M.L.J. Abercrombie, who was studying medical education (Bruffee, 1984). Abercrombie's *Anatomy of Judgment* (1964) discusses her research finding that in medical school the skills of diagnosis are better learned when small groups of students work together to establish a diagnosis than it is by students working individually. Based on the work of Abercrombie and others, some United States' medical schools today, such as that at Michigan State University, have created curriculums that revolve around group problem solving rather than traditional lecture formats.

Within the past ten years in the United States, collaborative group learning has been discussed and elaborated particularly by those who teach writing in colleges and universities.[2] It differs in both theory and practice from both the product and process approaches to teaching writing and has generated much debate within the field. Bruffee's text *A Short Course in Writing* (1985) gives an excellent overview of the use of collaborative group learning in the writing classroom. Much of my use of collaborative learning groups has been an applica-tion and extension of the principles and practices created by such teachers and researchers of writing as Bruffee (1982, 1984, 1985), Wiener (1986) and LeFevre (1987).

Often confused with the cooperative group learning models of Johnson and Johnson (1975) and Slavin (1983),[3] collaborative group learning can be defined as a 'group's effort to reach consensus by their own authority' (Wiener, 1986, p. 54). It differs from other models of group work primarily in its emphasis on how group consensus is negotiated and the placement of authority.

Group consensus and negotiation are key features in collaborative learning groups. Tasks are structured so that the group must arrive at some common understanding and agreement about an answer or completion of a task. However, as John Trimbur has pointed out, collaborative learning should not be construed as an activity that discourages divergent thinking or group differences. Rather it calls for a process of 'intellectual negotiation', and the demands for consensus in a task create a pressure that

> leads students to take their ideas seriously, to fight for them, and to modify or revise them in light of other's ideas. It can also cause students to agree to disagree — to recognize and tolerate differences and at best to see the value systems, set of beliefs, etc., that underlie these differences. (cited in Wiener, 1986, p. 54)

How the group arrives at an answer is as important as what their answer is. Ideally, the teacher should pose as questions those that do not have any one 'correct' answer and create problems that have different routes to solution or more than one correct solution. It is the difference between asking a group to answer the question, 'What are the cognitive and affective effects of tracking?' or the question, 'As teachers, how might you best convince a school board to consider an alternative to traditional tracking practices in your school district?' Such a question asks students to make a judgment and arrive at a decision. In doing so, they are allowed to hear how their peers think about the task and to determine together what the most sound decision is and what the criteria should be for judging its soundness.

In collaborative learning, there is a shift of authority from the teacher to the students. While the teacher may observe the groups as they work through a task, it is not his or her role to participate in the group's activity or discussion. The stress is on students learning from their peers and sharing in the construction of knowledge; this can not occur if the teacher still sees her or himself in the role of dispenser of knowledge. The context for learning changes from a classroom dominated by teacher thought and conversation to one dominated by student thought and conversation. As such, the teacher's role is to 'create conditions in which learning can occur and ... set the stage for learning' (Bruffee, 1985, p. 8). Thus, an apt metaphor might be that of teacher as play director. He or she makes sure the 'props' are in place, that the 'actors' have their materials and know their tasks, and then allows them to pull out of themselves the necessary knowledge for successful completion of the task. It is the student-actors, not the teacher-director, who create what happens on the classroom stage. Collaborative group learning is consistent with Dewey's (1975) belief that 'education is essentially a social process' in which 'the teacher loses the position of external boss or dictator but takes on that of leader of group activities' (pp. 58–9). The leader, however, in this case, is very much behind the scenes and puts in all of the work before and after, but not during, the 'performance'.

Why Use Collaborative Learning in the Teacher Education Classroom?

For those of us in teacher education who seek to foster in our students the beliefs, dispositions and skills necessary for them to become reflective practitioners, collaborative learning can be an effective means to the achievement of that goal. I use the term reflective here in the same sense as that of Zeichner and Liston (1987) and others who have based their definition on the distinction Dewey (1933) makes between reflective action and routine action, that is reflective action entails the active, persistent and careful consideration of any belief or supposed form of knowledge in light of the grounds that support it and the consequences to which it leads. Routine action is guided by tradition, external authority and circumstance (Zeichner and Liston, 1987, p. 24).

Much of the emphasis in the literature on reflective teaching has been placed on the development of reflective thought and action during the student teaching phase (and the seminars accompanying it) of the education professional sequence. Such methods as journal writing, action research, ethnographic studies, etc., are frequently used to encourage reflection. Some researchers have argued, however, that the development of the beliefs, dispositions and skills necessary for reflective teaching must begin early in a student's professional program and be a part of a variety of foundations and methods courses if a program is to successfully teach its students how to be reflective teachers (Zeichner and Liston, 1987; Korthagen, 1985; O'Loughlin, 1988). Collaborative learning is one technique that can be used in any course, at any stage in the professional sequence.

How might collaborative learning foster the development of reflective thinking? First of all, it provides a model of teaching that is based on an epistemology that knowledge is socially constructed[4] — a model, I would argue, that is more consistent with the goals of reflective teaching than that of a didactic or authoritarian one. Second, it structures assignments in such a manner that an attitude of 'open-mindedness', a prerequisite for reflective action (Dewey, 1933), is encouraged, as well as strengthening and exercising skills of inquiry. Third, it promotes a view of teaching that is based on collaboration, rather than competition or isolation.

It is quite probable that many students enter teacher education with a view that knowledge is something that must be transferred from the teacher to the student (Lortie, 1975; Feiman-Nemser, 1983; Jackson, 1986; Cohen, 1988). Students are to be passive recipients of knowledge and accept the teacher as the 'authority' because of her or his years of education and experience. It is their 'job' as students to sit quietly and receive that knowledge, while it's the teacher's 'job' to pass that knowledge on, usually in the form of lectures. Students' public school experience has no doubt contributed greatly to that view since 'the 'modus operandi' of the typical classroom is still didactics, practice, and little else' (Sirotnik, 1983, p. 16). Similarly, such a view of learning/teaching is seldom changed by a student's experience in college or university classrooms (Britzman, 1986; Comeaux, 1987). Likewise, little time is spent in teacher education courses studying the dynamics of student-student interaction (Johnson and Johnson, 1985).

If we are to begin challenging students to think about alternative views of knowledge, we must begin with our own approach in the classroom. Because its practice is based on an epistemology that views knowledge as socially constructed, collaborative learning can model for students an alternative to the 'traditional' view of teaching as didactics and little else. As Britzman (1986) notes, 'teacher education's conception of knowledge can promote a view of the teacher as either technician or intellectual, and the extent to which values are rendered explicit can either inhibit or encourage a more critical pedagogy' (pp. 443–4). Thus, I would suggest that if we use an alternative model such as collaborative learning, we must also make clear to students the underlying epistemology on which that model is built. Such a discussion has the additional benefit of enabling students to see their own teacher's process of reflective thinking.

Besides illustrating an alternative view of learning/teaching, collaborative learning helps to develop in students an attitude of 'open-mindedness' or the 'active desire to listen to more sides than one; to give heed to the facts from whatever source they come; to give full attention to alternative possibilities; and to recognize the possibility of error even in the beliefs that are dearest to us' (Dewey, 1933, p. 29). The stress on consensus in collaborative learning creates a situation in which students must listen carefully to each other, challenge each others' views, hold alternative interpretations in mind and, perhaps, admit errors in logic or judgment. I frequently hear students say to each other, 'You mean you think that the author meant _____? I never thought of that. Why do you think that?' or 'Why do you think I'm wrong? What's your evidence?' Assignments can be structured such that students are asked to examine their beliefs in relation to educational practice and to examine each other's conceptions of teaching, learning and education, as well as the grounds for those conceptions. (Examples of some assignments are discussed in the next section.)

Last, collaborative learning establishes a classroom climate that is neither competitive or isolationist. This is in sharp contrast to the typical environment in which a teacher practises his or her profession. As has been well-documented (Feiman-Nemser and Floden, 1986) the classroom can be a lonely place in which teachers feel isolated from their peers, struggling through the ups and downs of the day on their own. To admit a problem with a class or a fear of failing at teaching is often seen as a sign of weakness and something to cover up; similarly successes are frequently unreported as well. Group problem-solving is seldom practised in the teacher's lounge or high school department office.

Many educators/researchers are seeking to establish more collaborative ties with teachers and between teachers (Gomez, 1990; Grumet, 1989) in an effort to reduce the isolation of teachers and bring together their strengths in facing many of the problems confronting educators today. However, such skills of collaboration may be rusty or non-existent in some teachers, for most of us have gone through an educational system and grown up in a society that stresses competition and individual effort. By using collaborative learning in the classroom, we can help students acquire those skills and dispositions so that they see teaching as a collaborative adventure to be engaged in with their colleagues and students, rather than as a solo journey.

Does collaborative learning foster any of the beliefs, dispositions or skills of reflective thinking mentioned above? Little research has been done in the use of collaborative groups in the college classroom, particularly regarding reflective thinking?[5] However, based on the results of an open-ended survey I gave my last semester's class regarding the use of collaborative learning groups, I am optimistic that collaborative learning may accomplish much in terms of helping students develop the beliefs, skills, and dispositions needed for 'reflective action'. Nearly 75 per cent of the students voiced opinions similar to those that follow:

> It [collaborative learning groups] gives you an opportunity to hear more than your own opinion on what we've read. It also makes you look at why you support a certain position.

> It gives more insight into the topics. In the groups you saw various angles of an issue as well as having to express your own ideas; whereas in a large group or class discussion many people wouldn't speak up.

> This is wonderful because we had to think, analyze, and be somewhat creative, rather than having you analyze the text and summarize it for us in class. This way we got to make our conclusions and observations.

> Sometimes other students can explain better than the teacher and if you can explain something, it means you understand it.

> Reporting on what I read to others made it gel for me. I learned even more by having to explain it.

Many students also commented that the collaborative learning groups were a good way for them to get to know their peers as 'people' and to get ideas for teaching from them. Regarding the use of collaborative groups for responding to each other's writing, students most frequent comment was that their peers offered 'valuable suggestions for revision' in a 'non-threatening way'.

A Guide to the Use of Collaborative Learning

My experience with using groups in the classroom began over a decade ago, when I was still teaching high school English. I wanted to use groups as a way of creating a spirit of community in the classroom and to have students teach other how to problem-solve assignments on verbal reasoning more effectively (Comeaux and Waller, 1984). My efforts were not always successful and frequently the time the students spent in groups was a time spent talking about everything but the task on hand. I lacked both the strategies and underlying understanding of principles necessary to make group work an effective means of teaching. I soon gave up the use of groups. Recently, I have witnessed other teachers undergo the same experience (Comeaux, 1989) as they attempt to use groups in the teaching of writing, but without a prerequisite knowledge of the strategies or principles necessary to make group learning effective and successful. Such attempts can become rapidly frustrating for both the teachers and the students.

I offer the following guidelines on the use of collaborative learning, not as a list of 'do's and don'ts', but rather as suggestions that may prove useful to the teacher educator who would like to use collaborative learning, but has little or no prior experience with it. The suggestions are based on readings I have done,[6] workshops I have attended,[7] and, most importantly, discussions I have had with my students. They have taught me the most about how best to use collaborative learning in the classroom and what 'works' and what doesn't.

In the following section, I will first describe what types of collaborative learning tasks my students engage in and then discuss some guidelines that pertain to all the tasks.

Types of Collaborative Learning Tasks

I use collaborative learning in chiefly four ways in my 'Social Foundations of Education' course: for responding to each other's writing, for discussion of material they read, for peer teaching and for creation of some project. At least once every two weeks, students meet in small groups to read and react to each other's writing. Usually, the writing is in the form of a rough draft and students are asked to respond to both the form and content of their partner's writing. As such, they act as an immediate audience for each other (although the audience they are writing for may actually be quite different) and as a sounding board for testing their ideas or arguments. While some editing does occur during this meeting, the emphasis is on the content of the writing. What is discussed in the groups depends on the nature and purpose of the writing assignment and thus differs from week to week. For example, if the assignment is to write a research paper examining and evaluating the pros and cons of some current educational issue, the group discussion may focus on such questions as: Do you agree with the author's evaluation of the arguments? Why or why not? What evidence does he or she present for the conclusions drawn? Were the two sides of the issue both presented coherently or were there some parts you did not understand? Students are always asked to comment to each other what they liked about the paper or felt were strengths in the writing, as well as areas they felt could be improved or clarified. The author and readers must together decide what areas of the discussed paper need to be revised or reconsidered and what areas can be considered 'finished'.

A second use of collaborative learning is for discussion of material that all the students have read, such as a book chapter, a newspaper report or a journal article. In this case, the task is often to come to a consensus about their evaluation of the author's position on the topic or to agree on definitions of terms used and perhaps to apply those definitions to teaching. For example, after my students read chapter 3 in Joel Spring's *American Education* (1989), 'The Politics of Curriculum, Instruction, and Theories of Learning', I asked them to define the following terms discussed in the chapter (terms I knew that most were unfamiliar with) — (a) curriculum categories: social efficiency, humanism, social meliorism, developmentalism; (b) instruction categories: teacher-centred, student-centred; and (c) theories of learning: behavioral psychology, developmental psychology and cognitive psychology. Their second task was to decide which of these theories/ orientations they felt *I* endorsed or held, based on their observations of my teaching, and what evidence they could cite for that decision. The discussion that ensued was an exciting one both among and between groups as one group decided, for example, that I was a cognitive psychologist, while another felt I was a developmentalist (the two, they finally agreed, were not mutually exclusive!). A byproduct of the discussion, was my gaining a better understanding of how my classroom practices were being interpreted by my students!

Groups are also used to have students teach other some material.[8] First, the group is assigned a series of articles or group of chapters to cover, such as chapters 4–7 in Jeannie Oakes, *Keeping Track* (1985). Initially, each group member chooses one chapter to teach the others and agrees to be responsible for reading, synthesizing and teaching the material in that chapter. The next class period, all the members of the class who are teaching chapter 4, for example, meet to discuss what is important to teach from that chapter and how best to do it. Then, the 'teachers' present to their group the material, while the others listen, take notes, ask questions, etc. Thus, it is the students' responsibility to decide what the important concepts are in the chapters, as well as to explain to their peers the significance of these concepts. The material taught from those four chapters is later used by the students as they answer mid-term or final exam essay questions on the assumptions, practice and effects of tracking.

A final type of assignment I use is that of a group project, which results in the production and completion of some piece of writing, class presentation or teaching unit (or all three). One of the group projects my students complete during our unit on multicultural education is a unit lesson plan in their declared content/grade area major. Thus, all the students in secondary mathematics education, for example, will work together, while another group may be made up of elementary education majors.[9] The unit lesson plan must be multicultural in its presentation of material; the features of multicultural education been discussed beforehand in great detail in class and in their reading.[10] The group must turn in their unit for evaluation, as well as present a description of it to the class. Many chose to teach the class some part of their lesson plan as well. Evaluation is based on (a) how well the unit fits the criteria of multicultural education, (b) the conceptualization of the lesson plan and how it was written, (c) the class presentation of the material, and (d) the group's evaluation of how well they worked together as a group.

Guidelines for Use of Collaborative Learning

Group composition

Perhaps one of the first decisions facing the teacher using collaborative learning regards the composition of the group; that is, who should be in the group and how many? Although Johnson and Johnson (1975) and Slavin (1983) suggest that groups be made up of three to five students with varying ability level, I prefer to group the students in terms of experience or perspectives they bring to the task rather than by abilities. For example, some of the 'Social Foundations' students have completed a month long practicum, 'Career Orientation of Teaching', in an elementary or secondary school, while others have not. The practicum gives the students their first view of schooling from 'the other side of the desk' and helps them to examine schooling from a teacher's perspective. Those students often find it easier to relate the material we read to current practices and controversies in schools and bring lots of current 'stories to tell' to group discussions. Thus, I try to have groups composed of both those students who have had that experience and those who have not. Students also vary in terms of types of elementary and secondary schools they attended — from those of rural Minnesota's Iron Range to those of Edina, a wealthy suburb of Minneapolis. Similarly, I find the more heterogeneous the group composition in terms of background, the livelier and more thought-provoking the discussions. Of course, for the first few week or so of class I have little idea what the students' experiences or backgrounds are. In that case, I just make sure I have a mixture of elementary education and secondary education majors and males and females in the groups. Generally, I find four to five is the best number of students to have in a group — more than five and not everyone gets an opportunity to contribute to the conversation equally; fewer than four and not enough diverse opinions may be present. An exception to this number is the group writing response described above. In that case, two to three students in a group works best due to the time it takes to read and critique papers individually.

Group composition is changed frequently, generally after every two or three sessions, so that students get to meet and know all of their classmates. I have found that while a few students would prefer to stay with the same group because the 'chemistry' is just right and they feel comfortable with each other, the majority prefer to switch groups after several weeks of working together. Changing groups also gives students a greater exposure to a variety of viewpoints and opinions, which may help them in the change and re-formulation of their own.

Modeling/discussing of group behavior

Not all students know how to work together in groups, so I take some time at the beginning of the course to solicit from them what conditions make groups work well together. Students have much to add to this discussion, having had experience with groups that were dysfunctional throughout their years of schooling. We discuss, for example, effective listening behaviors, preparation of and responsibility for material assigned, and communication skills in asking/answering questions of each other (probing, clarifying, restating, etc.). At the end of the discussion, we compose on the blackboard a list of 'ground rules' for group participation, which is then typed and distributed to each student.

When the task for the group is to discuss a chapter or article or to solve some dilemma or problem, I ask them to assume and assign the following roles in their groups: recorder, reporter, time-keeper (not always necessary), and monitor(s). It is the recorder's job to keep track on paper the different answers given to a question or problem, as well as the final answer or solution arrived at. The reporter's job is to convey his or her group's decision or answer to the rest of the class during large-group discussion. The time-keeper keeps the group on task and moving toward resolution, especially when a specific amount of time is allocated to the discussion. The monitor(s) checks to make sure all members of the group are participating and that no one is monopolizing the conversation. Thus, following the cooperative learning model of Johnson and Johnson (1975), leadership responsibilities are split among all the members of the group.

Task definition

One of the first things I learned when using collaborative learning was that merely putting a group of students together and telling them to 'discuss' the material was a guarantee for failure. Students did not know where to begin in their discussion and so frequently felt frustrated. I had to spend much time going from group to group, answering their questions and clarifying what I meant by 'discuss'. Now, each person, no matter what the nature of the assignment, receives a sheet describing the task (e.g., 'Discuss the following points . . .; Define the following terms . . . .; List and evaluate the author's arguments regarding . . .; Discuss with the writer the following . . .'; etc.). These sheets are frequently collected at the end of the group meeting (and returned the next class period) so that I can have another means for evaluating the group's work. Students also use the sheets for review at exam time. These sheets are distributed and time is given for clarification of task, if needed, *before* the class breaks into groups.

Another way of using group discussion sheets, if they are related to a reading assignment, is to distribute them to students in the class period before they do the reading and have them answer the questions individually. When their group meets, they write the answers the group arrived at in a different color of ink, alongside their own answers.[11] By using that technique, it often becomes clearer to both them and me what misconceptions they may have had (or sometimes, I discover, still have even after discussion) and where they most differed in their interpretation of the material. Such a technique is used for evaluation of the *process* of the group work and are not graded as a product.

My goal in creating tasks is to design ones that are concrete and challenging, but not frustrating. I find that the assigned questions or problems that create the most exciting and thought-provoking discussions are those that are open-ended ones, calling for divergent thinking. For example, one group discussion task last semester, assigned after nearly eight weeks of their reading Spring's *American Education* (1989), Oakes' *Keeping Track* (1985) and numerous hand-outs from other sources, was to debate the question 'Do schools today succeed in providing equal educational opportunity for all students?' Groups were also required to cite evidence for their position, and that evidence was evaluated by all class members in a follow-up large group or class discussion.

Some teacher educators may be concerned that my focusing of the discussion content/topics for the students violates the philosophy on which collaborative learning is built, that of social construction of knowledge, and causes the classroom to still be more teacher-centred than student-centred. There may be some validity to those concerns.[12] I would argue, however, that students enter the post-secondary classroom with varying dispositions/abilities to reflect and inquire (Gore and Bartlett, 1987; Korthagen, 1988) and at differing developmental stages in how they think about issues (Perry, 1970; Belenky *et al.*, 1986). For those who have sat in classrooms for years in which they were told what, when and how to think, it is a large task (often threatening) to be asked to actually acknowledge, consider and hold in their mind varying viewpoints or interpretations of material; to evaluate arguments and evidence; and to examine the assumptions and underlying beliefs of various educational practices. To ask them also to decide exactly what educational dilemmas or issues to focus on in their discussions often results in total confusion and frustration, in my experience. While some initial frustration and confusion is probably necessary for growth, too much can lead to total rejection of the activity and refusal to participate.[13] As Dewey (1938) notes, 'The belief that all genuine education comes about through experience does not mean that all experiences are genuinely or equally educative' (p. 25). I feel it is my role to assume 'the responsibility for understanding the needs and capacities of the individuals who are learning [in my classroom] at a particular time' (p. 46) and insure that the learning tasks are appropriate, 'educative' ones that will further my goal as a teacher educator of fostering reflective thinking dispositions and skills in my students.

While I may provide the material or focus for the students' thought, it is the students themselves who serve as a 'scaffold' for each other's thinking, following the notion of Vygotsky's 'zone of proximal development' (1978). The interacting with peers of varying developmental stages of critical/reflective thinking, in activities that call for questioning, joint decision making and negotiating, provides the 'discrepancies and subsequent conflicts and uncertainties' (Sigel, 1978, p. 337) necessary for change in students' thinking habits and skills.

Concluding the activity

In my initial attempts at collaborative learning, I frequently neglected to have groups either reflect on their experience or share the results of their discussion with their classmates. Class would simply end, as the groups finished their task, turned in a report of their discussion and left the room. After some reflection myself and participation in collaborative learning workshops, I find my practice has changed. Now, at the end of each task (tasks may carry over several class periods), I ask students to (a) evaluate on paper their group work and (b) share with the class the discussion and arguments their group centered on. The paper evaluation asks them to assess their overall reaction to their group's discussion, the dynamics of the group (e.g., did everyone participate? was leadership shared? was it a non-threatening climate?) and their role(s) in the discussion.[14] After evaluation is completed and collected, time is allowed for each group to report to the class their answers/solutions to the assigned task. The report can sometimes take nearly all of a fifty minute period since groups frequently differ in their answers and debate the issues further. This is, of course, a valuable part of the exercise and further stimulates changes in student's thinking.

Monitoring

I find the less I directly observe the groups, the better they seem to do. If I am present, the students tend to look to me for support of their answer or for clarification of the terms/issues. They stop talking to each other and instead talk to me. Thus, I try to avoid joining any group or even walking around the room. This can be difficult for several reasons — one, because I am naturally curious as to what they are discussing and two, because it's hard to completely break free of the notion that they don't *need* me to guide them through or interpret the material for them (conditioned ways of perceiving knowledge do change, but slowly!).

Patience

I have learned over the past few years that it takes time for students to learn how to work well together and, sometimes, to even see that to do so is desirable. This type of learning is new to many of them and just as they had to learn how to take and organize notes as they listened to a lecture, so too do they have to learn the skills of negotiation and discussion. Furthermore, some of them have to be convinced that this method is not penalizing the 'brighter' students (who they fear will have to do all the work while the 'sluggards' profit from their toil) and that collaborative learning is a legitimate way to learn/teach. For many of them, the idea of them learning from each other is a novel concept and one they do not entirely trust. It is difficult and uncomfortable for some of them not to see the teacher as *the* authority.

Conclusion

Student teachers frequently 'teach as they've been taught' (Comeaux and Gomez, 1990; Gomez and Comeaux, 1990). If prospective teachers never encounter diverse methods of teaching or alternative views of learning, it is unlikely that they will teach any differently from those steeped in the tradition of didactic lecturing. By modeling and requiring the use of collaborative learning, as well as discussing why one might use such a method, teacher educators can give their students a powerful way to think about knowledge and teaching, as well as provide them with a new set of methodological skills.

For me as a teacher educator, the question remains, of course, if students will transfer what they experienced and learned about collaborative learning in my classroom to their own teaching, especially since this 'new' method may contradict much of what they've experienced before. Student responses from the survey given to my class at the end of last semester indicate that many will try using collaborative learning in their classes. To the question, 'Which teaching approaches, if any, that your instructor used in this course might you think of using in your own classroom someday?' Twenty-five out of thirty students in my last semester's class mentioned collaborative learning groups. Of course, without a longitudinal study it is impossible to know if they actually will use this approach. I would feel more confident in predicting their actual use of collaborative learning if I knew other instructors in my department and at the college, as well as their future cooperating teachers, were also using such an approach with them.

Equally unknown to me is whether or not the use of collaborative learning groups actually does foster reflective thinking/teaching and a spirit of collegiality in students' future work relationships. Further research will have to reveal that answer. For now, however, I will content myself with the probability that my students' views have changed enough to allow them to construe a class period spent in collaborative learning groups as a period of *teaching*, as well as *learning*, and with the knowledge that I have supplied them, through my words and actions, with a model of reflective teaching and a context which encourages reflective thought.

Notes

1 I have begun to use collaborative learning in the other courses I teach as well. However, 'Social Foundations' is the course in which I first developed my interpretation of collaborative learning and the context in which I have practised it the most.

2 Collaborative learning has been used in other disciplines, such as biology (Nelson, 1989). However, it is those in the writing field that have dominated the study of its uses and advanced the theory and practice.

3 While some may argue that the difference between collaborative learning and cooperative learning is chiefly one of semantics, I don't believe such is the case. Cooperative learning is offered as an alternative type of goal structure for classroom instruction to those of individual and competitive goals (Johnson and Johnson, 1985). Frequently 'teams' are organized that do compete against each other (Slavin, 1983) and/or the group is tested as a unit and a group grade assigned. Collaborative learning, however, has its roots in social construction of knowledge theory (Bruffee, 1984). While a group grade may be assigned for a project, there is no emphasis on between group competition.

4 It is beyond the scope or purpose of this paper to describe and examine the epistemology of social constructivism. Moreover, like 'reflection', the word has come to be used by groups with very different interpretations of it and with very different agendas and philosophies. To me, however, the term 'social constructivism' implies an epistemology with the following characteristics: learning is brought about through 'invention and reinvention' (Freire, 1970) and accomplished in a social setting in which dialogue and sharing of meaning takes place; knowledge is not viewed as fixed, but rather as fluid and subject to transformation; an individual's behavior is a function, not of rewards and punishments, but of how experiences are organized and made sense of; and reality is both individual and shared (Sigel, 1978).

5 While much research has been done on the use of cooperative learning groups (see Johnson and Johnson, 1985, for a summary), far less has been done on the use of collaborative learning in the college classroom except in its use in writing instruction (see, for example, Clifford, 1981).

6 Particularly helpful readings were Bruffee, 1984, 1985; and Wiener, 1986.

7 Two workshops I attended in 1989, one on critical thinking by Craig Nelson of Indiana University, and the other on collaborative learning by John Trimbur of Boston University, were most useful in elaborating the practice of collaborative learning.

8 This is, in fact, a variation of the 'Jigsaw' method described by Slavin (1983). It differs from his description, however, in that the group is not tested as a unit on the material they have taught each other.

9 In general, I try to avoid dividing students by major and separating elementary education majors from secondary since one of my goals is to have students understand and appreciate the concerns each group has regarding teaching and to emphasize the commonalities they share. However, when working with lesson-planning, students find it more practical and interesting to work with those in their chosen specialty.

10 Those features are based on state of Minnesota requirements for multicultural education and on my approach to multicultural education derived from readings and practice. They include an emphasis on (a) lesson plans that promote a transformation or decision making and social action approach (Banks, 1988); and (b) lesson plans that promote an understanding and appreciation of the cultural diversity of the United States, the historical and contemporary contributions of men and women to society, and the historical and contemporary contributions to society by handicapped persons (Minnesota Rule, part 3500.0550)

11 This technique was one described to me in a workshop by Craig Nelson, Department of Biology, Indiana University, Bloomington, Indiana.

12 I, as well as other teacher educators (see, for example, O'Loughlin, 1990) struggle with what it means to be a constructivist in the classroom. I find myself, like many of my student teachers, knowing what philosophy/epistemology I endorse,

but not knowing how best to put it into practice and make my beliefs consistent with my actions. The struggle is a source of constant tension, although not an unhealthy or unwelcome one.

13 Interestingly, those seniors who have me for a general methods course and were previous students of mine in 'Social Foundations' seem to be much more capable of shifting from a teacher-centred classroom to a student-centred one and are willing and able to share a greater responsibility for the creation of activities and tasks in the curriculum and for direction in the classroom.

14 The format I use is a modification of one designed by Craig Nelson. His, in turn, was based on one described by W.F. Hill in *Learning Through Discussion*, (1969) Sage Publication.

References

ABERCROMBIE, M.L.J. (1964) *Anatomy of Judgment*, Hammondsworth: Penguin.

BANKS, J. (1988) *Multiethnic Education: Theory and Practice*, 2nd edn, Boston: Allyn and Bacon.

BELENKY, M., CLINCHY, B., GOLDBERGER, N. and TARULE, J. (1986) *Womens' Ways of Knowing: The Development of Self, Voice, and Mind*, New York: Basic Books.

BRITZMAN, D.P. (1986) 'Cultural myths in the making of a teacher: Biography and social structure in teacher education', *Harvard Educational Review*, **56**, 4, pp. 442–56.

BRUFFEE, K.A. (1982) 'Liberal education and the social justification of belief', *Liberal Education*, **68**, 2, pp. 95–114.

BRUFFEE, K.A. (1984) 'Collaborative learning and the "conversation of mankind"', *College English*, **46**, 7, pp. 635–52.

BRUFFEE, K.A. (1985) *A Short Course in Writing*, 3rd edn, Boston: Little, Brown and Company.

CLIFFORD, J. (1981) 'Composing in stages: The effects of a collaborative pedagogy', *Research in the Teaching of English*, **15**, pp. 37–53.

COHEN, D.K. (1988) 'Teaching practice: Plus ca change', issue paper 88–3. E. Lansing, Michigan, National Center for Research on Teacher Education.

COMEAUX, M. (1987) 'Investigating my lecture teaching: A report of my action research project. Unpublished manuscript, University of Wisconsin-Madison.

COMEAUX, M. (1989) The reflective teacher: Fact or fiction? A study of the reflective processes of twelve high school English teacher. Unpublished dissertation, University of Wisconsin-Madison.

COMEAUX, M. and GOMEZ, M. (1990, April), Why Sarah doesn't teach like Sandra: Exploring the development of prospective teacher's' knowledge, beliefs, and dispositions about teaching writing. Paper presented at the Annual Meeting of the American Educational Research Association, Boston.

COMEAUX, M. and WALLER, M. (1984) The effects of teaching problem solving strategies in high school English classes. Paper presented at the annual meeting of the American Educational Research Association, New Orleans, Louisiana.

DEWEY, J. (1933) *How We Think*, Chicago, Regency.

DEWEY, J. (1975) *Experience in Education*, New York: Collier Books.

FEIMAN-NEMSER, S. (1983) 'Learning to teach', in SHULMAN, L. and SYKES, G. (Eds) *Handbook of Teaching and Policy*, New York: Longman.

FEIMAN-NEMSER, S. and FLODEN, R.E. (1986) 'The cultures of teaching' in WITTROCK, M.C. (Ed.) *Handbook of Research on Teaching*, 3rd edn, New York: Macmillan.

GOMEZ, M. (in press) 'Reflections on research for teaching: Collaborative inquiry with a novice teacher', *Journal of Education for Teaching*, **16**, 1, pp. 45–56.

GOMEZ, M. and COMEAUX, M. (1990) Always begin from where they are: Matching novices' needs with appropriate programs of induction. Paper presented at the Annual Meeting of the American Educational Research Association, Boston.

GORE, J. and BARTLETT, L. (1987) Pathways and barriers to reflective teaching in an initial teacher education program. Paper presented at the Australian Curriculum Studies Association National Conference, Macquarie University, Sydney.

GRUMET, M. (1989) 'Dinner at Abigail's: Nurturing collaboration', *NEA Today*, **7**, 7, pp. 20–4.

FREIRE, P. (1970) *Pedagogy of the Oppressed*, Middlesex, England: Penguin.

JACKSON, P. (1986) *The Practice of Teaching*, New York: Teachers College Press.

JOHNSON, D.W. and JOHNSON, R.T. (1975) *Learning Together and Alone: Cooperation, Competition, and Individualization*, Englewood Cliffs, New Jersey: Prentice-Hall.

JOHNSON, R.T. and JOHNSON, D.W. (1985) 'Student-student interaction: Ignored but powerful', *Journal of Teacher Education*, **36**, 4, pp. 22–6.

KORTHAGEN, F. (1985) 'Reflective teaching and preservice teacher education in the Netherlands', *Journal of Teacher Education*, **36**, 5, pp. 11–15.

KORTHAGEN, F. (1988) 'The influence of learning orientations on the development of reflective teaching', in CALDERHEAD, J. (Ed.). *Teachers' Professional Learning*, Basingstoke, Falmer Press.

LeFEVRE, K.B. (1987) *Invention as a Social Act*, Carbondale, Illinois: Southern Illinois University Press.

LORTIE, D. (1975) *Schoolteacher: A Sociological Study*, Chicago: University of Chicago Press.

NELSON, C.E. (1989) 'Skewered on the unicorn's horn: The illusion of a tragic tradeoff between content and critical thinking in the teaching of science? Unpublished MS., Bloomington: Indiana University.

OAKES, J. (1985) *Keeping Track: How Schools Structure Inequality*, New Haven, Connecticut: Yale University Press.

O'LOUGHLIN, M. (1988) 'Reconceptualizing educational psychology to facilitate teacher empowerment and critical reflection. Paper presented at the Annual Meeting of the Midwest Association for the Teaching of Educational Psychology, Indiana University, Bloomington, Indiana.

O'LOUGHLIN, M. (1990) Teachers' ways of knowing: A journal study of teacher learning in a dialogical and constructivist learning environment. Paper presented at the Annual Meeting of the American Educational Research Association, Boston.

PERRY, W.G. (1970) *Intellectual and Ethical Development in the College Years: A Scheme*, New York: Holt, Rinehart and Winston.

SIGEL, I. (1978) 'Constructivism and teacher education', *The Elementary School Journal*, **78**, 5, pp. 333–8.

SIROTNIK, K.A. (1983) 'What you see is what you get: Consistency, persistency, and mediocrity in classrooms', *Harvard Educational Review*, **53**, 1, pp. 16–31.

SLAVIN, R.E. (1983) *Student Team Learning: An Overview and Practical Guide*, Washington, D.C.: National Education Association.

SPRING, J. (1989) *American Education: An Introduction to Social and Political Aspects*, New York: Longman Publishing Company.

TEACHER EDUCATION REPORT (1989) prepared for the National Council on Accreditation of Teacher Education, Gustavus Adolphus College St. Peter, Minnesota.

VYGOTSKY, L.S. (1978) *Mind in Society* (Eds M. COLE, V. JOHN-STEINER, S. SCRIBNER, and E. SOUBERMAN) Cambridge: Harvard University Press.

WELSH, P. (1986) *Tales Out of School*, Penguin Publishing Company.

WIENER, H.S. (1986) 'Collaborative learning in the classroom: A guide to evaluation', *College English*, **48**, 1, pp. 52–61.

ZEICHNER, K.M. and LISTON, D.P. (1987) 'Teaching student teachers to reflect', *Harvard Educational Review*, **57**, 1, pp. 23–47.

10 Reading and Doing Ethnography: Teacher Education and Reflective Practice

Kenneth Teitelbaum and Deborah P. Britzman

Introduction

The introduction to and transformation of ethnographic study in education has not been smooth. Nor has it been, to date, easily accepted or universally known in the field. One reason may be that the term 'ethnography' is often interchanged with: qualitative research (Bogdan and Biklen, 1982), fieldwork (Agar, 1980), the phenomenological approach (Bogdan and Taylor, 1975), naturalistic research (Guba and Lincoln, 1981), the constructivist approach (Magoon, 1977), participant observation (Spradley, 1980), the human perspective (Bruyn, 1966), the holistic approach (Rist, 1977), action research (Longstreet, n.d.), an alternative methodology (Carini, 1975) and micro-ethnography (Erickson, 1977). By the early 1980s, confusion around terminology played a role in raising concerns about the growing popularity of ethnography. A dominant question was: 'But is it ethnography?' For example, those suspicious of its gaining recognition in education likened ethnography to: 'A hit and run drive', 'a blitzkreig' and 'a movement with an open admission policy' (Rist, 1980); 'an iceberg' (Hall, 1980); 'a buzz word' (Fetterman, 1982); and being 'mere' (Erickson, 1979). One author's panic, born from a traumatic experience with ethnography, compelled him to take the responsibility of 'sounding the alarm about the potential misuses of ethnographic research' (Hall, 1980, p. 350) in an attempt to restore ethnography's good name.

Despite years of academic debate, 'ethnography' continues to be an unknown or disorienting area of inquiry for many current and prospective classroom teachers and teacher educators. It may seem disorienting to some because ethnographic approaches to the doing and studying of research raise significant tensions about research that, supposedly, were settled long ago by the more traditional approaches of quantitative research. We are referring here to the messy relationships between the objective and the subjective, the researcher and the researched, theory and practice, and research and education. Indeed, ethnographic research embodies the fact that any ideal and real research relationships are never finalized.

Precisely because education is an applied field, those engaged there are constantly grappling with the ways research might sensitively inform practical understandings of the quality of daily life in schools, the education and pedagogy of educators and the democratic goals of educating every student. What the processes and products of ethnography offer the field of education is a healthy respect for complexity, diversity and the problems of understanding the competing perspectives and social practices that constitute lived experience in and out of schools. Perhaps Dell Hymes' (1980) definition best captures the elusive spirit of ethnographic projects in education:

> I should like to give 'ethnography' the connotation of inquiry that is open to questions and answers not forseen.... (E)thnography is inquiry that *begins* with the recognition that one is at work in situations that are massively pre-structured, but pre-structured by the history and ways among whom one inquires. (emphasis added, p. 4)

Our work with students focuses on *beginnings*: the reading of actual ethnographies in education and the doing of particular ethnographic practices as a means to structure classroom inquiries. Such a flexible approach makes ethnographic work quite significant to teacher education and to an image of reflection that can take into account both the given and the possible realities.

Ethnographic Research

Until the last decade or so, the overwhelming number of educational research studies were quantitative in nature. Emanating in the physical and biological sciences and rooted in a positivistic approach to scientific inquiry, this research model is perhaps best exemplified by the work of experimental psychologists. It has been characterized, generally speaking, as deductive, verificative, enumerative and objective (Goetz and LeCompte, 1984). Gaining increasing acceptance among educational researchers during the last ten years, however, has been qualitative research design. Initiated by anthropologists and sociologists as a way to provide more conceptually sophisticated accounts of the complexities of social reality, this research seeks to interrogate different kinds of questions using different kinds of sources and methods. For example, as Marion Dobbert (1982) has suggested, rather than seeking to 'measure reading abilities of school children', qualitative research investigates 'which reading method the students and teacher prefer, and why and how those methods change interpersonal relationships in the classroom' (pp. 7–8). More generally, qualitative research provides rich, 'thick' description (Geertz, 1973) of the socially constructed, negotiated and contextual nature of a cultural setting. It is concerned with description and interpretation rather than with prediction and measurement.

Ethnographic study, a predominant form of qualitative research, should be viewed as both a product and a process (Wolcott, 1988; Goetz and LeCompte, 1984; Agar, 1980). (For discussions of other kinds of qualitative research, see Sherman and Webb, 1988.) As an end *product*, ethnography comprises 'an indepth analytical description of an *intact* cultural scene' (Borg and Gall, 1989, p. 387). It typically includes a richness of descriptive data, an incisive interpretation of that description and an informed integration of findings within broader frameworks. It attempts to answer not just the question of 'What do I see these people doing?' but also 'What do these people see themselves doing?' (Spradley and McCurdy, 1972, p. 9). Additionally, from the subjects' viewpoint(s) as well as from the ethnographer's perspective, this research attempts to answer the more complex question of what underlying rules, patterns and orientations structure (and at times disturb) the meanings, understandings and practices of people.

The *process* of 'doing ethnography' is typically referred to as 'fieldwork'. It involves continuous observation, in an attempt to describe as much as possible of what occurs in the setting being studied. In schools, this might include focuses on the form and content of verbal interaction between subjects, and between subjects and researcher; nonverbal behavior (e.g., body postures and symbolic interaction); and patterns of action and nonaction (Wilson, 1977, p. 255). Extensive handwritten field notes are taken during or after observations and then usually enlarged upon and analyzed at the first opportunity. Almost two decades ago, Cusick (1973) described this aspect of ethnographic research in the following way:

> At the end of each day's field work, I would sit down and type everything that occurred that day. Needless to say, it was a long and painful process before I became reasonably accomplished at the art of remembering and recording events and conversations. (p. 239)

While the recent availability of personal computers has aided this process, it is usually still 'long and painful'.

Besides observations, different kinds of structured formal and informal interviews (e.g., key-informant, career histories, surveys) are conducted, and relevant written sources (e.g., personnel records, minutes of meetings, letters, diaries, memos, books) and nonwritten sources (e.g., audio and video recordings, maps, photographs, artifacts) are studied (Goetz and LeCompte, 1984; Bogdan and Biklen, 1982). Questionnaires, projective techniques (e.g., the Instrumental Activities Inventory of George and Louise Spindler), and standardized tests and other measurement techniques may also be utilized (Wolcott, 1988). Indeed, ethnographers do not rely on a single approach but rather attempt to obtain understanding through multiple data sources and multiple methods of data collection and analysis, a process referred to as 'triangulation'.

To varying degress, the ethnographer might be a participant or a nonparticipant in the cultural setting being studied. A more complete record is perhaps possible by non-participation but a participant observer can offer insights and develop interpersonal relationships that would not be possible for a nonparticipant. Of course, the extent to which one actively participates in a setting may not be a variable that can be easily controlled.

Harry Wolcott (1988) makes the point that perhaps one of the most difficult questions that is asked of the ethnographer by other researchers is, 'What is it that you look at when you conduct your research?' (p. 191). Wolcott suggests that an answer to this question depends on the interplay of five factors: first, the nature of the problem that initiated the need for ethnographic study; second, the personality (and training) of the researcher; third, the course of events that occur during one's fieldwork; fourth, the actual process of sorting through, analyzing and writing that one engages in during fieldwork; and fifth, what one's expectations are for the final account, including how and where it is to be circulated and who is to be the intended audience. Clearly, then, just as there is no one qualitative method that ethnographers adopt, there are many different kinds of questions and problems that ethnographers can and do study. There are, in essence, many variations within qualitative research itself (and human inquiry in general), what one observer has described as 'a rainbow' of approaches and concerns (Fetterman, 1987). What ethnographers do share is the attempt to recreate for the reader, in perhaps a fresh and different way, 'the shared beliefs, practices, artifacts, folk knowledge, and behaviors of some group of people' (Goetz and LeCompte, 1984, p. 2). More than a description, however, ethnography represents an interpretive effort at explaining complexity.

Educational ethnography in specific differs from its anthropological antecedents in its emphasis on local — as opposed to global — settings. In addition, unlike anthropologists who might enter as strangers in unfamiliar worlds, the educational ethnographer typically re-enters the familiar world of schools. Her or his work, then, is to render the familiar as strange and problematic, in an attempt to provide the reader with what a theorist of critical pedagogy has described as the experience of 'extraordinarily re-experiencing the ordinary' (Shor, 1980). In so doing, educational ethnography provides opportunities for the researchers' (and participants') own self-reflectiveness on the meanings of participation and the quality of everyday life for those who live it. Moreover, what distinguishes educational ethnography from other forms of research is the priority ethnographers give to the participants (e.g., administrators, teachers, counselors, students and parents) as intentional and meaning-driven beings. Because the ethnographer seeks to understand the participants' perspectives, ethnography always has the potential to validate and legitimize people's daily life struggles. Dell Hymes (1980) further suggests that the concomitant of that priority is 'the empowering of participants as sources of knowledge' (p. xiv). In fact, educational ethnography has often given voice to those most voiceless in educational research (e.g., Davies, 1989; Ryan, 1989; Fine, 1988; Mac an Ghaill, 1988; Medicine, 1988; Roman,1988; Deyhle, 1986; Sola and Bennett, 1985; Philips, 1983; McDermott and Hood, 1982; Ogbu, 1974). Finally, many educational ethnographies of recent years have been marked by a commitment to transforming existing educational practices in ways that can aid educators in disassembling persistent discriminatory practices, inequalities and ethnocentric orientations (e.g., Brodkey and Fine, 1988; Haug *et al.*, 1987; Goswami and Stillman, 1987; Heath, 1983). We suggest that such a goal is quite relevant to reflective practice.

Ethnography and Reflective Teacher Education

Over the last decade, a growing body of research has documented the value, procedures and potential of doing ethnography and of utilizing ethnographic techniques with those involved in their teacher education (e.g., Britzman, 1989; Smyth, 1987; Goodman, 1986; Woods, 1985a, 1985b; Connelly and Clandinin, 1985; Gitlin and Teitelbaum, 1983; Zeichner and Teitelbaum, 1982; McCutcheon, 1982). This literature is concerned primarily with helping students document and reflect upon their emerging practices (e.g., with reference to curriculum, pedagogy and evaluation) in ways that can move them beyond the immediacy of school life and the mere retelling of anecdotes, to the raising of questions about what is often taken for granted in educational practice. Suggested rationales and activities also focus on helping students to research and theorize about who they are becoming and to experience the process of theorizing not as an isolated activity separate from the experience of teaching, or as a grand truth one attempts to impose, but rather as a lived relationship that is grounded in the practical existence of people and dependent upon the shifting processes of interpretation. When students examine closely the rich complexities born of social interaction, subjective experience, dependency and struggle that characterize life in and outside of the classroom, as well as the moral and existential dilemmas that are so much a part of the work of teachers, reality does not take on an immutable and unitary meaning. When teachers are viewed and view themselves as sources of knowledge, a more constructivist understanding of knowledge is possible. Peter Woods (1987) refers to this type of knowledge as

> not simply an extant body of facts and theories, but a living, ex-
> perimental, processual, flexible, creative compilation of insights,
> memories, information, associations, articulations that go into resourc-
> ing on-the-spot teacher decision making and action. (p. 122)

Two significant intentions thus characterize ethnographic inquiry: the opening of research to its transformatory potential, and the establishment of the teacher's ownership of and centrality in the research process. These intentions are meant to help students move beyond their alienation from educational research and view research as a potential source of enlightenment and revitalization.

Yet while such directions do restore the centrality of teachers to the theorizing process, they should be approached as a point of departure in that the process of studying practices cannot conclude once practices are narrated. In other words, when practices become a text, they must be read not as guarantees of essential truths, or as automatic recipes for action, but as *partial representations* of particular discourses that implicate the voices of teachers and researchers in larger interests and investments. Unless the narrations of practices are read through the lens of discourses, that is, as representing particular ideological interests, orientations and meanings, and of embodying relations of power, there remains the danger of viewing personal knowledge as unencumbered by forms of authority and as unmediated by the relations of power that work through every teaching and research practice. Cameron McCarthy and Michael Apple (1988) are quite clear on this point: 'the production of educational theory and research is itself a site of ideological and political struggle' (p. 30). The particular forms of knowledge privileged in this research are not immune from this struggle. Indeed, such research is, in part, a response to the dominant research models that seek to normalize pedagogical interventions. Our point here is that unless the study of subjective knowledge moves beyond its celebratory appeal, there remains the danger of abstracting the teacher from the social context and from the borrowed discourses one claims as if they were one's own. As John Willingsky (1989) argues, 'researchers must find ways of stepping from behind the disembodied voice' (p. 249).

The above 'dangers' suggest that if ethnography is to be used as a way to refashion an understanding of discursive practices, students of education must have opportunities not just to document their practices but to engage with reading strategies particular to ethnography that allow for reading 'against the grain'. To date, the overwhelming body of literature on ethnography in education has focused on strategies for gathering and interpreting data. We strongly support such efforts and have, in fact, been contributors to their public advocacy. However, we want to claim here that, to the extent possible within a teacher education program, such strategies should not be abstracted from examining ethnographic literature. The danger in such a separation of the act and techniques of researching and writing from the practices of reading literature is that those learning to do ethnography may become unfamiliar with (and therefore unreflective about) competing traditions of ethnographic writing and consequently be unprepared for critiquing the product of their efforts. In effect, as Linda Brodkey (1987) asserts, 'New ways of writing require new ways of reading' (p. 74).

The work of David Hess (1989) offers a thoughtful way to reconceptualize and couple reading and writing ethnography. While specifically addressed to anthropologists, Hess' examination of how textual organization, voice and the politics of metaphor help to structure the narration of experience can provide a powerful lens from which to critically read and write the ethnographic account.

An understanding of textual organization helps the reader to consider the structure of the text, the choices involved in selection, the multiple identities of the narrator and the sense of chronology suggested by a tense of time known as the 'ethnographic present'. The reader might examine how literary conventions fashion partiality in ethnographic writing, thus focusing on what is said and left unsaid, and on the ethnographer's own investments. The concept of 'voice' is central to ethnographic writing. To attend to the voices that are included in every ethnography can help students to explore both the tensions of narration, all the voices that compose it, and multiple shifts of intonation. Because ethnography suggests a polyphony of voices, students should explore the politics of being known and making others known, and in this way be able to move beyond the 'disembodied voice of the researcher'. The omnipresent narrator of the educational ethnography, for example, embodies multiple identities: as participant/ observer, as researcher, as academic, as advocate and as interpretor of the lived experiences of others. Distinguishing these voices can orient students to discover the ways that the ethnographer authorizes and authors the voices of others. Moreover, when students analyze their own accounts, they can begin to critique the problems of ethnocentrism, the partiality of any understanding and the easy mistake of reading an ethnography as if it were a complete catalog of a selected culture. Finally, attention to the politics of metaphor concerns the analysis of ethnography as representation and the ways language works to embody a particular culture. Indeed, to approach an ethnography, as well as any research effort, as a metaphor may well encourage students to reflect upon the dual problems of objectivity and subjectivity in narrating one's own interpretive efforts.

Each of these aspects — textual organization, voice and the politics of metaphor — work to highlight the double issue of ethnography as an interpretive effort of *both* the ethnographer and the reader of ethnographies. As Hess concludes:

> ... teaching ethnographic writing nowadays means teaching an ethnography that is engaged not only with its informants but also with its implied readers, an ethnography that triangulates its path among the conflicting values which guide ethnographic writing and reverberate uneasily among [dialogue with? parody?] themselves. I refer to what remains at the core of this strategy of teaching ethnographic writing: the triple critique — turned outwardly as well as reflexively back on oneself — of political domination, ethnocentrism, and scientific methodology. (p. 173)

We suggest, then, that reflective teacher education programs provide students with the opportunities to become more knowledgeable about and skilled in two kinds of efforts: the critical reading of ethnographic accounts and the methods of ethnographic research. We briefly turn now to two examples of our own work in teacher education in which we have attempted to address these efforts.

Practices in Doing and Reading Ethnography

As Kenneth Zeichner (1987) points out, ethnography has been used both within campus-based courses and field experiences. In both cases, it is typical that 'students spend some time in schools studying various aspects of classrooms, curriculum, and teacher-pupil interactions, with varying degrees of guidance provided by teacher educators' (p. 569). Our first example follows the major emphasis that Zeichner describes in providing opportunities for students to experience aspects of ethnographic practices. Our second example gives more attention to the reading of ethnographic literature. Although in practice these two examples overlapped in significant ways, we have tried here to describe aspects of each one in ways that would not be repetitive.

Before coming to the State University of New York at Binghamton, one of the authors taught at Syracuse University and was director of a master's-level teacher education program in urban elementary teaching. Students (about twelve in any one year), most of whom were liberal arts graduates, enrolled in three courses with the director. One course ('The Urban School') was offered during the summer, one ('Urban Elementary Teaching') during the fall semester and one ('Multiculturalism and the American Classroom', with other students enrolled as well) during the following summer. While concerned with many different aspects of teaching (e.g., from lesson planning and the nature of the curriculum to a sociological examination of the urban school), the consecutive two-course sequence and the later third course provided the opportunity for ethnographic data collection and reading as part-time class activities. The attempt was made to interweave a focus on ethnographic study, albeit in very limited fashion, within the more traditional concerns of the three courses. Doing and reading ethnography were viewed as providing spaces for these prospective teachers to examine more closely the complexity and diversity of elementary school life. Emphasis was placed primarily on the skills that could be practiced, the questions that could be raised and the understandings that could be gained from ethnographic accounts.

After initial discussions about the nature of culture, students examined accounts of the hidden curriculum (Jackson, 1968), grouping practices (Oakes, 1985) and teacher-student interactions, in particular concerning the issue of sex equity (Sadker and Sadker, 1982), not because they were examples of ethnography (which they are not) but rather to encourage students to be more aware of the kinds of rather subtle but crucial aspects of school life that need to be addressed. Later, in the third course with the director, after students had limited experience in collecting, interpreting and sharing their own data, they read and critiqued various ethnographic accounts. These studies were assigned not so much for the ways they could inform students about ethnographic methodology but rather for how they could enhance students' awareness and understandings of the cultural problematics of school life (e.g., Sola and Bennett, 1985; Gilmore, 1985; Heath, 1982; Mohatt and Erickson, 1981; Au and Jordan, 1981; Carrasco, 1981; Rist, 1970).

During the first summer, the students were involved in a tutoring field experience at a local community center; during the fall semester they were assigned to an elementary school, where they did substitute teaching (sometimes in one classsroom on a long-term basis) or, when not asked to substitute, helped out in various other capacities at the school. During the second field experience, which was linked to a campus-based course with the director, students were expected to write up a 'mini-ethnography'. It is not possible in this brief space to entirely describe how this assignment evolved, but a few key aspects of it can be highlighted.

The first discussions centered on what it means to engage in ethnographic data collection. Among the points emphasized were the need to make problematic what is too often taken for granted about school life, the existence of multiple perspectives in any one school, the subjective nature of one's observations and the ethical tensions of formally observing others. Because the students were not being trained to be anthropologists or sociologists of education but rather reflective classroom teachers, and because of the very limited time available for attending to this assignment, these introductory discussions were relatively brief and simplified. In addition, five aspects of the project in particular were emphasized, what Susan Florio-Ruane (1990) has recently referred to as: looking, listening, asking, recording and analyzing.

What was stressed, then, was that 'observing' in the ethnographic sense meant, first, looking closely at the community, the school, the classroom, etc., in a way that differed substantively from when the sole concern is with improving one's classroom teaching skills. For example, initiated by a previous director of the program, during the first summer the students were expected to take walks in the neighborhood around the community center where they tutored for the purpose of noting what struck them most about it. They were not asked to focus on anything in particular but rather to gain a general view of the neighborhood and its participants and in effect to practice their observational skills. This effort was repeated in the fall, when they were at the elementary school. General observations included not just the neighborhood but also the school grounds, architecture, playground, hallways, classrooms, etc.

It was also stressed that good observing meant listening carefully as well as looking carefully, for example, with regard to teachers' verbal interactions with students and with other staff, students' verbal interactions with other students, and so forth. In addition, the education students were expected to more formally ask teachers, students, administrators and other staff members about what they were doing and why, and how they viewed school and classroom life. To enhance this aspect, the students in the program were required to conduct more formal 'interviews' with both teachers and students. Suggested questions were provided (e.g., see Posner, 1985) but the education students were encouraged to follow their own interests and concerns and view these encounters more like extended conversations than structured interviews. Of course, the interviews and observations were intended to inform each other. Thus, one student wrote: 'Watching Joyce and Susan during brief encounters throughout the day, I feel that they relate to their students in a way that corresponds to their [stated] philosophies' (CM, 26 September 1987). Although the students were encouraged to probe, it was emphasized that, especially with schoolchildren, it should not be done in a way that could make the interviewees uncomfortable.

The fourth aspect of this project that was emphasized was recording. The education students were asked to carry a small notebook and pen around with them whenever possible. However, given their high level of participation in the school setting, it could not be expected that they could take extensive notes at the time of having seen or heard something that they wanted to record. Oftentimes, they had to reconstruct later as accurately as possible what occurred, for example, during a break or at lunchtime or, if need be, after school. It was pointed out that, as Cusick (1973) found, this could be a somewhat 'long and painful' process. Extensive discussion of the content and form of fieldnotes was not held, but, in retrospect, perhaps should have been. Besides fieldnotes, students were also required to draw maps of several classrooms and analyze the organization of their arrangement of desks, materials, etc., with the work of Getzels (1974) and others helping to inform their discussions. Recording further meant that students were expected to submit a well-written account of what they observed in a form that could be read by someone else, namely the instructor. These accounts, submitted in three parts, were evaluated. In other words, the fieldwork itself was not assessed, only the students' final products. When 'supervising' was done, typically by a graduate assistant, it virtually always focused on the students' classroom teaching and not on the mini-ethnographic studies they were doing for the course. In retrospect, this was probably a 'lost opportunity' to link more closely what they were observing about school life to what they were experiencing as teachers.

Finally, the student's written account was to include not just descriptions of school life (gleaned from observing, interviews, examination of school documents and curriculum materials, etc.) but also interpretations of what participants were thinking or intending and an analysis of the implications of the different focuses of the study. Probably one of greatest difficulties encountered by the students involved differentiating as clearly as possible their interpretations from their 'objective' observations. A kind of 'rush to judgment' seemed to take place on the part of some students and a frequent written response by the instructor became something like, 'What exactly makes you think that this is the case?' This concern eventually became a specific focus of discussion but it is clear that it needed to be addressed more fully at the beginning of students' research.

The specifics of what students focused on were of course dependent on their own interests and concerns, as well as on the particular school in which they were placed. Many seemed to give special attention to teacher-student inter-actions, especially when 'problems' were observed, but a whole host of other aspects of school life were recorded as well. More structured assignments were also required by the instructor, such as the teacher interviews, student interviews, classroom maps and examination of school documents and curriculum materials mentioned earlier.

One example of school culture that the students were specifically asked to focus on was the hidden curriculum. Many features were highlighted in the students' data, such as 'teacher as the ultimate authority', patience, passivity, 'learning is work', competition and punctuality. Another feature was cleanliness, with one education student quoting a teacher who advised children (who had just come from gym class) to take showers so that they 'don't ... smell badly tomorrow'. The education student noted that the urban school where she was observing had many children from 'poorer families' and she wondered whether the teacher would feel it necessary to make such a comment to students from a different kind of school (ShG, 4 December 1987). Another observer noted that a kindergarten teacher told her five and six year olds 'what, how and when to play in the classroom'. It was suggested that in effect the children were subtly 'learning *not* to make personal decisions' on their own (AH, 1 December 1987). Another education student suggested that the children in an elementary class-room were implicitly being pressured to conform, indicating that for the teacher she was observing 'there is one right answer to the question and the possibility that there is another way of looking at it is not ... entertained'. She went on: 'Kids learn the unspoken rule that the teacher's point of view is the "right" way and their ideas are probably wrong although they may be simply "different"' (MB, 4 December 1987). Another observer noticed a similar aspect of the hidden curriculum in another elementary school. She described a family tree art project, in which one student 'glued one of his leaves to the bottom of the paper rather than putting all the leaves in the tree (like everyone else)'. The response of the teacher was, 'What happened? ... Why do you always have to be different; do it like everyone else' (CM, 4 December 1987). Similarly, in the same school, an art class construction project of a paper goose was pre-drawn on a sheet of paper for the children to cut the parts out and glue them together. The result was that 'when the geese were finished, they all looked the same. One child was even upset because his wings were a little farther up on the body than everyone else!' The education student summarized her thoughts on the matter this way:

> I have personally seen how difficult it is for very creative, divergent thinkers to fit into the classroom. The cases I remember are classmates I have had who were considered strange and weird because they did not think and act like everyone else. I was disappointed and concerned to see that many of these indirect feelings are transmitted to children in the very early grades of school. I wonder if the ridicule these divergent thinkers suffer is actually cultivated in children by their early grade school teachers. If this is the case, it would be nice to think that positive ideas could be transmitted to children as well. For example, teachers could help develop the idea that being unique and different is good and should be rewarded.... I am glad I have consciously observed this

aspect of the hidden curriculum because I will make a conscious effort to avoid conveying the message that divergent thinking and acting is [necessarily] negative. (CM, 4 December 1987)

We hope it is clear from the above examples that while students were strongly encouraged to adopt a critical posture toward what they were observing, no conscious attempt was made to coerce them into adopting particular positions on educational issues or specific educational practices. Indeed, as Zeichner and Teitelbaum (1982) said of their earlier work, there was not the intention 'to promote outright rejection of all that is taken to be natural within current forms of schooling; such a stance would be unreasonable'. What was hoped for instead was 'to create a situation where student teachers maintain more of a balance between the arrogance that blindly rejects and the servility that blindly receives' (p. 112). As the students themselves wrote:

The saying, 'never judge a book by its cover', should be applied when observing classrooms. The objectives that a classroom appears to promote may not be really taught.... [For example,] Mrs R's room appears to be like Mr S's room. But they do not engage in the same kind of teaching. (AH, 3 November 1987)

Lesson number one [that I learned]: don't believe what someone says just because they say it; watch, also, what they do. (RH, 3 November 1987)

[The 'mini-ethnography'] helped me to further my understanding of all that is involved in being a teacher. There is so much more than lesson plans and grading papers.... Throughout the rest of my observations of teachers, I will carefully be monitoring the decisions he or she makes and what might have affected that decision. (AN, 3 November 1987)

At the State University of New York at Binghamton, where teacher education programs are offered only on the master's level, an elective course on 'Introduction to Educational Anthropology' was designed by one of the authors primarily to acquaint students with the work of ethnographers. Preservice and inservice teachers are introduced to ethnography and the politics of reading the ethnographic account by way of Shirley Brice Heath's (1983) *Ways With Words: Language, Literacy, and Learning in Communities and Classrooms*. This text was selected because of the multiplicity of issues it raises: for example, how competing contexts of language, literacy and learning fashion the possibilities and impossibilities of school success; how different ways of knowing position the discontinuities among home, school and work; how the ethnographer participates in multiple communities of competing interests; how ethnographic data might refashion the practices, hopes and desires of participants; and how the classroom, with its possibilities for social change, is a site of struggle. Heath's text represents the dimensions of an ethnography as both a process and a product. As a process, it delineates clearly the nature of 'ethnographic doing 'and 'ethnographic learning' and narrates the lived experiences of different communities. As a product, it can be read as a description and an interpretation of complex cultural settings and as a 'blueprint' for transformative practice.

In this course, students are engaged in two simultaneous procedures: they read and critique Heath's text and they critique their own reading and writing practices. Initially, however, because one cannot discuss ethnography without talking about the concept of culture (and to assist students in actively reading Heath's text), fifteen different definitions of culture are provided. These definitions range from traditional views of culture as the acquired knowledge people use to interpret experience and generate social behavior (Spradley, 1979) and as a whole pattern of life (Dobbert, 1982), to more radical approaches that depict culture as the site where popular legitimacy and consent is constructed and fashioned (Hall, 1981) and where seriously contested codes and representations vie for power (Clifford, 1988). These latter definitions attempt to disrupt the unitary emphasis of the former by asserting culture as comprising multiple voices rather than as a seamless narrative.

In discussions of these definitions, emphasis is placed on the fact that any definition of culture represents an epistemological commitment, or a view of the nature and significance of meaning; an ontological stance, or what it means to be recognized as a human, and; a political investment, or where power and culture intersect. The starting point is that no definition of culture is neutral, objective or able to transcend the commitments, investments and desires of the definer. In addition, within any ethnographic account, the reader can identify competing definitions of culture. Throughout the discussions of the Heath text, particular episodes are analyzed in relation to a range of definitions of culture that are opened and suppressed. A favorite example from Heath's text concerns the question of whether culture is knowable to outsiders. At one point, when Heath is sitting in a church service of the Trackton community, she admits, albeit in academic ways, the difficulty of identifying the rules of participation during the 'raising of hymns': 'Outsiders, unfamiliar with the routines of the service and the norms of participation by members of the congregation, cannot understand the service in many parts, and often report their feeling that "too much is going on at the same time"' (p. 203). A few pages later, after being unsatisfied with how participants answered her questions about when they know it is time to participate, Heath gives up trying. In a rare admission, she realized that her line of questioning and her desire to analyze step by step the social practices of religious worship were 'fruitless' (p. 208). With this passage, Heath complicates the problem of defining a given culture and having access to its internal sense. Being there is no guarantee of truth and in this contest of codes — between the ethnographer and the culture she studies — the ethnographer may not always understand. In the same way, of course, the teacher education student utilizing ethnographic methods must become aware of the limitations of the observer's understanding of what school participants do and why.

The reading of Heath's text is further complicated with the introduction of Roland Barthes' (1974) narrative codes in order to provide students with different lenses from which to read and comment upon their reading practices. Central to Barthes' codes is the notion of intertextuality: that we bring to any text knowledges of other texts and this knowledge fashions our expectations of what a text should be and what a text should do, and that every text carries and suppresses traces of other texts. Barthes' narrative codes allow readers to get behind the text and consider what it is that structures both the text and their own reading practices.

Two of the six codes are most helpful to the students in this course: the cultural code and the communicative code. The cultural code represents the collective stock knowledge in the trade of human society, what people naturally believe about work, people, values, morals, race, gender, social class, age, status, power, etc. This stock knowledge helps readers and characters render social life intelligible. A second code, the communicative code, concerns the ways in which people dialogue with and address one another. It is concerned with the politics of voice: what it means to know and to be known in relation to others and what implicit rules of conduct structure talk. Again, to illustrate these codes, we can return to the above quoted passage from Heath. Heath does not have access to the cultural codes working through the church service. Nor can she make sense of the ways people describe their participation, particularly if she filters their descriptions through her own academic training, her own communicative code. She assumes that there might be a difference in the ways educated (i.e., well-schooled) and uneducated people answer her questions about church participation, an assumption grounded in academic cultural codes which position educated people as more articulate than uneducated people. Here the cultural and the communicative codes meet and, as conceived by Heath, also break down. That is, both groups of people are not intelligible in how they answer, Students who work with this passage, from the perspectives of culture and narrative codes, begin to appreciate both the complexity and incompleteness of the ethnographic narrative and the reading practices of the reader.

At mid-term, students begin the process of writing a 'mini-ethnographic account'. They are asked to select a cultural scene and through participant observation collect data so that they can represent this scene to others. The purpose of this assignment is not to write a fully-fledged ethnography, but rather to experience aspects of the ethnographer's work in description and cultural interpretation. These varied cultural scenes have included shopping malls, athletic events, free lunches for the elderly and theme restaurants for children, as well as classroom lessons. After data has been collected, students work in pairs to read each other's data and dialogue about the problems of identifying patterns and themes in the narration of experience. After the first attempt at interpretation, students read each other's drafts, and discuss the cultural and communicative codes and their assumptions about the nature of culture that work through both the narration and the reading of that narration. They are asked to analyze how power relations are positioned in each account and mark the multiple voices of the narrator. They are also asked to discuss the definitions of culture working through the narratives. Finally, students write a postscript that identifies possible omissions and gaps in their ethnographic account, what made certain details seem more significant than others, how they 'constructed' the participants and themselves, and the next steps to take should the cultural scene be revisited.

In discussions with the class, three points in particular are highlighted in relation to this series of activities. First, to 'do' ethnography requires self-reflexivity. One must be aware of what it means to take up and represent the perspectives of others and how the voices of the ethnographer are positioned. Second, there is a difference between experience and the narration of experience and this difference must be explored in both the reading and the writing of ethnographic texts. And third, ethnography always represents partiality in the sense that the whole story can never be told and in the sense of the researcher's interests. An awareness of these dynamics and the practical experiences of critiquing them can help students admit the tensions of becoming reflective agents in their own social practices and articulate reservations about their own reflections.

Can Ethnography Make a Difference?

While we have no longitudinal empirical evidence to support us (for a discussion of a few such studies, see Zeichner and Liston, 1987), we contend that our use of reading and doing ethnography with education students has been successful in promoting the goals of reflective teacher education. Other data in the form of student journals, class discussions, verbal feedback, and the like have convinced us of the efficacy of utilizing these strategies with our students, that they provide excellent opportunities for students to reflect upon, critique and discuss prevailing and alternative educational goals and practices.

This is not to assert, however, that problems have been absent from our use of ethnography with students. Some of these problems can in fact be viewed as resistances on the part of our students. For example, working with ethnographic traditions requires that students have the patience to read them. We have typically encountered students who believe too much detail was offered and that an ethnographic study could better be done in a short article. (Of course, this complaint may not be unique to reading ethnographies.) The 'thick' description and interpretation of the complex world of the school tends to demand book-length treatment and sometimes students resist spending the time necessary to fully critique the texts. In fairness to the students, however, it sometimes has not been possible to schedule the amount of time on individual texts that would allow for a careful reading.

A second kind of resistance seems more interesting to us. This takes the form of students' incredulity to the ethnographic account and the ethnographer's capacity to 'objectively' narrate the story. Because ethnographic research is inter-subjective, students may not necessarily 'believe' its findings. Typically, students have been socialized to read research from more traditional paradigms that seek to control the researcher's subjectivity. Yet such a stance seems more an effect of tradition than an inevitable conclusion. We thus encourage students to work through their understanding of subjectivity and objectivity in less dualistic ways.

A third kind of resistance has to do with taking up values that encourage cultural sensitivity and a healthy respect for diversity. For example, many students wonder, after engaging with ethnographic research, if it is 'fair' to treat students differently and attend to their cultural realities if the larger social world does not. The logic here goes something like this: one must simulate a harsh reality in order to prepare people for it. Ethnography in education often focuses on the problems of misunderstanding, ethnocentrism, marginalization and the contesting ways that communities define themselves and others. It requires that the student rethink her or his own investments and identifications in ways that may not be comfortable or seem necessary, or, at least at first glance, feel self-affirming. At the same time, an ethnography can challenge the student to reformulate practices and who they are becoming. Some students, then, approach ethnography in defensive terms and these terms themselves must be made problematic if ethnography is to make a difference in educational understandings and practices.

In addition, there have been instances in which we have felt it necessary to address explicitly the issue of the stereotyping that can accompany the collection of data about individual participants in a cultural setting. We have had to caution against misrepresenting whole groups of people with hastily arrived at and ill-founded conclusions. This is clearly a 'danger' that must be addressed at the beginning of this work. Heath's text, for example, is not about African-Americans in general, or poor African-Americans, or poor African-Americans living in the Piedmonts. It is about the Trackton community, and it is powerful for how it helps us to understand and interpret the world of others, not for any direct transfer of knowledge about groups of people.

It has also become clear that some students are initially resistant to the idea of collecting ethnographic data, especially when it takes place in field-based courses. Embracing a kind of celebration of 'the practical', they sometimes resent assignments that take away time from working and re-working lessons, meeting with teachers about classroom management problems, and so forth. However, although we do not claim that there has been unanimity on this issue, in most cases students come to appreciate the insights and skills that they have gained from their use of ethnographic methods. Indeed, the most common phrase that we have heard is, 'I never realized before that . . .' (It should be noted as well that a related resistance emanated from the schools. The idea that students should be allowed to take time to observe and collect data has always been a matter to be negotiated with the local school district and with individual school staff.)

Another problem in the doing of ethnography has been the difficulty that some students have had concerning the lack of ready 'answers' for what they observed. Again, this is no doubt a matter of tradition, specifically the propensity of teacher education programs to offer and education students to expect recipes of knowledge and skills to help them in the classroom (Britzman, 1986; Ohanian, 1985). This is also part of a larger problem, of students being primarily used to receiving a conceptual framework based on positivistic assumptions that there are ready answers to be found for carefully posed research questions. Here, they are being asked to assume a much more complex universe, in which answers are not necessarily obtainable and in which relationships are multidimensional and multifaceted (Shultz, 1983). We have found, again, that in most cases students do begin to appreciate that educational settings are much more complex than they originally supposed and that that complexity is something not to be overcome but rather thoughtfully wrestled with. To be sure, it is difficult to satisfy students who exclaim, as one of them did, that 'I ask myself so many questions now, I'm driving myself crazy. I've got questions, questions, questions, but no answers!' (SuG, 10 December 1987) We are sympathetic to this kind of frustration and feel that the potential for it to lead to discouragement or self-paralysis must be carefully addressed. Still, we claim that it is better to provide students with opportunities to figure out for themselves what is happening in their own and other's classrooms, even if it proves initially somewhat exasperating, than to have them 'trained' to always rely on the insights of others.

Another problem is not so much a matter of resistance by students as much as it relates to a frequently commented on criticism of ethnography by critical theorists. This involves the potential for ethnography to lack an awareness of history and of the social-economic realities of schooling and how these forces effect what is observed. We have found that because of the limited nature of the student's involvement with ethnography, there is a tendency for students not to see clearly the evolving dialectical relationship between social structure and human agency (Willis, 1977), what has sometimes been described as the macro-micro relationship. As Marcus and Fischer (1986) suggests,

> the 'outside forces' in fact are an integral part of the construction and constitution of the 'inside', the cultural unit itself, and must be so registered, even at the most intimate levels of cultural process. (p. 77)

Helping students to become aware of the political and economic interests inherent in the cultural construction of meaning, and the broader social forces that inform the lives of social actors in specific social settings, often has been one of the more problematic aspects of working with ethnography in such a limited fashion. Students' attention to the lives of participants in the cultural setting sometimes evolves into questions and suggestions related rather narrowly to personal change. The problem is that structural change becomes excluded from consideration. We find that we probably play our most active role in class discussions in helping to clarify for students the relationship between the experiences they observe within the school and the social structures that exist 'outside'.

While we have focused on some of the tensions of doing and reading ethnography in teacher education, we believe that these strategies do enable our students to move beyond an identity of the technician to taking up the perspectives of practitioners who are reflective. It is nonetheless apparent that what we have described in a sense represents the isolated efforts of individual teacher educators. Indeed, the danger exists that this method can become a curiosity or may be seen as idiosyncratic. In addition, the very limited nature of the students' engagement with ethnographic research in their teacher education programs severely lessens the extent to which this project of inquiry can aid them in actively observing, interpreting and analyzing what is taking place around them. These realizations, constructed from our own experiences, lead us to suggest that teacher educators seriously consider planning for a more comprehensive integration of ethnographic methods and ethnographic reading in their programs. Field-based programs that are in constant tension with encouraging deeper levels of reflectivity while students are daily involved in their own practical struggles with curriculum, pedagogy and assessment might be substantially strengthened if ethnographic study was introduced during a student's initiation into a program and then woven in and out of a student's teacher education. During the last ten years, ethnographers have addressed and extended the ways we understand the dynamics of learning (e.g., literacy and numeracy acquisition and development, and conceptual development in science, social studies, etc.). This body of research can be the foundation of pedagogical knowledge. Such an ethnographically-informed program in teacher education could challenge students to take up a more sophisticated rendering and understanding of the school as a setting of contesting cultures. We believe that this approach can encourage students to create flexible practices and ways of thinking about curriculum and pedagogy that can better take into account the multiple realities working through any classroom.

Even utilized in the limited fashion described earlier, five related benefits do seem significant to us. First, doing and reading ethnography provides opportunities for students to construct a knowledge base about culture, community, and school and classroom life that may be otherwise inaccessible to them. The use of ethnography enables students to explore in depth and with a high degree of engagement some of the very significant and complex but oftentimes subtle aspects of curriculum, pedagogy and evaluation. Second, students learn and practice specific skills in data collection, analysis, etc., that they can continue to utilize as classroom teachers. In specific, we view ethnographically-informed teacher education as providing important support for the 'teacher as researcher' emphasis of recent years. Third, for many of our students, ethnographic work provokes dialogue about research. Often, education students are mystified by the techniques of correlational studies and tend to 'receive' such research in silence. However, because the ethnographic account is grounded in social life, students begin to view themselves as more than passive consumers of research. They debate, argue and persuade one another about the difficult questions of what constitutes the nature and consequences of educational research. Fourth, some of our students bring ethnographic techniques into their own classrooms. They do this in two ways: their descriptive accounts of classrooms help them develop a curriculum that begins with the strengths of their students; and a few of our students have taught elementary and high school students to be 'ethnographers' of their own experiences. We find such directions promising in that both teachers and students are recognized as sources of knowledge and as producers of knowledge. Finally, many of our students begin to recognize the potentials of educational research as a source of revitalization, knowledge and empowerment. They begin to view research not as an alien product typically employed to prove them wrong, but as a site where teachers and researchers come together with shared concerns. We believe these directions are fundamental to reflective practices that make available that which is not yet.

References

AGAR, M. (1980) *The Professional Stranger: An Informal Introduction to Ethnography*, New York: Academic Press.

AU, K. and JORDAN, C. (1981) 'Teaching reading to Hawaiian children: Finding a culturally appropriate solution', in TRUEBA, H., GUTHRIE, G. and AU, K. (Eds) *Culture and the Bilingual Classroom: Studies in Classroom Ethnography*, Rowley, Massachusetts: Newbury House.

BARTHES, R. (1974) *S/Z*, (Trans. Richard Miller) New York: Hill and Wang.

BOGDAN, R. and BIKLEN, S. (1982) *Qualitative Research for Education: An Introduction to Theory and Methods*, Boston: Allyn and Bacon.

BOGDAN, R. and TAYLOR, S. (1975) *Introduction to Qualitative Research Methods: A Phenomenological Approach to the Social Sciences*, New York: John Wiley and Sons.

BORG, W. and GALL, M. (1989) *Educational Research: An Introduction*, New York: Longman.

BRITZMAN, D. (1986) 'Cultural myths in the making of a teacher: Biography and social structure in teacher education', *Harvard Educational Review*, **56**, 4, pp. 442–56.

BRITZMAN, D. (1989) 'Who has the floor? Curriculum, teaching, and the English student teacher's struggle for voice', *Curriculum Inquiry*, **19**, 2, pp. 143–62.

BRODKEY, L. (1987) 'Writing critical ethnographic narratives', *Anthropology and Education Quarterly*, **18**, 2, pp. 67–76.

BRODKEY, L. and FINE, M. (1988) 'Presence of mind in the absence of body', *Journal of Education*, **170**, 3, pp. 84–99.

BRUYN, S. (1966) *The Human Perspective in Sociology: The Methodology of Participant Observation*, Englewood Cliffs, New Jersey: Prentice Hall.

CARINI, P. (1975) *Observation and Description: An Alternative Methodology for the Investigation of Human Phenomena*, Grand Forks, North Dakota: University of North Dakota Study Group on Evaluation.

CARRASCO, R. (1981) 'Expanded awareness of student performance: A case study in applied ethnographic monitoring in a bilingual classroom', in TRUEBA, H., GUTHRIE, G. and AU, K. (Eds) *Culture and the Bilingual Classroom: Studies in Classroom Ethnography*, Rowley, Massachusetts: Newbury House.

CLIFFORD, J. (1988) *The Predicament of Culture: Twentieth-Century Ethnography, Literature, and Art*, Cambridge, Massachusetts: Harvard University Press.

CONNELLY, M. and CLANDININ, J. (1985) 'Personal practical knowledge and modes of knowing: Relevance for teaching and learning', in EISNER, E. (Ed.) *Learning and Teaching the Ways of Knowing*, Chicago: University of Chicago Press.

CUSICK, P. (1973) *Inside High School: The Student's World*, New York: Holt, Rinehart and Winston.

DAVIES, B. (1989) *Frogs and Snails and Feminist Tales: Preschool Children and Gender*, Boston: Allen and Urwin.

DEYHLE, D. (1986) 'Break dancing and breaking out: Anglos, Utes, and Navajos in a border reservation high school', *Anthropology and Education Quarterly*, **17**, 2, pp. 111–27.

DOBBERT, M. (1982) *Ethnographic Research: Theory and Application for Modern Schools and Societies*, New York: Praeger.

ERICKSON, F. (1977) 'Some approaches to inquiry in school-community ethnography', *Anthropology and Education Quarterly*, **8**, 2, pp. 58–69.

ERICKSON, F. (1979) 'Mere ethnography: Some problems in its use in educational practice', *Anthropology and Education Quarterly*, **10**, 3, pp. 182–8.

FETTERMAN, D. (1982) 'Ethnography in educational research: The dynamics of diffusion', *Educational Researcher*, **11**, 3, pp. 17–29.

FETTERMAN, D. (1987) 'A rainbow of qualitative approaches and concerns', *Education and Urban Society*, **20**, 1, pp. 4–8.

FINE, M. (1988) 'Sexuality, schooling, and adolescent females: The missing discourse of desire', *Harvard Educational Review*, **58**, 1, pp. 29–53.

FLORIO-RUANE, S. (1990) 'Creating your own case studies: A guide for early field experience', *Teacher Education Quarterly*, **17**, 1, pp. 29–41. (A version of this article first appeared in 1984 as a publication of the Institute for Research on Teaching at Michigan State University.)

GEERTZ, C. (1973) 'Thick description: Toward an interpretative theory of culture', in GEERTZ, C. *The Interpretation of Cultures*, New York: Basic Books.

GETZELS, J.W. (1974) 'Images of the classroom and visions of the learner', *School Review*, **82**, 4, pp. 527–40.

GILMORE, P. (1985) ' "Gimme Room": School resistance, attitude, and access to literacy', *Journal of Education*, **167**, 1, pp. 111–28.

GITLIN, A. and TEITELBAUM, K. (1983) 'Linking theory and practice: The use of ethnographic methodology by prospective teachers', *Journal of Education for Teaching*, **9**, 3, pp. 225–34.

GOETZ, J. and LeCOMPTE, M. (1984) *Ethnography and Qualitative Design in Educational Research*, Orlando, Florida: Academic Press.

GOODMAN, J. (1986) 'Teaching preservice teachers a critical approach to curriculum design: A descriptive account', *Curriculum Inquiry*, **16**, 2, pp. 179–201.

GOSWAMI, D. and STILLMAN, P. (Eds) (1987) *Reclaiming the Classroom: Teacher Researcher as an Agency for Change*, Upper Montclair, New Jersey: Boynton/Cook.

GUBA, E. and LINCOLN, Y. (1981) *Effective Evaluation: Improving the Usefulness of Evaluation Results through Responsive and Naturalistic Approaches*, San Francisco: Jossey Bass.

HALL, G. (1980) 'Ethnographers and ethnographic data: An iceberg of the first order for the research manager', *Education and Urban Society*, **12**, 3, pp. 349–66.

HALL, S. (1981) 'Teaching race', in JAMES, A. and JEFFCOATE, R. (Eds) *The School in the Multicultural Society: A Reader*, London: Harper and Row.

HAUG, F. *et al.* (1987) *Female Sexualization : A Collective Work of Memory*, (Trans. Erica Carter) London: Verso.

HEATH, S.B. (1982) 'Questioning at home and at school: A comparative study', in SPINDLER, G. (Ed.) *Doing the Ethnography of Schooling: Educational Anthropology in Action*, New York: Holt, Rinehart and Winston.

HEATH, S.B. (1983) *Ways With Words: Language, Life and Work in Communities and Classrooms*, New York: Cambridge University Press.

HESS, D. (1989) 'Teaching ethnographic writing: A review essay', *Anthropology and Education Quarterly*, **20**, 3, pp. 163–76.

HYMES, D. (1980) *Language and Education: Ethnolinguistic Essays*, Washington D.C.: Center for Applied Linguistics.

JACKSON, P. (1968) *Life in Classrooms*, New York: Holt, Rinehart and Winston.

LONGSTREET, W. (n.d.) Action research: A paradigm for the human services. Unpublished manuscript.

MAC AN GHAILL, M. (1988) *Young, Gifted and Black: Student-Teacher Relations in the Schooling of Black Youth*, Philadelphia: Open University Press.

MAGOON, J. (1977) 'Constructive approaches in educational research', *Review of Educational Research*, **47**, 4, pp. 651–93.

MARCUS, G. and FISCHER, M. (1986) *Anthropology as Cultural Critique: An Experimental Moment in the Human Sciences*, Chicago: University of Chicago Press.

McCARTHY, C. and APPLE, M. (1988) 'Race, class, and gender in American educational research: Toward a nonsynchronous parallelist position', in WEIS, L. (Ed.) *Class, Race, and Gender in American Education*, New York: SUNY Press.

McCUTCHEON, G. (1982) 'Educational criticisms: Reflections and reconsiderations'. *Journal of Curriculum Theorizing*, **4**, 1, pp. 171–6.

McDERMOTT, R. and HOOD, L. (1982) 'Institutionalized psychology and the ethnography of schooling', In GILMORE, P. (Ed.) *Children In and Out of Schools: Ethnography and Education*, Washington D.C.: Center for Applied Linguistics.

MEDICINE, B. (1988) 'Native American (Indian) women: A call for research', *Anthropology and Education Quarterly*, **19**, 2, pp. 86–92.

MOHATT, G. and ERICKSON, F. (1981) 'Cultural differences in teaching styles in an Odawa school: A sociolinguistic approach', In TRUEBA, H., GUTHRIE, G. and AU, K. (Eds) *Culture and the Bilingual Classroom: Studies in Classroom Ethnography*, Rowley, Massachusetts: Newbury House.

OAKES, J. (1985) *Keeping Track: How Schools Structure Inequality*, New Haven: Yale University Press.

OGBU, J. (1974) *The Next Generation: An Ethnography of Education in an Urban Neighborhood*, New York: Academic Press.

OHANIAN, S. (1985) 'On stir-and-serve recipes for teaching', *Phi Delta Kappan*, **66**, 10, pp. 696–701.

PHILIPS, S. (1983) *Invisible Culture: Communication in Classroom and Community on the Warm Springs Indian Reservation*, New York: Longman.

POSNER, G. (1985) *Field Experience: Methods of Reflective Teaching*, New York: Longman.

RIST, R. (1970) 'Student social class and teacher expectations: The self-fulfilling prophecy in ghetto education', *Harvard Educational Review*, **40**, 3, pp. 411–51.

RIST, R. (1977) 'On the relations among educational research paradigms: From disdain to detente', *Anthropology and Education Quarterly*, **8**, 2, pp. 42–50.

RIST, R. (1978) *The Invisible Children: School Integration in American Society*, Cambridge, Massachusetts: Harvard University Press.

RIST, R. (1980) 'Blitzkreig ethnography: On the transformation of a method into a movement', *Educational Researcher*, **9**, 2, pp. 8–10.

ROMAN, L. (1988) 'Intimacy, labor, and class: Ideologies of feminine sexuality in the punk slam dance', in ROMAN, L., CHRISTIAN-SMITH, L. and ELLSWORTH, E. (Eds) *Becoming Feminine: The Politics of Popular Culture*, Basingstoke: Falmer Press.

RYAN, J. (1989) 'Disciplining the Innuit: Normalization, characterization, and schooling', *Curriculum Inquiry*, **19**, 4, pp. 163–76.

SADKER, M. and SADKER, D. (1982) *Sex Equity Handbook for Schools*, New York: Longman.

SHERMAN, R. and WEBB, R. (Eds) (1988) *Qualitative Research in Education: Focus and Methods*, Basingstoke: Falmer Press.

SHOR, I. (1980) *Critical Teaching and Everyday Life, Boston*: South End Press.

SHULTZ, J. (1983) Ethnography in education: Implications for teacher education. Unpublished manuscript.

SMYTH, J. (Ed.) (1987) *Educating Teachers: Changing the Nature of Pedagogical Knowledge*, Basingstoke: Falmer Press.

SOLA, M. and BENNETT, A. (1985) 'The struggle for voice: Narrative, literacy and consciousness in an East Harlem school', *Journal of Education*, **167**, 1, pp. 88–109.

SPRADLEY, J. (1979) *The Ethnographic Interview*, New York: Holt, Rinehart and Winston.

SPRADLEY, J. (1980) *Participant Observation*, New York: Holt, Rinehart and Winston.

SPRADLEY, J. and McCURDY, D. (1972) *The Cultural Experience: Ethnography in Complex Society*, Chicago: Science Research Associates.

WILLINGSKY, J. (1989) 'Getting personal and practical with personal practical knowledge', *Curriculum Inquiry*, **19**, 3, pp. 247–64.

WILLIS, P. (1977) *Learning to Labour: How Working Class Kids Get Working Class Jobs*, Westmead, England: Saxon House.

WILSON, S. (1977) 'The use of ethnographic techniques in educational research', *Review of Educational Research*, **47**, 2, pp. 245–65.

WOLCOTT, H. (1988) 'Ethnographic research in education', in JAEGER, R.M. (Ed.) *Complementary Methods for Research in Education*, Washington D.C.: American Educational Research Association.

WOODS, P. (1985a) 'Conversations with teachers: Some aspects of life history method', *British Educational Research Journal*, **11**, 1, pp. 13–26.

WOODS, P. (1985b) 'Sociology, ethnography and teacher practice', *Teaching and Teacher Education*, **1**, pp. 51–62.

WOODS, P. (1987) 'Life histories and teacher knowledge', in SMYTH, J. (Ed.) *Educating Teachers: Changing the Nature of Pedagogical Knowledge*, Basingstoke: Falmer Press.

ZEICHNER, K. (1987) 'Preparing reflective teachers: An overview of instructional strategies which have been employed in preservice teacher education', *International Journal of Educational Research*, **11**, 5, pp. 565–75.

ZEICHNER, K. and LISTON, D. (1987) 'Teaching student teachers to reflect', *Harvard Educational Review*, **57**, 1, pp. 23–48.

ZEICHNER, K. and TEITELBAUM, K. (1982) 'Personalized and inquiry-oriented teacher education: An analysis of two approaches to the development of curriculum field-based experiences', *Journal of Education for Teaching*, **8**, 2, pp. 95–117.

11 Student Teachers Use Action Research: Issues and Examples*

Susan E. Noffke and Marie Brennan

For over five years, some student teachers at the University of Wisconsin-Madison have completed action research projects during their final semester of field experiences. Students are in classrooms four-and-a-half days per week, gradually assuming teaching responsibilities, and they attend a weekly university-based seminar with their supervisor. As supervisors in the program, we have included an action research project as one of the major requirements of the seminar. We see action research as a way of working toward a student teaching experience that provides opportunities and structures which facilitate and enhance the students' development as 'reflective' teachers (Grant and Zeichner, 1984). Our use of action research emanates from a strong conviction that, with all its pitfalls, constraints and under-examined theories, action research provides a lever to 'unpack' the complexities of thinking about teaching and schooling and to improve the quality of student teacher practices during their field experiences. Although we have yet to conduct longitudinal studies of our students beyond one semester (Noffke and Zeichner, 1987; Brennan and Noffke, 1988), we also hope that action research will assist in developing long-term habits and frameworks for teacher activism and reflective and critical pedagogy.

This chapter takes as its focus our use of action research to promote more critical and reflective teaching in preservice teacher education. In the first section, we explain the rationale behind and the expectations for the use of action research in teacher education. Secondly, we chart our experiences with and reflections about the main approaches we have used in introducing action research to student teachers. The next section covers how we help students to reflect as part of their action research projects. A particular teaching tool and an example of a student's project form the basis of this description. The final section considers issues and dilemmas which have emerged from our experiences. These are seen as in need of much wider debate within the action research and teacher education communities.

---

* An earlier version of this chapter was presented at the National Meeting of the Association of Teacher Educators, San Diego, February, 1988. The present version reflects the helpful comments of the editors.

Why Use Action Research?

Action research has been well documented as an approach to teacher inservice and staff development (Elliott, 1980). Its use with student teachers began in the 1950s (see Beckman, 1957; Perrodin, 1959), but only recently has it re-emerged as a focus for interest and debate. The rationale used for advocating action research with teachers has varied over time and place (Corey, 1953; Grundy, 1987; Kemmis and McTaggart, 1988a, 1988b), yet it may have much relevance to current (US) American teacher education. Although there are notable exceptions (Noffke and Zeichner, 1987; Ross, 1987), the overall lack of a rationale for and documentation of action research projects with preservice teachers inhibits judgments as to its usefulness in helping students and teachers to be reflective.

We use action research in our work with student teachers first because of its ability to help them see themselves as *producers* of educational knowledge. The 'democratic' epistemology of action research emphasizes that everybody is a producer of knowledge, thereby helping to demystify the whole area of research. Second, because of its collaborative nature and its focus on both one's own practice *and* the wider situation in which that practice occurs, it helps us as supervisors examine with the students the relationships between themselves and the university, as well as the teaching profession. This focus on the linkages between themselves and the wider practice of teaching continually brings to the forefront the connections between theory and practice: it helps to make questions of curriculum and pedagogy an integral part of their daily work. Action research efforts are, then, not 'reinventing the wheel', but ways one can learn to take ideas from research to one's own practice *and* bring one's own knowledge back into the analysis. Finally, its ongoing, cyclical nature, with both 'constructive' and 'deconstructive moments' (Kemmis and McTaggart, 1982), does not impose artificial boundaries on the research process. This allows one to recognize complexity over time, but it also means that one could stop after a shorter time and still learn.

Our use of action research must be seen as part of an overall rationale — one that puts the focus on the teacher as an 'inquirer' into his or her own practice. Yet to do so is to acknowledge that such an 'emancipatory' intent is not without its contradictions. Issues of 'empowerment' are not free of issues of control. Given the range of outcomes claimed in the literature on action research (Noffke and Zeichner, 1987; Oja and Smulyan, 1989) — from 'personal and professional growth' and increases in 'classroom awareness' on the one hand, to developing positive attitudes toward research (thereby narrowing the research-practice 'gap') on the other hand — we have come to strongly argue not only for the 'use' of action research, but for the 'doing' of action research *with* students. This allows us to raise the questions of who is 'inquiring' in 'inquiry-oriented' teacher education, and what the purpose of such an inquiry is.

Several important aspects of these questions demand further explanation. First, we are looking at action research from the 'inside'. A crucial element for us in engaging in action research is that it must not be used unproblematically. If our intent is an emancipatory one, we must first ask a question: By what right do we use action research? Many action research endeavors also include 'action research on action research'. Yet they rarely call their practices into question instead, they merely assess the 'effectiveness' of action research in achieving given aims.

The problem is that 'emancipatory' projects (in intent) are not free of issues of control. The history of 'group work' in the United Stated has often been tied to cooption and social control rather than real collaborative work (See Graebner, 1987; Noffke, 1989). This is one of the reasons that we engage in such research: to uncover that tension, not from the privileged position of 'outsiders', but rather as participants. We see part of that task as helping students to inquire into teacher education, to surface those contradictions and changing intentions over time. One of the good things about action research is that it does allow people to be contradictory — it's about trying to surface contradictions between what you think you're doing and what you're really doing. It develops an understanding of how both intentions and actions are problematic, and may need changing over time. Action research encourages this. It involves open-ended dialogue; it is historical. In the process of engaging in action research with prospective teachers, we are making learning to teach something that can be discussed, not a particular research 'technique' or method to be learned.

Our purpose in engaging in action research is not to help students to reach a particular 'stage' of development (Fuller, 1969) so that they can become 'reflective'. Rather, we seek to disclose the complexity that is *already* embedded in student teachers' thinking. Reflection on the 'survival' skills of teaching can be multi-dimensional (see Noffke and Brennan, 1988), including not only technical proficiencies but greater understanding of the implications of particular forms of teaching practice for the social and political context. To ensure that action research does not become merely a more sophisticated version of cooption, in a context where the rhetoric of greater 'school-based' decision making is coupled with greater 'accountability', it is increasingly important that the specific rationale behind the use of action research in preservice teacher education be made clear.

We have taken up action research partly as a way to explore its democratic impulse in our teaching and its potential for altering the conception of teacher education and the role of knowlege production. In an institution where the 'rules' are often bureaucratically defined and administratively arranged, there are many constraints working against achieving these goals, even if supervisors and student teachers themselves agree on their importance.

What are the alternatives for furthering habits of critical reflection and action in student teaching if we do not use action research? We could use (as has been done within the UW program) journals, observations, ethnographic studies or curriculum analysis projects along with readings and discussion during the seminar and the supervision process itself (Zeichner and Liston, 1987). Although the potential for critical reflection exists in these activities, none of them captures for us and for our students' work the political, social and ethical dimensions of reflective teaching practice. While observations, ethnographies and curriculum analysis do develop a broader understanding of teaching and schools and journals help to develop the students' awareness of themselves, they fail to help students to site themselves in the wider situation which could help them understand who they are *and* what they will do. Through action research we seek to expand the areas teachers consider in their everyday decisions, while also emphasizing the need for responsible action.

Action research differs from other forms of educational research in its methodology, but it is also a different way to conceive of what it means to 'know' and to 'act' — a different way to think about practice and change. It is democratic both in its emphasis on the production of knowledge by people from various sectors in education and in the topics and processes of the research itself. At its best, it can break through the barriers of individualism and isolation, all too often prevalent in US educational arenas. As such, it can provide an important experience and framework for the understanding and improvement of curriculum and teaching practices. In our case, it is an important focus for conceptualizing the role of teacher education in the development of 'reflective' teaching practices.

Action research could be presented as a way of increasing 'professionalism'. However, to us the term implies a view of knowledge which is undemocratic and therefore antithetical to action research. Emphasizing the use of knowledge to differentiate 'insiders' and 'outsiders' is to subscribe to a particular version of 'expertise'. We tend to avoid the term 'professional', focusing instead on the growth in understanding of practice, the improvement of practice and the linking of the student's own situation with those of others (Grundy and Kemmis, 1988).

How Do We Introduce Action Research to Teachers?

In the elementary education program at the UW-Madison, students take an introductory course before proceeding to twenty-seven credits of methods-related courses in a variety of subject areas. Two practicums are associated with the major areas of Language Arts/Reading and Science/Social Studies/Math. In their final semester, students are placed in schools for four-and-a-half days per week, gradually assuming responsibility for the entire classroom program. One afternoon per week is reserved for a seminar aimed at developing reflective thinking and covering a wide range of topics in relationship to their practice. The seminar is led by the university supervisor, who also observes and discusses the students' teaching approximately six times during the semester. It is within this seminar that action research is introduced and assigned, and in their own student teaching classrooms that the students' projects are carried out.

For some of the students, the idea of action research is novel. Action research is obviously a project that will require at least some time and commitment, and it has criteria that are not as easily quantified and attained as a multiple-choice question or a short answer exam. It is even more foreign than a long paper on a topic meaningful to them, with which some are still not familiar and comfortable, even at the end of their undergraduate studies. Action research projects provide students with an opportunity for longitudinal study. They learn to organize ideas and to think systematically in relation to their actions over time.

It is difficult to convince student teachers that they should be producers of knowledge if most of their university (and school) experience directly contradict this. As student teachers, their daily classroom experience can serve as constant reminders of their lack of knowledge and skill, of what they do *not* know and can*not* do. Such difficulties have to do, in part, then, with the nature of their university education. Some are a response to their understanding of the nature and processes of research itself. They are also a result of the students' desire to be spending all of their efforts on 'teaching', not seeing such university-based learning as a part of 'practice'.

In order to address these issues, we have tried several approaches to the introduction of action research with our students. In our first efforts, we began by asking students what they thought research was. Their responses, elicited as a 'word association', provided us with many questions about the program itself, and the students' experiences with 'research' in general. Their responses included: sitting in the library, boring, science, objective, bookwork, white lab coats and papers. Nothing was given that gave any sense that they themselves could be producers of knowledge or that research might have something to say to them. Theory was another word to 'unpack' in class as a means of articulating and identifying the tremendous hold of traditional science on the understanding of our students. The contrast between their 'traditional' notions of 'scientific research' and action research was used as a means to explain the differing principles of action research.

The students' initial reactions to this view of science, theory and research formed an area to be explored, making more problematic the meanings of the terms and their connection to the lives of teachers and children, as well as to the larger social and political context. We emphasized the importance of linking theory and practice, the production of knowledge as the basis of teacher development and the possibility of building a focus on one aspect of one's concerns as a teacher through integrating action research over time into the routines and daily experiences of the task of teaching.

This activity set action research as opposing conventional research views, which, in a sense, it does. Yet, such an oppositional stance also presented a dilemma. Although, on the one hand, action research does entail a differing definition of what it means to do research, it also holds a contrasting view of the theory-practice relationship. By formulating the view of action research as oppositional, we could also have been setting the stage for a continued reflection of 'university theory' in general, leading to, or reinforcing an anti-intellectual position. Rather than leading to a reformulation of theory and practice, our approach could merely have continued their separation.

At the very least, this oppositional stance may have rested uneasily with students whose main concern was often that of understanding and fitting in with the dominant practices present in the schools in which they were placed. The understanding of research that predominates in other sectors of society is also that of the mainstream student view. It is, therefore, not surprising that many of our students' projects were only minimally separated from the assumptions of other research forms, even though this was certainly not deliberate on their part. Oppositional stances, built on the so-called commonsense reactions of the students, cannot really be sustained without the political understanding and commitment that accompany such a position.

Nevertheless, feedback from students suggested that they found the projects interesting and useful, a change from other university work. Cooperating teachers also expressed interest in and support for this form of university project, into which they themselves could enter in a number of roles. One cooperating teacher, for example, continued the action research project after her student teacher had graduated (Wood, 1988). Both students and cooperating teachers liked the emphasis on investigating the 'practical' daily classroom life.

Although student and cooperating teacher comments do seem to have indicated both positive reactions and significant and favorable results in terms of our goals and their own practices, some difficulties remained that required changes in both our approach and our structuring of the assignment. As reported earlier (Noffke and Zeichner, 1987), surface level foci, lack of more than one 'cycle', lack of time and difficulty integrating the collected data into the written reports have been problems for the student teachers' projects. While the time aspect may have contributed to difficulties in completing more than one 'cycle' of action research, the other areas needed to be addressed in ways that did not add to, but rather created overlaps which would lessen, the overall workload during student teaching. It was hoped that such structuring of assignments would allow more time to continue into more 'cycles'.

In reaction to these concerns and those relating to the introduction of action research as an oppositional activity, we decided to decrease the emphasis on the 'foreignness' of action research by stressing that they knew quite a lot about action research already. The second way we introduced action research was to build some understanding of data-gathering and observation into their first few weeks in their classrooms, and then to develop a framework of action research around that. In this way, action research wasn't a university term appropriating what they already knew, but rather a way of being more systematic and rigorous in their own reflection and teaching — a way of gaining access to ways others have thought about and practised in relation to the topic, while developing their own reflective teaching practices, both individually and collectively. The rubric of 'reflective teaching' was emphasized more than 'action research' as the framework. As well, we arranged for the students to meet with other student teacher seminar groups to talk through their initial plans for their projects, before writing up their proposals. Some plans were also made for the students to present their completed projects to this larger group, but the students preferred to stay together in their seminar groups, allowing more time for each person to present and discuss his or her project.

Our emphasis in these two approaches to the introduction of action research was on asking students to choose one aspect of their practice which interested them and which they wanted to improve and better understand. It did not have to be a 'problem area'. This stipulation served both to distinguish action research and reflection from 'problem-solving' and to minimize the 'deficit model' that seems, at times, to pervade undergraduate teacher education.

Initial reports to the whole group of student teachers in the seminar were to be presented. These were to cover what the *issue* was, why the student found it important and necessary to investigate, its wider educational significance and how they would start their research. This final section usually outlined what data they would first collect and their first action step. Rather than separate written assignments, which would serve to keep things individual, the oral reports helped increase the complexity of the students' thinking about their issues and they helped to underline the process of action research as a collaborative effort.

The topics the students chose depended on a number of characteristics, including their own preferences and styles. They covered a range of foci from work with individual students and use of time by students, to issues of gender differentiation in teaching. Some students clearly chose their projects from issues that arose in supervisory conferences, which focused on questions about the students' own observed practice; others chose theirs through interaction with issues in reading and discussion.

Mostly, though, the students' projects arose from specific concerns about their teaching practice during the early part of the semester. While some do not fit traditional understandings of action research in that they are not centrally concerned with *investigating* their own practice, all need to be considered as affecting teaching practice and understanding in some form or another. Purist attempts at the definition of action research are not helpful in discussing these projects. What is noticeable is that students who chose not to do research on their own practice had projects which nonetheless gave them a useful way to investigate pupils, and to increase their understanding of their own classrooms. For instance, following a single pupil became less of a case study profiling a pupil's background and needs and more of a record of teaching plans and reflections. While this could be seen to be investigating one's practice, the difficulty lies in the way the investigation led to answers that were internal to that particular situation. While it helped in that site, it seemed as though it really didn't help these students to think about teaching in a wider way. The knowledge they gained had therefore more of a 'technical' nature, with unexamined connections to other situations.

As a result of our own action research on the students' action research — a process that was made explicit from the beginning and one which enabled us to give and receive feedback and to institute discussion during the seminar — we are still debating how to improve our use of action research in the overall course design for the elementary program. One recent approach conceives of the action research as an ongoing investigation of a broad issue: 'What it is to be a teacher?', as distinct from investigating over time a single, specific aspect of their practice such as discipline or individualizing instruction. Clearly, part of the new investigation must include developing specific elements and emphases during the semester. However, this is intended to be done as a way of focusing more attention on their own learning and practical development as a student teacher, enabling more direct discussion of the constraints and possibilities of that particular job. We hope that this approach will enable a more collaborative and self-conscious reflection and planning to emerge for the whole seminar group and will also allow for the possibility of bringing the cooperating teachers more into the conversation as partners. Before, the cooperating teacher might help to gather data or even to take part in the project, though this was by no means the norm. Now a conversation about what it is to become a teacher may help to make for a more equal partnership of reflection and critical development.

How Do We Help Students to Reflect Within Their Action Research?

Too often, teacher practice and reflection has been characterized as a hierarchical separation of the technical, the practical and the critical (Noffke and Brennan, 1988; Kemmis, 1985; Grundy, 1987). In our view, every issue has its technical (how to), practical (what to) and critical (why) dimensions. Reflection is not merely a 'critical' act, but also a practical and a technical one. Understanding an issue means examining all three. On a number of occasions, the focusing of attention by student teachers on the practical and the technical has been described as 'natural'. For example, the work on teacher thinking sometimes presents a progression through various 'stages' differentiating neophytes from experienced teachers. Such distinctions may be dangerous for the purposes of analyzing reflection because they separate out what we see as centrally connected ways of thinking and doing, creating an artificial hierarchy between the 'technical' and the 'reflective'. There is no sequence of practical and technical know-how that precedes the critical. In our view, different value positions imply different practical, technical and critical activities.

Once we discuss topics with student teachers, either in seminar or in supervision, we see that they do enter into all three dimensions — the critical, the practical and the technical — even though on first sight it may appear that their concern is exclusively with the technical. During student teaching (and here it is very difficult to avoid the language and concepts of stage theory ourselves!), the technical and practical aspects of their work are those which offer them the most challenge and are also the entry into the understanding of the way the critical operates for that topic or issue. Teaching is not an abstract act; nor are the students in their classrooms able to be put 'on hold' while they 'think' about what to do. This is where we find action research to be particularly suited to the teaching act. A teacher/student teacher can be investigating and improving her or his action at one and the same time. The different 'moments' in action research (Kemmis and McTaggart, 1988a) are not merely different temporally but also allow for a tight dialectic between reflecting and acting so that they are not different acts, but related. Many student teachers seem to feel that reflection is 'just thinking' (Hursh, 1988), a sort of linear process that happens automatically after 'doing'. As teachers of student teachers, one of our most difficult tasks is to help them to realize the dialectic of action and reflection in their daily experiences of reflective practice.

The 'cosmic egg' (See Figure 3) is a teaching tool developed to aid critical reflection by emphasizing the interrelatedness of all dimensions of an educational issue. It is a device to help in revealing and going beyond taken-for-granted assumptions and interpretations. At the center are the student teacher, her or his classroom and school. This is then surrounded, in outward moving, concentric circles by other institutions and habits (political, cultural and economic) in which the student is immediately involved, growing more distant-seeming, to the USA 1988. The power relations (race, class, gender, etc.), habits and structures which inform and construct these institutions and situations in which the student finds her or himself are made visible. All of these — self, situation, institution and power relations — need to be seen as operating at a specific point in time. Each has a history, often intertwined with other histories.

In explaining the 'egg' to the students, we say that the lines between each area are permeable, that is, there is a two-way flow of influence and construction. All parts operate simultaneously, but only some are in focus at any one time. The trick is to use the 'egg' to uncover our own habits, assumptions and interpretations in order to be able to reflect more deeply, and therewith alter not only how we think, but what we see, what we see as relevant, and what we will do as a

Figure 3   *The 'Cosmic Egg': A device to help in revealing and going beyond our taken-for-granted assumptions and interpretations*

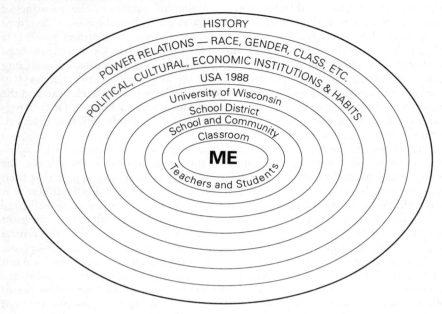

result. As an example, in seminar a student raises any issue. We try to fill in the dimensions of the issue by looking at all the layers of the 'egg'. The layer which seems to have least relevance often provokes the most discussion and illumination of the limits of our current understanding. It also gives an opportunity to surface differences of opinion and background and to 'play' with issues: 'What if gender really was operating here as an important hidden message of our discipline methods? How would you find out? What should/could you do to change it? How might your view of discipline be constrained by it being thought of and discussed in the present USA? What else have people thought and done about this issue? Why does the issue come up now and not earlier?'

Such questions are particularly helpful when students seem to be at a stand-still in their projects, for whatever reason. At times, especially when the original formulation of the question seems to have exhausted the possibilities for change, the use of this tool sparks further interest and challenge. It also appears to address the need for broadening the conception of the current issue — to see its inter-connectedness with other areas of teaching and educational life.

It is hard to explain a metaphor without reducing it or changing its purpose too much. The egg is a whole, an organic metaphor which does not deny its parts but which is also greater than the sum of its parts. The diagram we draw with students varies in that the concentric 'layers' of the egg may be labeled and ordered differently each time. Yet it always tries to capture some of the complex-ity of any situation in terms of its connection to other situations, power relations and ideologies, all of which have a history and occur at a particular place and point in time.

Learning Through Others' Experiences

The example of the 'cosmic egg' is only one of many ways in which we attempt to promote reflective action with our students. Working through the action research process itself, both individually and collectively, is another. Beginning in the initial seminar session on action research and building through reading, discussion, presentations and writing, students hear of the thoughts and efforts of others, and get a chance to explain and examine their own.

Getting started in action research is for many students, as well as their supervisors, a difficult process. It is important, for several reasons, that the introduction of action research to the seminar group does not take place until the third or fourth week of the semester. First, although the students have chosen their placements after several observation visits, they need time to learn more about and become comfortable in their classrooms, with their cooperating teachers, and with their supervisor. Second, they need time to sort through the mass of new information and experiences they encounter — to find those issues that are significant to them. Third, waiting a few weeks allows time for a trusting relationship to be built. Finally, we allow time for the supervisor to complete a 'letter of expectation' conference (to negotiate a time-line of activities for the semester), to conduct at least one cycle of supervision and to read the students' thoughts in their journals. Through these activities, not only trust, but an understanding of the students' goals and teaching is developed. This knowledge and trust plays an essential role in the introductory seminar session on action research.

After the general introductory discussion on action research described above, a specific example of a previous students' action research project is 'walked through' in detail. A typical description follows the course of the student's project from the early formulation of a 'general idea', through 'reconnaissance', to the plans for, data collection on and reflections about a series of action steps. The following account, adapted from an audiotape of such a seminar session, describes the process of action research as the students experienced it. It is important to note that the student whose work is described was not a 'superstar', nor was he a 'problem' student. He was thoroughly prepared for his work, and established appropriate and warm relationships with his seventh and eighth grade students. Yet he had a lot of trouble thinking of himself as an evaluator of his own practice.

Walking through a project

The student teacher was interested in what seemed to be a small problem, one that looked, at first, as if it might not lead anywhere. He was very concerned that he used the word 'OK' over and over in his teaching. He decided to tape-record one class period and to have a student check another class in order to see first what the situation was. His tape revealed 116 'OKs' in one class period; the student counted 132. Another student added that she had counted over 200 a week earlier. He started with a 'general idea' about his verbal behavior in his classroom. Then he entered a 'reconnaissance' phase — looking over the situation.

Although he still was not convinced that the tallies were accurate, he formulated an 'action plan' aimed at reducing the usage of that word. He analyzed the tape further, noting that he used 'OK' for questions, feedback, transitions, etc., and decided that he needed to focus on one aspect at a time. His first step involved developing more questions, instead of lecturing. He found that when he started asking questions of the students, instead of putting all of the conversation on himself, he stopped using the word entirely. Yet he also found a lot more.

His plans took into consideration suggestions from his cooperating teachers and his supervisor that he try to involve more students in discussions and attend to patterns of perhaps unconsciously 'calling on' more boys than girls, especially in math class. He then focused on broadening his repertoire of responses, making clearer transitions and attending more consciously to student responses. He also developed more and more varied questions. To help him in monitoring his efforts, both his supervisor and his cooperating teacher collected data, using charts and field notes. The data became the focus of post-observation conferences with his supervisor and were also part of his discussions with his cooperating teacher. Besides working on his own verbal behavior, he began to be able to attend more to the students and to broaden the basis for his own self-evaluation. He tried to involve more students in the lessons and looked for unconsciously enacted patterns of gender stereotyping.

Eventually this led him to reevaluate, not only the specific techniques he used, but their rationale and some of his general approach to teaching. He commented:

> I accomplished my goal of cutting down on 'OKs' and calling on students in a more even manner. Reasons I suggested for my accomplishment included physical prompters (notes on lessons) and more attention to the problem. There may be another answer, too. During my project, I thought about abandoning such a teacher-centered style ... I think the move to a more student-centered strategy may be as important of an accomplishment as cutting down on that naughty word. The only problem is, that was not the goal of this project!

His ongoing question changed, but also his understanding of the issue. He began with a narrow focus on his own language usage and moved to a broader understanding of the importance of student participation in class. While his original teaching style was almost exclusively teacher-centered lecture, his later lessons included large group discussion, small group problem solving in math, and experimentation in science.

His project reveals much of the nature of action research. It is ongoing, tentative, growing — often resulting in more questions than solutions. He found something that was important to him and this enabled him to look at other things. Other students have worked through the process in an opposite direction — for example, seeing a need to encorporate more of a feminist approach to pedagogy and seeing how those ideas worked out into concrete practices. Action research embodies thereby a different conception of the theory-practice relationship, one that is dialectical in nature.

After this 'walk through', a follow–up discussion asks students to identify the issues embedded in the students' projects. Through this, student teachers can see action research as a way to deal with all three dimensions — the technical, the practical and the critical — as they relate to an actual classroom situation. They can also see how the focus of a project and its consequent 'cycles' changes and broadens. It is appropriate at this point to discuss how data collection proceeds, including information on the use of 'triangulation', collecting various forms of data (e.g., tape, supervisor notes, student feedback, etc.) to focus in on the topic.

The final section of the class session involves asking the students to generate ideas for their own projects. Often students volunteer issues discussed at supervisory conferences. Others offer topics of interest from previous coursework or practice. It is useful to have them choose one or two and outline how one might begin — what information would be useful, how it could be gathered, and to what steps it might lead.

Over the next weeks students read more material about action research, including examples of others' project reports. The students also continue to discuss their progress informally at seminar and at supervisory conferences. Many times they request specific data related to their topic as part of a supervisory visit. It is important that there be time for students to share their thoughts about their projects. First, it gives them a chance to work through the process with others. It also allows for connections to be made to readings discussed in seminars related to curriculum, discipline/management, evaluation, grouping, racism, sexism, etc. It also allows for practice at articulating what they are doing and why, and for encouragement and suggestions from others as to how else they might proceed. While action research is not the central focus of the seminar, it often provides the opportunity to relate issues discussed to actual events in their classrooms.

Issues in Student Teacher Practice of Action Research

Some of the issues facing and emerging from our practice (experience and theorizing) of action research in the context of an undergraduate certification course are similar to those experienced in other fields and other places. Many of these issues are perennial for teacher education and have been debated for many years. Other issues are peculiar to the undergraduate teacher education experience at the University of Wisconsin-Madison. The specific histories of this institution and of the students involved, the UW Elementary Education program and ourselves as teachers alter and illuminate our understanding of what action research is, has been, and might be. Action research has for us been a useful and important way to organize our own practice and our thinking about it. Yet all issues focus attention on and raise questions about what we think action research is as it is being done — not only in the sense of refining a definition, but also in the evaluation of its emancipatory potential.

Researching action research can tell us about teacher education, some of its challenges, practices and problems for both students and instructors. Some of the difficulties involved in doing action research with student teachers have already been discussed in terms of how we help people learn about it. This section considers issues that are embedded in our efforts to make both action research and 'critical reflection' part of the experiences of teacher education.

Everyone who undertakes action research, for whatever reason, seems to complain and worry about the amount of time they will have available, and the kind of changes in their practice and in institutional practices that might be expected from it. The time element for student teachers is highly circumscribed and very little, if any, is under their direct control. First, they are in someone else's room. Even at the beginning of the school year, the teacher has set up routines, the curriculum of the school has certain elements of an inexorability which the student only gradually begins to understand in their institutional, teaching and personal dimensions. As well, students often work, have families and take other classes in addition to the full-time student teaching experience.

It is important to recognize that the seminar in which the action research project is included occurs within the context of a particular, state-accredited teacher certification program. This means that it is not easy for an individual supervisor to negotiate changes in the program. The university and to some extent the state Department of Public Instruction have a number of requirements for teacher preparation, none of which is onerous, but all of which need to be included. The very fact that some of these were required could be used to help them understand that they were joining a profession, not just having a private educational experience. It could also help them to see the preparation of teachers as a contested and political arena. The handbook for the program, for example, sets out activities which are required of all students. These include keeping a journal, writing lesson plans, making three observations of other classrooms, being observed by the university supervisor about six times, three three-way conferences between the teacher, student teacher and supervisor, preparing a unit of study, doing two weeks of lead teaching — with major responsibility for all teaching, preparation and assessment, and a weekly seminar. Although individual supervisors might have initiated changes in these requirements, these would not have altered the overall institutional practices.

For many students, the very existence of a two credit, conventionally graded seminar is a distraction from the 'real' job of the semester — their student teaching. Through our focus on action research, we attempt to explore the tension between the potential overemphasis on practice as the primary means of learning to teach and of becoming a teacher, and the need to examine critically the status of teaching practices and to generate alternatives. The demands are often perceived as conflicting in nature although for some students, the seminar works well and the tensions are perceived as fruitful for their learning. The time for university-required projects and reading is limited at the best of times; the more that the students perceive the project to be helpful to their practice, the more they are likely to set aside the time for it to be done. For most students, it seems that the writing-up is the most time-consuming area, even when they have used their journals and have plenty of data and ongoing reflective comments there. Yet the ongoing nature of the project tends to build its own momentum in the daily practice and routine of the classroom and seminar. However, this also tends to emphasize the practical and technical dimensions which may occur at the expense of the critical.

We can say, and so would other student teacher supervisors at the UW-Madison, that action research projects are a useful way to integrate various aspects of the student teaching semester. But whether or not the student teaching experience is redefined through a project which links school experience with the seminar is highly debatable. For some students, we can clearly say that they have made significant shifts in their understanding of the role of teacher, but whether this shift will last into their teaching is another matter entirely. The institutional experiences they have with us in seminar and supervisory conferences are important ones, but they may not be enough to balance their other experiences.

Because the seminar is graded, the action research project becomes part of the assessment relationship of supervisor to student. Even where grades are negotiated, the compulsory aspect of the project does tend to work against the democratic impulse for free and voluntary association which we see as desirable in action research. Each student also has to receive a separate grade. Given a local context in which a student's cumulative grade point average plays an increasing role in the selection of job candidates, the grade supports the continuation of the students' understanding of schooling as individual and competitive, and affects their approach to projects, papers and sharing in discussion. Students, even those who have been concerned with altering relationships of power both at the university and in their own teaching, have not often noted this aspect in their feedback. Yet none of us can afford to ignore the institutionalized patterns of action which must be reconciled with our own democratic intentions.

Continuing Dilemmas

As part of our ongoing debate at the UW-Madison, we continually return to the question — What are the minimum requirements for reflection? The formulation of the question alters, but the general area of our conception of reflection is important. Questions we are now asking include: How much is it intrinsic to action research to move between the three dimensions of technical, practical and critical? Exploring the multi-dimensionality of an issue seems essential in some ways, but how much of that is inherent to action research and how much is it a function that can occur with other forms of critical reflection which may not be so integrally tied to practice?

There seems to be little doubt that changes in understanding result from and accompany the process of doing action research as we have engaged in it, although it is hard to quantify and describe this. We also need to explore in much greater detail what it is to reflect on the practical and the technical, not just the critical, and whether there is a difference, as we suggest, in the kinds of reflection that occur within particular value positions.

Can we call what a student does 'action research', especially if it is only one cycle or a case study? Given the constraints of the situation, does it matter? How much does one have to do before it 'counts' as action research? These are questions which perhaps worry others more than they do the students. It may not be crucial that all projects match a particular definition of action research. However, it is important to understand what it is about our approach that leads to, in some cases, a concern for wider issues. For now, we have been content to call our work action research and to investigate its epistemological, normative, and practical aspects as we proceed with our teaching. At one level, though, the issue of definition is important because it helps us to clarify whether action research in fact matches our value commitments. The history of action research has often been a stormy one, especially in this country (Noffke, 1989), and its fate has often depended on its legitimacy according to criteria other than those to which we would subscribe.

Our future plans continue to focus on using action research with our student teachers. In particular, we are interested in ways of building more collaborative activity into their experiences, even though they may be in different schools and in different classrooms — themselves separated. We want to integrate better the university and school aspects of our work — to avoid seeing the university as theoretical and abstract and the school as the site for practical experience. Perhaps the greater involvement of the cooperating teacher in supervisor-student conversation will provide an important link in the process of reflection. Currently, teaching students about critical reflection is occurring much earlier in the program, with observation and data gathering leading to critical interpretation, as well as discussion of action research, built into the introductory course in elementary education. Hopefully, the load on final semester student teaching will not be so great because student teachers in the future will already have some familiarity with the practices and the theories.

We have found that engaging in action research, both on our own practices and with student teachers, continues to be useful in our efforts to enhance our understanding of teaching practices, to improve those practices and to improve the situation in which those practices take place.

References

BECKMAN, D.R. (1957) 'Student teachers learn by action research', *Journal of Teacher Education*, **8**, 4, pp. 369–75.

BRENNAN, M. and NOFFKE, S.E. (1988, April) Reflection in student teaching: The place of data in action research. Paper presented at the Annual Meeting of the American Educational Research Association, New Orleans.

COREY, S.M. (1953) *Action Research to Improve School Practices*, New York: Teachers College Press.

ELLIOTT, J. (1980) 'Implications of classroom research for professional development', in HOYLE, E. and Megarry, J. (Eds) *Professional Development of Teachers: World Yearbook of Education 1980* (pp. 308–24), London: Kogan Page.

FULLER, F. (1969) 'Concerns for teachers: A developmental conceptualization', *American Educational Research Journal*, **6**, pp. 207–26.

GRAEBNER, W. (1987) *The Engineering of Consent: Democracy and Authority in Twentieth Century America*, Madison: University of Wisconsin Press.

GRANT, C.A. and ZEICHNER, K.M. (1984) 'On becoming a reflective teacher', in GRANT, C.A. (Ed.) *Preparing for Reflective Teaching* (pp. 1–18), Boston: Allyn and Bacon.

GRUNDY, S. (1987) *Curriculum: Product or Praxis*, Basingstoke: Falmer Press.

GRUNDY, S. and KEMMIS, S. (1988) 'Educational action research in Australia: The state of the art (An overview)', in KEMMIS, S. and McTaggart, R. (Eds) *The Action Research Reader* (3rd edn), pp. 321–35, Victoria: Deakin University Press.

HURSH, D. (1988, February) Reflecting on teaching teachers to become reflective. Paper presented at the annual meeting of the American Association of Colleges of Teacher Education, New Orleans.

KEMMIS, S. (1985) 'Action research and the politics of reflection', in BOUD, D., KEOGH, R. and WALKER, D. (Eds) *Reflection: Turning Experience into Learning*, pp. 139–63, London: Kogan Page.

KEMMIS, S. and McTAGGART, R. (1982) *The Action Research Planner* (Rev edn), Geelong, Victoria: Deakin University Press.

KEMMIS, S. and McTAGGART, R. (Eds) (1988a) *The Action Research Planner* (3rd edn), Victoria: Deakin University Press.

KEMMIS, S. and McTAGGART, R. (Eds) (1988b) *The Action Research Reader* (3rd edn), Victoria: Deakin University Press.

NOFFKE, S.E. (1989, March) The social context of action research : A comparative and historical analysis. Paper presented at the annual meeting of the American Educational Research Association, San Francisco.

NOFFKE, S.E. and BRENNAN, M. (1988, April) The dimensions of reflection : A conceptual and contextual analysis. Paper presented at the annual meeting of the American Educational Research Association, New Orleans.

NOFFKE, S.E. and ZEICHNER, K.M. (1987, April) Action research and teacher thinking: The first phase of the action research on action research project at the University of Wisconsin -Madison. Paper presented at the annual meeting of the American educational Research Association, Washington, D.C.

OJA, S.N. and SMULYAN, L. (1989) *Collaborative Action Research: A Developmental Approach*, Basingstoke: Falmer Press.

PERRODIN, A.F. (1959, Dec.) 'Student teachers try action research', *Journal of Teacher Education*, **10**, 4, pp. 471–4.

ROSS, D.D. (1987, Spring) 'Action research for preservice teachers: A Description of why and how', *Peabody Journal of Education*, **64**, 3, pp. 131–50. (Published in 1989).

WOOD, P. (1988, April) Action research: A field perspective. Paper presented at the annual meeting of the American Educational Research Association, New Orleans.

ZEICHNER, K.M. and LISTON, D.P. (1987, February) 'Teaching student teachers to reflect', *Harvard Educational Review*, **57**, pp. 23–48.

12 The Cooperating Teacher's Role in Nuturing Reflective Teaching

Patricia O. Wood

Introduction

For the past fourteen years I have been an elementary teacher at the primary level in 'Open Classroom' settings. The goals of providing an active, child-centered and humanistic environment underscore my philosophy of child education and parallel my goals as a teacher educator. My classrooms have represented a non-traditional placement for student teachers from the University of Wisconsin. I use the term 'non-traditional' in that it is an open classroom attended by children from any of the schools in the District. The parents select the program and maintain a high level of involvement, the curriculum is integrated and the student teachers participate in creating much of the curriculum. I have served as a cooperating teacher with sixteen student teachers during their final practicums. In this paper I would like to share my views of the role a classroom teacher has as a teacher educator as well as a personal account of my experiences and methods for guiding student teachers to become more reflective in their teaching.

The motivations for being a cooperating teacher are varied and the rewards generally off-set the additional commitments that it requires. Student teachers bring a level of enthusiasm that is refreshing. I have found that by having a student teacher, my own teaching continues to evolve. Observing, questioning and guiding student teachers has made me more reflective about my own teaching. Working as a team introduces new ideas, questions and opportunities to challenge children more effectively. Cooperating teachers have access to newly emerging pedagogic methods and theories by their direct link with teacher education programs. My teaching philosophy and practices have benefited by my continued relationship with the teacher education programs. My prime motivation for being a cooperating teacher is that I believe it is important that teachers share responsibilities as teacher educators.

The Student Teacher/Cooperating Teacher Relationship

As a basis for discussing reflective teaching, I would first like to share some of my operating philosophy as a teacher educator. These ideas represent what I believe to be essential in forming an effective cooperating teacher/student teacher partnership.

Each student teacher has a unique background and enters within his or her own set of pedagogic experiences, expectations and values. Their levels of reflection range from concrete to abstract. While some are concerned with specific activities and projects, others are able to generate a variety of options for situations and see each activity as a part of a whole curriculum. The cooperating teacher should assess this entering knowledge and experience base and begin working at the appropriate level.

It is important to establish a sense of partnership in which the student teacher and cooperating teacher can both share observations and feedback. Student teachers should realize the value of teaching as a collaborative activity rather than one of isolation.

The classroom environment must support the student teacher's growth and encourage the development of their own style. Although student teaching takes place in an existing classroom structure, the student teacher must be allowed to experiment. With this experimenting comes accountability as well as the challenge to take on more responsibilities as the practicum progresses.

The cooperating teacher must be an active teacher educator and should serve as a model as a reflective teacher. Among other qualities, reflective teachers are aware of and able to articulate their views about teaching; are in touch with their pupils' interests, thinking, and learning styles; are open to change; and value staff development as an integral part of teaching.

The Student Teaching Semester

The students with whom I work have completed at least three semesters in subject related courses (that have also included some school experiences). In what is known as their final practice, or student teaching, they spend an entire semester in one specific classroom and are expected to spend at least two weeks as the 'lead teacher'. After a screening process at the university, the student visits several classrooms and talks with the teachers about their interests. A mutual choice is made and the assignment is completed. The students come from a program in which reflective teaching has been encouraged throughout the preservice sequence. The nature of the program reinforces reflection in that the cooperating teacher and student teacher actively contribute and determine the scope and particulars of the student teacher's experience.

For our first meeting, I prefer to meet with the student teacher outside of the classroom and before their first day. During this meeting I learn about their previous teaching experiences, areas of expertise, specific lessons they have successfully taught and their expectations for the semester. This information helps me identify the student's values and interests, as well as their possible strengths and weaknessses as a beginning teacher. This time also allows the opportunity to share ideas about working together. I state my requirements that we work positively, professionally and with the recognition that learning opportunities occur throughout the day and not simply when lessons are being taught. As a thinking exercise, we generate a list of things that we both agree each child in our class should experience as a part of each school day. I might begin with, 'I think each child should read for pleasure each day'. If the student agrees with that idea, we write it down and he or she generates another idea. We continue together until we have exhausted our ideas or do not agree. A disagreement provides an opportunity to clarify, question and discuss our differences and their impact on the semester. At that point I change the direction to include activities that we agree should happen once a week (e.g., work with children from a different classroom), each month (e.g., take a piece of their own writing to a 'final draft') and each semester (e.g., perform in front of a group, such as a reading or play). From these lists, we are able to generate a generalized schedule. As the semester moves along, we will find this valuable as a reference point for our planning. Finally, we begin an ongoing list of subjects and topics that interest us. We select one of these topics as our first integrated unit of study. We begin brainstorming activities around that topic and end the meeting with the agreement to both continue thinking about ways to implement this topic of study.

During the first week in the classroom, I make sure the student teacher has experiences that will help them get to know individual students and become familiar with our classroom environment. According to their entering skills, the student teacher will begin actively planning and implementing activities and lessons for small groups as well as some large group instruction. I give student teachers as much responsibility as they are able to handle from the first day. This immediate involvement introduces a baseline for reflection about their impact in the classroom.

On the first few days I have the student teacher:

1   Collect data about what one child is doing at various times during the school day.
2   Listen to each child read from a book the child has chosen and talk with them about the book. Make notes about the child's reading skill and attitudes.
3   Plan and carry out a simple sequence of small group lessons around a topic of their own choosing.

At the end of each day we meet and discuss our observations about the day. The agenda and focus of these meetings evolves during the semester. Usually we include our observations about individual children, methods for incorporating these observations into our planning for the next day, feedback concerning specific lessons and a confirmation that our daily plans fit into our long-range plans. Because the student has been involved from the first day, they have many thoughts, reactions and questions. I begin the early sessions by asking if there were things that happened during the day that the student didn't understand. There are naturally many questions about procedural matters to clarify. We then look at the data collected by the student and look for patterns, social groupings, time use, etc. For example, we might note a child having difficulties making an activity choice. We discuss ideas that might help this child with decision making and make sure that our plans for the next day incorporate a selected strategy.

When the routines of the school day and the student teacher's comfort with the class become established, it is time to identify our specific goals for the semester. These goals include curricular issues, topics of study and areas that we as educators want to explore and think about together. By this point in the semester I have identified areas in which I believe the student teacher will need more experience and growth. Throughout the semester we work on these goals and revise them on an ongoing basis.

During the final section of the semester, student teachers do their 'lead teaching'. At this time the student teacher moves from handling isolated lessons to coordinating the school day as well as maintaining continuity in the learning environment. My responsibilities change from active teaching to being an observer. My time is spent gathering data, reinforcing the student teacher's projects and doing more formal observations of lessons. Most importantly, I am there to help and to support the student teacher. It is during lead teaching that student teachers move from singular concerns about their teaching and begin putting all of their beliefs into action at once. Most student teachers become overwhelmed during this time and I feel it is my function to help them draw on what they have developed through reflection, question them about ways to pull things together and regain their confidence. Lead teaching is the time during which students gain independence and confirm for themselves their capabilities as teachers.

Specific Ways in Which I Guide Student Teachers to be More Reflective

There are a number of methods and approaches available in order to help student teachers become more reflective in their teaching. The strategies I use depend on the situations and form around the person's skills, attitudes and personality. Following is a discussion of some of the specific approaches that I use.

Curriculum Development

In the early stages, the student teacher and I plan each of his or her lessons carefully together. Initially, it is usually necessary for me to select the purposes and goals for the lessons and encourage the student teacher to design the activities. An example would be a lesson designed to reinforce the concept of place value. It might be appropriate that it be a teacher-directed lesson including instruction, use of manipulatives, as well as a paper and pencil activity. After the lesson the student teacher will share their reactions about the details of the lesson. This presents an opportunity to begin challenging the student to think beyond their immediacy by asking simple questions such as; 'Did the children learn what you intended?' . . . . 'How do you know?' As the semester progresses, the student teacher becomes more aware of the curriculum and the children's interests and needs and is able to take greater responsibility for overall planning.

After the student teacher has become comfortable in the classroom and is sharing in the daily curriculum planning, typically we plan and carry out an integrated unit of study. We choose a topic appropriate to the interests of the children in the class as well as the two of us. The student teacher and I agree to independently research this topic, identify important information, and select possible activities and lessons that will reinforce our learning goals.

At our next planning session, we share all of the possible learning objectives for the unit of study. As we talk about what children should learn and how children learn best, we narrow our list to specific objectives and begin to put them into a workable order. During this process we are reinforcing and questioning one another's ideas. As we identify the framework for our unit, we brainstorm ways to integrate the unit into all areas of the curriculum and discuss non-curricular goals as well (e.g., cooperative learning, social groupings, etc.). Next, we identify specific lessons for which we would each like to be responsible and the lessons we will present as a team. This process of developing a unit of study brings the student teacher and teacher together to evaluate and discuss the appropriateness and effectiveness of curriculum and materials. By planning the unit together we are in agreement and clear about the goals and purposes for the unit as well as the best ways to present the information. As the curriculum unit unfolds, the classroom response encourages us to continually reflect and modify our plans and goals. Writing curriculum collaboratively leads to an open dialogue in which we begin sharing our thoughts about the teaching process.

Questioning

A straightforward and always available approach to generate reflection in student teachers is simply to ask appropriate questions. Rather than telling a student teacher how to do something, asking the right questions at the right time will often lead the student to develop ideas on their own. Different situations present different opportunities for questioning, which might best be discussed through examples:

Questions during lesson planning

— Why are you choosing this lesson? How do you justify these objectives?
— Which children do you think will be challenged by this discussion/ activity? What about Kevin?
— What exact words will you use to begin this lesson?
— How much of the lesson will be your instruction? How much will be children discussion/input?
— How will you know that they are understanding the lesson?
— Will these activities reinforce your learning objectives?

Questions during post-lesson discussion

— What information were you really looking for with your question ...?
— Did you mind having Eric and Sarah reading during your lesson?
— What did you think about Kristin's comment ...?
— Why do you think Tom was frustrated?
— Do we need to spend more time with this topic?
— How could this particular objective be reinforced?
— Did this lesson fit into the long range goals of this unit?

General Questions

— During what part of the day are you most confident? What do you consider the most valuable part of our day?

— Which group of children do you work with most effectively?
— How can we better communicate with parents?
— Does this classroom integrate with the rest of the school?
— What do you think about the school district's mainstreaming policy?

These questions are asked with the intention of having student teachers reflect and change as well as reinforcing the beliefs they have developed during their reflection. As I gain more experience in the role as teacher educator, I find I am telling less and asking more. The questions I am asking have also changed. They have become more direct and quite simple.

Data Collection

Collecting data around a specific topic is another way to gather information and pose 'reflective' questions. At times during the semester I ask student teachers to step back and observe the entire classroom for a period of time. I provide a focus for this observation and ask them to collect data around a question that directly connects to a discussion or problem the student is trying to solve. Some questions for data collection have included:

— How are the children (or an individual child) spending their work time?
— What areas of the classroom are being used/not used effectively?
— How often do individual children go to adults for help?
— How do we as teachers spend our time in the classroom?
— What children are called upon most often/less often in group discussion? Is this consistent with both of us?
— What types of questions do we ask most often and which ones generate the most discussion?

To collect these data, the student observes for a designated amount of time and records specific information that is related to our question. Information that can be formed into a sociogram, graph, checklist or classroom mapping usually is concise and insightful. Being objective while collecting data is important; therefore, the question should be clear and specific.

As an example, Maria was concerned that the children were not using work time well. She proposed that the class have 'assigned seats'. Her rationale was that by reducing opportunities for socializing all of the children would complete more work. We designed a way to quickly record what each child was doing and collected this data every five minutes during several work periods. When we looked at the results, it was evident that five children were distracted and not at task, however, the rest of the class was attentive to their work. With this information, Maria was able to concentrate on helping the five children focus on their work without changing the entire classroom atmosphere. Collecting this information was helpful for Maria to reflect on the value of analyzing specifics, in this case, rather than acting on a generalization (from a few noticeable children to the whole class).

The use of a video-tape recorder can be very helpful for data collection procedures. Taping gives us the ability to review an important part of a day or a specific lesson and to focus on answering any of the above questions. Video-taping can also provide direct feedback to a teacher. Seeing yourself from the children's perspective initiates reflective thinking about your presence or an aspect of your teaching. One particular example of how effective video-taping can be concerned Robert, a student teacher who had trouble accepting responsibility for the difficulties he was experiencing in the classroom. Most of these problems were resulting from his overly-authoritarian demeanor and harsh tone with the children. In the many discussions and other ways in which I tried to point this out, he was defensive and was not open to thinking about or changing his approach. I taped several of his lessons and together we viewed them without much comment but with obvious effect (he also asked to take them home to review on his own). The very next day a new attitude was prevailing and some important obstacles started to be overcome.

Action Research

Action Research with its cycles of plan-act-observe-reflect provides a format for extending our questioning. The process itself requires reflection and has given positive direction for a number of student teachers with whom I have worked. Action research requires student teachers to revisit and revise their questions about teaching until their question changes or is answered. This revisiting of the same question provides a consistency for student teachers' reflection.

Some of the topics with which I have worked include improving cooperation among the children in the classroom, moving from concrete to abstract in math activities, and methods to transfer responsibilities for learning to children. One student teacher recognized the difficulties of leading a discussion beyond that which she had prepared in her lesson plans. We were able to refine the scope of an action research project: How do I recognize and extend learning opportunities beyond my lesson plans? After several days of collecting data centering on this question, it became clear that she was trying to cover too much information in each lesson, to the point that the children would become inattentitive. Furthermore, her presentations were unbalanced in that she was saving discussion/question time until the end of her lessons. Doing action research required her to think about the amount and appropriateness of the material that she was presenting to the class. The project was also successful in that she became more alert to the needs of the group and discovered ways to include discussions throughout her lessons.

When a student teacher and I are simultaneously doing action research projects, a unique support system emerges. We both feel vulnerable, we are taking risks and we are each working at making changes. Often we draw one another's attention to an activity or detail that concerns our projects. We are both reflecting about our own teaching and the opportunity is there for both of us to continually share observations and feedback.

Student teachers who are doing action research tend to ask more questions about teaching. They ask for help in understanding the results of their lessons, in how they could do things differently and for information about how I go about making instructional decisions, etc. This questioning often leads them to evaluate their own beliefs about teaching.

Obstacles to the Process of Reflection

As the student teacher gains confidence and begins assuming responsibilities in the classroom, many advantages may be gained by the nature of the co-teaching situation that emerges. There are a number of obstacles that can impede this development. Student teachers must work with the delicate balance of developing their own style while being respectful of the existing classroom systems and environment. Obviously, they are working in someone else's classroom and their confidence can be undermined by the sense that they are under continual evaluation. Common in the student teaching experience is the period, usually mid-semester, in which they become overwhelmed. They have experienced some failure by this time and they realize how much more there is to learn and do. They are now fully involved in the classroom, planning ahead for lead teaching, as well as maintaining their outside responsibilities (working other jobs, parenting, finishing course work, etc.). At this point it is necessary to reassure them and help them re-gain a perspective by reviewing and prioritizing plans and goals.

Serving as a teacher educator and classroom teacher, the cooperating teacher faces the challenges of the day in which many details and concerns compete with the time that otherwise might be available to develop student teacher reflective teaching. The school day is finite and the time given to a student teacher is often traded in for the teacher's own time for preparation or reflection. An additional time commitment is spent with parents who feel the quality of their child's education is being lessened because their child is being taught by a 'novice'. Another concern for the cooperating teacher is the chance of being placed with a student teacher who is not strong and requires an inordinate amount of additional time and help. This situation translates negatively to the children and parents, requires additional meetings with supervisors and other personnel, and gives the cooperating teacher a sense of failure as well as a hesitancy to take on another student teacher. This can best be prevented by allowing sufficient time with each prospective student teacher during the classroom selection process.

Summary

During their 'final practice', a student teacher is developing a concrete sense of pedagogical thinking, acting and decision making. While the student teacher is being challenged to learn about all aspects of classroom life, the cooperating teacher has the opportunity to guide a student teacher to become reflective about their teaching. There are a number of methods that can be helpful in encouraging reflection: developing curriculum collaboratively, questioning and collecting data around questions, video-taping and conducting action research projects.

In order for a cooperating teacher/student teacher relationship to develop that encourages reflective teaching, a number of needs must be met. Adequate time must be available to plan for the classroom; to observe, discuss and respond to each other; and to support the development of the program. A collaborative, team relationship must form (even though one is guide and mentor to the other). Both the student teacher and cooperating teacher must maintain an openness to question and to be questioned and show a willingness to re-examine their own teaching decisions. Both must be able to function positively while being continually observed and evaluated. When these conditions are met, having two adults in the classroom is a great benefit for everyone.

As a cooperating teacher I am involved with beginning teachers as they develop and refine their beliefs about teaching. I am reminded of the challenges and the amount of time, thought and effort that goes with learning to teach. Beginning teachers continually question, reflect and revise their teaching. The responsibility of a cooperating teacher is to guide their reflection from issues of daily survival into areas of meaningful pedagogical concerns. Student teachers' openness and ability to question and change are qualities that should be encouraged and that hopefully endure beyond their student teaching experience.

13   Writing and Reflection in Teacher Education

Jeffrey Maas

The Beginnings

> Sitting down to write about myself as a learner on what happens to be a beautiful spring day seems like it should be a difficult task. Quite the opposite is true. I'm feeling good about my student teaching experience coming to an end and feel I really need to tie together how I'm feeling about all those thoughts, concerns, and ideas that ran through my head all semester long. (student paper, 5/89)

> This is an extremely scary thought. Where do I begin? This semester has been a great learning experience for me. Not only have I learned more about children, but I have also learned a great deal about myself! (student paper, 5/89)

When I started teaching at the University of Wisconsin–Madison, I was given a handbook by my department entitled 'Supervised Teaching in the Elementary School'. Each student teacher was given a copy as well. The handbook outlined the policies and the approaches of the elementary education program, making clear the goals and expectations. The document emphasizes reflective teaching from the very first page. The department identifies four qualities that student teachers need to develop before being certified to teach. The university wants students who are technically competent, aware of ethical issues within teaching, sensitive to student diversity and analytic about practice (reflective).

Many supervisors (and, as I discovered, many preservice programs across the country) use writing as a tool to foster that elusive concept: 'reflective teaching'. Ten years ago, when I first began my search for the meaning of 'writing', talking about writing in broad generalities (writing as process, writing to learn, writer's voice, audience, etc.) filled a very real need. But today, after working with writers from kindergarten to graduate school, talking about 'writing' as a generic category simply conceals more than it reveals. 'Writing' just may not be the panacea for all our reflective teaching woes. It all depends. There are just too many nuances involved in its definition and application. This article attempts to describe one way of viewing writing and its complicated connection to that elusive thing we call 'reflective teaching'. While I will mention specific texts on writing and reflective teaching throughout this essay, using the ideas of 'others' to reformulate my own, I cannot begin this piece without sharing a bit of personal history.

Writing was my entry point into the world of reflective teaching. As a first grade teacher, the journal writing program I developed for my reading class influenced my own writing. I was the one who began keeping a journal, focusing my attention on the ways children learn. I joined colleagues to talk and write about teaching, first in the Great Rivers Writing Project in La Crosse, Wisconsin and then at Bread Loaf School of English in Middlebury, Vermont. As I read, wrote, reflected and reached out to others, I experimented with writing workshops and cooperative learning techniques in the classroom. My practice as a teacher became intertwined with my learning as a student. The classroom became my field laboratory. My supervision, and the weekly on-campus seminar that was a part of the student teaching program, were attempts to recreate many of the conditions that had influenced my own evolution as a 'reflective teacher'.

The seminar met every Wednesday afternoon for two-and-a-half hours. Of the twenty-five students over the year, most were kindergarten teachers, working for state teaching certification in both kindergarten and preschool. As seniors, they had gone through the university's array of method courses and practicums. They had encountered the concept of 'reflective teaching' in many of their courses. The student teaching experience was a time for them to make sense of it all, to discover their own teaching styles and their own approaches to learning. I wanted the seminar to function as a collaborative learning community, using language, both written and oral, as the medium of exchange. To accomplish my classroom goal, I chose the same strategy that many of the student teachers chose in their classrooms. I relied on my strengths. I approached teaching from an area I knew best: language arts.

The seminar was designed to heighten (and challenge) the students' awareness of their teaching theories, helping them evolve classroom practices consistent with those theories. Everyone was required to keep a teaching journal. The journals were the main tool in becoming reflective teachers. Most of the students had kept a teaching journal in other education courses. (As it turned out, their history with academic journal writing was one of the biggest inhibitors to their writing.) Students were also required to write two academic papers during the semester. They observed a child in their classrooms, using their journals as field notebooks, tracking the child's learning. They collected data: written anecdotes, drawings, writing assignments, worksheets, etc. They speculated about the ways children learn. Everyone wrote a brief mid-term summary statement and a final paper. Besides a child in the classroom, students tracked their own learning during the semester, again writing both a mid-term report and a final paper.

To help keep the pieces of the seminar together, I wrote a weekly newsletter. Each newsletter contained a section with my 'current thoughts', where I reported and reflected about events in the schools. The newsletter was a way to continually ground the seminar in the experiences of the students. It was an informal way for me to identify relevant issues and themes by drawing connections between teaching experiences. The letter served as a focal point for our group discussions. Part of my hope at the outset of the year was to create a network of experts within the seminar. The newsletters were a major tool in accomplishing that objective. In capturing the stories of student teaching, the newsletters informed students. It broke their feelings of isolation. Students knew who to contact for advice and a sympathetic ear.

Newsletter, 10/5/88
First of all, while it is still fairly fresh in my mind, I need to comment about last week's seminar. I thought it was our best yet. Your stories about teaching led us directly into several very important areas. P told a story about death. It raised key issues about our relationships with homes and the preconceived notions that we bring with us into the classroom. It also raised the issue of viewing our classrooms as a 'family unit'. I like the way roles are emerging within the group. Look at the way the roles have emerged over the weeks, as we have gotten to know each other better. (Are the same things happening in your classrooms?) Thank you B for telling us about the goal setting conferences in your school and thank you T for telling us about the elementary education newsletter and all the professional requirements. Do we need a speaker? How about a principal to conduct mock interviews?

Writing to Learn: The Limitations of a Cognitive Approach

This paper has really focused my thoughts. That is typical for me. Writing is my best tool to straighten out my head and learn. (student paper, 11/88)

As I taught the student teaching seminar, I took graduate courses on supervision. Much of the literature I read prescribed writing, and journal keeping in particular, as a method for developing 'reflective teaching'. Robert Yinger and Christopher Clark (1981), in their paper on reflective journal writing, provide a sound, cognitively-based approach to writing. But as in all cognitively-based models I have encountered in composition theory, only part of the picture seems to be portrayed. While I cannot deny the validity and importance of these models, the dynamics described did not reflect my own growth as a writer or the writing I saw taking place in my seminar. I can't help but feel that much has been left unsaid.

According to Yinger and Clark, writing 'forces people to think' (p. 2). The choice of the word 'forces' is interesting. It says much about their approach to writing. They view writing from a stimulus/response model. They have borrowed 'specific journal writing techniques to promote certain types of learning' (p. 4). Writers are assigned methodolgy. They practice the techniques of 'systematic reflection' and 'implicit theory exercises'. Writers respond to questions deemed important by others. The teacher's role is defined as a purveyor of models and solutions, a stimulant that 'forces' individual, cognitive responses (learning). This approach is usually counterproductive in the teaching of writing. It does not generate the personal involvement neccessary for writing to be, as James Britton (1970) defined it, 'close to the self' (p. 107). It transfers the writing away from the 'writer' and into the hands of the 'teacher' assuming teacher can stimulate certain kinds of thinking by assigning certain forms of writing.

Stephen Kemmis and Robin McTaggart (1988) employ journal writing as an important component in their approach to action research. They see advantages in journal writing 'because it imposes a discipline ..., forcing you to reflect and compose your thoughts' (p. 50). Again the language conjures images of writing as coercion. Kemmis and McTaggart prescribe 'four kinds of reflection' that the journals 'should contain' (p. 50). The ownership of the writing experience is again transferred. Writers are put in the position of forcing their thoughts into a given form. In a real writing situation, especially with beginning writers, thoughts usually precede deliberate form.

Much the same cognitive approach is set forth by Lois Stover (1986). Once again, 'writing assignments can be developed that force the student to engage in reflection' (p. 21). The writing , as in other programs, is determined by forces outside the writer. Stover offers 'principles' to consider in creating writing assignments. To integrate thinking, encourage exploration and enhance self-awareness are all fine objectives. But, as with all preordained objectives in learning situations, I am struck by a basic educational question: How do you accomplish these goals? The answer to this question may not rest in the cognitive domain of writing at all. The answers may be discovered in those areas that are left 'unsaid': the social and emotional worlds of writing.

Considerations of The Self and The Other

> I know I did a lousy job, too. Mostly because I have never been so frustrated for such an extended period of time. I took it out on you through my journals. (student paper, 5/89)

> A day has not passed in which I haven't learned something, trivial or important. I feel that I have learned more about myself while teaching. I have also learned about working with another individual and communicating effectively. (student paper, 5/89)

In describing writing, the major emphasis in most of the teacher education literature is focused on the cognitive growth of an individual student writing alone. But writing is a form of language. As language, its definition relies on the role of 'others'. When the role of 'others' in writing is suggested at all, it is in the vaguest of terms. 'The Other' is often stripped of significance, perhaps because the dynamics of interpersonal interactions are often a tangled knot of a thousand threads, difficult to sort and turn into educational prescriptions.

Frances Bolin (1988) examines the role of journals in learning. In interpreting a student's journal, she chooses to analyze a 'clean copy of the journal (without supervisory comments)' (p. 49). Bolin wants to focus on the learning experience of her student, but the student's learning is directly tied into the comments of his supervisor and all the 'others' in his experience. She says that 'student journals may not be as powerful a tool for self-revelation as a personal diary or journal since the journal is required and students know that a College Supervisor will read and respond to their entries' (p. 50). But she does not address the crucial issue of student/supervisor interaction. She chooses instead to interpret the words of the journal in isolation from the context of their creation. Student journals just may be a more powerful tool in understanding reflective teaching when inter-preted against the backdrop of 'others'.

Yinger and Clark (1981) depend on 'the other' in their discussion of action research. They say that journal writing 'puts writers into a position to learn at least four important things about themselves: (1) what they know, (2) what they feel, (3) what they do (and how they do it), and (4) why they do it' (p. 10). What people know, feel and do are determined in the light of what 'others' know, feel and do. Since teachers 'constantly function in social contexts, there are a number of cultural, social and interpersonal pressures that influence their thinking and performance' (p. 14). But in prescribing writing, they return to the walls of a cognitive model. A crucial component of their 'systematic reflection' is the 'dialogue' stage, talking to a peer. The language interactions between the 'writer' and the 'listener' may be more significant in the fostering of 'reflective teaching' than the cognitive benefits of writing alone.

Kemmis and McTaggart (1988) write extensively about the importance of human interactions. They recognize that 'human beings are social beings, and that language, activities and social relationships are socially constructed' (p. 16). The changes that take place through action research take place because the researchers are 'active participants in the living, local and concrete process of constructing and reconstructing language' (p. 17). They advise that researchers 'may even wish to share [their] journal with trusted colleagues' (p. 50). But the situation in preservice teacher education is different. Our seminar brought together a group of strangers with diverse backgrounds and experiences. We had only sixteen weeks to work together. Action research, as presented by Kremmis and McTaggart, does not address the power of writing and language to *create* 'trusted colleagues'.

The literature on writing and reflective teaching fails to explore the dynamics between the individual and the learning community. Less emphasis is given to the supervisor's role within those dynamics. Parallels can be seen in the teaching of writing in most elementary classrooms. Teachers employ methodology that stress 'writing process' and 'writing to learn', but the emphasis is upon the cognitive benefits for a writer working alone. By focusing on the language of my seminar and my role as supervisor within that language, I have reshaped my definition of teaching. I can no longer view writing/learning as a strictly cogni-tive process. I have set aside the monocular focus of the cognitive lens. I have expanded my definition of writing to include its social and emotional realities.

Emphasizing the Language in Language Arts

This semester I have become more aware of the importance of being a reflective teacher. I have been keeping a journal and feel that this has helped me to reflect on what has happened over the semester, changes in the students and in myself. (student paper, 12/88)

I mean, I learned so much this semester that I can't even compare it to other semesters and its all because of the freedom we were allowed in seminar. (student interview, 12/88)

You said we'd take over and we did. (student inerview, 12/88)

Two basic concepts from teaching writing served as overarching principles in my supervision. I was sensitive to issues of audience and ownership. My teaching included considerations of 'the other', extending beyond a strict, cognitive model of writing into the social and emotional domains. Writers write best when they know that their audience is authentic, someone who is sympathetic and involved with their work. By requiring dialogue journals and academic papers, I became an audience in my student teachers' writing. Because I wanted their writing to be legitimate, coming from the 'self', I did not 'force' the creation of words. I set up open-ended, flexible structures and enticed writing forward by becoming a caring audience. Likewise, learners learn best with the assistance of a tutor who is authentic. Because of my position as supervisor, I automatically became an audience in my students' learning experiences. In their writing and their learning, I needed to become, in Britton *et al.'s* (1975) terms, a trusted adult.

To diffuse the inherent power of my role as supervisor and to build trust, I gave the students a strong voice in the learning of the seminar. At our initial meeting, I explained the basic requirements and goals of the seminar. I made it clear that I would decide on topics to discuss the first few weeks, providing relevant readings and tending to administrative neccessities. After that, the professional issues would come from them. At our third seminar, I formed small groups based on a questionnaire the students completed at our initial meeting. I created groups that represented a diversity of experiences and interests. The groups generated a list of teaching topics, focusing on issues that were relevant to their situations. As a large group, we categorized our list to seven general topics to pursue through the semester. Each group chose a topic to research. They were responsible for providing articles on the topic and for leading the class in a discussion.

The small groups did many things for the social dynamics of the seminar. The groups served as a sounding board for lessons and unit plans. They were a study group and a support group. Students became acquainted through their work on a professional issue. Stories about teaching were told in small groups first, their dialogue serving as a low risk rehearsal for the academic discussions of the large group. As the talk of the small groups broke down social walls, the talk of the large group increased. More students discovered their voices, adding their realities to the flow of our conversations. The talk of the students allowed me to diversify and decentralize my role as a supervisor and teacher. I no longer was solely a dispenser of knowledge and evaluations. I assumed the roles of facilitator and observer. The students assumed ownership of their learning.

Our task in the seminar was learning how to teach, and, at the same time, to critique the effects of our teaching. Language helped us make sense of our experiences. It helped us to accommodate. John Dixon (1967) recognizes the 'power, always available in language, to give meaning and order to the flux and fragments of reality' (p. 8). The learning that took place in the seminar was generated by the power of language, in all its varied forms. Language created a living structure to support the social, emotional *and* cognitive needs of the learners. As one student teacher put it in an interview, 'It was nice to have a chance to talk about what happened [in the classroom]. It made you think about the week that went past, instead of just ripping through it' (5/89). I was asking my student teachers to attempt something new in their college education. I was asking them to define their own learning through their interactions with other learners. I was asking them to participate in language arts.

As a teacher, I created a network of language situations within the structure of the course. Each situation represented a different type of discourse. The situations became language tools to facilitate the collaborative learning. Like all classroom tools, their definition and their use evolved and shifted during the course of the year. In order to understand the complicated patterns of language interactions that took place, I cannot focus on writing, or any other form of discourse, in isolation from all other forms. To do so, would be to ignore language's strongest contribution to learning: its interrelatedness. To understand the complex dynamics at work in the writing of the seminar, I must talk about the interplay of discourses. I must recreate the language contexts that spawned the writing. So while the language situations are put into a nice, neat, framework for the purposes of this essay, let's not forget to toss them back into the classroom as they happened, complicated and inseparable.

Language Situations

Talking

There is often a distinction made in education between 'talk' and 'discussion'. While teachers usually admit the value of a 'good discussion', they rarely see the value in 'just talking'. All teachers, no matter their grade level, have a limited amount of time, and they envision a limitless field of knowledge ahead of their students. As teachers, we assume that our job is to know the easiest, most direct path through the field. We know the path because we have taken the trip. But we have also made many wrong turns, taken dead ends, and more than likely, accomplished all this with a good deal of 'talk'. But as 'teachers', we assume teaching means telling. In our effort to help our students, we often deny them the very experiences that have taught us what we know. We often deny them talk. We then deny ourselves the chance to listen.

In the student teaching seminar, talking always accompanied our learning. The talk was often not directly related to teaching. But it created an important social/emotional bond that allowed us to pursue teaching issues through the other language situations. In her self-evaluation at the end of the semester, one student wrote, 'This is the first group discussion that I've ever talked in. Perhaps it's because I liked the the topics, or felt comfortable with the people, but it was a surprise, and wonderful!!' (5/89). Talking kept the lines of communication open and accessible to everyone. Students became caring, authentic audiences for other students. The roles they assumed through their talk shifted through the weeks. They questioned and supported, criticized and praised. I would often come to class with an agenda of issues, an agenda that we could have talked about, if nothing else arose. That agenda usually took a back seat to the issues that the students themselves raised through their talk.

The language of talk was the language of students participating in learning. It was free flowing and spontaneous, but always grounded in the experiences of the students. Ownership was real. Issues raised in class were originally identified in journals. The talk of seminar covered a wide range of topics, from issues of parent involvement to the definition of key teaching terms, from loose teeth to safety in the classroom. But no matter the topic or the 'depth' of our talk, it always led us to issues of relevance to those involved. It was my job, in my role as facilitator, to link the professional issues carried within the talk to larger issues within the teaching profession.

One student teacher wrote about the value of talk in her paper for the course. In planning a science unit on bees with another student from the seminar, she wrote that they 'learned a great deal about bees, but we did it in a manner that was fun and motivating for us — TALKING! Yes, it's that scary word that no one wants to see happen in their own classroom' (5/89). The emphasis in the seminar was upon this helping nature of talk. The seniors at the university came to terms with the emotional, social and cognitive realities of their teaching situations through their talk with 'others'.

Telling stories

> The morning started out slowly. The kids came in and all had a word or two to say about the cold weather. Something sparked my attention when E came into the room and announced her birthday was on Saturday. She ended her announcement by saying, 'Bye-bye five!' That brief statement hit me and made me stop and realize how precious every year truly is. It seems like it is so easy to just let time go by without taking a look at what time has to offer. (student journal, 2/89)

Walter Benjamin (1969) writes that, 'Experience which is passed from mouth to mouth is the source from which all storytellers have drawn' (p. 84). The power of story, and storytelling, was at the base of our learning. The lessons of seminar, the information, were embedded within the language of stories. Each session began with stories, garnered from the contexts of the classroom. We went around the tables, telling tales from the week. Some of the stories were funny. Others were horribly sad. We learned about others, and about the worlds that surrounded them, through our stories. We ultimately learned about teaching.

I took notes in my journal, collecting the stories the students told: 'Stories led to parent discussion, family life, PK: story of father in jail, PW: accident outside of school, conversation about death' (9/88). The stories from this session eventually led to a presentation on parents' involvement in the schools by a small group a few weeks later. One of the student teachers, when interviewed, recalled this particular seminar. She did not have problems with parents when the seminar discussion took place. But several weeks later, when she was in a different classroom, the 'parent issue' suddenly surfaced. She used the seminar presentation as a base of knowledge to make sense of her new situation. That knowledge had its roots in story: 'But if we had a seminar on parents, and you had gotten up and done a half hour presentation on dealing with parents, I wouldn't have listened' (12/15).

Stories appeared as notes in student journals, to be retold later in seminar. As one student said in talking about writing in her journal: 'A lot of times I would start writing while something would happen, a specific incident or something, and I'd start writing like a story format. I'd just keep going' (5/89). Issues identified through the stories of seminar surfaced in papers as well. One student continually heard stories about the creative freedoms of a kindergarten in another school. Those stories spawned reflections in her journal about the role of teacher control in classroom learning. Her reflections led to a visit to the other school, where she realized that her room's system was just as effective and just as stimulating. Her final paper dealt with the complex issue of teacher control and student freedom: 'I see freedom and control as complementing each other. The control channels into the freedom. Freedom, I think, means more if you know how to use it' (5/89).

As I read journals and visited students in their classrooms, I collected their stories and redirected them through our newsletter, back into the learning of the seminar. The language of story was reflective, language in the 'spectator role' (Britton, 1970, 1982). It gave shape to the experiences of the classrooms, defined them and, like talk, served as departure points for much of the learning that occurred. Story represented the human beginnings of the cognitive work that followed.

Conferencing

From the beginning, I made connections between supervision and the teaching of writing. In my supervision, I roughly followed a clinical observation sequence which used a pre-observation conference, an observation and a follow-up conference. In both an observation conference with a student teacher and a writing conference with a writer, ownership is a key concern. Both conferences carry a highly emotional investment. The task in each is to reflect upon a 'work' without the 'author' becoming defensive. In the case of the student teacher, the 'work' was a lesson that included a personal performance as 'teacher'.

As in a writing conference, I tried to shift the responsibilities of ownership onto the student teacher. In our pre-observation conference, students were asked to assign me a task during the observation. My role within the observation was defined by the student teacher. I became an assistant in their learning, providing another set of eyes to view their teaching.

The conferences offered the students the opportunity to talk about their work on a technical, professional level. Often the conferences took place in small groups, but usually they were one to one. Conferences modeled a new way to talk about teaching, a kind of teacher-talk that focused on the theories and the practices of teaching, as well as the ethical and philosophical consequences. Topics from seminar, journal entries and previous conferences were layered into new conversations, creating an emerging vocabulary about teaching.

The conferences were designed to expose students to a diversity of responses and opinions. I stressed the importance of context in making decisions in the classroom. We often held triad conferences between the cooperating teacher, the student teacher and myself. I would often point out alternative positions on key issues to expose the student teacher to a greater diversity of opinion. In every conference, the decision-making power was left in the hands of the student.

As we engaged in our talks and our stories and our conferences and our writing, we created a reality called 'teaching'. In each language situation, I was listening to the source of the seminar's curriculum. I took notes on a clipboard during our discussions. I reflected in my journal and raised questions in the newsletters. As a reader of the classroom, I gathered the themes and issues from the many student teaching experiences and recirculated them directly into the learning of the seminar.

Writing/The Journals

> To be honest, journals are not my cup of tea. I guess writing down my thoughts isn't the hard part, it is writing on a schedule, day to day. I like to write when something meaningful happens, not just writing 'today this happened — blah, blah, blah'. (student journal, 1/89)

> Some days, I don't want to write in my journal. If I have to, I just think of stupid things to say to fill space. It doesn't feel like a journal I'm writing for myself then. It feels like I'm writing for seminar. It would be more my journal if I could write when I want to write. (student journal, 2/89)

There were two basic avenues for the writing in the student teaching seminar: journals and academic papers. Like the language situations themselves, it is impossible to talk about one without talking about the other. The two avenues together gave writing its power.

The journals were difficult things to describe. They had features of diaries, logs and journals as described by both Mary Louise Holly (1984) and James Moffett (1985). There were two main uses for the journals within the seminar. They were teachng journals, gathering data and experiences specific to teaching, and they were dialogue journals. Students turned in their journals throughout the semester. I read and responded to their thoughts and observations. Moffett (1985) calls the category of letters, diaries and journals 'Notation'. Journals contain the notes for future compositions. They 'accumulate the empirical fodder for the inductive process of generalization' (p. 48). The entries in our journals, besides being points of departure for our talk, served as the 'fodder' for our academic writing.

When I assigned the journals at the first seminar of the semester, I purposely left their definition vague. The writing I received in those first entries conformed to a norm that was safe and risk free. The students' writing and their responses to writing were influenced by a definition of academic journal writing built upon a long history of schooling. The students I interviewed drew distinct lines between private and academic writing. While they spoke kindly of diaries and letters written to friends, they portrayed academic writing in a different light. I was a new academic audience at the start of the semester. The students expected me to be evaluative and judgmental, someone whose written comments would be no more meaningful than a checkmark or a pat-two-word-phrase (Good point!). They expected a journal format that was prescribed, the form and the writing controlled by 'teacher'. As one student expressed it, 'I hated it with a passion. When you said we had to do one this year, I just didn't want to do it' (11/88).

Many of those first entries began with an apology for the quality of their writing. Students were convinced that they could not write. The penmanship was neat and legible. Their journals were uniform. Most wrote strictly from a spectator's role. Their entries read like a diary, notes written at night, removed from the frenzy of the day. While I endorsed the diary format, expecting everyone to write daily, I also opened new avenues of writing, nudging their writing closer to what Britton (1970) calls the 'participant role', or what Moffett

(1985) calls 'writing from within the events and not from the vantage point of their conclusion' (p. 4).

Our second seminar of the semester was devoted to expanding the definition of journal. Always sensitive to ownership, I wanted students to redefine the journal within their own contexts. In order for the cognitive benefits of writing to take place, I needed to expand the range of acceptable forms, not narrow it through a few, prescribed exercises. Holly (1984) understands the issue of ownership. In keeping a journal, she advises that 'each of us must develop procedures and organization according to our style and purposes' (p. 1). Her booklet describes several different types of journal writing, yet never prescribes their application.

I wanted students to discover and invent a combination of forms that fit their particular writing styles. As a student described it, 'It wasn't like there was a certain form. It was something that I could do that was me, my writing. I've never had the opportunity to do that before, even in high school or grade school' (5/89). I encouraged 'notes in action', 'to do' lists and brainstorming sheets. By the third week, a diversity of styles shyly emerged. The journals began to collect observations made in the classroom, reflections about lessons, problems encountered, triumphs achieved, notes to remember and reminders to accomplish. Students wrote me letters, some sent me folders stuffed with lists and loose leaf paper. Many photocopied lesson plans, turning them in with their reflective notes. Some stayed strictly with a diary format. Penmanship standards slackened. One student wrote notes on small hunks of paper during her teaching. Those notes became artifacts for her reflective computer writing later in the day. I received the hunks and the print out. Diversity became the norm. But no matter what form the journals took, the students began to write for themselves *and* for me. They depended on their journals to capture the fast pace reality of their classrooms.

I responded differently to the journal entries over the course of the semester. In the beginning, I worked to establish my position as a trusted adult. I read and responded to their journals in detail. My responses were informal, not teacherly. Their stories prompted stories from my days as a first grade teacher, stories that I shared. When I didn't have enough room to respond in the margins, I responded on another sheet of paper.

We talked about many things in the pages of those journals. Sometimes we dealt with pressing professional issues. Other times we wrote about new apartments and the excitment of graduation. As one student said, 'I just wrote about whatever I felt like writing. It had something to do with school. It's all part of me' (5/89). The journals allowed me to know the students as humans, emotionally and intellectually. My responses allowed them the opportunity to know me. As the semester progressed, we became authentic, caring audiences. The journals developed into a rich source of reflection that wound its way through all the language situations.

> In the beginning I thought the journals were just a waste of time. I realize now that they can be a real asset. They help you remember how a lesson went, whether it was good or bad. This may help you decide how you want to teach the lesson next year. How could you remember what happened if you did not have your journal? (student paper, 12/88)

> Observations and reflections have taught me numerous things about my class and how I would like to see my teaching style change, but most importantly the enormous value in observations and reflections themselves. (student paper, 12/88)

The last thing any classroom teacher needs is more work. Research in the classroom implies an approach, as much as anything else. It is a way to view the classroom. All good teachers practice basic elements of research. They observe their classes. They notice things. They reflect about their lessons in the light of the things they observe. And they ask questions: What if? How come? I wonder why? By acknowledging this research element of teaching, teachers can become more systematic in their evaluation and understanding of teaching. Research can be woven into a teacher's management systems so it is part of teaching, not another extra duty. All of us in the seminar, myself included, engaged in research. We inquired into our teaching, developing a systematic approach to help us understand the learning that took place in our rooms. The journal was at the center of most of the systems that developed.

Each student teacher wrote two major academic papers during the semester. One paper dealt with a child in the classroom, focusing on that individual's learning. Students also tracked their own learning in a second paper. The papers provided an opportunity for the students to think about the events of the classroom in a different discourse. By capturing classroom moments in their journals, students defined their daily classroom experiences. When those specific events were later reread and used as data in the writing of academic papers, the events generalized into statements of theory. A semester's worth of journal entries and conversations became pieces in an inductive puzzle. Observation of students, scraps of paper with 'notes in action', and lesson plans all became sources of information that defined the learning of the semester. Moffett (1985) calls this form of writing, 'Cogitation'. It is writing that is 'working from registration, recollection, and conscious collection of data to their distillation into a few general truths' (p. 372).

The academic papers opened yet another avenue of professional discourse. At mid-term, each student gave me a written report describing their progress. They noticed trends in the learning of their students and themselves. In my written responses and questions, I focused our attention on learning, encouraging students to build bridges between their own learning and the learning of the child they observed. I identified parallels when encouragement did not work. Follow-up discussions were based in the student's own teaching experiences, highlighting the connections between theory and practice. Students focused on the processes of their learning as well as their products, the 'how' as well as the 'what' of their knowledge. This is where the cognitive camps of composition reap their biggest dividends. Writing allowed the student teachers to tap their inner voices, to slow down their thoughts and to discover the realities of their learning that were hidden within them.

As I became a trusted adult, as students assumed ownership of the writing, our conversations, both written and oral evolved. The journals and the academic papers allowed me to question and respond on a personal and professional level.

They allowed me to push the limits of the student's teaching theories. The stories that were told in seminar came directly from the pages of the journals. Teaching issues raised in the papers were layered into our classroom discussions, creating the curriculum of our learning. But it was the social and emotional bonds established by all the language situations that allowed the cognitive benefits of writing to take place.

> I believe very strongly in reflective teaching ... I no longer believe that there is any correct way to write and reflect, but only a variety of ways to put your feelings and emotions into print ... Children deserve the same freedom adults do when involved in the learning process. (student paper, 5/89)

> This semester, I have my own goals and standards to make, which has not really been the case for me academically before. I would go for someone else's 'A' before, now I go for my own hypothetical 'A' — which comes harder and is much more important and valuable, and therefore motivating, which fuels real learning. (student paper, 12/88)

The Seminar as Novel

The seminar was a teaching workshop, rather than a discussion group. The language was a language of action. A workshop approach encouraged students into new areas of learning by sharing the processes of learning, as well as the products. The discourses employed in the seminar created an environment that fostered the free and open exchange of emotions, reactions and ideas. We became a community of learners involved in relevant learning experiences. Students experimented, took risks (and learned) with the emotional and social support of the seminar community. Their teaching in the classrooms, and the way they spoke about their teaching, shifted. Their vision of 'teacher' evolved from a giver-of-knowledge to a facilitator of learning. Students became more sensitive to the issue of ownership. They tried to create lessons that generated a motivation that was intrinsic, rather than extrinsic.

Throughout the semester, I read journals, conferenced on the phone, told stories, interviewed students, engaged in teacher-talk and responded to academic papers. I took 'notes in action'. I reflected in my journal. I used the seminar's newsletters to publish the themes I discovered. But while I was part of the seminar, I also occupied a different role. I created a workshop atmosphere for my seminar because I wanted the curriculum to come from the learners. Moffett (1986) refers to just such a curriculum when he suggests that the stimulants for writing 'arise out of the daily drama of the student's life in and out of school' (p. 208). It was one of my jobs, as supervisor, to keep track of the 'daily drama', to note the stories that the students told, to help build connections between teaching theories and practices. I continually interpreted the discourses that unfolded before me within the novel of the seminar.

The student teaching seminar was a gathering of emotional, social and cognitive contexts. Individuals contributed their context to the contexts of the others. The context of the seminar influenced the contexts of the individuals. The contexts of individuals fed into the larger context of the group. My job, as teacher, was to read, to listen, to interpret and to direct the interplay in the variety of contexts. This was a complicated novel to read! It was filled with the drama, the emotion and the joy of real human experience! Each student became a character nested within a history of contexts. I tried to make the professional, philosophical and ethical connections within our network of language. I collapsed the class upon itself.

Hours before a student teaching seminar, a cooperating teacher told me a story in the hallways of an elementary school. It was about an interaction between herself and her student teacher. Both teachers were tired after a long day in the kindergarten classroom. The student teacher was taken to task about her preparation in the teaching of a lesson. Tempers flared, somewhat, and the student teacher expressed disappointment about the time that was available for feedback on her teaching. The cooperating teacher thought that I should know so that I could address the issue of lesson preparation in seminar. Once again, I was working from a depth of context. From journal entries and from conferences, I knew that other student teachers had similiar conversations with their cooperating teachers.

I knew that the issue of student teacher/cooperating teacher communication needed to be addressed, but I wanted the issue to come from the class itself. I wanted the ownership to remain with the students. That day's seminar started as all others, with stories. I went first to student teacher number one, the one who had the squabble (she did not know that I knew). I asked her for a story. I provided an immediate opening for her to air her experience. She turned down the opportunity. As we went around the table, other students told stories and raised issues. After three stories, I recognized a connection to the plight of student teacher one. My connection was built on my reading of the classroom novel. I facilitated the conversation by restating the story of student teacher number four, providing a textual opening into our conversation. The opening was again turned down.

Three more teachers told their stories, and again, because I knew the contexts of the characters involved, another opening appeared. Again, I facilitated by restating the point. This time, student teacher number one took advantage of the opening. She told her story about the cooperating teacher. That story led to a twenty minute discussion on honesty in communication. The topic emerged because I had read the novel of the classroom, because I realized that the emotional, social and cognitive network of the classroom included 'teacher'.

Most models of classroom learning have relegated the role of 'teacher' to nothing more than a manager of the setting, a presenter of the proper stimulus. Learners are pictured struggling within the inner, private battle of cognition. The workshop approach used in the seminar created a learning environment that was emotional, cognitive and social. That environment engulfed all the learners, including myself. The language network hooked into everyone.

An Ending, With New Beginnings

My year can best be defined as a search for meaning. That search underlies all that I have learned. By keeping a teaching journal, by becoming involved in the learning of the classroom, I have tried to articulate the theories that underlie my use of 'writing' in teacher education. This essay is now part of my learning. In discussing the rough drafts with friends, answering their questions and rewriting my thoughts, the language process continues. 'Others' have helped me define (and redefine) the reasonings behind my practice. Next year will necessarily bring changes in my basic seminar structures. My approach will be more systematic. I will hold writing conferences at mid-term to focus the final student papers. I plan to tape-record all seminars, to better understand the current of the discourse. While I now understand the seminar in a different light, at least one thing still seems to remain a constant. My teaching this past year has reaffirmed a basic belief: humans learn best by interacting and solving problems with other humans through language. And 'writing', as a form of language, draws its power from roots that spread well beyond the walls of a cognitive curriculum, into the emotional and social realities of life. Surely, any attempt to foster reflective teaching through the use of writing must remember these basic realities.

References

BENJAMIN, W. (1969) *Illuminations: Essays and Reflections*, New York: Schocken Books

BOLIN, F.S. (1988) 'Helping Student Teachers Think about Teaching', *Journal of Teacher Education*, March–April, **39**, 2, pp. 48–53.

BRITTON, J. (1970) *Language and Learning*, Middlesex, England: Penguin Books Ltd.

BRITTON, J., BURGESS, T., MARTIN, N., McLEOD, A. and ROSEN, H. (1975) 'Sense of audience', *The Development of Writing Abilities*, London: Macmillan, pp. 58–73.

BRITTON, J. (1982) *Prospect and Retrospect*, Montclair: Boynton Cook Publishers, Inc.

DIXON, J. (1967) *Growth Through English*, London: Cox and Wyman Ltd.

HOLLY, M.L. (1984) *Keeping a Personal-Professional Journal*, Geelong Australia: Deakin University Press.

KEMMIS, S. and McTAGGART, R. (1988) *The Action Research Planner*, Victoria: Deakin University Press

MOFFETT, J. (1968) 'Learning to Write by Writing', *Teaching the Universe of Discourse*, Boston: Houghton Mifflin Company

MOFFETT, J. (1985) *Points of Departure: An Anthology of Nonfiction*, New York: Mentor Books.

STOVER, L. (1986) 'Writing to learn in teacher education', *Journal of Teacher Education*, **37**, 4, pp. 20–3.

YINGER, R. and CLARK, C. (1981) *Reflective Journal Writing: Theory and Practice*, East Lansing, MI: Institute for Research on Teaching. Occasional Paper no. 50.

14   War Stories: Invitations to Reflect on Practice

Jane J. White

All too often teachers' oral accounts of what is happening in their classrooms have been dismissed by educational researchers as trivial, unsophisticated chatter. Characterized as unobjective and, indeed, dangerously emotional, this idle talk is deemed fit only for the teachers' room: it is certainly not to be taken seriously by those trying to gain scientific insights into the workings of American classrooms. Even those researchers and phenomenologists who feel that the voice of the teacher should be heard in the recently renewed dialogue about what teachers know and do can only make very weak claims about teachers' representations of their experiences. For example, Connelly and Elbaz (1980) describe teachers as engaging in 'practical reasoning', and Bolster (1983) characterizes teachers as 'situational decision-makers' (p. 296) whose knowledge is 'idiographic in origin and therefore particularistic in character' (p. 298). Bolster contrasts the knowledge teachers construct with the more 'nomothetic' and 'universalistic' knowledge generated by conventional research (p. 301).

Just because the knowledge that teachers construct as they reflect on their lived experiences is generated within the context of a specific time and place, it does not mean that their reasoning is atheoretical, without a logic of its own. Are teachers to be categorically excluded from engaging in thoughtful dialogue because their stories about life in the classroom are perceived only as evidence of concrete thinking?

Labov shows us a way out of this conundrum. In his article, 'The Transformation of Experience in Narrative Syntax' (1972), he argues that while narratives by definition are 'one method of recapitulating past experience by matching a verbal sequence of clauses to the sequence of events which (it is inferred) actually occurred' (pp. 359–60), they also have a point to make, a *raison d'etre* for being told (p. 366).

Teachers' narratives, or 'war stories' as they are often called, encode both their specific experiences and go beyond them. Teachers tell stories for reasons other than being expressive, being entertaining or 'letting off steam'. When they tell stories, teachers are beginning a process of reflection on their practice. When teachers tell stories, they make claims about the premises of teaching, theoretically argue about priorities, inculcate those moving into the profession and cause others to reflect on their own practice.

Labov's careful analysis of the verbal skills used in narratives shows that there are regularized patterns and conventions by which a speaker transforms the events that occurred into words designed to rally maximum support for a central claim that the speaker is trying to make. Labov's argument that there is an evaluative agenda will be used as the basis for a discussion of

1 Stories told by a beginning teacher, Mr Nathan, as he returned to his alma mater to tell a field experience seminar what it was really like during his first year of teaching;
2 War stories written by student teachers in their journals and discussed in seminar; and
3 Stories told by experienced teachers to each other within a graduate seminar.

The purpose of this paper is to analyze stories told by teachers in terms of the central premises about teaching they are trying to transmit as they reflect upon their experiences. I will also describe how these war stories elicit reflection by others.

Mr Nathan's War Stories

Mr Nathan is a beginning teacher who, at a time when teaching positions were difficult to obtain, was hired as a long-term substitute in fourth grade at an inner city school. Given high ratings as a substitute, he was then hired as a full-time teacher in an inner city third grade. Mr Nathan is white and the children he teaches and a majority of the faculty are black. In the spring of his third year, Mr Nathan was invited to talk at the final meeting of a field experience seminar (with twenty-five education students) to tell them what his first years of teaching were 'really like'. Mr Nathan talked without notes for over an hour, dramatically presenting more than thirty war stories.

As will be seen from the opening story, although narratives are spontaneous oral productions, they are not random or ill-formed accountings of experience. The first war story contains characteristic and identifiable structural features including an orientation, a series of interwoven complicating actions and evaluative statements skillfully presented to heighten the tension, a climax, a resolution and a coda (Labov, 1972, pp. 362–70).

At the beginning of his talk, Mr Nathan tells how he obtained his first long-term substitute position in a fourth grade:

Mr Nathan: Early in the year their teacher fell and injured her
            shoulder
            and she's been out of school .. on disability.

            Well, since then
            they had many substitutes in and out.
            The year before
            they had been one of those classes that had been
            taught by substitutes.
            And so they *again*
            figured out that they can destroy any substitute
            that walks in the door

because they're not real teachers
and they don't *usually*
put in the *effort* .. to .. discipline.

So I walked in
and .. there they were ..
Everywhere.
I mean just everywhere in the classroom.
Forty-two children ..
NONE .. able to hear you ..
say anything about the rules
because they're all SCREAMING
at the top of their lungs.

It's just the ideal situation.

Mrs White: Don't you all fear
that on your first day
you'll walk in
and the kids will just be running all over?
I mean, that always used to be my night-before-school-
started nightmare.

Mr Nathan sets up his first problem as being hired to teach a group of children who up to now have been unteachable. The short uncomplicated clauses, the specification of the large class size, the description of the uncontrolled movement and noise, the stopping of the action to repeat, 'everywhere', 'I mean just everywhere in the classroom' and the slightly exaggerated-for-emphasis words augur well for a dramatic performance. The use of the strong verb 'destroy' ascribing negative motives to the class, and his sarcasm as he compares the situation with which he was confronted with the field experience students' more idealistic images of what their first class will be like, lead the audience toward framing the situation as an us-against-them power struggle, well qualifying this narrative for its vernacular characterization as a war story. The second speaker, Mrs White, spontaneously adds to this perspective by agreeing that an out-of-control classroom is one of the worst case fears of a teacher with a new group.

Mr Nathan then adds complicating action to the story by describing his initial attempts to solve his problem:

So .. so I tried speaking very loud.
Now I'm very strong on discipline.
That's my reputation in the city
and that's why they put me there.
They had this other substitute
that the parents wanted OUT

because she couldn't discipline the children
well enough to teach them anything.

So I walked in
knowing that everybody in the school
was expecting me to straighten them out.
And .. I raised my voice as loud as I could
and nothing happened at all.

I slammed the classroom door
and nothing happened at all.

Now generally those things DO something to my students
but it didn't happen.

So I walked around the room desperately trying to find
something I could use as a demonstration device,
and I found a piece of wood
about that long and about that thick
and I found an empty desk
and I beat it on the desk
and nothing happened.

Well usually when you hit a ruler or something on a desk
they stop, but nothing happened.

So I just hit it again
and again.

As he continues, the tension of the narrative is increased by Mr Nathan's use of specific detail and quantification: 'I tried speaking *very loud*'; and 'I raised my voice *as loud as I could*'. The rhythmic, poetic quality of the story is built up by the repetition of the lines at the end of each action: 'and nothing happened at all'.
   Finally the story reaches its climax and resolution:

I had to do it about ten times
and they finally .. quieted down.
At which point I said to them
we would not be doing that .. in here.

They disagreed. (Laughs)

So I beat it down again. (Audience laughs)
And this went on all day long
until there was nothing left of the piece of wood
except splinters all around the classroom.

Throughout his narrative Mr Nathan has made the point that by comparison to other groups, this is one of the most difficult groups to teach that he has ever met. Mr Nathan also makes the point that by comparison to other teachers, he has built up the reputation that he is 'very strong on discipline'. Thus, by the climax and resolution, the 'so-what' of the story becomes evident to the neophytes: no matter how difficult the students and the situation, the initial underlying premise of teaching is that one must first gain control of the students before one can begin any of the other activities conventionally construed as teaching.

Mr Nathan evaluates his actions by stating what other people might think, warns of possible negative consequences resulting from his actions but then, almost in defiance of public opinion, directly states his own thesis about teaching:

And, now that, that .. sounds terrible.
And I know a lot of people go berserk
when they hear of me doing that.
That evening I had two parents in
and I left several in the office when I went home.
And the thing is
like I'm supposed to teach these children
but I can't teach them anything until they listen.

So, .. I had to get them quiet and I did that.

This attention grabbing war story of Mr Nathan's was followed by stories that gave detailed technical advice about how to get students' attention. Mr Nathan told how he established a set of rules and demanded total adherence:

And I began giving them lots of work to keep them busy.
. . .
And I had very strict rules
the first things I tell them after I tell
'When you follow my rules you'll be happy.
When you do not follow my rules, . . .
you will be very unhappy'.
And . . . they always test me.
And for about a month I'm the most hated teacher
in any school I'm working in.

Mr Nathan explained that when he first started with these students' class, even the adults sympathetic to them in the school referred to them as 'the gorillas'. His class lost out on many pleasurable educational activities because of

their bad behavior. For example, they had not been on a field trip for three years.
Mr Nathan argued that:

> And one of the problems was
> with so many substitutes in the past couple of years
> they had not really learned how to behave.
> They did not know the simple procedures
> like passing things out.
> Which many people don't realize [is that]
> you have to teach that.

Thus, prior to giving a series of technical instructions about how to manage a classroom, Mr Nathan adds a second major premise to his philosophy of teaching: rather than believing that students are inherently bad and that it is hopeless to try to change them, Mr Nathan believes that students are bad because they have not yet been properly taught how to be good. Although initially harsh, Mr Nathan's message contains a measure of hope; if it is done properly, bad students can be taught how to be good.

Mr Nathan's stories repeatedly framed teaching as difficult as he described how students continually challenged his best efforts. For example, he told how he used vandalism to a bulletin board as an opportunity for learning. When a child angry at Mr Nathan for a reprimand poked a hole into a tree, Mr Nathan repaired it by adding a bird's nest. Building on the renewed interest in his bulletin board, each day he added something new to this representation of spring: two eggs; then baby birds, then the mother bird feeding worms to the babies, etc.

Mr Nathan also told stories about how he got the children interested in learning. In third grade he realized that the children were resentful of what they thought would be a boring science unit on the water cycle. He caught their attention by matter-of-factly stating that, 'Water is two hydrogen atoms bonded to an oxygen atom'. When the children argued that this was not the type of water they drank, he talked about the types of bonds between hydrogen and oxygen molecules, constantly repeating the chemical formula of water. When the children reviewed what they had learned prior to the test, the children not only remembered but were proud of what they had learned. One girl bragged how she had gone home and explained the molecular formula to her older sister who, although she was in junior high, had not learned that yet.

Mr Nathan recalled how he had used knowledge from science to break what he described as 'a terrible habit':

> They all picked their noses
> just all the time.

> So I thought, 'Well, I've got to teach science
> and I've got to stop this problem.
> I'll just teach them about clean hands'.

Although the fourth grade children claimed, that, of course, their hands were clean, Mr Nathan said:

> Well,
> you don't have clean hands
> because you've got these millions of little things...
> And they're all,
> 'Where are they? Where are they?'
> and they're staring at their hands.

> So I went through this lesson
> about bacteria, viruses.
> I taught them about DNA.
> I had a whole group of little fourth graders who,
> 'What's DNA?'
> 'DNA is deoxyribonucleic acid'.

> Half the faculty
> did not know what DNA was.
> My fourth graders are running around:
> they're saying, 'Deoxyribonucleic acid'.

Mr Nathan went on to describe how the class decided to grow bread mold as their science project. He gleefully reported how parents rushed into his room on P.T.A. night asking, 'Where's the bread mold? All I hear about is the mold!.. Look, my daughter's mold is really fuzzy!'

Mr Nathan concluded his talk by telling a story about taking his third grade class to the Smithsonian. As he reminded the field experience students, 'This was the first time in three years that this class had been out on a field trip':

> Well, I figured
> that this was the end of me.
> I had maintained everything
> until May
> and now
> we're going on a field trip...

> So I'm pondering,
> 'What can I give them
> that will give them direction?'

Mr Nathan spent a week connecting what the students would see at the Museum of Natural History with what they had been learning in their science units on geology and animals. He told them the legend of the Hope diamond and taught them what carats were. Mr Nathan gave them assignments. The children had to get the names of certain kinds of stones, 'they had to find three animals that lived in an Arctic area; five animals that lived in a desert area. They were to find out what the texture of the big elephant skin was like. And how big the blue whale was'.

Mr Nathan also carefully described how he spent three days teaching his students manners: how they were not to run, or to interrupt adults. He made out worksheets and stapled them to pieces of cardboard like clipboards. Mr Nathan found that other teachers at the school felt that he was being 'cruel' to give an assignment to his students for the field trip.

> So that morning they came in
> and I handed them out
> their little cardboard pieces with the worksheets
> and they thought they were
> the greatest thing on the face of the earth
> at that moment.

> They had these little clipboards
> and they had a pencil
> and they were going to the museum.
> And they got in line.

> They walked to the bus.
> They sat down.
> They didn't talk on the bus.
> Which, I didn't (laughs)
> tell them they couldn't talk on the bus.
> They didn't talk on the bus to Washington, D.C.
> They sat. (Laughter)
> The bus stopped.
> Everyone jumped up.
> Not my class.
> They sat there.
> They did not move on the bus.
> So I told them, 'Stand'.
> They stood.
> No one got into the aisle.
> So they just stood there.

> We walked out
> And then they were divided up.
> I had enough parents
> So that each parent only had four.
> And I didn't have anyone.
> Cause I figured that I was going to get Johnny and
> Marvin,
> Billy and Amos and James. . . .

But I didn't have any problems with them.

The children were walking around
with their little clipboards.
They were asking questions like,
'Did the astronauts package these moon rocks
before they brought them back
or were they just in a large container?'

And, on the way back from the museum
they talked,
all the way home:
'I didn't get three Arctic animals.
What did you get?'
They're finishing their worksheets.
And one child said,
'I didn't get a chance to see this one exhibit'.
And another child called out,
'Oh, I saw that one'.

For days they talked about it.
They remembered everything from the trip.
And, I had all these little follow-up activities.
And we discussed everything.

The other children had been out of school for a day.
Mine had been to a museum for a day
and they had learned things.

It was just a little activity
It wasn't intended to be hard for them
and I kind of built it up
as a treasure hunt type deal
where they could go and look for things
and it worked out.

Thus by the last story, several premises of teaching important to Mr Nathan have been established. In all of his stories, the teacher must first establish control, but by the end of the talk, the audience begins to understand that control is but a means to an end — that of transmitting academic knowledge to the students.

As the stories unfold, scientific knowledge is first introduced as one of the ways to gain control. Mr Nathan uses knowledge to surprise and then hold the attention of the students by mentioning that the water molecule is composed of two hydrogen and one oxygen atom. And, to stop the 'disgusting' habit of nose picking, Mr Nathan teaches the students about germs, viruses, mold and DNA. Paradoxically, by the end of his talk, Mr Nathan's need for control of a field trip results in enabling his students to act as if they are scientists gathering data on topics from the texture of elephant skin to the size of the Hope diamond.

There was not time left for questions at the end of Mr Nathan's presentation to the field experience students. While visibly enjoying his talk and applauding vigorously at the end, the field experience students did not automatically accept everything that he said. Several students stopped to talk with me immediately after class: although they were quick to assure me that they had nothing against Mr Nathan personally, the education students were bothered by the tone of his talk. They were shocked by what they described as Mr Nathan's 'harshness' and 'meanness'. They felt he showed callousness towards his students. They were particularly bothered by him conveying that the students were called 'gorillas', by the nose picking story, and by what was described as 'his delight and glee in the almost paramilitary manner in which his students behaved on the bus trip to Washington'. As one student remarked, 'There's control and there's control but this guy is excessively rigid'.

However, Mr Nathan's war stories were not dismissed out-of-hand. They disturbed the students who continued to mull over them to try to come to terms with them. A week after the final seminar, each field experience student met with the field experience instructor and supervisors for a twenty minute individual 'exit interview'. The student talked about both the strengths and problems of teaching and reflected on whether teaching would or would not be a good career choice. A week later, it was obvious that the field experience students were still trying to make meaning out of what Mr Nathan had said. For example, during the exit interviews, far more of the field experience students mentioned Mr Nathan than the numerous research articles on classroom management that they had read during the semester. Many found that there was much useful technical information embedded in his stories. Field experience students frequently mentioned what Mr Nathan said about getting a job and the notion that teachers are first judged by whether they do or do not have control. Questions asked included: 'Is it always like that when you go to get a job as a substitute?' and students worried if they would have to resort to banging a stick to get order. Students praised Mr Nathan's descriptions of teaching the students how to pass out papers and books and how to set up clipboards with questions to organize a field trip to a museum.

Although many field experience students had initially dismissed Mr Nathan as being too punitive towards students, they began to find reasons to reconsider some of the messages embedded in his war stories: 'Well at least he is honest and above board about the need for discipline' and 'You know, Mr Nathan is very clear with his students about the need for discipline'. Various field experience students began to argue that perhaps Mr Nathan was not totally negative towards his students because he was trying to help them learn. In fact, some students saw him as too powerful but very supportive. One student explained that Mr Nathan was not really in a struggle for power so that he won and the students lost. 'Really, when he wins everybody wins because the students learn'.

It should be noted that Mr Nathan's war stories violated many of the field experience students' deeply held but taken-for-granted values that they had about how children should be treated with friendship, with fairness, with dignity, with justice. However, Mr Nathan's war stories of life out in the 'real world' served notice that perhaps these values might not be easily or routinely implemented in their professional practice. Mr Nathan's war stories indirectly suggested that their values might be too one-sided, pristine and/or not contextualized. After all how does one go about immediately establishing fairness, dignity and justice in a situations in which children are labeled gorillas? Although one's commitment to children and/or to transmitting scholarship may be pure and true, how is a person to handle the more distasteful aspects of the occupation such as snotty hands, deliberate bulletin board vandalism, and disapproving parents and teachers?

Mr Nathan's war stories did not cause the field experience students to abandon their core values and beliefs. However, the establishment of a divergent view caused reflection by challenging some taken-for-granted beliefs. When students go out to student teach, war stories flourish in student journals and seminars as students once again find their beliefs and knowledge of teaching challenged (White, 1989).

War Stories Told by Student Teachers

Mr Nathan recounted his war stories within a more formal lecture mode. Unfortunately, there was no time for collegial feedback from the audience. In this next section, I describe a more dynamic group reflective process.

Student teachers arrive in the field with an unsorted set of beliefs about how teachers should act, beliefs about how children should act, memories of their own schooling, and a set of techniques from their university courses such as how to write lesson plans. However, war stories furiously written in journals and shared during the seminars during the first few weeks of student teaching reveal frustrations, doubts, bewilderment and sometimes a sense of 'injustice': life in the classroom does not operate in the way that it is supposed to. One student teacher, Sherry, placed in a first grade describes how her lessons were well-planned and well-executed but the pupils did not learn:

> One thing that didn't go well this week was my lesson on 'telling sentences'. On Monday I introduced the declarative sentence. On Tuesday and Wednesday I thought I made it very clear that there are two very special things about these sentences: (1) They always begin with capital letters. (2) They always end with a period. We went over countless examples orally, in the book and on the board. We did a worksheet together as a class and the class did really well. However, when I gave them a graded assignment on four sentences, more than half the class failed it!

Sherry then recounted how she had to figure out how to reteach the same content in a variety of different ways until the children finally 'got it' and could independently punctuate sentences properly.

Another student teacher, Pam, put in many hours meticulously planning a lesson that 'utterly bombed'. In the middle of the lesson she realized that the students did not have 'the slightest notion' of what she was talking about. As Pam wrote in her log:

> Panic set in. What do you do in two seconds? So I totally abandoned the charts I had worked on for three nights, all the activities and I had planned and the ditto sheets that I had run off. I pulled an activity out of the air. I let the kids ask me and each other questions until they could do it. Mrs C. said that it was the first good lesson that I've done so far. Is it really worth preparing lessons when the spur of the moment ones seem to work better?

As dramatically recounted in the student teaching seminar, this woman was outraged, not by her initial failure but by the success of her spontaneous lesson. Pam felt that her beliefs about the need for good preparation had been made meaningless. She claimed that all her notions of how teaching worked had 'blown up in her face' and that 'she didn't know what would work and what wouldn't'. The student teachers argued with Pam that her planning was still valuable: even if her first set of ideas didn't work, she had thought about the lesson enough to have a second set available.

Towards the end of a different semester, a student teacher, Tom, wrote scathingly about what he now sees as his misguided attempts to reach a troubled sixth grader:

> ... I was determined to help a child dumped into this wretched world by parents incapable of helping themselves and instilling Brian with any shred of self-worth. Brian would appreciate me for taking the time to offer personal encouragement, positive reinforcement and heavy doses of attention.
>
> Boy was I mistaken!! Brian not only resisted every one of my overtures and attempts to help him, but he retaliated with venomous disdain for my supposed noble efforts. Brian was deliberately disruptive, defiant, threatening and disaffected by my haughty pretensions. On several occasions he threatened: 'You better get out of my face!!' with the feisty spirit of an embittered and angry youth clawing at a stranger interested in him for no particular purpose or condition than that I liked him for being Brian. Brian deferred respectfully with no rumblings to Mrs B. but to me he was continually troublesome, insolent, apathetic and contemptuous of my total being.
>
> Along with other kids Brian was praised for his basketball prowess and physical education skills. He often made derisive and highly offensive comments and slurs to girls and the less popular children.
>
> I have come to realize that Brian's world was a constant battle to survive in an environment unsuitable for healthy and productive maturation. Brian was embattled and pulled down by forces plaguing many decaying urban environments. His learning, then, was how to take care of himself and survive the hellish shithole he had no control over or decision to enter. Brian is a product of any child's worst nightmare, only

Brian could not wake up and recover from the scary and frightening sensations temporary to poor bedtime slumber. Brian's world was permanent and he knew no other way to act or behave. Laying his emotional baggage at the school doorstep is tantamount to requiring a Vietnam Vet to forget the rages of the most vicious war we have fought.

I came to see or understand that Brian just wanted to be left alone — unattended — unscrutinized. Someone taking an interest in him was foreign to his understanding. I was, then, seen as a threat. When I loosened up and paid less attention to him, he settled down more and spoke out less and acted out less frequently.

I remember well the Indian proverb: 'Walk a mile in another man's moccasins'. I often tried to put myself in Brian's shoes in an attempt to understand his behavior. I became weighted down emotionally in his home life and struggle to survive.

My struggle with Brian shows that I cannot touch or help every child. For some children, education is not math or social studies but survival in a perilous world unfit for human habitation.

Student teachers begin reflecting when events in the classroom force them to confront that certain teaching strategies or beliefs about children have become suspect. As they leave the security of their previous knowledge base, student teachers often feel angry or overwhelmed by the ambiguity, complexity and interconnectedness of problems ranging from the mundane to the insolvable. The war stories of the first two student teachers initially involved frustration and rage: frustration at themselves for not being able to teach better and rage at the university for not preparing them better. Students in this seminar kept coming back to the issue of what do you do when you teach but no one learns. They shared stories of how to reteach exactly the same lesson using different techniques, they began to watch for different signs of whether the students were 'getting it' or not, and they shared stories of times that they or their cooperating teachers 'thought on their feet' to 'save the day'. These student teachers became interested in pacing, in trying to figure out how much they should try to teach to a class at any one time. They begin to watch how their cooperating teachers coped readily with problems that seemed overwhelming to them.

In a different seminar, Tom's anguish about not 'getting through' to a child in a different subculture split the seminar group. Middle-class students who had middle-class placements would not change their belief that one should always keep trying to 'get through' to children who had special needs. However, middle-class student teachers who were having experiences in racially different, inner city or lower socioeconomic classrooms agreed with Tom that they should be careful about forcing their structure of caring onto students from a different way of life. They argued about the morality of acting as if they could 'make a difference' to children, the ethics of raising expectations they probably could not meet because as student teachers, they were truly transient in these children's lives.

A further premise of Tom — that social studies and math were essentially irrelevant to Brian — led to wonderfully intense arguments and a converging of group consensus against's Tom's position. Although there was eventually an agreement to disagree about how 'close' a teacher should get to a pupil, everyone (including me, the supervisor) agreed that Tom should not conclude that academic subjects were meaningless to Brian. Arguing that the one difference a teacher could make was to expect and assist children 'in bad situations' to do well academically, student teacher after student teacher poured out war stories of how they had helped children of whom not much was expected to achieve break throughs: to give 'book talks' to the entire school, to conduct science experiments, to hold high level discussions about pollution. Tom only began to 'come around' to the group's way of thinking when several student teachers told back to him stories that he had told earlier in seminars of how Brian had provided the best questions and insights in lessons Tom had taught on Ancient Greeks and democracy. Faced with his own data, Tom was laughingly forced to agree that his actions indicated that he did hold high academic expectations for Brian who responded positively to them.

The premises in these war stories told by student teachers are different from the premises of Mr Nathan's war stories. All were elicited by discrepant events, by the need to make sense out of events that did not conform to their notions and beliefs about the way things should be. While Mr Nathan's battles seemed to locate the battle as one of control between 'us vs. them', these student teachers seem to be battling ignorance and confusion, their own as well as the students: the student teaching seminar decided that Tom's tale of deciding not to exhibit behaviors that seemed caring to him was really a way of caring.

War stories told by a first year teacher continue to contain reflections on these themes of power, ignorance and caring but in even more complicated situations with even a stronger sense of urgency. No longer protected by being an education student, this teacher perceived her actions as having even more serious consequences for herself and her pupils.

War Stories Told By A First Year Teacher

War stories emerged in yet another interactional format in a graduate course entitled 'Teaching Strategies for Problem Solving and Critical Thinking'. I taught six teachers from four different counties who had from zero to ten years of experience. Each week I modeled a different problem-solving lesson taken from a writing, reading, social studies, science or math curricula. Each week the teachers adapted the strategy I presented for the grade level and content of their curriculum and tried them out in their classrooms. Then each teacher presented a description and critique of what happened.

Lynn is an older white female who had been an executive in the banking industry but decided to go into teaching. It is her first year of teaching, she is teaching second grade and she is the only white staff member in an inner city all black elementary school. Emily is a younger white first grade teacher who has taught for four years in a large suburban county system, Karen is an older white science teacher from the more rural Eastern Shore and Daniel is a black male teacher who has taught English in a middle school in the city for ten years. Here is Lynn's story:

> *Lynn*: I had the most horrible thing happen to me today
> and I have to tell the class.

It was really upsetting to me
and the kids are all upset.

We were writing stories this week
and the kids were really going.
We spent a couple of hours verbalizing
all their ideas onto a chart.

The next day they did
a rough draft.
The next day they edited it.
and they did an excellent job.
They're only in second grade.
And I had one child who for the *first time*
wrote a complete sentence.
White: Oh, wow.
Lynn: And he had NEVER
put one single thing upon paper.
And he wrote a sentence and he said, 'I will be Hulk Hogan'.
Emily: Ohh.
White: Ohh.
Lynn: It floored me.
Lynn: And I thought it was wonderful.
And he rewrote it twice.
The first time rewriting the only mistake he made
was an upper case w instead of a lower case w.
White: Oh, well that's not serious at all.
Lynn: I put it on the bulletin board along with the kids' papers.
Well this morning my principal was in my room when I got
there.
She told me to take them off the bulletin board
because there were a few errors.
Some children had used upper case instead of lower case and
she didn't want any work that wasn't perfect on any bulletin
board!
White: Oh!
Karen: She's going to have empty bulletin boards
if everything has to be perfect.
Lynn: No, she wants the kind that you buy in the store.
Lynn: I was totally ...
Not only was I totally destroyed but
I didn't know how to deal with these kids when they walked in
the room this morning,
because they noticed that I had taken their papers off.

And they were so-o PROUD.
I mean there was just so much pri..

especially that one little kid
when he saw his paper hit the bulletin board
he was like a new person.
He couldn't wait to write again.
Emily: (In soft, shaky voice) It makes me want to cry.
Everyone talking at once: Utterly outrageous ... I can't
    believe it, etc.
Lynn: I couldn't just roll over and play dead!
Group: Laughter
Lynn: You have to understand that I wasn't going for grammar or
    capitalization here
    or their handwriting skills.
    Cause that's a whole different ball game.
    These children are finally able
    to get something from their mind onto the paper.

I said, 'They worked very hard.
This three days worth of work for them
and in second grade to have that much motivation to go for three
days..'
I said, 'I think they've acccomplished something here.
And I wanted to reinforce something good.
They haven't had much success in school'.
And SHE said, 'I don't want to hear it!
In our school only perfect papers go on the bulletin board'.
(Different members in group responded, angrily, supportively.
Emily suggested using the technique of having the students
'publish' in their writing folders.)
Lynn: I just had the feeling today
    that the rest of my day was not successful.
    I just had the feeling
    that I will play it by their rules
    and the hell with it.
    . . .
White: But you can't stand to be in constant conflict with her.
    You must stand up for your rights but you can't stand to be
    like this every day.
Lynn: But it was like:
    What am I supposed to do?
    There's this terrible feeling of impotence.
    Where do I go?
    If I think I'm right about something
    what do I DO with it?
    Do I GO along because this is the structure?

I mean I've been in private industry for years
and if you had a good idea

you documented it
you copyrighted it
you talked it out.

But if you had a theoretical idea
you were able to look at things objectively
and the reasons why.

And I thought to myself
I have no recourse here
other than a woman's subjective judgment.
Cause teaching is very subjective.
She's got
a subjective judgment call.
And I think mine is just as valid as hers.
I don't think

White: Well yours is more because you know the kids and you know
your purpose.
I mean it's the whole thing
if you're going to teach by objective
and you met your purpose.
Then can she superimpose
another purpose and other values?

Lynn: But I feel totally inadequate
to deal with this situation.

White: Well you felt totally powerless.

Lynn: Ya.

Daniel: Part of it is knowing
where you stand
in the . . . in the make-up of the school as well.
Uh and you know
I don't think..
For instance
If I'm at odds with my principal
she's going to win!
(Murmurs from group.)
And I understand that.
In a sense
she is the superior
(Uh the superior executive, whatever title you want to give
her.)
And,
if I'm going to make my life satisfying at that school
then I don't want to be in opposition to her.
. . .
You know..you have to
You have to answer these type questions for yourself.

Group: (All talk at once.)

Lynn: But you lose your professionalism.

Karen: Principals forget what it's like in the classroom.

Daniel: I think that has something to do with it.

Karen: I don't know how your principal could say that
   unless she doesn't remember teaching at all.

Lynn: It's been about ten years since she's taught.

Karen: And it just floors me.
   I always went to really small schools.
   In elementary school the principal was a teaching principal.
   And I think it makes a difference
   And there was a real big morale boost
   a year ago when our new principal started.
   We got two new assistant principals within a year.
   The entire building administration changed.
   And of course
   he had a lot of support to begin with
   because he had come up from within the ranks.
   Some little things he did that made a difference
   like
   if you had a doctor's appointment and had to leave
   an hour early,
   he said, 'Sure, go ahead, I'll cover your class'.

Group voices: Wow! My goodness.

Karen: He substitutes.
   And he sees to it that the two assistant principals substitute in a
   classroom
   and keep in touch with what
   what it's like to be in front of a group of kids.

Daniel: Yes. Oh yes.
   . . .

Lynn: I just keep putting my foot in my mouth.
   This has been a really rough week.
   I've had one kid.
   He has no eye-hand coordination
   And he's very destructive.
   I don't know what's going bad at home.
   When he came to school he wrote all over his desk with a pencil.
   Just totally covered the desk.
   And I tried not to lose my cool very much.
   I ripped into him in the classroom
   And asked him just to stand in the hall for a few minutes
   Until I got it together.

White: And he needed to get it together too.

Lynn: Right.

White: That's a really smart strategy.

Lynn: But one of the kids in the class when I walked back in
   said, 'why did he do that?'
   And I said, 'I don't know.

243

You'll have to ask him.
I don't know'.
So when he came back in a few minutes later I said,
'Donald, why don't you stand by your desk for a few seconds
because some of your classmates have questions they want to
ask you'.

White: Oh how neat'.

Lynn: So Richard, one of the other little boys, looked at hime and
he said, 'Why did you write on your desk?'
And Donald says, (in flat intonation) 'I don't know'.
And another one raised his hand
and DONALD CALLED ON HIM!
(And I'm going, 'I do not believe this!')

White: All right, OK!

Lynn: And this other one said, 'You know,
we don't like you anymore,
because it's our furniture and we won't get anymore
if you destroy it'.

White: (drawn out) WOW!

Lynn: On man, this is going good!
So I said, 'Does anyone have any suggestions?
What can we do?'
because I was afraid it was going to go too far.
And Adam said,
'I could help Donald clean off his desk'.

White: Wow.

Lynn: And that's what they did.
They cleaned off Donald's desk.
I was really impressed.
Things were going well.
I thought, 'We've got some understanding going'.
What happened an hour later —
Richard, who is always a problem with his mouth,
Very motivated child, very bright.
But always over-exuberant
Kept interrupting, interrupting, interrupting.
Well obviously he liked what happened with Donald.
And he proceeded to throw a pencil at me.
And he says, 'Now I go in front of the class'.

Emily: Uh-oooooh.

Lynn: And I thought, 'Richard, I'm not biting for this one.
I'm not going to give positive rewards for negative
behavior'.
So,
This is the first time —
Richard had been constantly warned all day.
I sent him to the principal.
I said, 'Out, that is enough'.

Well, that is a terrible thing to do from my end.
Because
Not only did she —
She sent Richard home.
And has him on three day suspension for that.
Not only that —
He came to school this morning and she made him go home.
But in front of me she called him a liar.
Cause I said, 'Richard left his note at home.
His mother was working last night.
Cause his mother's supposed to sign the note.
So he couldn't bring it back this morning'.

And she said, 'Well, you'll have to learn that he is a liar.'
Emily: You're kidding.
Lynn: This kid is bright.
 All this
 All this
 I was just
 I mean right on top of the bulletin board
 I said, 'this is too much'.
Emily: Yes.
Lynn: Because these children have had no success.
 It's homogeneous grouping.
 And they're all the kids that have failed.
 And they think that they're failures.
 They think they're lazy.
 They think they're dumb.
 They think they're liars.
 And here's the principal reinforcing everything.
Emily: I was going to say
 I haven't been teaching that long
 but through the years
 you find out what works for you.
 And one of the things you'll find out is
 that you'll just deal with these things within your class-
 room.
Lynn: RIGHT!
Emily: And it may take things like that to happen
 before you find out.
White: But we've got to figure out what you can do to keep your
 kids writing. We can't just leave it like this.
Emily: At our school
 they do say that you're not supposed to put anything up unless it's
 correct.
 It has to look nice
 and not be misspelled and so forth.

245

But how do we get around it
I was telling Lynn:
When we do a writing activity
if I know I am going to pick certain ones for a bulletin
board,
then I'll go through and sit down with several children
and correct it right on their paper in light pencil
or have them correct it right there with me
before we put it up.
So, the kids know they did a good job
but they also know that for the bulletin board
we have another standard.
   . . .

Lynn: Well, I guess I didn't shut down totally. I mean
I was really in the pits this afternoon.
I mean the constant attention to discipline.
I just stopped everything.
And I put the charts again
[signal to class that they are going to brainstorm ideas
for problem solving.]

And I said, 'Can somebody answer me?
I want to know what makes you feel good in school
and what makes you feel bad in school'.
And I brought the charts home and I just left them there
cause they
really feel good in school.

And they started listing
all the things that make them feel good in school
and made them feel happy
even homework they listed that made them feel good.
Reading.
When the teacher doesn't yell.
(Laughter. Group members talking)

I mean, they really got into it.
What they didn't like about school only came down to about
four things.
It was all the punishment things,
having to stay after school.
So I was looking at the two charts up there
and I said, 'Wow,
can anybody come up with a generalization?'
Group exclamations: What! Wow! What a question.
Lynn: I mean, it just came out.

And
my thinker
raised his hand and said,
'Yeah, look at how much more we LIKE about school than we
don't like'.
Wow.
And all the other kids said, 'Yeah'.
And I said, 'You know what,
you just turned a rough day into something great!'
(Lynn giggles.)
(Group murmurs and comments softly.)

And wouldn't you know just as we're writing the good
things on the board,
SHE had to walk in!
Wouldn't you know the law of averages.
And I saw the eyes go over my shoulder to the chart on the board
which said:
'We like when we behave good.
We like gym.
We like lunch'.

(Lynn giggles.)
It had all these words
which they're reading at the same time.
And I saw the eyes.
And she didn't say a word.
She didn't say a thing.
And I quick cut out of school
and I thought,
'Well, maybe I'll hear about it tomorrow and maybe I won't'.
(Laughs.)

These 'war stories' perform functions similar to those performed by the folk fairy tales as discussed by Bettelheim (1977, pp. 1–19). They help people achieve understanding by offering examples of both temporary and permanent solutions to pressing difficulties (p. 6). Teacher education courses, even student teaching seminars, often constrain talk because only discussions of what is right or what one should do are admissible. These war stories provide a structure in which the problematic nature of teaching can be expressed. Taboos, such as difficult children, difficult principals, one's own incompetence, ignorance or exhaustion, can be more acceptably discussed within the plot structure of a war story. The war stories allow the teachers to elaborate and give specific details of the problem without giving in to it or being defeated by it. Bettelheim argues that 'only by struggling courageously against overwhelming odds' can people succeed in wringing meaning out of existence (p. 8).

When teachers tell war stories they are in effect implicitly claiming that 'a struggle against severe difficulties in life is unavoidable, is an intrinsic part of human existence' (Bettelheim, p. 8). Thus, one is not a 'bad' teacher just because one has difficulties: everyone has difficulties; problems and often severe problems are indigenous to the profession of teaching. However, the second part of the claim is that, 'if one does not shy away, but steadfastly meets unexpected and often unjust hardships, one masters all obstacles and at the end emerges victorious' (Bettelheim, p. 8).

Like fairy tales, in the war stories by Mr Nathan, by Sherry, Pam, Tom and Lynn, the neophyte teachers:

— Face almost overwhelming dilemmas that threaten their very existence as teachers.
— Evil as well as virtue is present.
— They contain 'images of heroes who, although, originally ignorant of the ultimate things, find secure places in the world by following their right way with deep inner confidence' (Bettelheim, p. 11).

What is so fascinating about the spontaneous talk of Mr Nathan is that he is the unabashed, perhaps over-confident hero in all of his stories. When he meets ignorance and resistance in various forms from the children, he is always saved by teaching them how to behave. Much of what he teaches them is based on a very specific set of behavioral procedures — how to pass out books, how to go on a field trip as well as learning specific scientific knowledge: what DNA is, what elephant hide feels like.

The student teachers Sherry and Pam spontaneously tell about being overwhelmed because the techniques of lesson planning that they learned at the university did not work. They make several points in their stories: they tell us that the teacher must pay attention to how the students learn and don't learn rather than believing that there is one 'correct' way to plan or teach a lesson.

Their second message is also that one must not be deterred by initial failure but that one must persevere, teaching and reteaching, until the students show that they have acquired the information. Tom's war story is an interesting counterpoint. He too learns that what he had learned at the university and also believed about teaching — that it is important to care and to try to 'connect with' each individual — does not work. Tom's message, however, is that there are limits. Teachers must learn when to back off and not persevere if their actions make life too difficult for a child.

The stories spontaneously told by Lynn create the image of a heroine who, although originally naive, angry and powerless, is able to find a solution by following her principles with deep inner confidence. The story form allows her to acknowledge some harsh realities and power disputes. The principal desires form over substance: only perfect papers can go on the board. Although the second graders sometimes 'come through' as when they solve the problem of vandalizing the desk, one must be ever vigilant because certain students will constantly seek attention, often inappropriately. The principal adds to what Lynn sees as a problem of low self esteem by calling a student a liar in front of the class.

In this third example, we can see most clearly that teachers are not just aimlessly complaining about how bad life is. Rather they respond to the problems presented in Lynn's stories with counter narratives as a way of theorizing about what they do. As Lynn talks, various members of the group, myself included, function as an 'amen' section, giving support and legitimacy to her statement of the problem and goals by murmuring agreement or disbelief as the narrative requires. We confirm that it is most significant when a child writes for the first time and that perfect form is not an immediate requirement. (It should be noted here that this belief about the writing process is an innovative one from the university that is clashing with a more traditional view of writing held by the principal.)

Lynn rejects Emily's technical suggestion to have the students 'publish' privately in their writing folders. Instead, Lynn continues to explore the definition of the problem: her rights *vis-a-vis* the rights of the principal. Daniel argues that the principal is always right, even when she's wrong. Lynn also rejects this philosophy. Karen tells a story about a different principal that offers another explanation for the problem: the principal has 'forgotten' what it is like to teach. Lynn elaborates: she offers two more subcases and restates what she sees as the real problem (which the principal is only aggravating): 'Because these children have had no success ... they think that they're failures'.

The other teachers tell Lynn that this experience will teach her to handle problem students by herself and not to send them to the principal. They give suggestions as to how she can conform to the 'perfect' decree without compromising her principles. Lynn then describes the alternative she constructed in action, having the students brainstorm about why they like about school describes the feelings that occurred and one immediate consequence.

Conclusion

Bruner (1984) argues that: 'The psychology of thought has focused on the logical-scientific mode of thinking at the expense of the equally legitimate narrative mode'. By using war stories teachers are able to articulate principles on which their actions are based, examine premises and assumptions underlying their arguments, suggest possible alternatives and evaluate these alternatives in terms of their potential for success. The representations these neophytes make of their reality is much richer and more inclusive than conventional scientific representations. The stories convey feelings and intentionality, often through the use of morally loaded language. The exchanging of these stories helps teachers make their fears overt. They seek legitimacy that their problems are not just unique to them and that their solutions are acceptable, if not ideal. Eliciting reactions and counter-narratives helps beginning teachers gain access to alternative understandings of their situations.

Recently the conventional educational research literature has been filled with accounts that life in the classroom is complex and (rather patronizingly) celebrating the new finding that teachers must be highly intelligent to be able to manage such complex problems. For example Berliner (1986, p. 12) argues that, 'The 8-day orchestration and conduct of those lessons [on subtraction with grouping] with 25 low-income children is to us a much more monumental feat than the orchestration and conduct of a four movement symphony'. However, there are important differences between the problems that educational researchers think teachers are solving and the problems that teachers think they are solving.

Berliner and others study how expert and novice teachers solve logistical technical problems. Even in more open-ended ethnographies, researchers constrain and edit a teacher's perspective or the larger 'teachers' culture' by asking individual teachers for explanations of specific events that have been video-taped or observed in their classroom. Researchers are not yet studying how teachers themselves perceive and structure their problems which are often related to curricular goals, goals for specific individuals, and/or feelings that researchers may not value.

Eliciting War Stories

Social contexts can be set up to elicit war stories and reflections on practice from groups of beginning teachers. For example, Labov (1969) initially had difficulty getting a black inner city child to talk. Labov found that when Leon, a 8-year-old black inner city child, was interviewed by a large friendly white male who invited him to talk about some toys in front of them, Leon responded with long hesitations followed by one word answers. Labov changed the social context so that Clarence, a black male from Harlem highly skilled at interviewing, asked Leon questions about everyday experiences such as fighting and television: this interview still resulted in Leon responding with long pauses, 'mmm's', 'nopes' and one word answers. It was only after changing the social context from an asymmetrical formal interview situation into an informal gathering in which Clarence:

— brought along a supply of potato chips, changing the 'interview' into something more in the nature of a party;
— brought along Leon's best friend, 8 year old Gregory;
— reduced the height imbalance (when Clarence got down on the floor of Leon's room, he dropped from 6 foot 2 to 3 foot 6)
— introduced taboo words and taboo topics, and proved to Leon's surprise that one can say anything into our microphone without any fear of retaliation. (1983, p. 188)

that there was a great increase in the verbosity, volume and style of Leon's speech. Leon then actively competed for the floor and talked to his friend Gregory as much as he did to the interviewer.

Teacher talk must be elicited without the constraints of an asymmetrical situation. In the student teaching seminars and in the graduate course there are discussions in which I deliberately give up control as the leader and encourage a more informal conversation. For example, in the graduate seminar I and the students began to:

— bring a lavish supply of food to class — cold cuts, bread, materials to make sandwiches, coffee and soft drinks. This changed the class into something more informal and social.
— Different faculty friends of mine and friends of the teachers were invited to drop in to see what we were doing. Several sat in for a session or two and participated actively.

—I introduced taboo topics by starting one class period with an impassioned monologue about why what you are taught in university education courses won't work in your classrooms. I explained why what I was teaching them would lead immediately to failure and challenged them to transform my ideas into ideas that worked for them.

If the situation can be set up that is informal, if there is no correct answer, if nothing is taboo, than education students and teachers will tell stories that help the group to articulate and reflect on the problems of teaching as they perceive them.

Structuring Reflection

However, the problem is not the elicitation of the war stories. The problem is challenging both the storytellers and the listeners to use the stories to create new insights. Merely telling and retelling the same old stories can self-servingly be used for self-justification and/or to display membership in a group mindset. However, if after a story has been supportively elicited, it can be questioned, countered, compared or affirmed with other stories, then educational neophytes can use war stories to examine and perhaps criticize their goals, their practices and/or their work environment.

What is it about these stories that makes them so powerful a form of data? The structure or grammar of a story allows the narrator to tell of a conflict or a violation of expectations at a specific time and place. The spontaneous rhythmic, poetic cadences are compelling as strong verbs are used to complicate and further complicate the action until the climax is reached. Precisely because they are not objective, detached, abstract, logical claims, war stories are often dismissed when they could serve a major source of information. Precisely because each story that 'works' conveys a sense of verisimilitude, a sense of 'Gee, that could happen to me sometime', war stories carry powerful explanatory meaning for teachers' experiences, meanings that transcend the uniqueness of the time and place as well as legitimate their teaching as a struggle for achievement.

If teacher educators are aware that war stories always contain a *raison d'etre*, they and neophyte teachers can begin to look for and examine the underlying assumptions. After a war story has been told, participants can look for alternative perspectives. Teachable moments were created when the field experience students wondered if being Mr Nathan's arguments for rigid control were the only way to succeed when working with lower socioeconomic black students. If teacher educators have a collection of war stories from comparable situations, greater reflection can be generated. Reflection occurred when the student teachers were moved by, and then argued with Tom about his caring and expectations for Brian. No claims are made that reflections result in the ability to rewrite stories with a happy ending. Yet, as when the class reacted to Lynn's account of her horrible day, reflections on stories of lived events allow neophyte teachers to obtain support as they learn to function in a world with surprisingly harsh realities.

Acknowledgment

I wish to thank Deborah Tannen, Georgetown University, who first introduced me to the beauty and structure of narratives.

References

BERLINER, D. (1986) 'In pursuit of the expert pedagogue', *Educational Researcher*, **15**, 7, pp. 5–13.

BETTELHEIM, B. (1977) *The Uses of Enchantment: The Meaning and Importance of Fairy Tales*, New York: Random House.

BOLSTER, A. (1983) 'Toward a more effective model of research on teaching', *Harvard Education Review*, **53**, 3, pp. 294–308.

BRUNER, J. (1984) 'Narrative and paradigmatic modes of thought', in *Learning and Teaching: The Ways of Knowing*, 1985 Yearbook of the National Society for the Study of Education.

CONNELLY, F.M. and ELBAZ, F. (1980) 'Conceptual bases for curriculum thought: A teacher's perspective', In *Considered Action for Curriculum Improvement*, Alexandria, VA: ASCD.

LABOV, W. (1969) 'The logic of nonstandard English', in *Georgetown Monographs on Language and Linguistices*, **22**. Reprinted in GIGLIOLI, P. (Ed.) *Language and Social Context*, pp. 179–215, Penguin Books.

LABOV, W. (1972) 'The transformation of experience in narrative syntax', in *Language in the Inner City*, Philadelphia: University of Pennsylvania Press.

WHITE, J.J. (1989) 'Student teaching as a rite of passage', *Anthropology and Education Quarterly*, **20**, 3, pp. 177–95.

15 Practicing What We Preach: Action Research and the Supervision of Student Teachers

Jennifer M. Gore

Teacher education programs which aim to facilitate the development of 'reflective teachers', like other teacher education programs, make a number of demands on their students. These demands, or requirements, include such pedagogical practices as writing journals, engaging in peer supervision, using readings in particular ways and conducting action research (practices which are reported more fully in other chapters of this volume).

If we conceive of pedagogy as the process of knowledge production (Lusted, 1986), we can distinguish between the pedagogy we talk *about* and the pedagogy *of* our talk. Both are important in the production of knowledge about teaching. I contend that in some of our talk about alternative approaches to teaching and teacher education (the pedagogy we talk *about*) we have not paid sufficient attention to the way we have talked (the pedagogy *of* our talk). The changes needed to improve schooling are not only those most commonly articulated in inquiry-oriented and 'critical' approaches to education — changes in teachers' definitions of their work or changes in teachers' practices, or broader changes in the political, social, economic conditions of schooling and society — but also changes in teacher education. Hence, we must consider changes in the way we conceive of and conduct our practice.

This chapter is based on my belief that, as teacher educators, we should attempt to facilitate our own reflectivity and should be wary of inconsistencies between our message and our example. Considerable research on the 'hidden curriculum' of teacher education and on teacher socialization (e.g., Bartholomew, 1976; Ginsburg, 1988; Giroux, 1980; Popkewitz, 1985) has illustrated that the 'impact of preservice preparation lies in ... images of teacher, learner, knowledge, and curriculum which are subtly communicated to prospective teachers through the covert processes of the hidden curriculum of teacher education programs' (Zeichner and Gore, 1990). Without attention to the pedagogy of our arguments, inquiry-oriented teacher education surely risks the same fate as much traditional university teacher education; namely, that it is seen as 'university stuff' with little relevance to the everyday task of teaching.

One way of strengthening the message students glean from our unquiry-oriented teacher education programs is to demonstrate the usefulness, for our own teaching, of the practices we are encouraging or requiring of students. Such demonstration should not amount to simply 'going through the motions' but should be based on commitment. Otherwise, our students will surely see through insincere or half-hearted attempts, just as they can see our passion and enthusiasm for ideas and activities we cherish. Again, we need to attend to the pedagogy of our arguments. We need to ask ourselves questions such as the following: Do we really believe in these practices of inquiry-oriented teacher education: Why don't we use them regularly in our own teaching? If we argue that we do not have time, can we blame teachers for not adopting them as a regular part of their teaching? If we argue that teaching is not a priority among the many academic tasks before us, can we justify our location in teacher education? These questions are not to suggest that teacher educators must do all that they ask their students to do. However, I believe that if we really value, for example, action research to promote reflective teaching, we will learn from the conduct of our own action research and, in so doing, will help students learn from and appreciate such practices.

In the following, and major, part of this chapter I share an action research project I conducted while a supervisor in a teacher education program that aimed to facilitate the development of reflective teachers at the University of Wisconsin-Madison. The project involved researching an aspect of my teaching I wanted to understand better and hopefully improve; namely, the functioning of the 'student teaching triad'. Given the purpose of this book to provide detailed accounts of issues and practices of inquiry-oriented teacher education, my account here is a very personal one. It is offered as an example of a teacher educator researching her own practice. After presenting my action research, I return to my introductory arguments and reiterate them in light of the 'data'.

Facilitating the Student Teaching Triad through Action Research

The student teaching triad — student teacher, cooperating teacher, university supervisor — has a long history in the practicum component of teacher education programs. The action research project reported here commenced from a feeling of dissonance about the use of the label 'triad'. The term itself simple implies a group of three closely related persons or things, or, in music, a chord of three tones which constitutes the harmonic basis of tonal music (Webster's New Collegiate Dictionary, 1975). These definitions satisfactorily characterize the student teaching triad; the three persons are closely related through their common endeavor of facilitating the student teaching experience, and ideally, they work in harmony.

The catalyst for my dissonance was the depiction of the triad on an equilateral triangle in the handbook distributed to all students and cooperating teachers involved in the senior practicum in elementary education at the University of Wisconsin-Madison. My experience of supervision, at various times in each of the roles, did not match this representation of all sides as being equal. Rather, my experience was of unequal power, unequal investment and unequal consequences.

Nevertheless, the ideal of the harmonious, equilateral triangle of student teaching seemed a worthwhile goal — a goal that was consistent with my own commitment to altering relations of power in teacher education — and so became my focus in an action research project.

This report of the action research is organized into the following sections:

1   a rationale for the focus on the student teaching triad in which I elaborate my own commitments;
2   a descriptive account of the development of the project;
3   an analytic discussion of the project around the major issues that emerged;
4   reflections on the process of action research as a vehicle for enhancing my learning, my performance, and my satisfaction, as a supervisor, and finally;
5   a return to the symbols of triad and triangle.

Why be Concerned about the Student Teaching Triad?

It is not my intention here to go into a lengthy justification of the triad itself. It is widely acknowledged that the student teacher often has less experience to draw on in making sense of his or her experiences (Calderhead, 1988) and that 'teacher educators must be actively present in student teaching to give prospective teachers a concrete sense of pedagogical thinking and acting' (Feiman-Nemser and Buchmann, 1987, p. 272). Although it can be debated whether or not a university supervisor is necessary or desirable in the student teaching experience,[1] in my particular situation, the position of university supervisor was a given. That was my role. My concern was to do a good job and to live up to the image I had of the student teaching program at the University of Wisconsin-Madison. This image included notions of a more critical and democratic approach to supervision than is found in traditional teacher education programs. I leapt at the opportunity to work in such a program and to test out an approach which seemed congruent with my own 'educational platform' (Sergiovanni and Starratt, 1988); an approach that fits well with Zeichner and Tabachnick's (1982) portrayal of a 'critical orientation' to supervision. That is, I believe that supervision must be cognizant of the broad socio-political context in which schooling and teacher education take place and should raise issues such as unequal power relations and oppressive social formations in the structures and processes of schooling at all levels, as well as concerned about technical skills of teaching and other aspects of teachers' work.

The equilateral representation of the student teaching triad raised several questions for me about my role and abilities as a supervisor. Could I be this sort of supervisor? If these teachers were used to a role in the triad which was unfamiliar to me, would I be able to discern it soon enough? Would I be able and willing to make the necessary adjustments in my own supervisory style? Clearly, it was in this relationship within the triad that I considered I had the most work to do as a supervisor.

My doubts and uncertainties were balanced by a strong commitment to 'democratizing' the student teaching triad. I was uncomfortable with the construction of roles within the triad which sometimes placed teacher and supervisor in antagonistic relation to one another and which worked against a partnership conception of the teacher education process during student teaching. Furthermore, I wanted the student teachers to be able to exert much more control over their student teaching experience than is frequently the case when students feel compelled to conform to the teaching approaches or philosophies of their cooperating teachers or university supervisors. I was concerned to alter the unequal power relations of the student teaching triad in which the student generally comes out on the bottom.

It seemed to me that the student teaching experience, the learning of all members of the triad and particularly the student teacher, would be enhanced by as open and honest a communication as possible between all members. I was eager to enter into debate and willing to be challenged. I was keen to sit down with teacher and student teacher after a lesson to share all of our perspectives on the lesson and work together in helping the student teacher. I wanted to enter into critical dialogue, together.

Moreover, as a newcomer to this country and education system, I felt that I had much to learn. It was easy for me to want the full and active participation of cooperating teacher and student teacher when I knew would be in settings that were unfamiliar, such as US schools and kindergarten classrooms. (My previous school teaching and supervising experiences had been in Australian elementary and secondary schools.)

However, my commitment to democratizing the triad went much deeper than my own needs for immediate or short-term survival and success. While my focus was necessarily on the specific triads of which I was a part, my interest in this question was not simply a psychologistic or individualistic one. Rather, I entered into the action research eager to better understand the structural constraints affecting this aspect of student teaching through the systematic and close study of several specific triads. That is, I wanted to explore the connections between the individual and the societal, the psychological and the sociopolitical. While working closely and caringly with 'my' student teachers and cooperating teachers, I wanted to better understand the institutional and social conditions which were manifested in, and affected by (if only reproduced), the relations of power in those triads.

Democratizing the Student Teaching Triad

During the semester in which I conducted this action research (Fall 1988), I worked with twelve student teachers, supervising their practice in schools and leading a weekly seminar on campus. Like students in many other elementary teacher education programs, these were predominantly white women from middle-class backgrounds. Two males, one of whom is African American, were exceptions. Among the requirements I set for these students was an 'action research project' which drew on the theories and guidelines for action research found in the work of Kemmis and McTaggart (1988). Primarily, I required students to research an aspect of their own practice or situation that they felt they could do something about and to which they felt a commitment, and to try to make their research collaborative by involving the people in their situation or, at least, engaging with other student teachers. I set this requirement for many reasons. In terms of democratizing the triad I thought action research would help student teachers develop a sense of their contribution to the classrooms in which they had been placed and an ownership which is often missing when the classroom is considered to be someone else's.

With four years of experience in Australia as a university teacher educator trying to facilitate reflective teaching, I had amassed considerable experience in supervising action research and had found students to be very positive about their experience with action research. Until this semester however, I had not conducted my own action research. (I wonder how frequently we advocate practices we have never tried *for* ourselves?) Nevertheless, I felt confident that the process would at least help me to understand the way that the triad was constructed, and functioned, and would hopefully help me to improve my practice as a member of that triad. So as not to appear to be presenting myself as 'holier than thou' I should make clear that it was not without provocation that I decided to join my students in the conduct of an action research project during that semester. I was enrolled in an advanced seminar in the supervision of student teaching and chose action research from the assessment options. A group of graduate students from that class worked collaboratively on action research projects. I shall leave further comment on the motivation to conduct our own action research (or to write our own journals, and so on) for the concluding sections of this chapter. Suffice it to say that after this experience I feel even more strongly about the importance of practicing what we preach.

In trying to clarify the jumble of events which took place, or which I constructed, throughout the semester, I have found it helpful to separate those actions which were aimed at setting the right tone from those which occurred later and were mainly aimed at responding to, or making new sense out of, earlier events. The whole process was not clear or tidy and so a strictly chronological account of the project's development (or 'cycles' of action research) is not possible, nor my aim, here. Rather, I will refer to main events or critical incidents in order to trace the development of the project.

Setting it up

1   One aspect of setting up a democratic triad related to establishing particular relations and dispositions of trust with my students. The initial meetings with the students were very important. Even before deciding on a focus for my action research I wanted to be very open with my students, to take risks, to encourage them to take risks and to communicate as openly as possible with me and with each other, and to instil confidence in them. I articulated much of this, told them that I was deliberately not talking too often and asked them to address their comments and questions to each other and not just to me. I also completed many of the tasks I was asking them to complete and was careful to share some of my experiences, thoughts and feelings before asking them to reveal aspects of themselves. I hoped this would indicate my willingness to work *with* rather than *over* them.

2   Another aspect of setting up a democratic triad, related to establishing particular ways of functioning when the members of the triad were together. The Statement of Expectations conference (part of the University of Wisconsin-Madison program), in which all three members of the triad state and negotiate their expectations of each other, was very important here, not only for its

substance (the pedagogy we were *about*), but for the process (the pedagogy *of* our talk). My statement[2] included several items which were directly aimed at setting up a triad in which all members were active (see Appendix A). I also presented it in a way which I hoped was opening myself up to challenge and demonstrating my willingness to reveal my own beliefs and thus paving the way for dialogue. I therefore offered to share what I had written before asking student teacher or teacher to share theirs. I did not presume that I would take the lead, but rather than putting the student or the teacher on the spot, I wanted to show that I was willing to practice what I was asking of the triad through my written document. My presentation of the statement was negotiable, tentative, and as honest as possible. Some evidence that the Statement of Expectations conference facilitated the relationships of the triad was apparent when one student informed me that his teacher thought it was the best Statement of Expectations that he had seen from a university person because it was 'more human'; there was 'more of *me* in it', and he liked that (Journal, 10/4).

3   A third aspect of getting things underway involved the conduct of other three-way discussions. Again I showed my willingness to take risks, to take the lead. This action seemed to be particularly important in establishing some credibility with the teachers. One student reported to me that her teacher had been impressed with my conduct of our first post observation conference; that I was perceptive and expressed myself well. This teacher was considerably warmer to me after that experience. As I put it in my journal 'It's as if I have to prove that I'm capable/competent/confident (as a supervisor) before they (the cooperating teachers) are willing to accept me as a partner in the supervision' (Journal, 10/4).

Keeping it going, responding to feelings, events and conditions

After my early visits to classrooms I noticed that I felt more comfortable in some rooms than I did in others. I attributed my comfort to a number of factors: how I felt interpersonally with the teachers, how I felt ideologically about what was going on in the classroom and the way the student teacher was being treated, and how comfortable the student appeared to be. I felt very much a stranger in some rooms, for example in rooms where Assertive Discipline was used, and more at ease in others. Given that I felt most comfortable in a room where the teacher was someone with whom I had taken a course the previous semester, I thought one way to improve what was happening in the triads might be to get to know the teachers better.

4   Hence, my next step was to design a brief survey to send out to teachers as a way of finding out a little more about them (see Appendix B). As a way of expediting the process and minimizing expense, I had the students deliver these surveys, with a cover letter, to the teachers. This may have been a mistake. I know some teachers received the letter weeks after the event. Other students reported that their teachers simply filed this letter along with all the other information sent by the university. In the end, I received four responses (from the eleven sent), three written, one verbal. However, there was little time to follow up on the responses. Largely because of time constraints, my manner in the schools was rather task-oriented with communication between supervisor and cooperating teacher often limited to discussions of the student teacher's progress.

5   One question I asked in the survey called for suggestions as to how to get

the triad functioning in a way which pleased the teachers. Most mentioned the constraints of time and emphasized the importance of arranging visits to coincide with 'specials' (periods when the children would be out of the room for art, music, physical education, and so on), which I was already doing. Something I needed to do became apparent with the suggestion, by one teacher, that the student and I make sure the cooperating teacher shared in the purposes of the observation and so was able to more fully participate in the post-observation conference (I was using a clinical supervision approach). I had been trying to encourage the teachers to comment on the lessons. Now I realized that perhaps the teachers lacked some of the focus and/or language that was being employed to discuss the lesson. This problem became particularly clear when the students' action research projects were mentioned. Many of the teachers lacked a clear sense of what the project (its process, or substance) was all about. At times this was deliberate on the part of the students who had made critical comments about their teachers or their teachers' practices in their journals. They wanted to maintain the privacy of their journals. In cases where the project was less controversial, some teachers were very supportive and worked in collaborative ways with the students. Others were not particularly interested in anything they perceived as primarily academic (pertaining to the university) and therefore never really understood the potential of the action research projects that the students were involved in, let alone my own project.

6   I was frustrated at times when it was clear that there was not open and honest communication within the triad. This became particularly clear when teachers took me aside to share their concerns about their student teacher and, when it came down to it, to ask me to deal with the 'problem(s)' in a way which did not implicate them. As just one example, a teacher who wanted her student to arrive at school earlier, prepare more exciting lessons, stop writing in her journal during school time, and stop chewing gum, did not want to say these things because she had become 'such good friends' with the student teacher. Even when I tried to encourage teachers in such situations to talk with the students, and pointed out that it was in the student's interest to know how the teacher felt, I was often left with this responsibility.

7   Finally, I continued the attempt to conduct the seminar in a way which encouraged debate and the idea that students' own insights were valuable. I also solicited a great deal of feedback throughout the process, feedback about my supervision as well as the seminar, and tried to remain open to correction. The following representative comments from students' final course evaluations are presented here to provide evidence of the relationship(s) that developed through our work together:

> [Jenny] developed a trust with me that allowed me to feel comfortable around her.

> Jenny never expected us to do anything that she herself did not intend to do. She was very willing to help and was willing to make changes if we felt they were necessary.

> I thought the seminar was worthwhile. I felt very comfortable and was not uneasy about discussing anything.

Constraints and Possibilities for the Student Teaching Triad

The previous section has outlined some of the major steps or events in the development of my action research project. In this section I identify some of the key issues which emerged out of my writing and reflecting on both the process of the project and the process of writing about it thus far; namely, issues of interpersonal relationships, power relations, time and institutions. These issues emerged in dialectical relation to each other as I shall attempt to illustrate in the following discussion.

First, a caveat: while I would not claim that this is a comprehensive taxonomy of factors which influence all student teaching triads I think these issues are pertinent to all such triads. That is, all student teaching triads require the development of interpersonal relationships within limited periods of time and bring together, and are affected by, (at least) the institutions of school and university. Particular relations of power are brought to, and worked out in, these conditions of the student teaching triad, some of which are relatively common to all triads and some of which will be manifested differently in each specific triad.

Interpersonal Relationships

One of the earliest observations I made about the different triads was that varying degrees of comfort were apparent among members. That comfort seemed to be related to friendship, familiarity, trust and respect. It is difficult to build a deep sense of trust and respect with the cooperating teachers when, as university supervisor, I am essentially a 'school visitor' (Boydell, 1986). It is easier to build such trust and respect with my students, with whom the contact is more frequent and also in situations where only two members of the triad are involved. As Yee (1968) argued, groups of three are inherently unstable.

An example of a situation which promoted the building of trust occurred when one student phoned me in tears and ready to give up teaching. In order to manage Kate's[3] very real crisis I invited her to my home. Many hours later, we both felt strengthened and felt a bond of trust and friendship. Kate acknowledged the importance of that moment with a card which she sent just prior to her departure for England where she was completing her student teaching. The printed words read: 'Thanks for listening ... and listening ... and listening ... and listening...'. Kate had added 'I honestly couldn't have made it through without you!' This incident points to many issues in the functioning of the triad not the least of which is that the relationship established between Kate and myself took time: time that few supervisors could make available to each of their students.

Had the incident not been a direct result of the unreasonable demands of the cooperating teacher, this situation might have been a catalyst to improved trust throughout the triad. That is, if the crisis was not felt to have been precipitated by Margaret (Kate's teacher), and if Kate's initial attempts to reason with Margaret had proved at all productive, the three of us might have worked together to help Kate continue with her student teaching and deal with the problem. As it was, the bond between Kate and myself may well have been strengthened at the expense of the cohesiveness of the triad. I sympathized with her situation and felt some anger toward the teacher for creating what I saw as an unpleasant, unnecessary and unprofessional environment for a student teacher. But how could I have told Margaret that it was unreasonable to expect Kate to be at school for at least nine hours a day (and often twelve) when Margaret was doing that herself? She maintained that such long hours were necessary in the type of classroom she had established.

I was guilty of not being as open and honest as I had proposed that we all be because I did not want to upset my personal, and more importantly, the institutional, relationship with the cooperating teachers. We all needed to remain together for the entire period of student teaching. Diplomacy was a must. When I reflect on this situation in light of Noddings' (1986) comments on fidelity to persons, I feel uncomfortable with not having been more outspoken with Margaret. But it was difficult to assess what could and could not be articulated particularly when we did not know each other well. Frustratingly, there was not really enough time to get to know each other well. On the other hand, it can be just as hard to criticize someone with whom you have developed strong feelings of trust. For example, another student teacher, Melissa, reacted particularly defensively one day when I raised some questions about her lesson. I thought my questions were pushing her in important intellectual and pedagogical ways. She was hurt. Perhaps as Noddings (1986) suggests: 'an unfavorable report from a friendly and apparently knowledgeable [supervisor] hurts doubly. The hurt is aggravated by a feeling of betrayal: this person, with whom a relation of trust has been established, has said these dreadful things' (p. 395).

In trying to resolve such incidents in supervision, the personal relationships sometimes become more important than the intellectual or pedagogical one. For example, instead of insisting that Kate, Margaret and I sit down and have the difficult and painful discussions that were needed over conceptions of the student teaching experience (pedagogical discussions), Kate and I together chose instead to try to maintain civil and tolerable communication (at a primarily personal level). Likewise, teachers, usually, are concerned to make the student teaching experience a pleasant one (Calderhead, 1988) and sometimes emphasize their personal relationship with the student teacher over pedagogical concerns. Consider, for instance, the teacher who took me aside rather than confronting her student teacher with concerns about her performance. Moreover, students were reluctant to confront their teachers, and perhaps even me, because we held the power of respectable grades and references over them. Here the personal/institutional relationship might have prevented the students from asking the questions or making the statements that would have facilitated a more educative experience.

Power Relations

A related aspect of the student teaching triad is the relative 'voice' of the student teacher. We can understand questions of student voice if we explicitly address relations of power within the triads. In several of the triads in which I was working, even apparently successful ones, students were unable/unwilling to confront their teachers with their concerns. Kate was more outspoken than many of the others. In two other cases this 'problem' was so great that it became a focus of students' action research projects. For example, Louise titled her project 'Gaining access to a private domain: A student teacher's struggle for authority in the classroom' but never really confronted her teacher with her deepest feelings about this. Amy titled her project 'Becoming a kindergarten teacher', a focus that she traced to an incident which occurred before the semester began. Her teacher had asked whether she wanted to be called by her first name. Having come from preschool experiences in which all the teachers went by their first names, Amy agreed. She was not informed, nor did she ask, how her teacher wished to be addressed, but felt that many of the management problems she encountered arose from the fact that she was 'Amy' and her teacher was 'Mrs Johns'. Amy felt unable to confront her teacher about this.

These circumstances are related to both personal biographies and the historical construction of roles within the triad. Consider my earlier comments about feeling that a leadership role was ascribed to me in the triad. I suggested that teachers waited for me to prove my credibility. Perhaps the teachers also waited for me, because that is how they have usually experienced discussions in the triad. All of the teachers with whom I worked had experiences with other university supervisors; two of them had been supervisors at some point themselves. Through these experiences they clearly had certain expectations of our particular student teaching triad. It is possible that they even abdicated some of their own responsibility for the student teacher, given conceptions of the university supervisor as 'the teacher educator'. Of course, similar preconceptions of the roles of cooperating teacher and student teacher were also in place as the semester began. The interpersonal working out of these power relations occurs in the context of personal and structural histories as teachers and supervisors draw on their own student teaching experiences in the construction of present triads. I contend that during the time of my action research such preconceptions were probably strongest for the cooperating teachers. The students were fairly new to the whole experience and a little unsure of what to expect. As a newcomer to the US and to the Elementary Education program, I believe I was quite open to a reconstruction or reconceptualization of roles and relations in the student teaching triad.

Preconceptions of roles and relations in the student teaching triad include particular power relations whereby, for instance, the university supervisor is considered to be the authority in teacher education, to carry the final say in questions of assessment, and to hold a greater store of academic knowledge. The teacher is considered to be the authority in the school and classroom, to carry the final say in what is permitted in the classroom, and to hold much more relevant practical knowledge. As examples of preconceptions of power relations consider that my initial questions about my work as a supervisor pertained more to my relationship with the cooperating teachers than to my relationship with the students. In the power relations of the student teaching triad the student teacher often 'comes out on the bottom', but it is not at all clear who is 'on top'. There seems to be a struggle for power between university supervisor and cooperating teacher in a way which affects our dialogue. Consider also the different tone of address to student teacher and cooperating teacher in my Statement of Expectations (see Appendix A). It is not surprising to note that my Statement of Expectations was hardly challenged or even discussed. Teachers most often called for clarification of some of my 'academic jargon' such as 'reflective teaching' and 'action research'. As a final example, consider the evaluation process in this student teaching program: university supervisor and teacher formally evaluate the student; student teacher formally evaluates university supervisor; there is no formal evaluation of cooperating teacher; there is certainly no formal evaluation of university supervisor and cooperating teacher by each other. However, it would have been interesting to solicit direct feedback from the teachers on my performance. Given that we did not establish the same kind of relationships as developed with my students, I expect their comments would not be as positive as those I reported earlier from the students' final evaluations of my supervision and that I would learn from such feedback.

With respect to power relations and questions of democracy and hierarchy, a related issue is that there is not really a sense of reciprocity in the student teaching triad (Richardson-Koehler, 1988). Investments and consequences are not equal. Most obviously, teachers did not often open their teaching for critique; my teaching, in seminar and in the context of pre- and post-observation conferences, was not available for critique in the same way; and yet the students' performance was constantly open to the critique of cooperating teacher, university supervisor and others (such as principals, parents and students).

Knowledge plays a central part in the construction of relations of power: as just one example, consider the unequal investments in my action research project. My aim that it should be a collaborative endeavor was not realized. Teachers were not particularly interested in the project *per se* as was clear from the lack of responses to the survey which I had developed with the aim of getting to know the teachers better and feeling less of a visitor. I suspect that this lack of interest was partly a function of teachers' unfamiliarity with the concept or process of action research. With the word 'research' in the title, as is the case with student teachers (Noffke and Brennan, 1988), no doubt teachers had visions of experiments and outsiders. Those teachers who simply filed the letter and survey with other information sent by the university, revealed some of the tension over relations of power between university and school, where university 'stuff' is considered irrelevant to teachers' work. Teachers' reluctance to respond might also have been a function of the extra demand I was making on their time. Their lack of response might also have been because of a major oversight on my behalf; that is, I neglected to enter into the process reciprocally. I did not think to include in the letter, information on my own background!?! This oversight was partly a result of the feeling that the teachers had already solicited considerable information about my background during our initial meetings. Of course, questions of reciprocity remain. Why is it that the teachers had asked many questions of me and I had felt less comfortable in asking such questions of them? Perhaps it was that the teachers placed me, and I placed myself, as outsider and foreigner to their classrooms.

Furthermore, in the power-knowledge relation there was a question of ownership. This action research project was seen as mine. Collaborative research is foreign to most of us. Even though I made concerted attempts to inform the teachers about action research, my feeling is that action research still seemed quite foreign to them. As one of my students pointed out, some teachers saw me as 'the academic', having travelled all the way from Australia to undertake PhD studies and no doubt felt considerable distance from my work.

This alienation from the action research process was less an issue for the student teachers. Each of them was also involved in an action research project and had read parts of the *Action Research Planner* (Kemmis and McTaggart, 1988). Even if the substance of my project was not a direct concern of the students, the process of action research was. The situation in which I felt the greatest shared investment in the project was in the triad involving Kate and her teacher, Margaret. Kate's project on working cooperatively with other adults in her classroom was closest in substance to my focus. Unfortunately it was an investment shared by only two members of the triad for reasons already discussed and because of the perennial problem of insufficient time.

Time

As already mentioned, time seemed to be a major constraint on the student teaching triad. There was insufficient time to really get to know each other and to develop deep trust and respect across all relationships of the triad. This constraint was particularly true of the relationship between teacher and supervisor. There was insufficient time to educate teachers about action research or to involve them thoroughly in my project or the student teachers' projects. (There was insufficient time even for me to be as thorough as I would have liked with the action research process!) Time was also a problem when it came to having three-way discussions; a lesson would begin, another meeting would remove one member of the triad, or I had to keep my next appointment with another triad. The 'task-oriented' approach to my supervision was no doubt partly constructed out of time pressures. Furthermore, there was never enough time in seminar to do everything we wanted to do — to share the action research process as we might have, to discuss the readings as we might have, to share experiences as we might have.

The problem to which I am referring is not simply one of time. Rather, the problem stems from the way each of our roles has been defined and constructed through the institutions in which we work. Teachers' days are filled with pressing concerns. Rare moments of peace are cherished to the extent that it is easy to understand the reluctance of a teacher to give her or his lunch time over to talking with a supervisor and student teacher. The university supervisor's situation (in this program) which often involves taking nine credits of graduate study as well as responsibility for twelve students teachers in five different schools is hardly one which lends itself to leisurely discussions of . . . anything! Similarly, student teachers, many of whom are working and/or taking courses in addition to their student teaching, are stretched to their limits. These problems are neither uncommon nor temporary. They reflect the institutional, social and political value given to teaching and teacher education.

Institutions

While teaching, schooling and education feature as valued social practices in much rhetoric, the value actually accorded these social functions is difficult to fathom. In universities, teaching and teacher education are undervalued as is clear in the struggle for funding and other support which is a constant source of tension for the organizers of the program in which I was working at the time of this research, and in many other programs. Thus, at the University of Wisconsin-Madison graduate students who need an income to pay their tuition fees and, often literally, to survive and who, at the same time, care about teaching and teacher education, find themselves accepting positions in which their workload far exceeds the hours for which they are paid.

It is not just the university supervisor who is affected by the lack of financial support given to teaching. Cooperating teachers who are keen to be involved in the process of teacher education, accept student teachers but find there is little time for them to perform that role. Teacher learning is often not valued to the extent that teachers are provided with time to work with their peers, to reflect systematically on their teaching, to attend workshops to strengthen what they bring to either their teaching or their involvement in student teaching.

One way in which the triad could be strengthened is to help teachers gain greater insight into the elementary program, the nature of supervision and the relevance of action research, through some sort of program-specific workshop conducted by the university. Most of the workshops currently conducted are not program specific and so bring together teachers who will supervise in elementary education, secondary education, special education and librarianship. Program specific workshops would provide a context in which teacher and supervisor knowledge could be shared and demystified which could help establish conditions for the triad in which these two 'teacher educators' could work together from a more common knowledge base. But how could such workshops take place? Exhausted and disenchanted teachers are reluctant to give up extra 'spare' time for such meetings. Many school districts are unwilling/unable to release teachers from their teaching duties. The university is unwilling/unable to make funds available for such an endeavor. However, if at all possible, I would argue for program-specific workshops to replace the general workshops which teachers are currently required to attend.

As Feiman-Nemser and Buchmann (1983) have written, schools are not really set up for teacher education. 'The legitimate purposes of teachers center on their classrooms' (p. 203), and student teacher learning (and indeed teacher learning) often are accorded low importance. I believe that action research by student teachers can help overcome this problem if it is restructured in a way which enables the student teacher's 'problem' to be viewed as one which can help the functioning of the classroom and can enhance the educational experience of the pupils. This restructuring would require that student teacher and cooperating teacher worked much more closely in the identification and articulation of the problem. Once established, the project should be considered a shared investment. As an example, Margaret agreed with Kate that working cooperatively with other adults in her classroom was an important issue. There were two teachers, two student teachers, an aide and occasional visitors. But it became Kate's problem to the extent that Margaret was unwilling to engage with the difficult questions Kate was raising, particularly when they pertained to her own practices. With the kind of program-specific workshop to which I referred earlier, teacher involvement in student teacher action research could be explained and, perhaps, expected. Of course, such a mandate would not erase the problems of time and other school structures which work against teacher education but it would go part way toward redressing the 'cross-purposes' (Feiman-Nemser and Buchmann, 1983) of school and university teacher education.

Another institution which influences the student teaching triad is the State Department of Public Instruction (DPI). While it could act to facilitate school-university communication in a supportive and educative way, it tends to function instead as a regulatory agency, providing legislation and surveillance. For example, the DPI requires that at least four three-way conferences take place during the senior student teaching experience and that quadruplicate records are kept of at least four visits per student per semester. While these requirements are intended to ensure that the student teaching experience is educative, the time demanded means that for many supervisors and teachers these requirements become, understandably, a nuisance. The processes are entered into half-heartedly to satisfy the bureaucracy. Meanwhile, the education of the student teacher is further limited. The DPI *could* legislate extra time for these processes or provide other support mechanisms. Instead, it simply legislates the requirements.

In summary, individual supervisors can continue to struggle to improve the functioning of student teaching triads and to find some satisfaction in that struggle. However the democratic triad which is suggested as a goal in the Elementary Education Program will not be widely achieved through such individual struggles. Developing such a triad is not a simple question of imploring teachers, student teachers and university supervisors to talk more openly and honestly with each other. The individual and psychological struggles must be connected to institutional and societal conditions and tensions. This project has encouraged my commitment to those struggles. The interpersonal relationships established within the specific triads of this supervision experience were affected by power relations, time constraints and institutional conditions. Strengthening the student teaching triad requires a wider focus and action at levels beyond the immediacy of the classroom or staffroom. The democratic ideal is unlikely to be achieved without massive institutional changes; changes which are unlikely to occur without significant social, economic and political change in the wider society.

The data gleaned from my action research project suggest that the constraints on our work as supervisors are many, thus making it difficult to always 'practice what we preach'. Acknowledging the constraints and using them as excuses is not enough. Future action should be directed at altering those conditions which militate against the learning of teacher educators as well as the learning of student teachers and cooperating teachers.

Action Research as a Vehicle for Improving Supervision

The collaboration with other supervisors working on action research projects proved to be a major strength of the whole experience. The five of us met approximately once a week to discuss our progress and concerns and to seek each other's help with our supervision. Each of us brought something different to the group in a way which seemed to add to its vitality and strength. No two projects had the same focus, and yet we found that we began to take on each other's 'problems' in our supervision practice. The group quickly developed a level of trust and mutual respect that allowed us to challenge each other; indeed, to ask some of the difficult questions that I wanted to be able to ask in my student teaching triads. We began to develop as a community of supervisor researchers investigating aspects of student teaching and teacher education.

The process of doing action research, even if it had been completed without that emotional and intellectual support, was extremely useful as a way of thinking about my functioning as a supervisor. Action research, as I understand it, forces systematic reflection about a particular aspect of one's practice and/or situation. The complexities of all educational practice make it easy to be 'lost among the trees'. Adopting a focus allows one to find some clarity. Thus, I believe the main advantage of doing action research as a teacher educator was that it forced me to focus and to articulate; it forced me to create the time to think systematically about issues that concerned me.

The experience was also very positive in the collaboration it facilitated with my students. Action research provided a legitimate way of soliciting constant feedback from my students. The fact that students were also conducting action research meant that there were shared intentions and experiences which seemed to strengthen the connections we were able to make. In the past, when I only supervised action research projects without engaging in one myself, the hierarchical distinction between supervisor and student teacher seemed much clearer. Here, there was a much stronger and more genuine sense of working together. Consequently, I feel I was a better supervisor than I might otherwise have been.

Triads and Triangles: Symbols for Student Teaching?

As a conclusion, I want to return to focus briefly on the two symbols which undergirded this project: triad and triangle. Although the choice of symbols to describe aspects of student teaching may be somewhat arbitrary and pragmatic, they have implications for the way we think about and conduct our work. After all, the symbols of triad and triangle created some of the initial dissonance which led to my identification of the student teaching triad as the focus of my action research project.

In music a triad is a chord made up of a root and its third and fifth. Who is the root in the student teaching triad? One might assume that it is the student teacher but ... it seems that the supervisor plays the major role in establishing the triad, in setting out the requirements for the semester, even where that involves negotiating a statement of expectations, even when that involves trying to create more open and honest communication and the active participation of all members of the triad. Perhaps this has been historically constructed through notions of the expertise of the university supervisor and his/her key role in evaluation. On the other hand, perhaps it *is* appropriate to talk of the student teacher as the root; in music, the root gives the central focus to the tonality. The supervisor might then be considered the third; in music, the third is perhaps the most important note because it determines whether it is a major or minor triad. Perhaps the supervisor determines how the triad functions while the student provides its central focus, its *raison d'etre*. But what of the cooperating teacher? Perhaps I *see* myself as the most important in determining the functioning or the relations of the triad because I am speaking from my own perspective, my own position. Nevertheless, the data from my action research project certainly support my contention that the supervisor, or perceptions of the supervisor (me)/ Supervisor (the role), had a major impact on the triad.

The symbol triad also implies harmony, 'a pleasing or congruent arrangement of parts', musical notes in a harmonious chord. The roles of the student teaching 'triad' are complementary, although not necessarily. An unsuccessful triad is characterized as dissonant, a clashing musical interval, an unresolved musical chord, a lack of agreement. Certainly some of the triads in which I participated, were, at least at times, dissonant.

The second symbol which has been used, perhaps even which created this project, is that of the equilateral triangle, of equal sides. In mathematics the three sides are identical in length, although they are positioned differently in space so as to connect with one another. The lines of the triangle intersect because of their different direction. The central image of the equilateral triangle is one of equality. But the members of the student teaching triad are never equal; perhaps most obviously, the evaluations of the student teacher are important to his or her career. Any evaluations of teacher or supervisor by the other, or even by student teachers, generally have less significant consequences.

Without wishing to make too much of the equilateral triangle, which may simply have been pragmatic choice in minimizing the work of a graphic artist, it appears to me to conflict with and contradict the concept of a triad. A triad is made up of different parts, parts which are not the same. This seems a realistic portrayal of the student teaching triad. The notion of an equilateral triangle seems an unrealistic, and perhaps even undesirable, goal. If a triangle was to be used to represent the student teaching triad, it would almost always have sides of different lengths and these would vary at different 'moments' of the experience.

Does it even make sense to talk of equalizing a triad? The triad gets its strength from the difference of its components. Compare the student teaching triad to the chamber music trio. Each individual contributes a different note, the sum of which is greater, more pleasing, than any of the individual parts.

Another interesting analogy is raised when we consider that occasionally in music, dissonance is deliberately created to enhance the pleasure in the following consonance. One or more members of the triad will deliberately disrupt the harmony for the result which may ensue. In student teaching we do not have to assume that consonance will always predominate, or is always necessary. Moments of dissonance can actually enhance the triad; for example the student teacher might benefit from being privy to a disagreement between supervisor and teacher about an aspect of a lesson just observed.

I do not want to push these musical and mathematical metaphors too far. Clearly there are some limitations, not the least of which is the appropriateness of inanimate phenomena for explaining human relationships. Nevertheless I believe there is some value in thinking of the student teaching triad as chamber music.

Acknowledgment

I wish to thank James Ladwig, Kelly Larsen, Mary Campbell and the editors for their insightful comments and criticisms on earlier drafts of this chapter.

Notes

1   Although 'teacher educators' could refer to cooperating teachers or other members
    of the school staff, it is often argued that a university supervisor is in a better
    position, as an outsider, to help students make connections between their specific
    experiences in the classroom and broader frames of reference (Buchmann, 1984).
    Others have argued that a university supervisor helps provide direction for the
    student teaching experience, enhances communication between student teacher
    and cooperating teacher, and makes more critical contributions to the student
    teacher's progress (Zimpher, deVoss and Nott, 1980). On the other hand, argu-
    ments have been made that the university supervisor is ineffective and a waste of
    limited resources for teacher education (Bowman, 1979).
2   This statement of expectations was very closely based on that of another super-
    visor who had been working in the program for two semesters. I thank Marie
    Brennan for allowing me access to her Statement.
3   Pseudonyms are used throughout this chapter.

References

BARTHOLOMEW, J. (1976) 'Schooling teachers: The myth of the liberal college', in
    WHITTY, G. and YOUNG, M. (Eds) *Explorations in the Politics of School Knowledge*,
    pp. 114–24, Driffield, England: Nafferton.
BOWMAN, N. (1979) 'College supervision of student teaching: A time to reconsider',
    Journal of Teacher Education, **30**, 3, pp. 29–30.
BOYDELL, D. (1986) 'Issues in teaching practice supervision research', *Teaching and
    Teacher Education*, **2**, 2, pp. 115–26.
BUCHMANN, M. (1984) 'The priority of knowledge and understanding in teaching', in
    KATZ, L.G. and RATHS, J.D. (Eds) *Advances in Teacher Education*, Vol. 1, pp.
    29–48, Norwood, NJ: Ablex.
CALDERHEAD, J. (1988) 'The contribution of field experience to student primary
    teachers' professional learning', *Research in Education*, **40**, pp. 33–49.
FEIMAN-NEMSER, S. and BUCHMANN, M. (1983) 'Pitfalls of experience in teacher
    preparation', in TAMIR, P., HOFSTEIN, A. and BEN-PERETZ, M. (Eds) *Preservice and
    Inservice Training of Science Teachers*, pp. 197–205, Philadelphia: Balaban Interna-
    tional Science Serv s.
FEIMAN-NEMSER, S. and UCHMANN, M. (1987) 'When is student teaching teacher
    education'? *Teaching   Teacher Education*, **3**, 4, pp. 255–73.
GINSBURG, M. (1988) *Contradictions in Teacher Education and Society: A Critical Analysis*,
    Basingstoke, Falmer Press.
GIROUX, H. (1980) 'Teacher education and the ideology of social control', *Journal of
    Education*, **162**, pp. 5–27.
GORE, J.M. (1987) 'Reflecting on reflective teaching', *Journal of Teacher Education*, **38**,
    2, pp. 33–9.
GORE, J.M. (1990) 'Pedagogy as text in physical education teacher education: Beyond
    the preferred reading', in KIRK, D. and TINNING, R. (Eds) *Physical Education,
    Curriculum and Culture: Critical Studies in the Contemporary Crisis*. Basingstoke,
    Falmer Press, pp. 101–38.
KEMMIS, S. and McTAGGART, R. (1988) *The Action Research Planner*, Victoria: Deakin
    University Press.
LUSTED, D. (1986) 'Why pedagogy?' *Screen*, **27**, 5, pp. 2–14.

NODDINGS, N. (1986) 'Fidelity in teaching, teacher education and research for teaching', *Harvard Educational Review*, **56**, 4, pp. 496–510.

NOFFKE, S. and BRENNAN, M. (1988) Action Research and Reflective Student Teaching at UW-Madison. A paper presented at the annual meeting of the American Educational Research Association, New Orleans.

POPKEWITZ, T. (1985) 'Ideology and social formation in teacher education', *Teaching and Teacher Education*, **1**, pp. 91–107.

RICHARDSON-KOEHLER, V. (1988) 'Barriers to the effective supervision of student teaching: A field study', *Journal of Teacher Education*, **39**, 2, pp. 28–35.

SERGIOVANNI, T. and STARRATT, R. (1988) 'The supervisors' educational platform', in *Supervision: Human perspectives*, pp. 233–46, New York: McGraw Hill.

YEE, A.H. (1968) 'Interpersonal relationships in the student teaching triad', *Journal of Teacher Education*, **19**, pp. 95–112.

ZEICHNER, K.M. and GORE, J.M. (1990) 'Teacher socialization', in HOUSTON, W.R. (Ed.) *Handbook of Research on Teacher Education*, New York: Macmillan.

ZEICHNER, K. and TABACHNICK, B.R. (1982) 'The belief systems of university supervisors in an elementary student teaching program', *Journal of Education for Teaching*, **8**, pp. 34–54.

ZIMPHER, N.L., DEVOSS, G.G. and NOTT, D. (1980) 'A closer look at university student teacher supervision', *Journal of Teacher Education*, **31**, 4, pp. 11–15.

Appendix A

STATEMENT OF EXPECTATIONS: 463/464/465   Jennifer Gore
Fall 1988

My expectations of myself

1 I will turn up prepared for each seminar and on time to each appointment made in a school.

2 I will respond to all journal entries and work submitted by students in as short a time as possible.

3 I will learn as much as possible about each student, their hopes and expectations, their strengths and interests, their school situation, and areas for focus/improvement, and take these things into account in designing a curriculum for the seminar and in giving feedback.

4 I will try to pace myself across the semester so that I last the distance and fit in all commitments, including my own study and personal life. I will not try to be superwoman.

5 I will find out as much as possible about the school and the cooperating teacher, what they can offer and how I can best offer support in each different situation.

6 I will ask questions, challenge openly and honestly and be available to students and cooperating teachers for discussion.

7 I will make clear what expectations and requirements are necessary for all of us to fulfill.

8 I will use as criteria for success and progress the criteria laid out in the handbook.

9 I will ask for and expect criticism and suggestions about the seminar and about my own teaching in the seminar as well as about my supervision.

10 I will try, as much as possible, to share what I know and put people in touch with other resources, people, ideas.

11 I will contribute to the discussions and concerns of the students and co-operating teachers, always endeavoring to be honest and open to criticism myself.

12 I will focus the seminar work to include all students and, while making clear the expectations, will try to retain a sense of balance about what can be realistically achieved in the short- and long-term.

13 I will model what I mean by reflective teaching and action research by undertaking both myself and making them a topic of discussion.

14 I will be available, within the constraints of my timetable and other tasks, to arrange observations when most convenient to student and cooperating teacher. The needs of other students and cooperating teachers particularly in the same school will be taken into account when making arrangements. Advance notice through the student teacher will be given if changes need to be made to arrangements.

15 I will offer support to the student, for both short-term and long-term needs as a prospective teacher.

My expectations of the student teacher

1 That you will do your best to become a reflective and critical teacher, balancing the development of different skills including the highly specific and practical and the more intangible skills associated with teaching and working in a school.

2 That you will become familiar with the handbook and the outline for seminar so that you are in a position to be in charge of your own learning this semester (which includes but is not bounded by meeting all necessary requirements).

3 That your first priority is to the learning and educational well-being of the students in your classroom.

4 That you will set yourself realistic and important goals to achieve this semester.

5 That you will attend all seminars and contribute to the success of the seminar by ensuring that you prepare and share your learning.

6 That you will become involved in extra school activities as appropriate in your own school setting and as negotiated with your cooperating teacher; that you will participate with your cooperating teacher in such activities as grading, record keeping, staff meetings, inservice and links with the other staff in the school.

7 That you will be open and honest with both your cooperating teacher and me about what you need, your progress, your concerns.

8 That *you* will arrange for me to observe you at least every three weeks, more frequently if possible; that you will negotiate times for pre-observation conferencing and a post-observation conference which includes the cooperating teacher wherever possible; and that you will ensure that these arrangements are convenient for your cooperating teacher and me.

9 That you will notify me as soon as possible of any changes to your schedule and arrangements.

10 That you will meet on a regular weekly basis with your cooperating teacher to discuss your concerns, progress and plans.

11 In the event that you cannot attend school (e.g., when sick or death in the family) please follow school rules for notification procedures. Contact at least the school, your cooperating teacher and me.

My expectations of the cooperating teacher

1 Meetings, on a weekly basis, with the student teacher at which time the *student teacher's* concerns, interests, plans and progress are the focus.

2 Participation in the development of a timeline describing the student teacher's gradual assumption of teaching duties and the build up to two weeks of lead teaching (lead teaching to be completed by April 28).

3 Clarification of school, district and state policies affecting curriculum or procedures.

4 Introduction of the student to other staff and to the extra curricular activities of teaching.

5 Commitment to the long-term and short-term development of the student as a teacher.

6 Assistance and advice to the student in becoming reflective as well as in becoming technically proficient in the skills of teaching.

7 Fulfillment of responsibilities and requirements as laid out in the handbook and advice to the student on the balancing of commitments.

8 Willingness to give feedback to me as well as to the student, especially if difficulties should arise.

9 Participation in initial, mid-term and final evaluation conferences at least, and as many three-way discussions as possible.

10 Willingness to discuss and explore the reasons you teach the way you do.

11 Assistance, where possible, and at the request of the student teacher, in the student's action research project.

Appendix B

Questions Sent To Cooperating Teachers

1 What teaching experiences have you had (e.g., grade levels, locations, different 'types' of schools)?

2 Are there any other 'special experiences' (defined however you like) relevant to your role as a cooperating teacher?

3 What do you see as your major strengths/expertise?

4 Would you like to be involved in a seminar/demonstration of any sort during this semester? Is it feasible? Do you have any specific ideas as to the sort of involvement you might like? (Semester is rapidly disappearing. Please don't be too upset if we are unable to act on your suggestion.)

5 I have a specific interest at the moment in facilitating the functioning of the student teaching *triad* as a three-way dialogue. Do you have any suggestions as to how this can be improved (either generally, or specifically in relation to our current triad)?

6 Anything else ...

Notes on Contributors

Susan A. Adler is Assistant Professor of Teacher Education and of Curriculum and Instruction at the University of Missouri-Kansas City. She is a member of the Board of Directors of the National Council for the Social Studies, a past member of the Publication and Advisory Board of the Association of Teacher Educators and is active in a variety of teacher education and social studies professional organizations. Her research interests include the curriculum of teacher education and the development of the perspectives of preservice teachers. Adler completed her doctoral program at the University of Wisconsin and, while there, was the coordinator of the secondary social studies student teaching program.

Landon E. Beyer supervised student teachers for three years, and served as an instructor for one year, in the elementary education program at the University of Wisconsin-Madison. His central interests are in the areas of critical theory and its implications for educational studies, curriculum theory and development, and teacher education. Recent publications include, *Knowing and Acting: Inquiry, Ideal-ogy, and Educational Studies: The Curriculum: Problems, Politics, and Possibilities* (senior editor, with Michael W. Apple); and *Preparing Teachers as Professionals: The Role of Educational Studies and Other Liberal Disciplines* (with Walter Feinberg, Jo Anne Pagano and James A. Whitson). He is currently chair of the Department of Education at Knox College in Galesburg, Illinois.

Marie Brennan is currently Manager of School Improvement in the Victorian Ministry of Education, Melbourne, Australia. She formerly supervised elementary student teachers at the University of Wisconsin-Madison. Marie's current interests, like those of her co-author Susan Noffke, are in curriculum theory, educational reform, and collective, democratic, and feminist schooling.

Deborah P. Britzman is an Assistant Professor in the School of Education and Human Development at the State University of New York at Binghamton. She teaches and does school supervision in secondary English education and teaches courses in the field of multicultural education. She is author of a forthcoming ethnographic study of secondary teacher education titled, *Practice Makes Practice: A Critical Study of Learning to Teach* (Albany: SUNY-Press, 1991), and recent publications in *The Harvard Educational Review* and *Curriculum Inquiry*.

Robert V. Bullough Jr. is Professor of Educational Studies, the University of Utah, Salt Lake City,. Utah. Among his major areas of interest, aside from being a father to four children, gardening, book collecting and the restoration of antiques, are the study of teacher culture and socialization, and curriculum criticism and history. His most recent books include *The Forgotten Dream of American Public Education* (Iowa State University Press, 1988), *First Year Teacher: A Case Study* (Teachers College Press, 1989) and *Emerging as a Teacher* (Routledge, 1991).

Michelle Comeaux is an Assistant Professor of Education at Gustavus Adolphus College, located in St Peter, Minnesota. She received a PhD in Educational Psychology from the University of Wisconsin-Madison in 1989. While in graduate school, she was a teaching assistant for the educational psychology department and completed an action research project on her teaching. Her current research interests include, teacher beliefs and cognition, preservice education, the teaching of writing, and teacher evaluation. Her most recent publication is 'Evaluating the systems: Teachers' perspectives on teacher evaluation' (with Penelope Peterson), in *Educational Evaluation and Policy Analysis*, spring, 1990.

Andrew Gitlin is Associate Professor of Educational Studies, University of Utah. He has taught and published in the areas of curriculum, critical theory, and teacher education. His major areas of interest include the effects of school structure on teachers' work, evaluation, and school reform. His most recent book is *Teacher Evaluation: Educative Alternatives*, coauthored with John Smyth.

Mary Louise Gomez is Assistant Professor in the Department of Curriculum and Instruction at the University of Wisconsin-Madison and a Senior Researcher with the National Center for Research on Teacher Education at Michigan State University. Her teaching and research focuses on the education of preservice and inservice teachers to work with diverse populations of learners; she is particularly concerned with the preparation of teachers of writing. Professor Gomez is the Associate Director of the Wisconsin Writing Project and works extensively at the state and national level on issues related to equity in schooling.

Jesse Goodman received his PhD degree in 1982 from the University of Wisconsin in Madison, and he is now an Associate Professor at Indiana University in Bloomington. His primary interests include teacher education/socialization and the development and implementation of emancipatory pedagogy. He has had over twenty articles on these topics published in a variety of scholarly journals. Since 1986, his research of teacher socialization has received four national awards for distinguished scholarship and was selected as a finalist for a fifth award. Recently, the Indiana Association of Colleges for Teacher Education presented him with the Teacher Educator of the Year Award. He is currently working on a book that examines the potential development of elementary education for critical democracy.

Jennifer M. Gore is a Doctoral student in the Department of Curriculum and Instruction, University of Wisconsin-Madison. In addition to her involvement as a supervisor in the Elementary Education program there, she has worked as a teacher educator at the University of Queensland and Newcastle College of Advanced Education, Australia. She has published articles and contributed to books dealing with such topics as reflective teaching, teacher socialization, action research, teacher empowerment and pedagogy as 'text' in teacher education. Her doctoral research is aimed at clarifying the currently fragmented and ambiguous discourses of critical and feminist pedagogies through the lens of Michel Foucault's analyses of power-knowledge.

Jeffrey Maas is currently teaching a combination fourth/fifth grade open classroom in the Madison Metropolitan School District and is a PhD candidate at the University of Wisconsin-Madison. He was an elementary student teacher supervisor at the University of Wisconsin-Madison from 1988–90. Prior to teaching in Madison, he taught first grade in West Salem, Wisconsin, developing a writing program that was selected as a Center of Excellence by the National Council of Teachers of English. He also taught language arts at the Wisconsin Center for Gifted Learners in Milwaukee, Wisconsin. A participant in the National Writing Program, he received his Masters Degree from Bread Loaf School of English, Middlebury, Vermont. He has given numerous inservices across Wisconsin on writing, language and learning. Since 1988, he has been an independent writing consultant, serving as a writer-in-residence for elementary schools.

Frances Maher is Associate Professor of Education at Wheaton College in Norton, Massachusetts, where she directs a small undergraduate preservice teacher education program. Her research is in feminist pedagogy, about which she has published several articles, and she has been coordinator of Wheaton's Balanced Curriculum Project for integrating the study of women into undergraduate courses. She is currently at work with Mary Kay Tetreault on an ethnographic study of the classrooms of feminist college teachers in several institutions.

Susan E. Noffke is a former elementary school teacher and is presently Assistant Professor of Learning and Instruction at the State University of New York at Buffalo. She was also a lecturer and student teaching supervisor in the Elementary Teacher Education program at the University of Wisconsin-Madison. Susan's current interests are in curriculum theory, educational reform, and collective, democratic and feminist schooling.

Anna Richert is an Assistant Professor in the Department of Education at Mills College in Oakland, California. In addition to this chapter which discusses the use of case methods in preservice teacher education, she has written two other pieces currently in press on case methods in staff development: 'Using cases to promote reflective and enhanced understanding', in *Teachers: Their World and Their Work*, Ann Lieberman and Lynn Miller (Eds) (Second edn) New York: Teachers College Press and 'Writing cases, a vehicle for inquiry into the teaching process', in *Case methods in Teacher Education*, Judith Shulman (Ed.), New York: Teachers College Press.

B. Robert Tabachnick is Professor of Curriculum and Instruction and of Educational Policy Studies at the University of Wisconsin-Madison. His major interests are in the study of teacher education and in educational planning and curriculum change in developing countries. Major publications include *The Myth of Educational Reform* (with T. Popkewitz and G. Wehlage) and *The Development of Teacher Perspectives* (with K. Zeichner). He has participated in developing the elementary preservice teacher education program at the University of Wisconsin-Madison, having been associated with the program since 1959. He has been involved in research and in programs to strengthen teacher education and university education in Nigeria, Uganda, Sierra Leone Botswana, Indonesia and Thailand.

Kenneth Teitelbaum received a PhD in General Curriculum Studies from the University of Wisconsin at Madison. While at Madison, he supervised and taught classes in the elementary education and social studies education programs. He is currently Associate Professor in the Division of Education at the State University of New York at Binghamton. His teaching and research interests include curriculum theory and history, teacher education, the social foundations of education, multicultural education and social studies education. He has published in journals such as *Curriculum Inquiry, Journal of Education for Teaching, Journal of Curriculum Studies, History of Education Quarterly* and *Social Education.*

Jane J. White is an Associate Professor and the Elementary Education Coordinator at the University of Maryland Baltimore County. Trained as an anthropologist, she has written articles about 'Student teaching as a rite of passage' and 'The teacher as a broker of scholarly knowledge'.

Patricia Wood currently is an elementary school teacher in Madison, Wisconsin. She has a Masters Degree in Curriculum and Instruction from the University of Wisconsin-Madison where she has also served as a supervisor of student teachers. Patricia is the author of 'Action research: A field perspective', published in the *Journal of Education for Teaching* in 1988.

Ken M. Zeichner is Professor of Curriculum and Instruction at the University of Wisconsin-Madison. He has published work in the US, Europe and in Australia related to various issues in teacher education. His recent publications include 'Teacher socialization' in the *Handbook of Research on Teacher Education* (with Jennifer Gore, 1990) and *Teacher Education and the Social Conditions of Schooling* (with Dan Liston) New York: Routledge. He teaches graduate courses in the study of Teacher Education at Wisconsin and directs the elementary student teaching program.

Index